The Editor

HILDEGARD HOELLER is Associate Professor of English at the College of Staten Island, City University of New York. She is the author of *Edith Wharton's Dialogue with Realism and Sentimental Fiction* and co-author with Rebecca Brittenham of *Key Words for Academic Writers*. Her essays on nineteenth- and early-twentieth-century American literature have been published in journals such as *American Literature, Studies in American Fiction, ESQ, American Transcendental Quarterly, African-American Review, American Literary Realism, Edith Wharton Review*, and *Dreiser Studies*.

A NORTON CRITICAL EDITION

Horatio Alger, Jr.

RAGGED DICK
or, Street Life in New York with Boot Blacks

AN AUTHORITATIVE TEXT

CONTEXTS

CRITICISM

Edited by

HILDEGARD HOELLER
COLLEGE OF STATEN ISLAND

W • W • NORTON & COMPANY • *New York* • *London*

W. W. Norton & Company has been independent since its founding in 1923, when William Warder Norton and Mary D. Herter Norton first published lectures delivered at the People's Institute, the adult education division of New York City's Cooper Union. The Nortons soon expanded their program beyond the Institute, publishing books by celebrated academics from America and abroad. By mid-century, the two major pillars of Norton's publishing program—trade books and college texts—were firmly established. In the 1950s, the Norton family transferred control of the company to its employees, and today—with a staff of four hundred and a comparable number of trade, college, and professional titles published each year—W. W. Norton & Company stands as the largest and oldest publishing house owned wholly by its employees.

This title is printed on permanent paper containing
30 percent post-consumer waste recycled fiber.

Copyright © 2008 by W. W. Norton & Company, Inc.

All rights reserved.
Printed in the United States of America.
First Edition.

The text of this book is composed in Fairfield Medium
with the display set in Bernhard Modern.
Series design by Antonina Krass.
Composition by Binghamton Valley Composition.
Manufacturing by the Maple-Vail Book Group, Binghamton.
Production manager: Benjamin Reynolds.

Library of Congress Cataloging-in-Publication Data

Alger, Horatio, 1832–1899.
  Ragged Dick, or, Street Life in New York with boot-blacks : an authoritative text, contexts, criticism / Horatio Alger, Jr.; edited by Hildegard Hoeller.
    p. cm. — (A Norton critical edition)
  Includes bibliographical references (p.   ).

ISBN-13: 978-0-393-92589-0 (pbk.)
ISBN-10: 0-393-92589-7 (pbk.)

  1. Boys—Fiction.   2. Shoes shiners—Fiction.   3. Poor children—Fiction.   4. New York (N.Y.)—Fiction.   5. Street children—Fiction.   6. Alger, Horatio 1832–1899. Ragged Dick, or, Street life in New York with boot-blacks.   I. Hoeller, Hildegard, 1960–   II. Title.   III. Title: Ragged Dick.   IV. Title: Street life in New York with boot-blacks.

PS1029.A3R34 2007
813'.4—dc22   2006053090

W. W. Norton & Company, Inc., 500 Fifth Avenue, New York,
N. Y. 10110-0017
www.wwnorton.com

W. W. Norton & Company Ltd., Castle House,
75/76 Wells Street, London WIT 3QT

4 5 6 7 8 9 0

Contents

Illustrations

Preface

"Only fools laugh at Horatio Alger, and his poor boys who make good. The wiser man who thinks twice about that sterling author will realize that Alger is to Americans what Homer was to the Greeks," wrote Nathaneal West and Boris Ingster in 1940 (quoted by Scharnhorst, epigraph to *The Lost Life*). In his 1962 introduction to *Ragged Dick* and *Mark, the Match Boy* Rychard Fink warns in a similar fashion: "Anyone who wants to know his country should get acquainted with Horatio Alger. It is dangerous to ignore a man whose ideas hang on so stubbornly" (31). This Norton Critical Edition presents Alger's quintessential rags-to-riches story in the way these writers suggest: it hopes to illuminate the cultural context and centrality of Alger's novel, showing how and why this juvenile work resonated so strongly when published and remained a central American text. Alger, like the master of entertainment P. T. Barnum, had his finger on the pulse of America and was able to offer a version of its central myth, the American dream, that his readers could—for a long time—embrace. How and why was that so? What was it about Alger's narratives about New York bootblacks that captured America's imagination?

Alger was a rather unlikely candidate to become such a central American voice. Born in 1832 to Reverend Horatio Alger and Olive Fenno, he grew up in a financially struggling middle-class home. In 1844 Alger's father was bankrupt, and the family moved from Boston to Marlborough. Alger began to attend Harvard University in 1848, and he started publishing early works such as essays and poems in the Boston *Pictorial National Library*. After graduation he was unable to make a living as a writer and returned home. He continued to write, began to teach and tutor, and also entered theological school. He went back and forth between writing under various pseudonyms and aspiring to become a minister. In 1860 Alger graduated from Cambridge Theological School and started to work as a minister and continued employment as a private tutor. In 1863 due to his unusual height (5 feet 2 inches) and his near-sightedness he was not enlisted in the war and therefore remained a minister and published with increasing success as a writer of juvenile fiction. For example, his first novel *Frank's Campaign* (1864) was well received. By 1866, however, his life took a serious turn when rumors emerged that Alger had been sexually abusing boys in his parish. When charges were brought against him, he did not deny them and was dismissed as a minister. Now exclusively a writer, Alger moved to New York to study the "street arabs," young homeless urban boys, and in them he found *his* subject. Only a year later, in 1867, *Ragged Dick* appeared in serialized form, the novel that made Horatio Alger a household name in America and that remained his greatest success.

From its beginning, the novel captured something readers wanted to read. After a successful serialized run, the 1868 book edition was victorious. According to Gary Scharnhorst, "The first edition of several thousand copies was sold out within a few weeks of its publication on May 5, 1868, and a second edition appeared in August. It was the most successful story Alger ever wrote, technically his only best-seller" (*Lost Life*, 86). Alger himself could never replicate the hit of this particular novel, even though he certainly tried writing more than a hundred books for young readers in his career (Scharnhorst, "Demythologizing Alger," 20). But there was something about *Ragged Dick* that sounded particularly right to a lot of readers at the time and that later made it an iconic American text. This Norton Critical Edition is interested in accounting for this success and for delineating the strange centrality the novel acquired. It begins by looking at the book's immediate context—both Alger's life and the literature about New York City in the 1860s—and then moves to the larger context of its later reception and the many responses it has elicited. If Alger's story, and the story of the novel, is not exactly a rags-to-riches story of the kind Alger tells, it is a story of a voice from an unlikely source becoming utterly central. Not all people, however, who use the Horatio Alger name and the myth they associate with it, know about its historical references, the context of its author's life, or even the novel's actual content. That Horatio Alger's *Ragged Dick* would become a central American text that for many would remain a shorthand for America itself and the opportunities it offered to all is one of the most amazing elements of the story of *Ragged Dick*, which this Norton Critical Edition tries to tell.

As troubling and ironic as it may today appear in light of his past as a pederast, Alger's liking for and affiliation with New York City street boys was probably one factor that accounted for the novel's popularity. Certainly Alger cited his immersion in the boys' lives and his extraordinary sympathy for them as one reason for his novel's particular success. Alger had become involved with the Children's Aid Society and other reform organizations trying to help homeless children, and, throughout his life, he also invited young boys into his home, adopted them, and took care of them. The section on "Alger on His Art and Life" includes Alger's own statements about his writing and his relation to his subjects; I am also including amongst

Alger's writings about himself his poem "Friar Anselmo," written shortly after he left the ministry because he had been accused of—and did not deny—having had performed "unnatural acts" with boys.

While Alger's liking for New York City's poor boys was personal, this Norton Critical Edition suggests in the next section on "The New York City Background" that the reading public had also become fascinated with these boys and the city. The immediate success of *Ragged Dick* thus also had to do with the way in which Alger's novel tapped into an already existing market of books representing the "lures" and "snares" of the city to an American middle-class readership. America's eyes, particularly its middle-class eyes, were focused on New York and its rapidly growing population and poverty. Many urban poors were immigrants, and anti-foreign sentiments were one response to their presence. Perhaps because they were easier to romanticize than adults, street children began to be a popular subject for books about the city. In them, the so-called "street arabs," audiences found a way to look at this new New York population and find both hope and danger in it. Alger's novel *Ragged Dick* fits remarkably neatly into this new literature about urban poverty, and particularly its children. It spoke to a common fear of and fascination with New York City's poor children, and Alger's invented character "Ragged Dick" was a most ingenious and charming version of a "street arab" everyone could embrace, love, and enjoy.

But despite *Ragged Dick*'s topicality in 1868, it has also had remarkable staying power. Indeed, as Gary Scharnhorst delineates, the novel's greatest success came much later, in the early twentieth century ("Demythologizing Alger," 20). The remainder of this Norton Critical Edition is devoted to considering the ways in which Alger has been read and re-read and in which *Ragged Dick* has become an iconic American text. The "Criticism" section begins with contemporary reviews of the novel and then moves to a conversation by librarians in the 1880s about the merits and dangers of Alger's novels. In these debates, the reception and fate of Alger's books get discussed. Who should read them and for what reason? Then, I offer a selection of parodies and responses to Alger that exemplify his lasting influence; that he was ridiculed and parodied speaks to his enduring presence and to the ways in which he offered a central argument about American culture that seemed again and again worthy of a response. Gary Scharnhorst's essay "Demythologizing Alger" caps this section on Alger's legacy because it traces the ways in which Alger's work was read and made into a household word in American ideology.

The final section "Critical Essays" includes literary scholarship on Alger, showcasing four different critical approaches to his work as a way of representing the scope of the ongoing critical conversation about Alger's novel. Mary Roth Walsh's essay is particularly useful in engendering discussions about the masculine nature of the American dream as told by Alger. Gender and masculinity are also at the center of Michael Moon's essay, which discusses Alger's fiction in light of the homosocial strains in American market culture. "Pandering in the Public Sphere" by Glenn Hendler contemplates Alger's fiction in the context of reading practices and definitions of public and private spheres. Following up on Alger's allusions to Barnum's museum, my own essay compares Ragged Dick to Tom Thumb and Alger's narrative techniques to P. T. Barnum's exhibition strategies in his freak shows in order to account for the novel's success.

This Norton Critical Edition could not have come into being without the faith and support of my editor, Carol Bemis. This work was supported by a grant from the City University of New York PSC-CUNY Research Award Program; furthermore, the College of Staten Island gave me a Dean's Award in support of my writing the essay "Freaks and the American Dream: Horatio Alger, P. T. Barnum, and the Art of Humbug," included in this volume. I give many thanks to the City University of New York. My dear thanks go to my friend Laura Saltz who read my work on Alger and made many helpful suggestions, and I am grateful to all my other friends who were willing to listen to me talking about Alger in the last few years. Also, I am indebted to Cindy VandenBosch and my other colleagues at the Lower East Side Tenement Museum for making me part of their marvelous enterprise of representing later nineteenth-century life on the Lower East Side to the public. The knowledge I gained from offering tours at the museum and hearing many stories from our visitors has given me the kind of detailed insight into the background of *Ragged Dick* I could not have gathered in any other fashion. Finally, I thank the librarians at the College of Staten Island and the New York Public Library for their generous help.

The Text of
RAGGED DICK

Preface

by Horatio Alger, Jr.

"Ragged Dick" was contributed as a serial story to the pages of the *Schoolmate*, a well-known juvenile magazine, during the year 1867. While in course of publication, it was received with so many evidences of favor that it has been rewritten and considerably enlarged, and is now presented to the public as the first volume of a series intended to illustrate the life and experiences of the friendless and vagrant children who are now numbered by thousands in New York and other cities.

Several characters in the story are sketched from life. The necessary information has been gathered mainly from personal observation and conversations with the boys themselves. The author is indebted also to the excellent superintendent of the Newsboys' Lodging House, in Fulton Street, for some facts of which he has been able to make use. Some anachronisms may be noted. Wherever they occur, they have been admitted, as aiding in the development of the story, and will probably be considered as of little importance in an unpretending volume, which does not aspire to strict historical accuracy.

The author hopes that, while the volumes in this series may prove interesting as stories, they may also have the effect of enlisting the sympathies of his readers in behalf of the unfortunate children whose life is described, and of leading them to co-operate with the praiseworthy efforts now making [sic] by the Children's Aid Society and other organizations to ameliorate their condition.

New York, April, 1868

Chapter 1

Ragged Dick Is Introduced to the Reader

"Wake up there, youngster," said a rough voice.

Ragged Dick opened his eyes slowly, and stared stupidly in the face of the speaker, but did not offer to get up.

"Wake up, you young vagabond!" said the man, a little impatiently; "I suppose you'd lay there all day, if I hadn't called you."

"What time is it?" asked Dick.

"Seven o'clock."

"Seven o'clock! I oughter 've been up an hour ago. I know what 'twas made me so precious sleepy. I went to the Old Bowery[1] last night, and didn't turn in till past twelve."

"You went to the Old Bowery? Where'd you get your money?" asked the man, who was a porter in the employ of a firm doing business on Spruce Street.

"Made it by shines, in course. My guardian don't allow me no money for theatres, so I have to earn it."

"Some boys get it easier than that," said the porter significantly.

"You don't catch me stealin', if that's what you mean," said Dick.

"Don't you ever steal, then?"

"No, and I wouldn't. Lots of boys does it, but I wouldn't."

"Well, I'm glad to hear you say that. I believe there's some good in you, Dick, after all."

"Oh, I'm a rough customer!" said Dick. "But I wouldn't steal. It's mean."

"I'm glad you think so, Dick," and the rough voice sounded gentler than at first. "Have you got any money to buy your breakfast?"

"No, but I'll soon get some."

While this conversation had been going on, Dick had got up. His bedchamber had been a wooden box half full of straw, on which the young bootblack[2] had reposed his weary limbs, and slept as soundly as if it had been a bed of down. He dumped down into the straw without taking the trouble of undressing. Getting up too was an equally short process. He jumped out of the box, shook himself, picked out one or two straws that had found their way into the rents of his clothes, and, drawing a well-worn cap over his uncombed locks, he was all ready for the business of the day.

Dick's appearance as he stood beside the box was rather peculiar. His pants were torn in several places, and had apparently belonged in the first instance to a boy two sizes larger than himself. He wore a

1. Popular theatre, mostly frequented by working-class audiences.
2. Boy who polishes shoes for a living.

vest, all the bottons of which were gone except two, out of which peeped a shirt which looked as if it had been worn a month. To complete his costume he wore a coat too long for him, dating back, if one might judge from its general appearance, to a remote antiquity.

Washing the face and hands is usually considered proper in commencing the day, but Dick was above such refinement. He had no particular dislike to dirt, and did not think it necessary to remove several dark streaks on his face and hands. But in spite of his dirt and rags there was something about Dick that was attractive. It was easy to see that if he had been clean and well dressed he would have been decidedly good-looking. Some of his companions were sly, and their faces inspired distrust; but Dick had a frank, straight-forward manner that made him a favorite.

Dick's business hours had commenced. He had no office to open. His little blacking-box was ready for use, and he looked sharply in the faces of all who passed, addressing each with, "Shine yer boots, sir?"

"How much?" asked a gentleman on his way to his office.

"Ten cents," said Dick, dropping his box, and sinking upon his knees on the sidewalk, flourishing his brush with the air of one skilled in his profession.

"Ten cents! Isn't that a little steep?"

"Well, you know 'taint all clear profit," said Dick, who had already set to work. "There's the *blacking* costs something, and I have to get a new brush pretty often."

"And you have a large rent too," said the gentleman quizzically, with a glance at a large hole in Dick's coat.

"Yes, sir," said Dick, always ready to joke; "I have to pay such a big rent for my manshun up on Fifth Avenoo, that I can't afford to take less than ten cents a shine. I'll give you a bully shine, sir."

"Be quick about it, for I am in a hurry. So your house is on Fifth Avenue, is it?"

"It isn't anywhere else," said Dick, and Dick spoke the truth there.

"What tailor do you patronize?" asked the gentleman, surveying Dick's attire.

"Would you like to go to the same one?" asked Dick, shrewdly.

"Well, no; it strikes me that he didn't give you a very good fit."

"This coat once belonged to General Washington," said Dick comically. "He wore it all through the Revolution, and it got torn some, 'cause he fit so hard. When he died he told his widder to give it to some smart young feller that hadn't got none of his own; so she gave it to me. But if you'd like it, sir, to remember General Washington by, I'll let you have it reasonable."

"Thank you, but I wouldn't want to deprive you of it. And did your pants come from General Washington too?"

"No, they was a gift from Lewis Napoleon.[3] Lewis had outgrown 'em and sent 'em to me,—he's bigger than me, and that's why they don't fit."

"It seems you have distinguished friends. Now, my lad, I suppose you would like your money."

"I shouldn't have any objection," said Dick.

"I believe," said the gentleman, examining his pocket-book, "I haven't got anything short of twenty-five cents. Have you got any change?"

"Not a cent," said Dick. "All my money's invested in the Erie Railroad."[4]

"That's unfortunate."

"Shall I get the money changed, sir?"

"I can't wait; I've got to meet an appointment immediately. I'll hand you twenty-five cents, and you can leave the change at my office any time during the day."

"All right, sir. Where is it?"

"No. 125 Fulton Street. Shall you remember?"

"Yes, sir. What name?"

"Greyson,—office on second floor."

"All right, sir; I'll bring it."

"I wonder whether the little scamp will prove honest," said Mr. Greyson to himself, as he walked away. "If he does, I'll give him my custom regularly. If he don't, as is most likely, I shan't mind the loss of fifteen cents."

Mr. Greyson didn't understand Dick. Our ragged hero wasn't a model boy in all respects. I am afraid he swore sometimes, and now and then he played tricks upon unsophisticated boys from the country or gave a wrong direction to honest old gentlemen unused to the city. A clergyman in search of the Cooper Institute[5] he once directed to the Tombs Prison,[6] and, following him unobserved, was highly delighted when the unsuspicious stranger walked up the front steps of the great stone building on Centre Street, and tried to obtain admission.

"I guess he wouldn't want to stay long if he did get in," thought Ragged Dick, hitching up his pants. "Leastways I shouldn't. They're so precious glad to see you that they won't let you go, but board you gratooitous, and never send in no bills."

3. Allusion to famous performer Tom Thumb, a "miniature man" whose early performances in P. T. Barnum's freak show included Napoleon.
4. Ironic allusion to the very well-known Erie Railroad stock scandal, which would have left Dick, like many investors, penniless.
5. Private New York City trade school, founded in 1859 by Peter Cooper; it initially offered evening engineering and arts classes and was free for U.S. residents.
6. New York City prison completed in 1838 and named for its structure, which was based on an illustration of an Egyptian tomb.

Another of Dick's faults was his extravagance. Being always wide-awake and ready for business, he earned enough to have supported him comfortably and respectably. There were not a few young clerks who employed Dick from time to time in his professional capacity, who scarcely earned as much as he, greatly as their style and dress exceeded his. Dick was careless of his earnings. Where they went he could hardly have told himself. However much he managed to earn during the day, all was generally spent before morning. He was fond of going to the Old Bowery Theatre, and to Tony Pastor's,[7] and if he had any money left afterwards, he would invite some of his friends in somewhere to have an oyster stew; so it seldom happened that he commenced the day with a penny.

Then I am sorry to add that Dick had formed the habit of smoking. This cost him considerable, for Dick was rather fastidious about his cigars, and wouldn't smoke the cheapest. Besides, having a liberal nature, he was generally ready to treat his companions. But of course the expense was the smallest objection. No boy of fourteen can smoke without being affected injuriously. Men are frequently injured by smoking, and boys always. But large numbers of the newsboys and boot-blacks form the habit. Exposed to the cold and wet they find that it warms them up, and the self-indulgence grows upon them. It is not uncommon to see a little boy, too young to be out of his mother's sight, smoking with all the apparent satisfaction of a veteran smoker.

There was another way in which Dick sometimes lost money. There was a noted gambling-house on Baxter Street, which in the evening was sometimes crowded with these juvenile gamesters, who staked their hard earnings, generally losing of course, and refreshing themselves from time to time with a vile mixture of liquor at two cents a glass. Sometimes Dick strayed in here, and played with the rest.

I have mentioned Dick's faults and defects, because I want it understood, to begin with, that I don't consider him a model boy. But there were some good points about him nevertheless. He was above doing anything mean or dishonorable. He would not steal, or cheat, or impose upon younger boys, but was frank and straight-forward, manly and self-reliant. His nature was a noble one, and had saved him from all mean faults. I hope my young readers will like him as I do, without being blind to his faults. Perhaps, although he was only a bootblack, they may find something in him to imitate.

And now, having fairly introduced Ragged Dick to my young readers, I must refer them to the next chapter for his further adventures.

---

7. Another popular theatre on the Bowery named after its director, Tony Pastor, a former clown and entertainer.

Chapter 2

Johnny Nolan

After Dick had finished polishing Mr. Greyson's boots he was fortunate enough to secure three other customers, two of them reporters in the Tribune establishment, which occupies the corner of Spruce Street and Printing House Square.

When Dick had got through with his last customer the City Hall clock indicated eight o'clock. He had been up an hour, and hard at work, and naturally began to think of breakfast. He went up to the head of Spruce Street, and turned into Nassau. Two blocks further, and he reached Ann Street. On this street was a small, cheap restaurant, where for five cents Dick could get a cup of coffee, and for ten cents more, a plate of beef-steak with a plate of bread thrown in. These Dick ordered, and sat down at a table.

It was a small apartment with a few plain tables unprovided with cloths, for the class of customers who patronized it were not very particular. Our hero's breakfast was soon before him. Neither the coffee nor the steak were as good as can be bought at Delmonico's;[1] but then it is very doubtful whether, in the present state of his wardrobe, Dick would have been received at that aristocratic restaurant, even if his means had admitted of paying the high prices there charged.

Dick had scarcely been served when he espied a boy about his own size standing at the door, looking wistfully into the restaurant. This was Johnny Nolan, a boy of fourteen, who was engaged in the same profession as Ragged Dick. His wardrobe was in very much the same condition as Dick's.

"Had your breakfast, Johnny?" inquired Dick, cutting off a piece of steak.

"No."

"Come in, then. Here's room for you."

"I ain't got no money," said Johnny, looking a little enviously at his more fortunate friend.

"Haven't you had any shines?"

"Yes, I had one, but I shan't get any pay till tomorrow."

"Are you hungry?"

"Try me, and see."

"Come in. I'll stand treat this morning."

Johnny Nolan was nowise slow to accept this invitation, and was soon seated beside Dick.

---

1. Restaurant that opened in 1830 as an expansion of a pastry shop owned by Swiss immigrants Giovanni and Pietro Del-Monico. It is generally considered the first restaurant in America where customers could order from a menu rather than eat a fixed meal. By 1865 the Delmonico brothers had four restaurants in New York City, at 14th Street, Chambers Street, South William Street, and Broad Street.

"What'll you have, Johnny?"

"Same as you."

"Cup o' coffee and beefsteak," ordered Dick.

These were promptly brought, and Johnny attacked them vigorously.

Now, in the boot-blacking business, as well as in higher avocations, the same rule prevails, that energy and industry are rewarded, and indolence suffers. Dick was energetic and on the alert for business, but Johnny was the reverse. The consequence was that Dick earned probably three times as much as the other.

"How do you like it?" asked Dick, surveying Johnny's attacks upon the steak with evident complacency.

"It's hunky."

I don't believe "hunky" is to be found in either Webster's or Worcester's[2] big dictionary; but boys will readily understand what it means.

"Do you come here often?" asked Johnny.

"Most every day. You'd better come too."

"I can't afford it."

"Well, you'd ought to, then," said Dick. "What do you do with your money, I'd like to know?"

"I don't get near as much as you, Dick."

"Well, you might if you tried. I keep my eyes open,—that's the way I get jobs. You're lazy, that's what's the matter."

Johnny did not see fit to reply to this charge. Probably he felt the justice of it, and preferred to proceed with the breakfast, which he enjoyed the more as it cost him nothing.

Breakfast over, Dick walked up to the desk, and settled the bill. Then, followed by Johnny, he went out into the street.

"Where are you going, Johnny?"

"Up to Mr. Taylor's, on Spruce Street, to see if he don't want a shine."

"Do you work for him reg'lar?"

"Yes. Him and his partner wants a shine most every day. Where are you goin'?"

"Down front of the Astor House.[3] I guess I'll find some customers there."

At this moment Johnny started, and, dodging into an entry way, hid behind the door, considerably to Dick's surprise.

"What's the matter now?" asked our hero.

"Has he gone?" asked Johnny, his voice betraying anxiety.

2. Noah Webster (1758–1843) published *The American Dictionary of the English Language* first in 1828; Joseph Emerson Worcester (1784–1865) published his *Comprehensive Pronouncing and Explanatory Dictionary of the English Language* in 1830. While Worcester claimed to have based his work on Webster's, Webster accused him of plagiarism, starting a battle known as the "Dictionary War." In 1860 Worcester published the last revision of his dictionary, while Webster's dictionary has remained in print.

3. John Jacob Astor's prestigious Park Hotel, opened 1836, located on Broadway directly west of City Hall park, and later called Astor House.

"Who gone, I'd like to know?"

"That man in the brown coat."

"What of him. You aint scared of him, are you?"

"Yes, he got me a place once."

"Where?"

"Ever so far off."

"What if he did?"

"I ran away."

"Didn't you like it?"

"No, I had to get up too early. It was on a farm, and I had to get up at five to take care of the cows.⁴ I like New York best."

"Didn't they give you enough to eat?"

"Oh, yes, plenty."

"And you had a good bed?"

"Yes."

"Then you'd better have stayed. You don't get either of them here. Where'd you sleep last night?"

"Up an alley in an old wagon."

"You had a better bed than that in the country, didn't you?"

"Yes, it was as soft as—as cotton."

Johnny had once slept on a bale of cotton, the recollection supplying him with a comparison.

"Why didn't you stay?"

"I felt lonely," said Johnny.

Johnny could not exactly explain his feelings, but it is often the case that the young vagabond of the streets, though his food is uncertain, and his bed may be any old wagon or barrel that he is lucky enough to find unoccupied when night sets in, gets so attached to his precarious but independent mode of life, that he feels discontented in any other. He is accustomed to the noise and bustle and ever-varied life of the streets, and in the quiet scenes of the country misses the excitement in the midst of which he has always dwelt.

Johnny had but one tie to bind him to the city. He had a father living, but he might as well have been without one. Mr. Nolan was a confirmed drunkard, and spent the greater part of his wages for liquor. His potations made him ugly, and inflamed a temper never very sweet, working him up sometimes to such a pitch of rage that Johnny's life was in danger. Some months before, he had thrown a flat-iron at his son's head with such terrific force that unless Johnny had dodged he would not have lived long enough to obtain a place in our story. He fled the house, and from that time had not dared to re-enter it. Somebody had given him a brush and box of blacking, and

4. Allusion to the so-called orphan trains, a program organized by the Children's Aid Society to relocate urban boys into rual locations. For details, see the article by Clark Kidder, on p. 144 of this volume.

he had set up in business on his own account. But he had not energy enough to succeed, as has already been stated, and I am afraid the poor boy had met with many hardships, and suffered more than once from cold and hunger. Dick had befriended him more than once, and often given him a breakfast or dinner, as the case might be.

"How'd you get away?" asked Dick, with some curiosity. "Did you walk?"

"No, I rode on the cars."

"Where'd you get your money. I hope you didn't steal it."

"I didn't have none."

"What did you do, then?"

"I got up about three o'clock, and walked to Albany."[5]

"Where's that?" asked Dick, whose ideas on the subject of geography were rather vague.

"Up the river."

"How far?"

"About a thousand miles," said Johnny, whose conceptions of distance were equally vague.

"Go ahead. What did you do then?"

"I hid on top of a freight car, and came all the way without their seeing me.[6] That man in the brown coat was the man that got me the place, and I'm afraid he'd want to send me back."

"Well," said Dick, reflectively, "I dunno as I'd like to live in the country. I couldn't go to Tony Pastor's, or the Old Bowery. There wouldn't be no place to spend my evenings. But I say, it's tough in winter, Johnny, 'specially when your overcoat's at the tailor's, an' likely to stay there."

"That's so, Dick. But I must be goin', or Mr. Taylor'll get somebody else to shine his boots."

Johnny walked back to Nassau Street, while Dick kept on his way to Broadway.[7]

"That boy," soliloquized Dick, as Johnny took his departure, "ain't got no ambition. I'll bet he won't get five shines today. I'm glad I aint like him. I couldn't go to the theatre, nor buy no cigars, nor get half as much as I wanted to eat.—Shine yer boots, sir?"

Dick always had an eye to business, and this remark was addressed to a young man, dressed in a stylish manner, who was swinging a jaunty cane.

"I've had my boots blacked once already this morning, but this confounded mud has spoiled the shine."

"I'll make 'em all right, sir, in a minute."

"Go ahead, then."

5. State capital of New York since 1797, about 150 miles from New York City.
6. A fact [Alger's note].
7. Nassau and Broadway run parallel to each other in lower Manhattan.

The boots were soon polished in Dick's best style, which proved very satisfactory, our hero being a proficient in the art.

"I haven't got any change," said the young man, fumbling in his pocket, "but here's a bill you may run somewhere and get changed. I'll pay you five cents extra for your trouble."

He handed Dick a two-dollar bill, which our hero took into a store close by.

"Will you please change that, sir?" said Dick walking up to the counter.

The salesman to whom he proffered it took the bill, and, slightly glancing at it, exclaimed angrily, "Be off, you young vagabond, or I'll have you arrested."

"What's the row?"

"You've offered me a counterfeit bill."

"I didn't know it," said Dick.

"Don't tell me. Be off, or I'll have you arrested."

Chapter 3

Dick Makes a Proposition

Though Dick was somewhat startled at discovering that the bill he had offered was counterfeit, he stood his ground bravely.

"Clear out of this shop, you young vagabond," repeated the clerk.

"Then give me back my bill."

"That you may pass it again? No sir, I shall do no such thing."

"It doesn't belong to me," said Dick. "A gentleman that owes me for a shine gave it to me to change."

"A likely story," said the clerk, but he seemed a little uneasy.

"I'll go and call him," said Dick.

He went out, and found his late customer standing on the Astor House steps.

"Well, youngster, have you brought back my change? You were a precious long time about it. I began to think you had cleared out with the money."

"That aint my style," said Dick proudly.

"Then where's the change?"

"I haven't got it."

"Where's the bill then?"

"I haven't got that either."

"You young rascal!"

"Hold on a minute, mister," said Dick, "and I'll tell you all about it. The man what took the bill said it wasn't good, and kept it."

"The bill was perfectly good. So he kept it, did he? I'll go with you to the store, and see whether he won't give it back to me."

Dick led the way, and the gentleman followed him into the store. At the reappearance of Dick in such company, the clerk flushed a little, and looked nervous. He fancied that he could browbeat a ragged boot-black, but with a gentleman he saw that it would be a different matter. He did not seem to notice the new-comers, but began to replace some goods on the shelves.

"Now," said the young man, "point out the clerk that has my money."

"That's him," said Dick, pointing out the clerk.

The gentleman walked up to the counter.

"I will trouble you," he said a little haughtily, "for that bill which that boy offered you, and which you still hold in your possession."

"It was a bad bill," said the clerk, his cheek flushing, and his manner nervous.

"It was no such thing. I require you to produce it, and let the matter be decided."

The clerk fumbled in his vest-pocket, and drew out a bad-looking bill.

"This is a bad bill, but it is not the one I gave the boy."

"It is the one he gave me."

The young man looked doubtful.

"Boy," he said to Dick, "is this the bill you gave to be changed?"

"No, it isn't."

"You lie, you young rascal!" exclaimed the clerk, who began to find himself in a tight place, and could not see the way out.

This scene naturally attracted the attention of all in the store, and the proprietor walked up from the lower end, where he had been busy.

"What's all this, Mr. Hatch?" he demanded.

"That boy," said the clerk, "came in and asked change for a bad bill. I kept the bill, and told him to clear out. Now he wants it again to pass on somebody else."

"Show the bill."

The merchant looked at it. "Yes, that's a bad bill," he said. "There is no doubt about that."

"But it is not the one the boy offered," said Dick's patron. "It is one of the same denomination, but on a different bank."[1]

"Do you remember what bank it was on?"

"It was on the Merchants' Bank of Boston."

"Are you sure of it?"

"I am."

"Perhaps the boy kept it and offered the other."

"You may search me if you want to," said Dick, indignantly.

---

1. Bank notes were issued by individual banks.

"He doesn't look as if he was likely to have any extra bills. I suspect that your clerk pocketed the good bill, and has substituted the counterfeit note. It is a nice little scheme of his for making money."

"I haven't seen any bill on the Merchants' Bank," said the clerk, doggedly.

"You had better feel in your pockets."

"This matter must be investigated," said the merchant, firmly. "If you have the bill, produce it."

"I haven't got it," said the clerk; but he looked guilty notwithstanding.

"I demand that he be searched," said Dick's patron.

"I tell you I haven't got it."

"Shall I send for a police officer, Mr. Hatch, or will you allow yourself to be searched quietly?" said the merchant.

Alarmed at the threat implied in these words, the clerk put his hand into his vest-pocket, and drew out a two-dollar bill on the Merchants' Bank.

"Is this your note?" asked the shopkeeper, showing it to the young man.

"It is."

"I must have made a mistake," faltered the clerk.

"I shall not give you a chance to make such another mistake in my employ," said the merchant sternly. "You may go up to the desk and ask for what wages are due you. I shall have no further occasion for your services."

"Now, youngster," said Dick's patron, as they went out of the store, after he had finally got the bill changed, "I must pay you something extra for your trouble. Here's fifty cents."

"Thank you, sir," said Dick. "You're very kind. Don't you want some more bills changed?"

"Not to-day," said he with a smile. "It's too expensive."

"I'm in luck," thought our hero complacently. "I guess I'll go to Barnum's[2] tonight, and see the bearded lady, the eight-foot giant, the two-foot dwarf, and the other curiosities, too numerous to mention."

Dick shouldered his box and walked up as far as the Astor House. He took his station on the sidewalk, and began to look about him.

Just behind him were two persons,—one, a gentleman of fifty; the other, a boy of thirteen or fourteen. They were speaking together, and Dick had no difficulty in hearing what was said.

"I am sorry, Frank, that I can't go about, and show you some of the sights of New York, but I shall be full of business to-day. It is your first visit to the city too."

"Yes, sir."

2. P. T. Barnum's museum.

"There's a good deal worth seeing here. But I'm afraid you'll have to wait till next time. You can go out and walk by yourself, but don't venture too far, or you may get lost."

Frank looked disappointed.

"I wish Tom Miles knew I was here," he said. "He would go around with me."

"Where does he live?"

"Somewhere up town, I believe."

"Then, unfortunately, he is not available. If you would rather go with me than stay here, you can, but as I shall be most of the time in merchants' countingrooms, I am afraid it would not be very interesting."

"I think," said Frank, after a little hesitation, "that I will go off by myself. I won't go very far, and if I lose my way, I will inquire for the Astor House."

"Yes, anybody will direct you here."

"Very well, Frank, I am sorry I can't do better for you."

"Oh, never mind, uncle, I shall be amused in walking around, and looking at the shop-windows. There will be a great deal to see."

Now Dick had listened to all this conversation. Being an enterprising young man, he thought he saw a chance for a speculation, and determined to avail himself of it.

Accordingly he stepped up to the two just as Frank's uncle was about leaving, and said, "I know all about the city, sir; I'll show him around, if you want me to."

The gentleman looked a little curiously at the ragged figure before him.

"So you are a city boy, are you?"

"Yes, sir," said Dick, "I've lived here ever since I was a baby."

"And you know all about the public buildings, I suppose?"

"Yes, sir."

"And the Central Park?"

"Yes, sir. I know my way all round."

The gentleman looked thoughtful.

"I don't know what to say, Frank," he remarked after a while. "It is rather a novel proposal. He isn't exactly the sort of guide I would have picked out for you. Still he looks honest. He has an open face, and I think can be depended upon."

"I wish he wasn't so ragged and dirty," said Frank, who felt a little shy about being seen with such a companion.

"I'm afraid you haven't washed your face this morning," said Mr. Whitney, for that was the gentleman's name.

"They didn't have no wash-bowls at the hotel where I stopped," said Dick.

"What hotel did you stop at?"

"The Box Hotel."

"The Box Hotel?"

"Yes, sir, I slept in a box on Spruce Street."

Frank surveyed Dick curiously.

"How did you like it?" he asked.

"I slept bully."

"Suppose it had rained?"

"Then I'd have wet my best clothes," said Dick.

"Are these all the clothes you have?"

"Yes, sir."

Mr. Whitney spoke a few words to Frank, who seemed pleased with the suggestion.

"Follow me, my lad," he said.

Dick in some surprise obeyed orders, following Mr. Whitney and Frank into the hotel, past the office, to the foot of the staircase. Here a servant of the hotel stopped Dick, but Mr. Whitney explained that he had something for him to do, and he was allowed to proceed.

They entered a long entry, and finally paused before a door. This being opened a pleasant chamber was disclosed.

"Come in, my lad," said Mr. Whitney.

Dick and Frank entered.

Chapter 4

Dick's New Suit

"Now," said Mr. Whitney to Dick, "my nephew here is on his way to a boarding-school. He had a suit of clothes in his trunk about half worn. He is willing to give them to you. I think they will look better than those you have on."

Dick was so astonished that he hardly knew what to say. Presents were something that he knew very little about, never having received any to his knowledge. That so large a gift should be made to him by a stranger seemed very wonderful.

The clothes were brought out, and turned out to be a neat gray suit.

"Before you put them on, my lad, you must wash yourself. Clean clothes and a dirty skin don't go very well together. Frank, you may attend to him. I am obliged to go at once. Have you got as much money as you require?"

"Yes, uncle."

"One more word, my lad," said Mr. Whitney, addressing Dick; "I may be rash in trusting a boy of whom I know nothing, but I like your looks, and I think you will prove a proper guide for my nephew."

"Yes, I will, sir," said Dick, earnestly. "Honor bright!"[1]

"Very well. A pleasant time to you."

The process of cleansing commenced. To tell the truth Dick needed it, and the sensation of cleanliness he found both new and pleasant. Frank added to his gift a shirt, stockings, and an old pair of shoes. "I am sorry I haven't any cap," he said.

"I've got one," said Dick.

"It isn't so new as it might be," said Frank, surveying an old felt hat, which had once been black, but was now dingy, with a large hole in the top and a portion of the rim torn off.

"No," said Dick; "my grandfather used to wear it when he was a boy, and I've kep' it ever since out of respect for his memory. But I'll get a new one now. I can buy one cheap on Chatham Street."

"Is that near here?"

"Only five minutes' walk."

"Then we can get one on the way."

When Dick was dressed in his new attire, with his face and hands clean, and his hair brushed, it was difficult to imagine that he was the same boy.

He now looked quite handsome, and might readily have been taken for a young gentleman, except that his hands were red and grimy.

"Look at yourself," said Frank, leading him before the mirror.

"By gracious!" said Dick, staring back in astonishment, "that isn't me, is it?"

"Don't you know yourself?" asked Frank, smiling.

"It reminds me of Cinderella," said Dick, "when she was changed into a fairy princess. I see it one night at Barnum's. What'll Johnny Nolan say when he sees me? He won't dare to speak to such a young swell as I be now. Aint it rich?" and Dick burst into a loud laugh. His fancy was tickled by the anticipation of his friend's surprise. Then the thought of the valuable gifts he had received occurred to him, and he looked gratefully at Frank.

"You're a brick," he said.

"A what?"

"A brick! You're a jolly good fellow to give me such a present."

"You're quite welcome, Dick," said Frank, kindly. "I'm better off than you are, and I can spare the clothes just as well as not. You must have a new hat though. But that we can get when we go out. The old clothes you can make into a bundle."

"Wait a minute till I get my handkercher," and Dick pulled from the pocket of the pants a dirty rag, which might have been white once, though it did not look like it, and had apparently once formed a part of a sheet or shirt.

---

1. An assurance of truth and fidelity.

"You mustn't carry that," said Frank.

"But I've got a cold," said Dick.

"Oh, I don't mean you to go without a handkerchief. I'll give you one."

Frank opened his trunk and pulled out two, which he gave to Dick.

"I wonder if I aint dreamin'," said Dick, once more surveying himself doubtfully in the glass. "I'm afraid I'm dreamin', and shall wake up in a barrel, as I did night afore last."

"Shall I pinch you so you can wake here?" asked Frank, playfully.

"Yes," said Dick, seriously, "I wish you would."

He pulled up the sleeve of his jacket, and Frank pinched him pretty hard, so that Dick winced.

"Yes, I guess I'm awake," said Dick; "you've got a pair of nippers,[2] you have.

"But what shall I do with my brush and blacking?" he asked.

"You can leave them here till we come back," said Frank. "They will be safe."

"Hold on a minute," said Dick, surveying Frank's boots with a professional eye, "you ain't got a good shine on them boots. I'll make 'em shine so you can see your face in 'em."

And he was as good as his word.

"Thank you," said Frank; "now you had better brush your own shoes."

This had not occurred to Dick, for in general the professional boot-black considers his blacking too valuable to expend on his own shoes or boots, if he is fortunate enough to possess a pair.

The two boys now went downstairs together. They met the same servant who had spoken to Dick a few minutes before, but there was no recognition.

"He don't know me," said Dick. "He thinks I'm a young swell like you."

"What's a swell?"

"Oh, a feller that wears nobby[3] clothes like you."

"And you, too, Dick."

"Yes," said Dick, "who'd ever have thought as I should have turned into a swell?"

They had now got out on Broadway, and were slowly walking along the west side by the Park, when who should Dick see in front of him, but Johnny Nolan?

Instantly Dick was seized with a fancy for witnessing Johnny's amazement at his change in appearance. He stole up behind him, and struck him on the back.

2. A scissorlike instrument.
3. Stylish, fashionable, elegant.

"Hallo, Johnny, how many shines have you had?"

Johnny turned round expecting to see Dick, whose voice he recognized, but his astonished eyes rested on a nicely dressed boy (the hat alone excepted) who looked indeed like Dick, but so transformed in dress that it was difficult to be sure of his identity.

"What luck, Johnny?" repeated Dick.

Johnny surveyed him from head to foot in great bewilderment.

"Who be you?" he said.

"Well, that's a good one," laughed Dick; "so you don't know Dick?"

"Where'd you get all them clothes?" asked Johnny. "Have you been stealin'?"

"Say that again, and I'll lick you. No, I've lent my clothes to a young feller as was goin' to a party, and didn't have none fit to wear, and so I put on my second-best for a change."

Without deigning any further explanation, Dick went off, followed by the astonished gaze of Johnny Nolan, who could not quite make up his mind whether the neat-looking boy he had been talking with was really Ragged Dick or not.

In order to reach Chatham Street it was necessary to cross Broadway. This was easier proposed than done. There is always such a throng of omnibuses, drays, carriages, and vehicles of all kinds in the neighborhood of the Astor House, that the crossing is formidable to one who is not used to it. Dick made nothing of it, dodging in and out among the horses and wagons with perfect self-possession. Reaching the opposite sidewalk, he looked back, and found that Frank had retreated in dismay, and that the width of the street was between them.

"Come across!" called out Dick.

"I don't see any chance," said Frank, looking anxiously at the prospect before him. "I'm afraid of being run over."

"If you are, you can sue 'em for damages," said Dick.

Finally Frank got safely over after several narrow escapes, as he considered them.

"Is it always so crowded?" he asked.

"A good deal worse sometimes," said Dick. "I knowed a young man once who waited six hours for a chance to cross, and at last got run over by an omnibus, leaving a widder and a large family of orphan children. His widder, a beautiful young woman, was obliged to start a peanut and apple stand. There she is now."

"Where?"

Dick pointed to a hideous old woman, of large proportions, wearing a bonnet of immense size, who presided over an apple-stand close by.

Frank laughed.

"If that is the case," he said, "I think I will patronize her."

"Leave it to me," said Dick, winking.

He advanced gravely to the apple-stand, and said, "Old lady, have you paid your taxes?"

The astonished woman opened her eyes.

"I'm a gov'ment officer," said Dick, "sent by the mayor to collect your taxes. I'll take it in apples just to oblige. That big red one will about pay what you're owin' to the gov'ment."

"I don't know nothing about no taxes," said the old woman, in bewilderment.

"Then," said Dick, "I'll let you off this time. Give us two of your best apples, and my friend here, the President of the Common Council, will pay you."

Frank, smiling, paid three cents apiece for the apples, and they sauntered on, Dick remarking, "If these apples aint good, old lady, we'll return 'em and get our money back." This would have been rather difficult in his case, as the apple was already half consumed.

Chatham Street, where they wished to go, being on the East side, the two boys crossed the Park. This is an enclosure of about ten acres, which years ago was covered with a green sward, but is now a great thoroughfare for pedestrians and contains several important public buildings. Dick pointed out the City Hall, the Hall of Records, and the Rotunda. The former is a white building of large size, and surmounted by a cupola.[4]

"That's where the mayor's office is," said Dick. "Him and me are very good friends. I once blacked his boots by particular appointment. That's the way I pay my city taxes."

Chapter 5

Chatham Street and Broadway

They were soon in Chatham Street, walking between rows of ready-made clothing shops, many of which had half of their stock in trade exposed on the sidewalk. The proprietors of these establishments stood at the doors, watching attentively the passers-by, extending urgent invitations to any who even glanced at the goods, to enter.

"Walk in, young gentlemen," said a stout man, at the entrance of one shop.

"No, I thank you," replied Dick, "as the fly said to the spider."

"We're selling off at less than cost."

"Of course you be. That's where you makes your money," said Dick. "There aint nobody of any enterprise that pretends to make any profit on his goods."

4. A roof in the form of a dome.

The Chatham Street trader looked after our hero as if he didn't quite comprehend him; but Dick, without waiting for a reply, passed on with his companion.

In some of the shops auctions seemed to be going on.

"I am only offered two dollars, gentlemen, for this elegant pair of doeskin pants, made of the very best of cloth. It's a frightful sacrifice. Who'll give an eighth? Thank you, sir. Only seventeen shillings! Why the cloth cost more by the yard!"

This speaker was standing on a little platform haranguing to three men, holding in his hand meanwhile a pair of pants very loose in the legs, and presenting a cheap Bowery look.

Frank and Dick paused before the shop door, and finally saw them knocked down to rather a verdant-looking individual at three dollars.

"Clothes seem to be pretty cheap here," said Frank.

"Yes, but Baxter Street is the cheapest place."

"Is it?"

"Yes. Johnny Nolan got a whole rig-out there last week, for a dollar,—coat, cap, vest, pants, and shoes. They was very good measure, too, like my best clothes that I took off to oblige you."

"I shall know where to come for clothes next time," said Frank, laughing. "I had no idea the city was so much cheaper than the country. I suppose the Baxter Street tailors are fashionable?"

"In course they are. Me and Horace Greeley[1] always go there for clothes. When Horace gets a new suit, I always have one made just like it; but I can't go the white hat. It aint becomin' to my style of beauty."

A little farther on a man was standing out on the sidewalk, distributing small printed handbills. One was handed to Frank, which he read as follows,—

"GRAND CLOSING-OUT SALE!—A variety of Beautiful and Costly Articles for Sale, at a Dollar apiece. Unparalleled Inducements! Walk in, Gentlemen!"

"Whereabouts is this sale?" asked Frank.

"In here, young gentlemen," said a black-whiskered individual, who appeared suddenly on the scene. "Walk in."

"Shall we go in, Dick?"

"It's a swindlin' shop," said Dick, in a low voice. "I've been there. That man's a reg'lar cheat. He's seen me before, but he don't know me coz of my clothes."

"Step in and see the articles," said the man, persuasively, "You needn't buy, you know."

"Are all the articles worth more'n a dollar?" asked Dick.

---

1. Influential American journalist and political leader (1811–1872). Trained as a printer, Greeley worked for the *New Yorker*, established the *New York Tribune* in 1841 and edited it for over thirty years.

"Yes," said the other, "and some worth a great deal more."

"Such as what?"

"Well, there's a silver pitcher worth twenty dollars."

"And you sell it for a dollar. That's very kind of you," said Dick, innocently.

"Walk in, and you'll understand it."

"No, I guess not," said Dick. "My servants is so dishonest that I wouldn't like to trust 'em with a silver pitcher. Come along, Frank. I hope you'll succeed in your charitable enterprise of supplyin' the public with silver pitchers at nineteen dollars less than they are worth."

"How does he manage, Dick?" asked Frank, as they went on.

"All his articles are numbered, and he makes you pay a dollar, and then shakes some dice, and whatever the figgers come to, is the number of the article you draw. Most of 'em aint worth sixpence."

A hat and cap store being close at hand, Dick and Frank went in. For seventy-five cents, which Frank insisted on paying, Dick succeeded in getting quite a neat-looking cap, which corresponded much better with his appearance than the one he had on. The last, not being considered worth keeping, Dick dropped on the sidewalk, from which, on looking back, he saw it picked up by a brother boot-black who appeared to consider it better than his own.

They retraced their steps and went up Chambers Street to Broadway. At the corner of Broadway and Chambers Street is a large white marble warehouse, which attracted Frank's attention.

"What building is that?" he asked, with interest.

"That belongs to my friend A. T. Stewart," said Dick. "It's the biggest store on Broadway.[2] If I ever retire from boot-blackin', and go into mercantile pursuits, I may buy him out, or build another store that'll take the shine off this one."

"Were you ever in the store?" asked Frank.

"No," said Dick; "but I'm intimate with one of Stewart's partners. He is a cash boy, and does nothing but take money all day."

"A very agreeable employment," said Frank laughing.

"Yes," said Dick, "I'd like to be in it."

The boys crossed to the West side of Broadway, and walked slowly up the street. To Frank it was a very interesting spectacle. Accustomed to the quiet of the country, there was something fascinating in the crowds of people thronging the sidewalks, and the great variety of vehicles constantly passing and repassing in the street. Then again the shop-windows with their multifarious contents interested and amused him, and he was constantly checking Dick to look in at some well-stocked window.

"I don't see how so many shopkeepers can find people enough to

2. Mr. Stewart's Tenth Street store was not open at the time Dick spoke [*Alger's note*].

buy of them," he said. "We haven't got but two stores in our village, and Broadway seems to be full of them."

"Yes," said Dick; "and its pretty much the same in the avenoos, 'specially the Third, Sixth, and Eighth avenoos. The Bowery, too, is a great place for shoppin'. There everybody sells cheaper'n anybody else, and nobody pretends to make no profit on their goods."

"Where's Barnum's Museum?" asked Frank.

"Oh, that's down nearly opposite the Astor House," said Dick. "Didn't you see a great building with lots of flags?"

"Yes."

"Well, that's Barnum's.[3] That's where the Happy Family live, and the lions, and bears, and curiosities generally. It's a tip-top place. Haven't you ever been there? It's most as good as the Old Bowery, only the plays isn't quite so excitin'."

"I'll go if I get time," said Frank. "There is a boy at home who came to New York a month ago, and went to Barnum's, and has been talking about it ever since, so I suppose it must be worth seeing."

"They've got a great play at the Old Bowery now," pursued Dick. " 'Tis called the 'Demon of the Danube.' The Demon falls in love with a young woman, and drags her by the hair up to the top of a steep rock where his castle stands."

"That's a queer way of showing his love," said Frank, laughing.

"She didn't want to go with him, you know, but was in love with another chap. When he heard about his girl bein' carried off, he felt awful, and swore an oath not to rest till he had got her free. Well, at last he got into the castle by some underground passage, and he and the Demon had a fight. Oh, it was bully seein' 'em roll round the stage, cuttin' and slashin' at each other."

"And which got the best of it?"

"At first the Demon seemed to be ahead, but at last the young Baron got him down, and struck a dagger into his heart, sayin', 'Die, false and perjured villain! The dogs shall feast upon thy carcass!' and then the Demon give an awful howl and died. Then the Baron seized his body, and threw it over the precipice."

"It seems to me the actor who plays the Demon ought to get extra pay, if he has to be treated that way."

"That's so," said Dick; "but I guess he's used to it. It seems to agree with his constitution."

"What building is that?" asked Frank, pointing to a structure several rods back from the street, with a large yard in front. It was an unusual sight for Broadway, all the other buildings in that neighborhood being even with the street.

---

3. Since destroyed by fire, and rebuilt farther up Broadway, and again burned down in February [Alger's note].

"That is the New York Hospital,"[4] said Dick. "They're a rich insti-tution, and take care of sick people on very reasonable terms."

"Did you ever go in there?"

"Yes," said Dick; "there was a friend of mine, Johnny Mullen, he was a newsboy, got run over by a omnibus as he was crossin' Broad-way down near Park Place. He was carried to the Hospital, and me and some of his friends paid his board while he was there. It was only three dollars a week, which was very cheap, considerin' all the care they took of him. I got leave to come and see him while he was here. Everything looked so nice and comfortable, that I thought a little of coaxin' a omnibus driver to run over me, so I might go there too."

"Did your friend have to have his leg cut off?" asked Frank, inter-ested.

"No," said Dick; "though there was a young student there that was very anxious to have it cut off; but it wasn't done, and Johnny is around the streets as well as ever."

While this conversation was going on they reached No. 365, at the corner of Franklin Street.[5]

"That's Taylor's Saloon," said Dick. "When I come into a fortun' I shall take my meals there reg'lar."

"I have heard of it very often," said Frank. "It is said to be very ele-gant. Suppose we go in and take an ice-cream. It will give us a chance to see it to better advantage."

"Thank you," said Dick; "I think that's the most agreeable way of seein' the place myself."

The boys entered, and found themselves in a spacious and elegant saloon, resplendent with gilding, and adorned on all sides by costly mirrors. They sat down to a small table with a marble top, and Frank gave the order.

"It reminds me of Aladdin's palace," said Frank, looking about him.

"Does it?" said Dick; "he must have had plenty of money."

"He had an old lamp, which he had only to rub, when the Slave of the Lamp would appear, and do whatever he wanted."

"That must have been a valooable lamp. I'd be willin' to give all my Erie shares for it."

There was a tall, gaunt individual at the next table, who apparently heard this last remark of Dick's. Turning towards our hero, he said, "May I inquire, young man, whether you are largely interested in this Erie Railroad?"

"I haven't got no property except what's invested in Erie," said Dick, with a comical side-glance at Frank.

"Indeed! I suppose the investment was made by your guardian."

4. Opened in 1776 for colonial soldiers; opened to the public in 1791.
5. Now the office of the Merchant's Union Express Company [*Alger's note*].

"No," said Dick; "I manage my property myself."

"And I presume your dividends have not been large?"

"Why, no," said Dick; "you're about right there. They haven't."

"As I supposed. It's poor stock. Now, my young friend, I can rec-
ommend a much better investment, which will yield you a large
annual income. I am agent of the Excelsior Copper Mining Company,
which possesses one of the most productive mines in the world. It's
sure to yield fifty per cent on the investment. Now, all you have to do
is to sell out your Erie shares, and invest in our stock, and I'll insure
you a fortune in three years. How many shares did you say you had?"

"I didn't say, that I remember," said Dick. "Your offer is very kind
and obligin', and as soon as I get time I'll see about it."

"I hope you will," said the stranger. "Permit me to give you my card.
'Samuel Snap, No — Wall Street.' I shall be most happy to receive a
call from you, and exhibit the maps of our mine. I should be glad to
have you mention the matter also to your friends. I am confident you
could do no greater service than to induce them to embark in our
enterprise."

"Very good," said Dick.

Here the stranger left the table, and walked up to the desk to settle his bill.

"You see what it is to be a man of fortune, Frank," said Dick, "and
wear good clothes. I wonder what that chap'll say when he sees me
blackin' boots to-morrow in the street?"

"Perhaps you earn your money more honorably than he does, after
all," said Frank. "Some of these mining companies are nothing but
swindles, got up to cheat people out of their money."

"He's welcome to all he gets out of me," said Dick.

Chapter 6

Up Broadway to Madison Square

As the boys pursued their way up Broadway, Dick pointed out the
prominent hotels and places of amusement. Frank was particularly
struck with the imposing fronts of the St. Nicholas and Metropolitan
Hotels, the former of white marble, the latter of a subdued brown
hue, but not less elegant in its internal appointments. He was not
surprised to be informed that each of these splendid structures cost
with the furnishing not far from a million dollars.

At Eighth Street Dick turned to the right, and pointed out the Clinton Hall Building now occupied by the Mercantile Library, comprising at that time over fifty thousand volumes.[1]

1. Now not far from one hundred thousand [*Alger's note*].

A little farther on they came to a large building standing by itself just at the opening of Third and Fourth Avenues, and with one side on each.

"What is that building?" asked Frank.

"That's the Cooper Institute," said Dick; "built by Mr. Cooper, a particular friend of mine. Me and Peter Cooper used to go to school together."

"What is there inside?" asked Frank.

"There's a hall for public meetin's and lectures in the basement, and a readin' room and a picture gallery up above," said Dick.

Directly opposite Cooper Institute, Frank saw a very large building of brick, covering about an acre of ground.

"Is that a hotel?" he asked.

"No," said Dick; "that's the Bible House. It's the place where they make Bibles. I was in there once,—saw a big pile of 'em."

"Did you ever read the Bible?" asked Frank, who had some idea of the neglected state of Dick's education.

"No," said Dick; "I've heard it's a good book, but I never read one. I aint much on readin'. It makes my head ache."

"I suppose you can't read very fast."

"I can read the little words pretty well, but the big ones is what stick me."

"If I lived in the city, you might come every evening to me, and I would teach you."

"Would you take so much trouble about me?" asked Dick, earnestly.

"Certainly; I should like to see you getting on. There isn't much chance of that if you don't know how to read and write."

"You're a good feller," said Dick, gratefully. "I wish you did live in New York. I'd like to know somethin'. Whereabouts do you live?"

"About fifty miles off, in a town on the left bank of the Hudson. I wish you'd come up and see me sometime. I would like to have you come and stop two or three days."

"Honor bright?"

"I don't understand."

"Do you mean it?" asked Dick, incredulously.

"Of course I do. Why shouldn't I?"

"What would your folks say if they knowed you asked a boot-black to visit you?"

"You are none the worse for being a boot-black, Dick."

"I aint used to genteel society," said Dick. "I shouldn't know how to behave."

"Then I could show you. You won't be a boot-black all your life, you know."

"No," said Dick; "I'm goin' to knock off when I get to be ninety."

"Before that, I hope," said Frank, smiling.

"I really wish I could get somethin' else to do," said Dick, soberly. "I'd like to be a office boy, and learn business, and grow up 'spectable."

"Why don't you try, and see if you can't get a place, Dick?"

"Who'd take Ragged Dick?"

"But you aint ragged now, Dick."

"No," said Dick; "I look a little better than I did in my Washington coat and Louis Napoleon pants. But if I got in a office, they wouldn't give me more'n three dollars a week, and I couldn't live 'spectable on that."

"No, I suppose not," said Frank, thoughtfully. "But you would get more at the end of the first year."

"Yes," said Dick; "but by that time I'd be nothin' but skin and bones."

Frank laughed. "That reminds me," he said, "of the story of an Irishman, who, out of economy, thought he would teach his horse to feed on shavings. So he provided the horse with a pair of green spectacles which made the shavings look eatable. But unfortunately, just as the horse got learned, he up and died."[2]

"The hoss must have been a fine specimen of architectur' by the time he got through," remarked Dick.

"Whereabouts are we now?" asked Frank, as they emerged from Fourth Avenue into Union Square.

"That is Union Park,"[3] said Dick, pointing to a beautiful enclosure, in the centre of which was a pond, with a fountain playing.

"Is that the statue of General Washington?" asked Frank, pointing to a bronze equestrian statue, on a granite pedestal.

"Yes," said Dick; "he's growed some since he was President. If he'd been as tall as that when he fit in the Revolution, he'd have walloped the British some, I reckon."

Frank looked up at the statue, which is fourteen and a half feet high, and acknowledged the justice of Dick's remark.

"How about the coat, Dick?" he asked. "Would it fit you?"

"Well, it might be rather loose," said Dick, "I aint much more'n ten feet high with my boots off."

"No, I should think not," said Frank, smiling. "You're a queer boy, Dick."

"Well, I've been brought up queer. Some boys is born with a silver spoon in their mouth. Victoria's boys is born with a gold spoon, set with di'monds; but gold and silver was scarce when I was born, and mine was pewter."

2. Reference to Charles Dickens's novel *Oliver Twist*, Chapter II.
3. Union Square Park, established where Broadway and the Bowery came together in the early nineteenth century. It is famous for its equestrian statue of George Washington created by Henry Kirk Brown and unveiled in 1856.

"Perhaps the gold and silver will come by and by, Dick. Did you ever hear of Dick Whittington?"[4]

"Never did. Was he a Ragged Dick?"

"I shouldn't wonder if he was. At any rate he was very poor when he was a boy, but he didn't stay so. Before he died, he became Lord Mayor of London."

"Did he?" asked Dick, looking interested. "How did he do it?"

"Why, you see, a rich merchant took pity on him, and gave him a home in his own house, where he used to stay with the servants, being employed in little errands. One day the merchant noticed Dick picking up pins and needles that had been dropped, and asked him why he did it. Dick told him he was going to sell them when he got enough. The merchant was pleased with his saving disposition, and when soon after, he was going to send a vessel to foreign parts, he told Dick he might send anything he pleased in it, and it should be sold to his advantage. Now Dick had nothing in the world but a kitten which had been given him a short time before."

"How much taxes did he have to pay for it?" asked Dick.

"Not very high, probably. But having only the kitten, he concluded to send it along. After sailing a good many months, during which the kitten grew up to be a strong cat, the ship touched at an island never before known, which happened to be infested with rats and mice to such an extent that they worried everybody's life out, and even ransacked the king's palace. To make a long story short, the captain, seeing how matters stood, brought Dick's cat ashore, and she soon made the rats and mice scatter. The king was highly delighted when he saw what havoc she made among the rats and mice, and resolved to have her at any price. So he offered a great quantity of gold for her, which, of course, the captain was glad to accept. It was faithfully carried back to Dick, and laid the foundation of his fortune. He prospered as he grew up, and in time became a very rich merchant, respected by all, and before he died was elected Lord Mayor of London."

"That's a pretty good story," said Dick; "but I don't believe all the cats in New York will ever make me mayor."

"No, probably not, but you may rise in some other way. A good many distinguished men have once been poor boys. There's hope for you, Dick, if you'll try."

"Nobody ever talked to me so before," said Dick. "They just called me Ragged Dick, and told me I'd grow up to be a vagabone (boys who are better educated need not be surprised at Dick's blunders) and come to the gallows."

"Telling you so won't make it turn out so, Dick. If you'll try to be somebody, and grow up into a respectable member of society, you

---

4. Mayor of London (1350–1423). Alger refers to a famous legend about Whittington.

will. You may not become rich,—it isn't everybody that becomes rich, you know,—but you can obtain a good position, and be respected."

"I'll try," said Dick, earnestly. "I needn't have been Ragged Dick so long if I hadn't spent my money in goin' to the theatre, and treatin' boys to oyster-stews, and bettin' money on cards, and such like."

"Have you lost money that way?"

"Lots of it. One time I saved up five dollars to buy me a new rig-out, cos my best suit was all in rags, when Limpy Jim wanted me to play a game with him."

"Limpy Jim?" said Frank, interrogatively.

"Yes, he's lame; that's what makes us call him Limpy Jim."

"I suppose you lost?"

"Yes, I lost every penny, and had to sleep out, cos I hadn't a cent to pay for lodgin'. 'Twas a awful cold night, and I got most froze."

"Wouldn't Jim let you have any of the money he had won to pay for a lodging?"

"No; I axed him for five cents, but he wouldn't let me have it."

"Can you get lodging for five cents?" asked Frank, in surprise.

"Yes," said Dick, "but not at the Fifth Avenue Hotel. That's it right out there."

Chapter 7

The Pocket-Book

They had reached the junction of Broadway and of Fifth Avenue. Before them was a beautiful park of ten acres. On the left-hand side was a large marble building, presenting a fine appearance with its extensive white front. This was the building at which Dick pointed.

"Is that the Fifth Avenue Hotel?" asked Frank. "I've heard of it often. My Uncle William always stops there when he comes to New York."

"I once slept on the outside of it," said Dick. "They was very reasonable in their charges, and told me I might come again."

"Perhaps sometime you'll be able to sleep inside," said Frank.

"I guess that'll be when Queen Victoria goes to the Five Points[1] to live."

"It looks like a palace," said Frank. "The queen needn't be ashamed to live in such a beautiful building as that."

Though Frank did not know it, one of the queen's palaces is far from being as fine a looking building as the Fifth Avenue Hotel. St. James' Palace is a very ugly-looking brick structure, and appears

---

1. A New York City neighborhood. See n. 1, p. 57.

much more like a factory than like the home of royalty. There are few hotels in the world as fine-looking as this democratic institution.

At that moment a gentleman passed them on the sidewalk, who looked back at Dick, as if his face seemed familiar.

"I know that man," said Dick, after he had passed, "He's one of my customers."

"What is his name?"

"I don't know."

"He looked back as if he thought he knew you."

"He would have knowed me at once if it hadn't been for my new clothes," said Dick. "I don't look much like Ragged Dick now."

"I suppose your face looked familiar."

"All but the dirt," said Dick, laughing. "I don't always have the chance of washing my face and hands in the Astor House."

"You told me," said Frank, "that there was a place where you could get lodging for five cents. Where's that?"

"It's the Newsboys' Lodgin' House[2] on Fulton Street," said Dick, "up over the 'Sun'[3] office. It's a good place. I don't know what us boys would do without it. They give you supper for six cents, and a bed for five cents more."

"I suppose some boys don't even have the five cents to pay,—do they?"

"They'll trust the boys," said Dick. "But I don't like to get trusted. I'd be ashamed to get trusted for five cents, or ten either. One night I was comin' down Chatham Street, with fifty cents in my pocket. I was goin' to get a good oyster-stew, and then go to the lodgin' house; but somehow it slipped through a hole in my trowses-pocket, and I hadn't a cent left. If it had been summer I shouldn't have cared, but it's rather tough stayin' out winter nights."

Frank, who had always possessed a good home of his own, found it hard to realize that the boy who was walking at his side had actually walked the streets in the cold without a home, or money to procure the common comfort of a bed.

"What did you do?" he asked, his voice full of sympathy.

"I went to the 'Times' office.[4] I knowed one of the pressmen, and he let me set down in a corner, where I was warm, and I soon got fast asleep."

"Why don't you get a room somewhere, and so always have a home to go to?"

---

2. Founded in 1854, this lodging house offered shelter to boys.
3. The *New York Sun*, leading daily New York newspaper, established by Moses Yale Beach (1800–1868).
4. The *New York Times* newspaper was founded in 1851. In 1868 the *Times* took on the Erie Railroad scandal.

"I dunno," said Dick. "I never thought of it. P'rhaps I may hire a furnished house on Madison Square."

"That's where Flora McFlimsey lived."

"I don't know her," said Dick, who had never read the popular poem of which she is the heroine.[5]

While this conversation was going on, they had turned into Twenty-fifth Street, and had by this time reached Third Avenue.

Just before entering it, their attention was drawn to the rather singular conduct of an individual in front of them. Stopping suddenly, he appeared to pick up something from the sidewalk, and then looked about him in rather a confused way.

"I know his game," whispered Dick. "Come along and you'll see what it is."

He hurried Frank forward until they overtook the man, who had come to a stand-still.

"Have you found anything?" asked Dick.

"Yes," said the man, "I've found this."

He exhibited a wallet which seemed stuffed with bills, to judge from its plethoric appearance.

"Whew!" exclaimed Dick; "you're in luck."

"I suppose somebody has lost it," said the man, "and will offer a handsome reward."

"Which you'll get."

"Unfortunately I am obliged to take the next train to Boston. That's where I live. I haven't time to hunt up the owner."

"Then I suppose you'll take the pocket-book with you," said Dick, with assumed simplicity.

"I should like to leave it with some honest fellow who would see it returned to the owner," said the man, glancing at the boys.

"I'm honest," said Dick.

"I've no doubt of it," said the other. "Well, young man, I'll make you an offer. You take the pocket-book—"

"All right. Hand it over, then."

"Wait a minute. There must be a large sum inside. I shouldn't wonder if there might be a thousand dollars. The owner will probably give you a hundred dollars reward."

"Why don't you stay and get it?" asked Frank.

"I would, only there is sickness in my family, and I must get home as soon as possible. Just give me twenty dollars, and I'll hand you the pocket-book, and let you make whatever you can out of it. Come, that's a good offer. What do you say?"

---

5. The poem is "Miss M'Flimsey, or, Nothing to Wear, an Episode of City Life" (1857) by William Allen Butler; Flora McFlimsey became an idiom to describe women who were overly interested in fashion and consumerism.

Dick was well dressed, so that the other did not regard it as at all improbable that he might possess that sum. He was prepared, however, to let him have it for less, if necessary.

"Twenty dollars is a good deal of money," said Dick, appearing to hesitate.

"You'll get it back, and a good deal more," said the stranger, persuasively.

"I don't know but I shall. What would you do, Frank?"

"I don't know but I would," said Frank, "if you've got the money." He was not a little surprised to think that Dick had so much by him.

"I don't know but I will," said Dick, after some irresolution. "I guess I won't lose much."

"You can't lose anything," said the stranger briskly. "Only be quick, for I must be on my way to the cars. I am afraid I shall miss them now."

Dick pulled out a bill from his pocket, and handed it to the stranger, receiving the pocket-book in return. At that moment a policeman turned the corner, and the stranger, hurriedly thrusting the bill into his pocket, without looking at it, made off with rapid steps.

"What is there in the pocket-book, Dick?" asked Frank in some excitement. "I hope there's enough to pay you for the money you gave him."

Dick laughed.

"I'll risk that," said he.

"But you gave him twenty dollars. That's a good deal of money."

"If I had given him as much as that, I should deserve to be cheated out of it."

"But you did,—didn't you?"

"He thought so."

"What was it, then?"

"It was nothing but a dry-goods circular got up to imitate a bank-bill."

Frank looked sober.

"You ought not to have cheated him, Dick," he said, reproachfully.

"Didn't he want to cheat me?"

"I don't know."

"What do you s'pose there is in that pocket-book?" asked Dick, holding it up.

Frank surveyed its ample proportions, and answered sincerely enough, "Money, and a good deal of it."

"There aint stamps enough in it to buy an oyster-stew," said Dick. "If you don't believe it, just look while I open it."

So saying he opened the pocket-book, and showed Frank that it was stuffed out with pieces of blank paper, carefully folded up in the shape of bills. Frank, who was unused to city life, and had never heard anything of the "drop-game," looked amazed at this unexpected development.

"I knowed how it was all the time," said Dick. "I guess I got the best of him there. This wallet's worth somethin'. I shall use it to keep my stiffkit's of Erie stock in, and all my other papers what aint of no use to anybody but the owner."

"That's the kind of papers it's got in it now," said Frank, smiling.

"That's so!" said Dick.

"By hokey!" he exclaimed suddenly, "if there aint the old chap comin' back ag'in. He looks as if he'd heard bad news from his sick family."

By this time the pocket-book dropper had come up.

Approaching the boys, he said in an undertone to Dick, "Give me back that pocket-book, you young rascal!"

"Beg your pardon, mister," said Dick, "but was you addressin' me?"

"Yes, I was."

"'Cause you called me by the wrong name. I've knowed some rascals, but I aint the honor to belong to the family."

He looked significantly at the other as he spoke, which didn't improve the man's temper. Accustomed to swindle others, he did not fancy being practised upon in return.

"Give me back that pocket-book," he repeated in a threatening voice.

"Couldn't do it," said Dick, coolly. "I'm go'n' to restore it to the owner. The contents is so valooable that most likely the loss has made him sick, and he'll be likely to come down liberal to the honest finder."

"You gave me a bogus bill," said the man.

"It's what I use myself," said Dick.

"You've swindled me."

"I thought it was the other way."

"None of your nonsense," said the man angrily. "If you don't give up that pocket-book, I'll call a policeman."

"I wish you would," said Dick. "They'll know most likely whether it's Stewart or Astor[6] that's lost the pocket-book, and I can get 'em to return it."

The "dropper," whose object it was to recover the pocket-book, in order to try the same game on a more satisfactory customer, was irritated by Dick's refusal, and above all by the coolness he displayed. He resolved to make one more attempt.

"Do you want to pass the night in the Tombs?" he asked.

"Thank you for your very obligin' proposal," said Dick; "but it aint convenient to-day. Any other time, when you'd like to have me come

6. Robert Stewart and John Jacob Astor owned the Astor House, with Ramsey Crooks.

and stop with you, I'm agreeable; but my two youngest children is down with the measles, and I expect I'll have to set up all night to take care of 'em. Is the Tombs, in gineral, a pleasant place of residence?"

Dick asked this question with an air of so much earnestness that Frank could scarcely forbear laughing, though it is hardly necessary to say that the dropper was by no means so thrilled.

"You'll know sometime," he said, scowling.

"I'll make you a fair offer," said Dick. "If I get more'n fifty dollars as a reward for my honesty, I'll divide with you. But I say, aint it most time to go back to your sick family in Boston?"

Finding that nothing was to be made out of Dick, the man strode away with a muttered curse.

"You were too smart for him, Dick," said Frank.

"Yes," said Dick, "I aint knocked round the city streets all my life for nothin'."

Chapter 8

Dick's Early History

"Have you always lived in New York, Dick?" asked Frank, after a pause.

"Ever since I can remember."

"I wish you'd tell me a little about yourself. Have you got any father or mother?"

"I aint got no mother. She died when I wasn't but three years old. My father went to sea; but he went off before mother died, and nothin' was ever heard of him. I expect he got wrecked, or died at sea."

"And what became of you when your mother died?"

"The folks she boarded with took care of me, but they was poor, and they couldn't do much. When I was seven the woman died, and her husband went out West, and then I had to scratch for myself."

"At seven years old!" exclaimed Frank, in amazement.

"Yes," said Dick, "I was a little feller to take care of myself, but," he continued with pardonable pride, "I did it."

"What could you do?"

"Sometimes one thing, and sometimes another," said Dick. "I changed my business accordin' as I had to. Sometimes I was a news-boy, and diffused intelligence among the masses, as I heard somebody say once in a big speech he made in the Park. Them was the times when Horace Greeley and James Gordon Bennett[1] made money."

---

1. American newspaper proprietor (1841–1918); he took over the New York *Herald* in 1867.

"Through your enterprise?" suggested Frank.

"Yes," said Dick; "but I give it up after a while."

"What for?"

"Well, they didn't always put news enough in their papers, and people wouldn't buy 'em as fast as I wanted 'em to. So one mornin' I was stuck on a lot of Heralds, and I thought I'd make a sensation. So I called out 'GREAT NEWS! QUEEN VICTORIA ASSASSINATED!'[2] All my Heralds went off like hot cakes, and I went off, too, but one of the gentlemen what got sold remembered me, and said he'd have me took up, and that's what made me change my business."

"That wasn't right, Dick," said Frank.

"I know it," said Dick; "but lots of boys does it."

"That don't make it any better."

"No," said Dick, "I was sort of ashamed at the time, 'specially about one poor old gentleman,—a Englishman he was. He couldn't help cryin' to think the queen was dead, and his hands shook when he handed me the money for the paper."

"What did you do next?"

"I went into the match business," said Dick; "but it was small sales and small profits. Most of the people I called on had just laid in a stock, and didn't want to buy. So one cold night, when I hadn't money enough to pay for a lodgin', I burned the last of my matches to keep me from freezin'. But it cost too much to get warm that way, and I couldn't keep it up."

"You've seen hard times, Dick," said Frank, compassionately.

"Yes," said Dick, "I've knowed what it was to be hungry and cold, with nothin' to eat or to warm me; but there's one thing I never could do," he added, proudly.

"What's that?"

"I never stole," said Dick. "It's mean and I wouldn't do it."

"Were you ever tempted to?"

"Lots of times. Once I had been goin round all day, and hadn't sold any matches, except three cents' worth early in the mornin'. With that I bought an apple, thinkin' I should get some more bimeby.[3] When evenin' come I was awful hungry. I went into a baker's just to look at the bread. It made me feel kind o' good just to look at the bread and cakes, and I thought maybe they would give me some. I asked 'em wouldn't they give me a loaf, and take their pay in matches. But they said they'd got enough matches to last three months; so there wasn't any chance for a trade. While I was standin' at the stove warmin' me, the baker went into the back room, and I felt so hungry I thought I

2. In actuality, there had been many assassination attempts on the Queen, in 1839, 1847 (twice), 1849, 1850, and later again in 1872 and 1882.
3. By and by.

would take just one loaf, and go off with it. There was such a big pile I don't think he'd have known it."

"But you didn't do it?"

"No, I didn't, and I was glad of it, for when the man came in ag'in, he said he wanted some one to carry some cake to a lady in St. Mark's Place. His boy was sick, and he hadn't no one to send, so he told me he'd give me ten cents if I would go. My business wasn't very pressin' just then, so I went, and when I come back, I took my pay in bread and cakes. Didn't they taste good, though?"

"So you didn't stay long in the match business, Dick?"

"No, I couldn't sell enough to make it pay. Then there was some folks that wanted me to sell cheaper to them; so I couldn't make any profit. There was one old lady—she was rich, too, for she lived in a big brick house—beat me down so, that I didn't make no profit at all; but she wouldn't buy without, and I hadn't sold none that day; so I let her have them. I don't see why rich folks should be so hard upon a poor boy that wants to make a livin'."

"There's a good deal of meanness in the world, I'm afraid, Dick."

"If everybody was like you and your uncle," said Dick, "there would be some chance for poor people. If I was rich I'd try to help 'em along."

"Perhaps you will be rich sometime, Dick."

Dick shook his head.

"I'm afraid all my wallets will be like this," said Dick, indicating the one he had received from the dropper, "and will be full of papers what aint of no use to anybody except the owner."

"That depends very much on yourself, Dick," said Frank. "Stewart wasn't always rich, you know."

"Wasn't he?"

"When he first came to New York as a young man he was a teacher, and teachers are not generally very rich. At last he went into business, starting in a small way, and worked his way up by degrees. But there was one thing he determined in the beginning: that he would be strictly honorable in all his dealings, and never overreach any one for the sake of making money. If there was a chance for him, Dick, there is a chance for you."

"He knowed enough to be a teacher, and I'm awful ignorant," said Dick.

"But you needn't stay so."

"How can I help it?"

"Can't you learn at school?"

"I can't go to school 'cause I've got my livin' to earn. It wouldn't do me much good if I learned to read and write, and just as I'd got learned I starved to death."

"But are there no night-schools?"

"Yes."

"Why don't you go? I suppose you don't work in the evenings."

"I never cared much about it," said Dick, "and that's the truth. But since I've got to talkin' with you, I think more about it. I guess I'll begin to go."

"I wish you would, Dick. You'll make a smart man if you only get a little education."

"Do you think so?" asked Dick, doubtfully.

"I know so. A boy who has earned his own living ever since he was seven years old must have something in him. I feel very much interested in you, Dick. You've had a hard time of it so far in life, but I think better times are in store. I want you to do well, and I feel sure you can if you only try."

"You're a good fellow," said Dick, gratefully. "I'm afraid I'm a pretty rough customer, but I aint as bad as some. I mean to turn over a new leaf, and try to grow up 'spectable."

"There've been a great many boys begin as low down as you, Dick, that have grown up respectable and honored. But they had to work pretty hard for it."

"I'm willin' to work hard," said Dick.

"And you must not only work hard, but work in the right way."

"What's the right way?"

"You began in the right way when you determined never to steal, or do anything mean or dishonorable, however strongly tempted to do so. That will make people have confidence in you when they come to know you. But, in order to succeed well, you must manage to get as good an education as you can. Until you do, you cannot get a position in an office or counting-room[4] even to run errands."

"That's so," said Dick, soberly. "I never thought how awful ignorant I was till now."

"That can be remedied with perseverance," said Frank. "A year will do a great deal for you."

"I'll go to work and see what I can do," said Dick, energetically.

Chapter 9

A Scene in a Third Avenue Car

The boys had turned into Third Avenue, a long street, which, commencing just below the Cooper Institute, runs out to Harlem. A man came out of a side street, uttering at intervals a monotonous cry which sounded like "glass puddin'."

"Glass pudding!" repeated Frank, looking in surprised wonder at Dick. "What does he mean?"

4. House or room where a merchant or trader keeps books and transacts business.

"Perhaps you'd like some," said Dick.

"I never heard of it before."

"Suppose you ask him what he charges for his puddin'."

Frank looked more narrowly at the man, and soon concluded that he was a glazier.

"Oh, I understand," he said. "He means 'glass puttin.'"

Frank's mistake was not a singular one. The monotonous cry of these men certainly sounds more like "glass puddin," than the words they intend to utter.

"Now," said Dick, "where shall we go?"

"I should like to see Central Park," said Frank. "Is it far off?"

"It is about a mile and a half from here," said Dick. "This is Twenty-ninth Street, and the Park begins at Fifty-ninth Street."

It may be explained, for the benefit of readers who have never visited New York, that about a mile from the City Hall the cross-streets begin to be numbered in regular order. There is a continuous line of houses as far as One Hundred and Thirtieth Street, where may be found the terminus of the Harlem line of horse-cars.[1] When the entire island is laid out and settled, probably the numbers will reach two hundred or more. Central Park, which lies between Fifty-ninth Street on the South and One Hundred and Tenth Street on the north, is true to its name, occupying about the centre of the island. The distance between two parallel streets is called a block, and twenty blocks make a mile. It will therefore be seen that Dick was exactly right, when he said they were a mile and a half from Central Park.

"That is too far to walk," said Frank.

"'Twon't cost but six cents to ride," said Dick.

"You mean in the horse-cars?"

"Yes."

"All right then. We'll jump aboard the next car."

The Third Avenue and Harlem line of horse-cars is better patronized than any other in New York, though not much can be said for the cars, which are usually dirty and overcrowded. Still, when it is considered that only seven cents are charged for the entire distance to Harlem, about seven miles from the City Hall, the fare can hardly be complained of. But of course most of the profit is made from the way-passengers who only ride a short distance.

A car was at that moment approaching, but it seemed pretty crowded.

"Shall we take that, or wait for another?" asked Frank.

"The next'll most likely be as bad," said Dick.

The boys accordingly signalled to the conductor to stop, and got on the front platform. They were obliged to stand up till the car reached

1. Horse-drawn trolleys.

Fortieth Street, when so many of the passengers had got off that they obtained seats.

Frank sat down beside a middle-aged woman, or lady, as she probably called herself, whose sharp visage and thin lips did not seem to promise a very pleasant disposition. When the two gentlemen who sat beside her arose, she spread her skirts in the endeavor to fill two seats. Disregarding this, the boys sat down.

"There aint room for two," she said looking sourly at Frank.

"There were two here before."

"Well, there ought not to have been. Some people like to crowd in where they're not wanted."

"And some like to take up a double allowance of room," thought Frank; but he did not say so. He saw that the woman had a bad temper, and thought it wisest to say nothing.

Frank had never ridden up the city as far as this, and it was with much interest that he looked out of the car windows at the stores on either side. Third Avenue is a broad street, but in the character of its houses and stores it is quite inferior to Broadway, though better than some of the avenues further east. Fifth Avenue, as most of my readers already know, is the finest street in the city, being lined with splendid private residences, occupied by the wealthier classes. Many of the cross streets also boast houses which may be considered palaces, so elegant are they externally and internally. Frank caught glimpses of some of these as he was carried towards the Park.

After the first conversation, already mentioned, with the lady at his side, he supposed he should have nothing further to do with her. But in this he was mistaken. While he was busy looking out of the car window, she plunged her hand into her pocket in search of her purse, which she was unable to find. Instantly she jumped to the conclusion that it had been stolen, and her suspicions fastened upon Frank, with whom she was already provoked for "crowding her," as she termed it.

"Conductor!" she exclaimed in a sharp voice.

"What's wanted, ma'am?" returned the functionary.

"I want you to come here right off."

"What's the matter?"

"My purse has been stolen. There was four dollars and eighty cents in it. I know, because I counted it when I paid my fare."

"Who stole it?"

"That boy," she said pointing to Frank, who listened to the charge in the most intense astonishment. "He crowded in here on purpose to rob me, and I want you to search him right off."

"That's a lie!" exclaimed Dick, indignantly.

"Oh, you're in league with him, I dare say," said the woman spitefully. "You're as bad as he is, I'll be bound."

"You're a nice female, you be!" said Dick, ironically.

"Don't you dare to call me a female, sir," said the lady, furiously.

"Why, you aint a man in disguise, be you?" said Dick.

"You are very much mistaken, madam," said Frank quietly. "The conductor may search me, if you desire it."

A charge of theft, made in a crowded car, of course made quite a sensation. Cautious passengers instinctively put their hands on their pockets, to make sure that they, too, had not been robbed. As for Frank, his face flushed, and he felt very indignant that he should even be suspected of so mean a crime. He had been carefully brought up, and been taught to regard stealing as low and wicked.

Dick, on the contrary, thought it a capital joke that such a charge should have been made against his companion. Though he had brought himself up, and known plenty of boys and men, too, who would steal, he had never done so himself. He thought it mean. But he could not be expected to regard it as Frank did. He had been too familiar with it in others to look upon it with horror.

Meanwhile the passengers rather sided with the boys. Appearances go a great ways, and Frank did not look like a thief.

"I think you must be mistaken, madam," said a gentleman sitting opposite. "The lad does not look as if he would steal."

"You can't tell by looks," said the lady, sourly. "They're deceitful; villains are generally well dressed."

"Be they?" said Dick. "You'd ought to see me with my Washington coat on. You'd think I was the biggest villain ever you saw."

"I've no doubt you are," said the lady, scowling in the direction of our hero.

"Thank you, ma'am," said Dick. " 'Tisn't often I get such fine compliments."

"None of your impudence," said the lady, wrathfully. "I believe you're the worst of the two."

Meanwhile the car had been stopped.

"How long are we going to stop here?" demanded a passenger, impatiently. "I'm in a hurry, if none of the rest of you are."

"I want my pocket-book," said the lady, defiantly.

"Well, ma'am, I haven't got it, and I don't see as it's doing you any good detaining us all here."

"Conductor, will you call a policeman to search that young scamp?" continued the aggrieved lady. "You don't expect I'm going to lose my money, and do nothing about it."

"I'll turn my pockets inside out if you want me to," said Frank, proudly. "There's no need of a policeman. The conductor, or any one else, may search me."

"Well, youngster," said the conductor, "if the lady agrees, I'll search you."

The lady signified her assent.

Frank accordingly turned his pockets inside out; but nothing was revealed except his own porte-monnaie[2] and a penknife.

"Well, ma'am, are you satisfied?" asked the conductor.

"No, I aint," said she, decidedly.

"You don't think he's got it still?"

"No, but he's passed it over to his confederate, that boy there that's so full of impudence."

"That's me," said Dick, comically.

"He confesses it," said the lady; "I want him searched."

"All right," said Dick, "I'm ready for the operation, only, as I've got valooable property about me, be careful not to drop any of my Erie Bonds."

The conductor's hand forthwith dove into Dick's pocket, and drew out a rusty jack-knife, a battered cent, about fifty cents in change, and the capacious pocket-book which he had received from the swindler who was anxious to get back to his sick family in Boston.

"Is that yours, ma'am?" asked the conductor, holding up the wallet which excited some amazement, by its size, among the other passengers.

"It seems to me you carry a large pocket-book for a young man of your age," said the conductor.

"That's what I carry my cash and valooable papers in," said Dick.

"I suppose that isn't yours, ma'am," said the conductor, turning to the lady.

"No," said she, scornfully. "I wouldn't carry round such a great wallet as that. Most likely he's stolen it from somebody else."

"What a prime detective you'd be!" said Dick. "P'rhaps you know who I took it from."

"I don't know but my money's in it," said the lady, sharply. "Conductor, will you open that wallet, and see what there is in it?"

"Don't disturb the valooable papers," said Dick, in a tone of pretended anxiety.

The contents of the wallet excited some amusement among the passengers.

"There don't seem to be much money here," said the conductor, taking out a roll of tissue paper cut out in the shape of bills, and rolled up.

"No," said Dick. "Didn't I tell you them were papers of no valoo to anybody but the owner? If the lady'd like to borrow, I won't charge no interest."

"Where is my money, then?" said the lady, in some discomfiture. "I shouldn't wonder if one of the young scamps had thrown it out of the window."

"You'd better search your pocket once more," said the gentleman

2. A wallet.

opposite. "I don't believe either of the boys is in fault. They don't look to me as if they would steal."

"Thank you, sir," said Frank.

The lady followed out the suggestion, and plunging her hand once more into her pocket, drew out a small porte-monnaie. She hardly knew whether to be glad or sorry at this discovery. It placed her in rather an awkward position after the fuss she had made, and the detention to which she had subjected the passengers, now, as it proved, for nothing.

"Is that the pocket-book you thought stolen?" asked the conductor.

"Yes," said she, rather confusedly.

"Then you've been keeping me waiting all this time for nothing," he said, sharply. "I wish you'd take care to be sure next time before you make such a disturbance for nothing. I've lost five minutes, and shall not be on time."

"I can't help it," was the cross reply; "I didn't know it was in my pocket."

"It seems to me you owe an apology to the boys you accused of a theft which they have not committed," said the gentleman opposite.

"I shan't apologize to anybody," said the lady, whose temper was not of the best; "least of all to such whipper-snappers[3] as they are."

"Thank you, ma'am," said Dick, comically; "your handsome apology is accepted. It aint of no consequence, only I didn't like to expose the contents of my valooable pocket-book, for fear it might excite the envy of some of my poor neighbors."

"You're a character," said the gentleman who had already spoken, with a smile.

"A bad character!" muttered the lady.

But it was quite evident that the sympathies of those present were against the lady, and on the side of the boys who had been falsely accused, while Dick's drollery had created considerable amusement.

The cars had now reached Fifty-ninth Street, the southern boundary of the Park, and here our hero and his companion got off.

"You'd better look out for pickpockets, my lad," said the conductor, pleasantly. "That big wallet of yours might prove a great temptation."

"That's so," said Dick. "That's the misfortin' of being rich. Astor and me don't sleep much for fear of burglars breakin' in and robbin' us of our valooable treasures. Sometimes I think I'll give all my money to an Orphan Asylum, and take it out in board. I guess I'd make money by the operation."

While Dick was speaking, the car rolled away, and the boys turned up Fifty-ninth Street, for two long blocks yet separated them from the Park.

3. Insignificant or pretentious persons.

Chapter 10

Introduces a Victim of Misplaced Confidence

"What a queer chap you are, Dick!" said Frank laughing. "You always seem to be in good spirits."

"No, I aint always. Sometimes I have the blues."

"When?"

"Well, once last winter it was awful cold, and there was big holes in my shoes, and my gloves and all my warm clothes was at the tailor's. I felt as if life was sort of tough, and I'd like it if some rich man would adopt me, and give me plenty to eat and drink and wear, without my havin' to look so sharp after it. Then agin' when I've seen boys with good homes, and fathers, and mothers, I've thought I'd like to have somebody to care for me."

Dick's tone changed as he said this, from his usual levity, and there was a touch of sadness in it. Frank, blessed with a good home and indulgent parents, could not help pitying the friendless boy who had found life such up-hill work.

"Don't say you have no one to care for you, Dick," he said, lightly laying his hand on Dick's shoulder. "I will care for you."

"Will you?"

"If you will let me."

"I wish you would," said Dick, earnestly. "I'd like to feel that I have one friend who cares for me."

Central Park was now before them, but it was far from presenting the appearance which it now exhibits. It had not been long since work had been commenced upon it, and it was still very rough and unfinished. A rough tract of land, two miles and a half from north to south, and a half a mile broad, very rocky in parts, was the material from which the Park Commissioners have made the present beautiful enclosure. There were no houses of good appearance near it, buildings being limited mainly to rude temporary huts used by the workmen who were employed in improving it. The time will undoubtedly come when the Park will be surrounded by elegant residences, and compare favorably in this respect with the most attractive parts of any city in the world. But at the time when Frank and Dick visited it, not much could be said in favor either of the Park or its neighborhood.

"If this is Central Park," said Frank, who naturally felt disappointed, "I don't think much of it. My father's got a large pasture that is much nicer."

"It'll look better some time," said Dick. "There aint much to see now but rocks. We will take a walk over it if you want to."

"No," said Frank, "I've seen as much of it as I want to. Besides, I feel tired."

"Then we'll go back. We can take the Sixth Avenue cars. They will bring us out at Vesey Street, just beside the Astor House."

"All right," said Frank. "That will be the best course. I hope," he added, laughing, "our agreeable lady friend won't be there. I don't care about being accused of *stealing* again."

"She was a tough one," said Dick. "Wouldn't she make a nice wife for a man that likes to live in hot water, and didn't mind bein' scalded two or three times a day?"

"Yes, I think she'd just suit him. Is that the right car, Dick?"

"Yes, jump in, and I'll follow."

The Sixth Avenue is lined with stores, many of them of very good appearance, and would make a very respectable principal street for a good-sized city. But it is only one of several long business streets which run up the island, and illustrate the extent and importance of the city to which they belong.

No incidents worth mentioning took place during their ride down town. In about three-quarters of an hour the boys got out of the car beside the Astor House.

"Are you goin' in now, Frank?" asked Dick.

"That depends upon whether you have anything else to show me."

"Wouldn't you like to go to Wall Street?"

"That's the street where there are so many bankers and brokers,— isn't it?"

"Yes, I s'pose you aint afraid of bulls and bears,—are you?"

"Bulls and bears?" repeated Frank, puzzled.

"Yes."

"What are they?"

"The bulls is what tries to make the stock go up, and the bears is what try to growl 'em down."[1]

"Oh, I see. Yes, I'd like to go."

Accordingly they walked down on the west side of Broadway as far as Trinity Church, and then, crossing, entered a street not very wide or very long, but of very great importance. The reader would be astonished if he could know the amount of money involved in the transactions which take place in a single day in this street. It would be found that although Broadway is much greater in length, and lined with stores, it stands second to Wall Street in this respect.

"What is that large marble building?" asked Frank, pointing to a massive structure on the corner of Wall and Nassau Streets. It was in the form of a parallelogram, two hundred feet long by ninety wide, and about eighty feet in height, the ascent to the entrance being by eighteen granite steps.

---

1. Stock exchange slang for someone who tries to either raise or depress the price of stock respectively.

"That's the Custom House,"[2] said Dick.

"It looks like pictures I've seen of the Parthenon at Athens,"[3] said Frank, meditatively.

"Where's Athens?" asked Dick. "It aint in New York State,—is it?"

"Not the Athens I mean, at any rate. It is in Greece, and was a famous city two thousand years ago."

"That's longer than I can remember," said Dick. "I can't remember distinctly more'n about a thousand years."

"What a chap[4] you are, Dick! Do you know if we can go in?"

The boys ascertained, after a little inquiry, that they would be allowed to do so. They accordingly entered the Custom House and made their way up to the roof, from which they had a fine view of the harbor, the wharves crowded with shipping, and the neighboring shores of Long Island and New Jersey. Towards the north they looked down for many miles upon continuous lines of streets, and thousands of roofs, with here and there a church-spire rising above its neighbors. Dick had never before been up there, and he, as well as Frank, was interested in the grand view spread before them.

At length they descended, and were going down the granite steps on the outside of the building, when they were addressed by a young man, whose appearance is worth describing.

He was tall, and rather loosely put together, with small eyes and a rather prominent nose. His clothing had evidently not been furnished by a city tailor. He wore a blue coat with brass buttons, and pantaloons[5] of rather scanty dimensions, which were several inches too short to cover his lower limbs. He held in his hand a piece of paper, and his countenance wore a look of mingled bewilderment and anxiety.

"Be they a-payin' out money inside there?" he asked, indicating the interior by a motion of his hand.

"I guess so," said Dick. "Are you a goin' in for some?"

"Wal, yes. I've got an order here for sixty dollars,—made a kind of speculation this morning."

"How was it?" asked Frank.

"Wal, you see I brought down some money to put in the bank, fifty dollars it was, and I hadn't justly made up my mind what bank to put it into, when a chap came up in a terrible hurry, and said it was very unfortunate, but the bank wasn't open, and he must have some money right off. He was obliged to go out of the city by the next train. I asked him how much he wanted. He said fifty dollars. I told him I'd

2. Built in 1842 and located on Wall Street between Broad and William Streets, it was the first U.S. Custom House.
3. Temple of Athena, built in the fifth century B.C.E. on the acropolis of Athens, Greece.
4. A boy or fellow.
5. Trousers, pants.

got that, and he offered me a check on the bank for sixty, and I let him have it. I thought that was a pretty easy way to earn ten dollars, so I counted out the money and he went off. He told me I'd hear a bell ring when they began to pay out money. But I've waited most two hours, and I haint heard it yet. I'd ought to be goin', for I told dad I'd be home to-night. Do you think I can get the money now?"

"Will you show me the check?" asked Frank, who had listened attentively to the countryman's story, and suspected that he had been made the victim of a swindler. It was made out upon the "Washington Bank," in the sum of sixty dollars, and was signed "Ephraim Smith."

"Washington Bank!" repeated Frank. "Dick, is there such a bank in the city?"

"Not as I knows on," said Dick. "Leastways I don't own any shares in it."

"Aint this the Washington Bank?" asked the countryman, pointing to the building on the steps of which the three were now standing.

"No, it's the Custom House."

"And won't they give me any money for this?" asked the young man, the perspiration standing on his brow.

"I am afraid the man who gave it to you was a swindler," said Frank, gently.

"And won't I ever see my fifty dollars again?" asked the youth in agony.

"I am afraid not."

"What'll dad say?" ejaculated the miserable youth. "It makes me feel sick to think of it. I wish I had the feller here. I'd shake him out of his boots."

"What did he look like? I'll call a policeman and you shall describe him. Perhaps in that way you can get track of your money."

Dick called a policeman, who listened to the description, and recognized the operator as an experienced swindler. He assured the countryman that there was very little chance of his ever seeing his money again. The boys left the miserable youth loudly bewailing his bad luck, and proceeded on their way down the street.

"He's a baby," said Dick, contemptuously. "He'd ought to know how to take care of himself and his money. A feller has to look sharp in this city, or he'll lose his eye-teeth before he knows it."

"I suppose you never got swindled out of fifty dollars, Dick?"

"No, I don't carry no such small bills. I wish I did," he added.

"So do I, Dick. What's that building at the end of the street?"

"That's the Wall-Street Ferry to Brooklyn."

"How long does it take to go across?"

"Not more'n five minutes."

"Suppose we just ride over and back."

"All right!" said Dick. "It's rather expensive; but if you don't mind, I don't."

"Why, how much does it cost?"

"Two cents apiece."

"I guess I can stand that. Let us go."

They passed the gate, paying the fare to a man who stood at the entrance, and were soon on the ferry-boat, bound for Brooklyn.

They had scarcely entered the boat, when Dick, grasping Frank by the arm, pointed to a man just outside of the gentlemen's cabin.

"Do you see that man, Frank?" he inquired.

"Yes, what of him?"

"He's the man that cheated the country chap out of his fifty dollars."

Chapter 11

Dick as a Detective

Dick's ready identification of the rogue who had cheated the countryman, surprised Frank.

"What makes you think it is he?" he asked.

"Because I've seen him before, and I know he's up to them kind of tricks. When I heard how he looked, I was sure I knowed him."

"Our recognizing him won't be of much use," said Frank. "It won't give back the countryman his money."

"I don't know," said Dick, thoughtfully. "May be I can get it."

"How?" asked Frank, incredulously.

"Wait a minute, and you'll see."

Dick left his companion, and went up to the man whom he suspected.

"Ephraim Smith," said Dick, in a low voice.

The man turned suddenly, and looked at Dick uneasily.

"What did you say?" he asked.

"I believe your name is Ephraim Smith," continued Dick.

"You're mistaken," said the man, and was about to move off.

"Stop a minute," said Dick. "Don't you keep your money in the Washington Bank?"

"I don't know any such bank. I'm in a hurry, young man, and I can't stop to answer any foolish questions."

The boat had by this time reached the Brooklyn pier, and Mr. Ephraim Smith seemed in a hurry to land.

"Look here," said Dick, significantly; "you'd better not go on shore unless you want to jump into the arms of a policeman."

"What do you mean?" asked the man, startled.

"That little affair of yours is known to the police," said Dick; "about how you got fifty dollars out of a greenhorn[1] on a false check, and it mayn't be safe for you to go ashore."

"I don't know what you're talking about," said the swindler with affected boldness, though Dick could see that he was ill at case.

"Yes you do," said Dick. "There isn't but one thing to do. Just give me back that money, and I'll see that you're not touched. If you don't, I'll give you up to the first p'liceman we meet."

Dick looked so determined, and spoke so confidently, that the other, overcome by his fears, no longer hesitated, but passed a roll of bills to Dick and hastily left the boat.

All this Frank witnessed with great amazement, not understanding what influence Dick could have obtained over the swindler sufficient to compel restitution.

"How did you do it?" he asked eagerly.

"I told him I'd exert my influence with the president to have him tried by *habeas corpus*,"[2] said Dick.

"And of course that frightened him. But tell me, without joking, how you managed."

Dick gave a truthful account of what occurred, and then said, "Now we'll go back and carry the money."

"Suppose we don't find the poor countryman?"

"Then the p'lice will take care of it."

They remained on board the boat, and in five minutes were again in New York. Going up Wall Street, they met the countryman a little distance from the Custom House. His face was marked with the traces of deep anguish; but in his case even grief could not subdue the cravings of appetite. He had purchased some cakes of one of the old women who spread out for the benefit of passers-by an array of apples and seed-cakes, and was munching them with melancholy satisfaction.

"Hilloa!" said Dick. "Have you found your money?"

"No," ejaculated the young man, with a convulsive gasp. "I shan't ever see it again. The mean skunk's cheated me out of it. Consarn his picter![3] It took me most six months to save it up. I was workin' for Deacon Pinkham in our place. Oh, I wish I'd never come to New York! The deacon, he told me he'd keep it for me; but I wanted to put in in the bank, and now it's all gone, boo hoo!"

And the miserable youth, having despatched[4] his cakes, was so overcome by the thought of his loss that he burst into tears.

---

1. An inexperienced person; someone who is easily deceived.
2. (Latin: you should have the body.) Order written by a judge to bring an imprisoned person forward to a designated place at a designated time; established to release an individual from unlawful imprisonment.
3. Damn his picture!
4. Dispatched.

"I say," said Dick, "dry up, and see what I've got here."

The youth no sooner saw the roll of bills, and comprehended that it was indeed his lost treasure, than from the depths of anguish he was exalted to the most ecstatic joy. He seized Dick's hand, and shook it with so much energy that our hero began to feel rather alarmed for its safety.

"'Pears to me you take my arm for a pump-handle," he said. "Couldn't you show your gratitood some other way? It's just possible I may want to use my arm ag'in some time."

The young man desisted, but invited Dick most cordially to come up and stop a week with him at his country home, assuring him that he wouldn't charge him anything for board.

"All right!" said Dick. "If you don't mind I'll bring my wife along, too. She's delicate, and the country air might do her good."

Jonathan stared at him in amazement, uncertain whether to credit the fact of his marriage. Dick walked on with Frank, leaving him in an apparent state of stupefaction, and it is possible that he has not yet settled the affair to his satisfaction.

"Now," said Frank, "I think I'll go back to the Astor House. Uncle has probably got through his business and returned."

"All right," said Dick.

The two boys walked up to Broadway, just where the tall steeple of Trinity[5] faces the street of bankers and brokers, and walked leisurely to the hotel. When they arrived at the Astor House, Dick said, "Good-by, Frank."

"Not yet," said Frank; "I want you to come in with me."

Dick followed his young patron up the steps. Frank went into the reading-room, where, as he had thought probable, he found his uncle already arrived, and reading a copy of "The Evening Post," which he had just purchased outside.

"Well, boys," he said, looking up, "have you had a pleasant jaunt?"

"Yes, sir," said Frank. "Dick's a capital guide."

"So this is Dick," said Mr. Whitney, surveying him with a smile. "Upon my word, I should hardly have known him. I must congratulate him on his improved appearance."

"Frank's been very kind to me," said Dick, who, rough street-boy as he was, had a heart easily touched by kindness, of which he had never experienced much. "He's a tip-top[6] fellow."

"I believe he is a good boy," said Mr. Whitney. "I hope, my lad, you will prosper and rise in the world. You know in this free country poverty in early life is no bar to a man's advancement. I haven't risen

---

5. Trinity Church, a Gothic Revival structure consecrated in 1846, located at 74 Trinity Place in lower Manhattan. At the time, the church dominated New York's skyline.
6. First-rate.

very high myself," he added, with a smile, "but have met with moderate success in life; yet there was a time when I was as poor as you."

"Were you, sir?" asked Dick, eagerly.

"Yes, my boy, I have known the time when I have been obliged to go without my dinner because I didn't have enough money to pay for it."

"How did you get up in the world?" asked Dick, anxiously.

"I entered a printing-office as an apprentice, and worked for some years. Then my eyes gave out and I was obliged to give that up. Not knowing what else to do, I went into the country, and worked on a farm. After a while I was lucky enough to invent a machine, which has brought me in a great deal of money.[7] But there was one thing I got while I was in the printing-office which I value more than money."

"What was that, sir?"

"A taste for reading and study. During my leisure hours I improved myself by study, and acquired a large part of the knowledge which I now possess. Indeed, it was one of my books that first put me on the track of the invention, which I afterwards made. So you see, my lad, that my studious habits paid me in money, as well as in another way."

"I'm awful ignorant," said Dick, soberly.

"But you are young, and, I judge, a smart boy. If you try to learn, you can, and if you ever expect to do anything in the world, you must know something of books."

"I will," said Dick, resolutely. "I aint always goin' to black boots for a livin'."

"All labor is respectable, my lad, and you have no cause to be ashamed of any honest business; yet when you can get something to do that promises better for your future prospects, I advise you to do so. Till then earn your living in the way you are accustomed to, avoid extravagance, and save up a little money if you can."

"Thank you for your advice," said our hero. "There aint many that takes an interest in Ragged Dick."

"So that's your name," said Mr. Whitney. "If I judge you rightly, it won't be long before you change it. Save your money, my lad, buy books, and determine to be somebody, and you may yet fill an honorable position."

"I'll try," said Dick. "Good-night, sir."

"Wait a minute, Dick," said Frank. "Your blacking-box and old clothes are upstairs. You may want them."

"In course," said Dick. "I couldn't get along without my best clothes, and my stock in trade."

"You may go up to the room with him, Frank," said Mr. Whitney. "The clerk will give you the key. I want to see you, Dick, before you go."

---

7. Reference to Eli Whitney (1765–1825), who invented the cotton gin, a machine that automated the separation of cotton seed from cotton fiber.

"Yes, sir," said Dick.

"Where are you going to sleep to-night, Dick?" asked Frank, as they went upstairs together.

"P'r'aps at the Fifth Avenue Hotel—on the outside," said Dick.

"Haven't you any place to sleep, then?"

"I slept in a box, last night."

"In a box?"

"Yes, on Spruce Street."

"Poor fellow!" said Frank, compassionately.

"Oh, 'twas a bully bed—full of straw! I slept like a top."

"Don't you earn enough to pay for a room, Dick?"

"Yes," said Dick; "only I spend my money foolish, goin' to the Old Bowery, and Tony Pastor's, and sometimes gamblin' in Baxter Street."

"You won't gamble any more,—will you, Dick?" said Frank, laying his hand persuasively on his companion's shoulder.

"No, I won't," said Dick.

"You'll promise?"

"Yes, and I'll keep it. You're a good feller. I wish you was goin' to be in New York."

"I am going to a boarding-school in Connecticut. The name of the town is Barnton. Will you write to me, Dick?"

"My writing would look like hens' tracks," said our hero.

"Never mind. I want you to write. When you write you can tell me how to direct,[8] and I will send you a letter."

"I wish you would," said Dick. "I wish I was more like you."

"I hope you will make a much better boy, Dick. Now we'll go in to my uncle. He wishes to see you before you go."

They went into the reading-room. Dick had wrapped up his blacking-brush in a newspaper with which Frank had supplied him, feeling that a guest of the Astor House should hardly be seen coming out of the hotel displaying such a professional sign.

"Uncle, Dick's ready to go," said Frank.

"Good-by, my lad," said Mr. Whitney. "I hope to hear good accounts of you sometime. Don't forget what I have told you. Remember that your future position depends mainly upon yourself, and that it will be high or low as you choose to make it."

He held out his hand, in which was a five-dollar bill. Dick shrunk back.

"I don't like to take it," he said. "I haven't earned it."

"Perhaps not," said Mr. Whitney; "but I give it to you because I remember my own friendless youth. I hope it may be of service to you. Sometime when you are a prosperous man, you can repay it in the form of aid to some poor boy, who is struggling upward as you are now."

8. Which address to use.

"I will, sir," said Dick, manfully.

He no longer refused the money, but took it gratefully, and, bidding Frank and his uncle good-by, went out into the street. A feeling of loneliness came over him as he left the presence of Frank, for whom he had formed a strong attachment in the few hours he had known him.

Chapter 12

Dick Hires a Room on Mott Street

Going out into the fresh air Dick felt the pangs of hunger. He accordingly went to a restaurant and got a substantial supper. Perhaps it was the new clothes he wore, which made him feel a little more aristocratic. At all events, instead of patronizing the cheap restaurant where he usually procured his meals, he went into the refectory attached to Lovejoy's Hotel, where the prices were higher and the company more select. In his ordinary dress, Dick would have been excluded, but now he had the appearance of a very respectable, gentlemanly boy, whose presence would not discredit any establishment. His orders were therefore received with attention by the waiter, and in due time a good supper was placed before him.

"I wish I could come here every day," thought Dick. "It seems kind o' nice and 'spectable, side of the other place. There's a gent at that other table that I've shined boots for more'n once. He don't know me in my new clothes. Guess he don't know his boot-black patronizes the same establishment."

His supper over, Dick went up to the desk, and, presenting his check, tendered in payment his five-dollar bill, as if it were one of a large number which he possessed. Receiving back his change he went out into the street.

Two questions now arose: How should he spend the evening, and where should he pass the night? Yesterday, with such a sum of money in his possession, he would have answered both questions readily. For the evening, he would have passed it at the Old Bowery, and gone to sleep in any out-of-the-way place that offered. But he had turned over a new leaf, or resolved to do so. He meant to save his money for some useful purpose,—to aid his advancement in the world. So he could not afford the theatre. Besides, with his new clothes, he was unwilling to pass the night out of doors.

"I should spile[1] 'em," he thought, "and that wouldn't pay."

So he determined to hunt up a room which he could occupy

1. Spoil.

regularly, and consider as his own, where he could sleep nights, instead of depending on boxes and old wagons for a chance shelter. This would be the first step towards respectability, and Dick determined to take it.

He accordingly passed through the City Hall Park, and walked leisurely up Centre Street.

He decided that it would hardly be advisable for him to seek lodgings in Fifth Avenue, although his present cash capital consisted of nearly five dollars in money, besides the valuable papers contained in his wallet. Besides, he had reason to doubt whether any of his line of business lived on that aristocratic street. He took his way to Mott Street, which is considerably less pretentious, and halted in front of a shabby brick lodging-house kept by a Mrs. Mooney, with whose son Tom, Dick was acquainted.

Dick rang the bell, which sent back a shrill metallic response.

The door was opened by a slatternly[2] servant, who looked at him inquiringly, and not without curiosity. It must be remembered that Dick was well dressed, and that nothing in his appearance bespoke his occupation. Being naturally a good-looking boy, he might readily be mistaken for a gentleman's son.

"Well, Queen Victoria," said Dick, "is your missus at home?"

"My name's Bridget,"[3] said the girl.

"Oh, indeed!" said Dick. "You looked so much like the queen's picter what she gave me last Christmas in exchange for mine, that I couldn't help calling you by her name."[4]

"Oh, go along wid ye!" said Bridget. "It's makin' fun ye are."

"If you don't believe me," said Dick, gravely "all you've got to do is to ask my partic'lar friend, the Duke of Newcastle."

"Bridget!" called a shrill voice from the basement.

"The missus is calling me," said Bridget, hurriedly. "I'll tell her ye want her."

"All right!" said Dick.

The servant descended into the lower regions, and in a short time a stout, red-faced woman appeared on the scene.

"Well, sir, what's your wish?" she asked.

"Have you got a room to let?" asked Dick.

"Is it for yourself you ask?" questioned the woman, in some surprise.

Dick answered in the affirmative.

---

2. Sluttish, negligent, dirty, especially used for women.
3. Term used for domestic servants since many Irish immigrant women ended up working as such.
4. Performers in freak shows sold and exchanged pictures of themselves; Tom Thumb's pictures were highly coveted.

"I haven't got any very good rooms vacant. There's a small room in the third story."

"I'd like to see it," said Dick.

"I don't know as it would be good enough for you," said the woman, with a glance at Dick's clothes.

"I ain't very partic'lar about accommodations," said our hero. "I guess I'll look at it."

Dick followed the landlady up two narrow staircases, uncarpeted and dirty, to the third landing, where he was ushered into a room about ten feet square. It could not be considered a very desirable apartment. It had once been covered with an oilcloth carpet, but this was now very ragged, and looked worse than none. There was a single bed in the corner, covered with an indiscriminate heap of bedclothing, rumpled and not over-clean. There was a bureau, with the veneering scratched and in some parts stripped off, and a small glass, eight inches by ten, cracked across the middle; also two chairs in rather a disjointed condition. Judging from Dick's appearance, Mrs. Mooney thought he would turn from it in disdain.

But it must be remembered that Dick's past experience had not been of a character to make him fastidious. In comparison with a box, or an empty wagon, even this little room seemed comfortable. He decided to hire it if the rent proved reasonable.

"Well, what's the tax?" asked Dick.

"I ought to have a dollar a week," said Mrs. Mooney, hesitatingly.

"Say seventy-five cents, and I'll take it," said Dick.

"Every week in advance?"

"Yes."

"Well, as times is hard, and I can't afford to keep it empty, you may have it. When will you come?"

"To-night," said Dick.

"It aint lookin' very neat. I don't know as I can fix it up to-night."

"Well, I'll sleep here to-night, and you can fix it up to-morrow."

"I hope you'll excuse the looks. I'm a lone woman, and my help is so shiftless, I have to look after every-thing myself; so I can't keep things as straight as I want to."

"All right!" said Dick.

"Can you pay me the first week in advance?" asked the landlady, cautiously.

Dick responded by drawing seventy-five cents from his pocket, and placing it in her hand.

"What's your business, sir, if I may inquire?" said Mrs. Mooney.

"Oh, I'm professional!" said Dick.

"Indeed!" said the landlady, who did not feel much enlightened by this answer.

"How's Tom?" asked Dick.

"Do you know my Tom?" said Mrs. Mooney in surprise. "He's gone to sea,—to Californy.[5] He went last week."

"Did he?" said Dick. "Yes, I knew him."

Mrs. Mooney looked upon her new lodger with increased favor, in finding that he was acquainted with her son, who, by the way, was one of the worst young scamps in Mott Street, which is saying considerable.

"I'll bring over my baggage from the Astor House this evening," said Dick in a tone of importance.

"From the Astor House!" repeated Mrs. Mooney, in fresh amazement.

"Yes, I've been stoppin' there a short time with some friends," said Dick.

Mrs. Mooney might be excused for a little amazement at finding that a guest from the Astor House was about to become one of her lodgers—such transfers not being common.

"Did you say you was purfessional?" she asked.

"Yes, ma'am," said Dick, politely.

"You aint a—a—" Mrs. Mooney paused, uncertain what conjecture to hazard.

"Oh, no, nothing of the sort," said Dick, promptly. "How could you think so, Mrs. Mooney?"

"No offense, sir," said the landlady, more perplexed than ever.

"Certainly not," said our hero. "But you must excuse me now, Mrs. Mooney, as I have business of great importance to attend to."

"You'll come round this evening?"

Dick answered in the affirmative, and turned away.

"I wonder what he is!" thought the landlady, following him with her eyes as he crossed the street. "He's got good clothes on, but he don't seem very particular about his room. Well; I've got all my rooms full now. That's one comfort."

Dick felt more comfortable now that he had taken the decisive step of hiring a lodging, and paying a week's rent in advance. For seven nights he was sure of a shelter and a bed to sleep in. The thought was a pleasant one to our young vagrant, who hitherto had seldom known when he rose in the morning where he should find a resting-place at night.

"I must bring my traps round," said Dick to himself. "I guess I'll go to bed early to-night. It'll feel kinder good to sleep in a reg'lar bed. Boxes is rather hard to the back, and aint comfortable in case of rain. I wonder what Johnny Nolan would say if he knew I'd got a room of my own."

---

5. Many immigrants moved to the West, either in search of gold or in hopes of settling and farming.

Chapter 13

Micky Maguire

About nine o'clock Dick sought his new lodgings. In his hands he carried his professional wardrobe, namely, the clothes which he had worn at the commencement of the day, and the implements of his business. These he stowed away in the bureau drawers, and by the light of a flickering candle took off his clothes and went to bed. Dick had a good digestion and a reasonably good conscience; consequently he was a good sleeper. Perhaps, too, the soft feather bed conduced to slumber. At any rate his eyes were soon closed, and he did not awake until half-past six the next morning.

He lifted himself on his elbow, and stared around him in transient bewilderment.

"Blest if I hadn't forgot where I was," he said to himself. "So this is my room, is it? Well, it seems kind of 'spectable to have a room and a bed to sleep in. I'd orter be able to afford seventy-five cents a week. I've throwed away more money than that in one evenin'. There aint no reason why I shouldn't live 'spectable. I wish I knowed as much as Frank. He's a tip-top feller. Nobody ever cared enough for me before to give me good advice. It was kicks, and cuffs, and swearin' at me all the time. I'd like to show him I can do something."

While Dick was indulging in these reflections, he had risen from bed, and, finding an accession to the furniture of his room, in the shape of an ancient wash-stand bearing a cracked bowl and broken pitcher, indulged himself in the rather unusual ceremony of a good wash. On the whole, Dick preferred to be clean, but it was not always easy to gratify his desire. Lodging in the street as he had been accustomed to do, he had had no opportunity to perform his toilet in the customary manner. Even now he found himself unable to arrange his dishevelled locks, having neither comb nor brush. He determined to purchase a comb, at least, as soon as possible, and a brush too, if he could get one cheap. Meanwhile he combed his hair with his fingers as well as he could, though the result was not quite so satisfactory as it might have been.

A question now came up for consideration. For the first time in his life Dick possessed two suits of clothes. Should he put on the clothes Frank had given him, or resume his old rags?

Now, twenty-four hours before, at the time Dick was introduced to the reader's notice, no one could have been less fastidious as to his clothing than he. Indeed, he had rather a contempt for good clothes, or at least he thought so. But now, as he surveyed the ragged and dirty coat and the patched pants, Dick felt ashamed of them. He was unwilling to appear in the streets with them. Yet, if he went to work in his new suit, he was in danger of spoiling it, and he might not have it in his power to purchase a new one. Economy dictated a return to the old garments. Dick tried them on, and surveyed himself in the cracked glass; but the reflection did not please him.

"They don't look 'spectable," he decided; and, forthwith taking them off again, he put on the new suit of the day before.

"I must try to earn a little more," he thought, "to pay for my room, and to buy some new clo'es when these is wore out."

He opened the door of his chamber, and went down-stairs and into the street, carrying his blacking-box with him.

It was Dick's custom to commence his business before breakfast; generally it must be owned, because he began the day penniless and must earn his meal before he ate it. To-day it was different. He had four dollars left in his pocket-book; but this he had previously determined not to touch. In fact he had formed the ambitious design of starting an account at a savings' bank, in order to have something to fall back upon in case of sickness or any other emergency, or at any rate as a reserve fund to expend in clothing or other necessary articles when he required them. Hitherto he had been content to live on from day to day without a penny ahead; but the new vision of respectability which now floated before Dick's mind, owing to his recent acquaintance with Frank, was beginning to exercise a powerful effect upon him.

In Dick's profession as in others there are lucky days, when everything seems to flow prosperously. As if to encourage him in his new-born resolution, our hero obtained no less than six jobs in the course of an hour and a half. This gave him sixty cents, quite abundant to purchase his breakfast, and a comb besides. His exertions made him hungry, and, entering a small eating-house he ordered a cup of coffee and a beefsteak. To this he added a couple of rolls. This was quite a luxurious breakfast for Dick, and more expensive than he was accustomed to indulge himself with. To gratify the curiosity of my young readers, I will put down the items with their cost,—

Coffee, ...	5 cts.
Beefsteak, ...	15 cts.
A couple of rolls, ...	5 cts.
	——25 cts.

It will thus be seen that our hero had expended nearly one-half of his morning's earnings. Some days he had been compelled to breakfast on five cents, and then he was forced to content himself with a couple of apples, or cakes. But a good breakfast is a good preparation for a busy day, and Dick sallied forth from the restaurant lively and alert, ready to do a good stroke of business.

Dick's change of costume was liable to lead to one result of which he had not thought. His brother boot-blacks might think he had grown aristocratic, and was putting on airs,—that, in fact, he was getting above his business, and desirous to outshine his associates. Dick had not dreamed of this, because in fact, in spite of his new born ambition, he entertained no such feelings. There was nothing of what boys call "big feeling" about him. He was a thorough democrat, using the word not politically, but in its proper sense, and was disposed to fraternize with all whom he styled "good fellows," without regard to their position. It may seem a little unnecessary to some of my readers to make this explanation; but they must remember that pride and "big feeling" are confined to no age or class, but may be found in boys as well as men, and in boot-blacks as well as those of a higher rank.

The morning being a busy time with the boot-blacks, Dick's changed appearance had not as yet attracted much attention. But when business slackened a little, our hero was destined to be reminded of it.

Among the down-town boot-blacks was one hailing from the Five Points,[1]—a stout, red-haired, freckled-faced boy of fourteen, bearing the name of Micky Maguire. This boy, by his boldness and recklessness, as well as by his personal strength, which was considerable, had acquired an ascendency among his fellow professionals, and had a gang of subservient followers, whom he led on to acts of ruffianism, not unfrequently terminating in a month or two at Blackwell's Island.[2] Micky himself had served two terms there; but the confinement appeared to have had very little effect in amending his conduct, except, perhaps, in making him a little more cautious about an encounter with the "copps," as the members of the city police, are, for some unknown reason, styled among the Five-Point boys.

Now Micky was proud of his strength, and of the position of leader which it had secured him. Moreover he was democratic in his tastes, and had a jealous hatred of those who wore good clothes and kept their faces clean. He called it putting on airs, and resented the implied superiority. If he had been fifteen years older, and had a trifle more education, he would have interested himself in politics, and been prominent at ward meetings, and a terror to respectable voters on election day. As it was, he contented himself with being the leader of a gang of young ruffians, over whom he wielded a despotic power.

Now it is only justice to Dick to say that, so far as wearing good clothes was concerned, he had never hitherto offended the eyes of Micky Maguire. Indeed, they generally looked as if they patronized the same clothing establishment. On this particular morning it chanced

1. Sixth ward in New York, bounded by Reade Street, West Street, Canal Street, and Broadway. It was named in the 1830s after the intersection of five streets (Mulberry, Anthony [now Worth Street], Cross [now Park], Orange [now Baxter], and Little Water Street [no longer exists]). The neighborhood was known for crime, vice, and terrible tenement living conditions.
2. Reference to Blackwell's Penitentiary, a prison built in 1832 on what is now called Roosevelt Island.

that Micky had not been very fortunate in a business way, and, as a natural consequence, his temper, never very amiable, was somewhat ruffled by the fact. He had had a very frugal breakfast,—not because he felt abstemious, but owing to the low state of his finances. He was walking along with one of his particular friends, a boy nicknamed Limpy Jim, so called from a slight peculiarity in his walk, when all at once he espied our friend Dick in his new suit.

"My eyes!" he exclaimed, in astonishment; "Jim, just look at Ragged Dick. He's come into a fortun', and turned gentleman. See his new clothes."

"So he has," said Jim. "Where'd he get 'em, I wonder?"

"Hooked 'em, p'r'aps. Let's go and stir him up a little. We don't want no gentlemen on our beat. So he's puttin' on airs,—is he? I'll give him a lesson."

So saying the two boys walked up to our hero, who had not observed them, his back being turned, and Micky Maguire gave him a smart slap on the shoulder.

Dick turned round quickly.

Chapter 14

A Battle and a Victory

"What's that for?" demanded Dick, turning round to see who had struck him.

"You're gettin' mighty fine!" said Micky Maguire, surveying Dick's new clothes with a scornful air.

There was something in his words and tone, which Dick, who was disposed to stand up for his dignity, did not at all relish.

"Well, what's the odds if I am?" he retorted. "Does it hurt you any?"

"See him put on airs, Jim," said Micky, turning to his companion. "Where'd you get them clo'es?"

"Never mind where I got 'em. Maybe the Prince of Wales gave 'em to me."[1]

"Hear him, now, Jim," said Micky. "Most likely he stole 'em."

"Stealin' aint in *my* line."

It might have been unconscious the emphasis which Dick placed on the word "my." At any rate Micky chose to take offence.

"Do you mean to say that *I* steal?" he demanded, doubling up his fist, and advancing towards Dick in a threatening manner.

"I don't say anything about it," answered Dick, by no means alarmed at this hostile demonstration. "I know you've been to the

---

1. Tom Thumb met the Prince of Wales in 1840 in Buckingham Palace. Barnum publicized this visit widely.

island twice. P'r'aps 'twas to make a visit along of the Mayor and Aldermen. Maybe you was a innocent victim of oppression. I aint a goin' to say."

Micky's freckled face grew red with wrath, for Dick had only stated the truth

"Do you mean to insult me," he demanded, shaking his fist already doubled up in Dick's face. "Maybe you want a lickin'?"

"I aint partic'larly anxious to get one," said Dick, coolly. "They don't agree with my constitution which is nat'rally delicate. I'd rather have a good dinner than a lickin' any time."

"You're afraid," sneered Micky. "Isn't he, Jim?"

"In course he is."

"P'r'aps I am," said Dick, composedly, "but it don't trouble me much."

"Do you want to fight?" demanded Micky, encouraged by Dick's quietness, fancying he was afraid to encounter him.

"No, I don't," said Dick. "I aint fond of fightin'. It's a very poor amusement, and very bad for the complexion, 'specially for the eyes and nose, which is apt to turn red, white, and blue."

Micky misunderstood Dick, and judged from the tenor of his speech that he would be an easy victim. As he knew, Dick very seldom was concerned in any street fight,—not from cowardice, as he imagined, but because he had too much good sense to do so. Being quarrelsome, like all bullies, and supposing that he was more than a match for our hero, being about two inches taller, he could no longer resist an inclination to assault him, and tried to plant a blow in Dick's face which would have hurt him considerably if he had not drawn back just in time.

Now, though Dick was far from quarrelsome, he was ready to defend himself on all occasions, and it was too much to expect that he would stand quiet and allow himself to be beaten.

He dropped his blacking-box on the instant, and returned Micky's blow with such good effect that the young bully staggered back, and would have fallen, if he had not been propped up by his confederate, Limpy Jim.

"Go in, Micky!" shouted the latter, who was rather a coward on his own account, but liked to see others fight. "Polish him off, that's a good feller."

Micky was now boiling over with rage and fury, and required no urging. He was fully determined to make a terrible example of poor Dick. He threw himself upon him, and strove to bear him to the ground; but Dick, avoiding a close hug, in which he might possibly have got the worst of it, by an adroit movement, tripped up his antagonist, and stretched him on the sidewalk.

"Hit him, Jim!" exclaimed Micky, furiously.

Limpy Jim did not seem inclined to obey orders. There was a quiet strength and coolness about Dick, which alarmed him. He preferred that Micky should incur all the risks of battle, and accordingly set himself to raising his fallen comrade.

"Come, Micky," said Dick, quietly, "you'd better give it up. I wouldn't have touched you if you hadn't hit me first. I don't want to fight. It's low business."

"You're afraid of hurtin' your clo'es," said Micky, with a sneer.

"Maybe I am," said Dick. "I hope I haven't hurt yours."

Micky's answer to this was another attack, as violent and impetuous as the first. But his fury was in the way. He struck wildly, not measuring his blows, and Dick had no difficulty in turning aside so that his antagonist's blow fell upon the empty air, and his momentum was such that he nearly fell forward headlong. Dick might readily have taken advantage of his unsteadiness, and knocked him down; but he was not vindictive, and chose to act on the defensive, except when he could not avoid it.

Recovering himself, Micky saw that Dick was a more formidable antagonist than he had supposed, and was meditating another assault, better planned, which by its impetuosity might bear our hero to the ground. But there was an unlooked-for interference.

"Look out for the 'copp,'" said Jim, in a low voice.

Micky turned round and saw a tall policeman heading towards him, and thought it might be prudent to suspend hostilities. He accordingly picked up his blacking-box, and, hitching up his pants, walked off, attended by Limpy Jim.

"What's that chap been doing?" asked the policeman of Dick.

"He was amoosin' himself by pitchin' into me," replied Dick.

"What for?"

"He didn't like it 'cause I patronize a different tailor from him."

"Well, it seems to me you *are* dressed pretty smart for a boot-black," said the policeman.

"I wish I wasn't a boot-black," said Dick.

"Never mind, my lad. It's an honest business," said the policeman, who was a sensible man and a worthy citizen. "It's an honest business. Stick to it till you get something better."

"I mean to," said Dick. "It aint easy to get out of it, as the prisoner remarked, when he was asked how he liked his residence."

"I hope you don't speak from experience."

"No," said Dick; "I don't mean to get into prison if I can help it."

"Do you see that gentleman over there?" asked the officer, pointing to a well-dressed man who was walking on the other side of the street.

"Yes."

"Well, he was once a newsboy."

"And what is he now?"

"He keeps a bookstore, and is quite prosperous."

Dick looked at the gentleman with interest, wondering if he should look as respectable when he was a grown man.

It will be seen that Dick was getting ambitious. Hitherto he had thought very little of the future, but was content to get along as he could, dining as well as his means would allow, and spending the evenings in the pit of the Old Bowery, eating peanuts between the acts if he was prosperous, and if unlucky supping on dry bread or an apple, and sleeping in an old box or a wagon. Now, for the first time, he began to reflect that he could not black boots all his life. In seven years he would be a man, and, since his meeting with Frank, he felt that he would like to be a respectable man. He could see and appreciate the difference between Frank and such a boy as Micky Maguire, and it was not strange that he preferred the society of the former.

In the course of the next morning, in pursuance of his new resolutions for the future, he called at a savings bank, and held out four dollars in bills besides another dollar in change. There was a high railing, and a number of clerks busily writing at desks behind it. Dick, never having been in a bank before, did not know where to go. He went, by mistake, to the desk where money was paid out.

"Where's your book?" asked the clerk.

"I haven't got any."

"Have you any money deposited here?"

"No sir, I want to leave some here."

"Then go to the next desk."

Dick followed directions, and presented himself before an elderly man with gray hair, who looked at him over the rims of his spectacles.

"I want you to keep that for me," said Dick, awkwardly emptying his money out on the desk.

"How much is there?"

"Five dollars."

"Have you got an account here?"

"No, sir."

"Of course you can write?"

The "of course" was said on account of Dick's neat dress.

"Have I got to do any writing?" asked our hero, a little embarrassed.

"We want you to sign your name in this book," and the old gentleman shoved round a large folio volume containing the names of depositors.

Dick surveyed the book with some awe.

"I aint much on writin'," he said.

"Very well; write as well as you can."

The pen was put into Dick's hand, and, after dipping it in the inkstand, he succeeded after a hard effort, accompanied by many contortions of the face, in in scribing upon the book of the bank the name

DICK HUNTER.

"Dick!—that means Richard, I suppose," said the bank officer, who had some difficulty in making out the signature.

"No; Ragged Dick is what folks call me."

"You don't look very ragged."

"No, I've left my rags at home. They might get wore out if I used 'em too common."

"Well, my lad, I'll make out a book in the name of Dick Hunter, since you seem to prefer Dick to Richard. I hope you will save up your money and deposit more with us."

Our hero took his bank-book, and gazed on the entry "Five Dollars" with a new sense of importance. He had been accustomed to joke about Erie shares; but now, for the first time, he felt himself a capitalist; on a small scale, to be sure, but still it was no small thing for Dick to have five dollars which he could call his own. He firmly determined that he would lay by every cent he could spare from his earnings towards the fund he hoped to accumulate.

But Dick was too sensible not to know that there was something more than money needed to win a respectable position in the world. He felt that he was very ignorant. Of reading and writing he only knew the rudiments, and that, with a slight acquaintance with arithmetic, was all he did know of books. Dick knew he must study hard, and he dreaded it. He looked upon learning as attended with greater difficulties than it really possesses. But Dick had good pluck. He meant to learn, nevertheless, and resolved to buy a book with his first spare earnings.

When Dick went home at night he locked up his bank-book in one of the drawers of the bureau. It was wonderful how much more independent he felt whenever he reflected upon the contents of that drawer, and with what an important air of joint ownership he regarded the bank building in which his small savings were deposited.

Chapter 15

Dick Secures a Tutor

The next morning Dick was unusually successful, having plenty to do, and receiving for one job twenty-five cents,—the gentleman refusing to take change. Then flashed upon Dick's mind the thought that he had not yet returned the change due to the gentleman whose boots he had blacked on the morning of his introduction to the reader.

"What'll he think of me?" said Dick to himself. "I hope he won't think I'm mean enough to keep the money."

Now Dick was scrupulously honest, and though the temptation to be otherwise had often been strong, he had always resisted It. He was not willing on any account to keep money which did not belong to him, and he immediately started for 125 Fulton Street (the address which had been given him) where he found Mr. Greyson's name on the door of an office on the first floor.

The door being open, Dick walked in.

"Is Mr. Greyson in?" he asked of a clerk who sat on a high stool before a desk.

"Not just now. He'll be in soon. Will you wait?"

"Yes," said Dick.

"Very well; take a seat then."

Dick sat down and took up the morning "Tribune," but presently came to a word of four syllables, which he pronounced to himself a "sticker," and laid it down. But he had not long to wait, for five minutes later Mr. Greyson entered.

"Did you wish to speak to me, my lad?" said he to Dick, whom in his new clothes he did not recognize.

"Yes, sir," said Dick. "I owe you some money."

"Indeed!" said Mr. Greyson, pleasantly; "that's an agreeable surprise. I didn't know but you had come for some. So you are a debtor of mine, and not a creditor?"

"I b'lieve that's right," said Dick, drawing fifteen cents from his pocket, and placing in Mr. Greyson's hand.

"Fifteen cents!" repeated he, in some surprise. "How do you happen to be indebted to me in that amount?"

"You gave me a quarter for a-shinin' your boots, yesterday mornin', and couldn't wait for the change. I meant to have brought it before, but I forgot all about it till this mornin'."

"It had quite slipped my mind also. But you don't look like the boy I employed. If I remember rightly he wasn't as well dressed as you."

"No," said Dick. "I was dressed for a party, then, but the clo'es was too well ventilated to be comfortable in cold weather."

"You're an honest boy," said Mr. Greyson. "Who taught you to be honest?"

"Nobody," said Dick. "But it's mean to cheat and steal. I've always knowed that."

"Then you've got ahead of some of our business men. Do you read the Bible?"

"No," said Dick. "I've heard it's a good book, but I don't know much about it."

"You ought to go to some Sunday School. Would you be willing?"

"Yes," said Dick, promptly. "I want to grow up 'spectable. But I don't know where to go."

"Then I'll tell you. The church I attend is at the corner of Fifth Avenue and Twenty-first Street."

"I've seen it," said Dick.

"I have a class in the Sunday School there. If you'll come next Sunday, I'll take you into my class, and do what I can to help you."

"Thank you," said Dick, "but p'r'aps you'll get tired of teaching me. I'm awful ignorant."

"No, my lad," said Mr. Greyson, kindly. "You evidently have some good principles to start with, as you have shown by your scorn for dishonesty. I shall hope good things of you in the future."

"Well, Dick," said our hero, apostrophizing himself, as he left the office; "you're gettin' up in the world. You've got money invested, and are goin' to attend church, by partic'lar invitation, on Fifth Avenue. I shouldn't wonder much if you should find cards, when you get home, from the Mayor, requestin' the honor of your company to dinner, along with other distinguished guests."

Dick felt in very good spirits. He seemed to be emerging from the world in which he had hitherto lived, into a new atmosphere of respectability, and the change seemed very pleasant to him.

At six o'clock Dick went into a restaurant on Chatham Street, and got a comfortable supper. He had been so successful during that day that, after paying for this, he still had ninety cents left. While he was despatching his supper, another boy came in, smaller and slighter than Dick, and sat down beside him. Dick recognized him as a boy who three months before had entered the ranks of the boot-blacks, but who, from a natural timidity, had not been able to earn much. He was ill-fitted for the coarse companionship of the street boys, and shrank from the rude jokes of his present associates. Dick had never troubled him; for our hero had a certain chivalrous feeling which would not allow him to bully or disturb a younger and weaker boy than himself.

"How are you, Fosdick?"[1] said Dick, as the other seated himself.

"Pretty well," said Fosdick. "I suppose you're all right."

"Oh, yes, I'm right side up with care. I've been havin' a bully supper. What are you goin' to have?"

"Some bread and butter."

"Why don't you get a cup o' coffee?"

"Why," said Fosdick, reluctantly, "I haven't got money enough to-night."

"Never mind," said Dick; "I'm in luck to-day. I'll stand treat."

"That's kind in you," said Fosdick, gratefully.

"Oh, never mind that," said Dick.

1. Allusion to writer Charles Austin Fosdick, pseudonym H. Castlemom (1842–1915), whose juvenile *Gunboat* and *Rocky Mountain* series appeared between 1865 and 1869.

Accordingly he ordered a cup of coffee, and a plate of beef-steak, and was gratified to see that his young companion partook of both with evident relish. When the repast was over, the boys went out into the street together, Dick pausing at the desk to settle for both suppers.

"Where are you going to sleep to-night, Fosdick?" asked Dick, as they stood on the sidewalk.

"I don't know," said Fosdick, a little sadly. "In some door-way, I expect. But I'm afraid the police will find me out, and make me move on."

"I'll tell you what," said Dick, "you must go home with me. I guess my bed will hold two."

"Have you got a room?" asked the other, in surprise.

"Yes," said Dick, rather proudly, and with a little excusable exultation. "I've got a room over in Mott Street; there I can receive my friends. That'll be better than sleepin' in a door-way,—won't it?"

"Yes, indeed it will," said Fosdick. "How lucky I was to come across you! It comes hard to me living as I do. When my father was alive I had every comfort."

"That's more'n I ever had," said Dick. "But I'm goin' to try to live comfortable now. Is your father dead?"

"Yes," said Fosdick, sadly. "He was a printer; but he was drowned one dark night from a Fulton ferry-boat, and, as I had no relations in the city, and no money, I was obliged to go to work as quick as I could. But I don't get on very well."

"Didn't you have no brothers nor sisters?" asked Dick.

"No," said Fosdick; "father and I used to live alone. He was always so much company to me that I feel very lonesome without him. There's a man out West somewhere that owes him two thousand dollars. He used to live in the city, and father lent him all his money to help him go into business; but he failed, or pretended to, and went off. If father hadn't lost that money he would have left me well off; but no money would have made up his loss to me."

"What's the man's name that went off with your father's money?"

"His name is Hiram Bates."

"P'r'aps you'll get the money again, sometime."

"There isn't much chance of it," said Fosdick. "I'd sell out my chances of that for five dollars."

"Maybe I'll buy you out some time," said Dick. "Now, come round and see what sort of a room I've got. I used to go to the theatre evenings, when I had money; but now I'd rather go to bed early, and have a good sleep."

"I don't care much about theatres," said Fosdick. "Father didn't use to let me go very often. He said it wasn't good for boys."

"I like to go to the Old Bowery sometimes. They have tip-top plays

there. Can you read and write well?" he asked, as a sudden thought
came to him.

"Yes," said Fosdick. "Father always kept me at school when he was
alive, and I stood pretty well in my classes. I was expecting to enter
at the Free Academy[2] next year."

"Then I'll tell you what," said Dick; "I'll make a bargain with you.
I can't read much more'n a pig; and my writin' looks like hens' tracks.
I don't want to grow up knowin' no more'n a four-year-old boy. If
you'll teach me readin' and writin' evenin's, you shall sleep in my
room every night. That'll be better'n door-steps or old boxes, where
I've slept many a time."

"Are you in earnest?" said Fosdick, his face lighting up hopefully.

"In course I am," said Dick. "It's fashionable for young gentlemen
to have private tootors to introduce 'em into the flower-beds of literatoor and science, and why shouldn't I foller the fashion? You shall
be my perfessor; only you must promise not to be very hard if my
writin' looks like a rail-fence on a bender."

"I'll try not to be too severe," said Fosdick, laughing. "I shall be
thankful for such a chance to get a place to sleep. Have you got anything to read out of?"

"No," said Dick. "My extensive and well-selected library was lost
overboard in a storm, when I was sailin' from the Sandwich Islands[3]
to the desert of Sahara. But I'll buy a paper. That'll do me a long time."

Accordingly Dick stopped at a paper-stand, and bought a copy of a
weekly paper, filled with the usual variety of reading matter,—stories,
sketches, poems, etc.

They soon arrived at Dick's lodging-house. Our hero, procuring a
lamp from the landlady, led the way into his apartment, which he
entered with the proud air of a proprietor.

"Well, how do you like it, Fosdick?" he asked, complacently.

The time was when Fosdick would have thought it untidy and not
particularly attractive. But he had served a severe apprenticeship in
the streets, and it was pleasant to feel himself under shelter, and he
was not disposed to be critical.

"It looks very comfortable, Dick," he said.

"The bed aint very large," said Dick; "but I guess we can get along."

"Oh, yes," said Fosdick, cheerfully. "I don't take up much room."

"Then that's all right. There's two chairs, you see, one for you and
one for me. In case the mayor comes in to spend the evenin' socially,
he can sit on the bed."

The boys seated themselves, and five minutes later, under the guid-
ance of his young tutor, Dick had commenced his studies.

2. Now the College of the City of New York [*Alger's note*].
3. Name given to Hawaii by discoverer James Cook on January 18, 1778.

Chapter 16

The First Lesson

Fortunately for Dick, his young tutor was well qualified to instruct him. Henry Fosdick, though only twelve years old, knew as much as many boys of fourteen. He had always been studious and ambitious to excel. His father, being a printer, employed in an office where books were printed, often brought home new books in sheets, which Henry was always glad to read. Mr. Fosdick had been, besides, a subscriber to the Mechanics' Apprentices' Library, which contains many thousands of well-selected and instructive books. Thus Henry had acquired an amount of general information, unusual in a boy of his age. Perhaps he had devoted too much time to study, for he was not naturally robust. All this, however, fitted him admirably for the office to which Dick had appointed him,—that of his private instructor.

The two boys drew up their chairs to the rickety table, and spread out the paper before them.

"The exercises generally commence with ringin' the bell," said Dick; "but as I aint got none, we'll have to do without."

"And the teacher is generally provided with a rod," said Fosdick. "Isn't there a poker handy, that I can use in case my scholar doesn't behave well?"

" 'Taint lawful to use fire-arms," said Dick.

"Now, Dick," said Fosdick, "before we begin, I must find out how much you already know. Can you read any?"

"Not enough to hurt me," said Dick. "All I know about readin' you could put in a nutshell, and there'd be room left for a small family."

"I suppose you know your letters?"

"Yes," said Dick, "I know 'em all, but not intimately. I guess I can call 'em all by name."

"Where did you learn them? Did you ever go to school?"

"Yes; I went two days."

"Why did you stop?"

"It didn't agree with my constitution."

"You don't look very delicate," said Fosdick.

"No," said Dick, "I aint troubled much that way, but I found lickins didn't agree with me."

"Did you get punished?"

"Awful," said Dick.

"What for?"

"For indulgin' in a little harmless amoosement," said Dick. "You see the boy that was sittin' next to me fell asleep, which I considered improper in school-time; so I thought I'd help the teacher a little by wakin' him up. So I took a pin and stuck into him; but I guess it went a little too far, for he screeched awful. The teacher found out what it was that made him holler, and whipped me with a ruler till I was black and blue. I thought 'twas about time to take a vacation; so that's the last time I went to school."

"You didn't learn to read in that time, of course?"

"No," said Dick; "but I was a newsboy a little while; so I learned a little, just so's to find out what the news was. Sometimes I didn't read straight, and called the wrong news.[1] One mornin' I asked another boy what the paper said, and he told me the King of Africa was dead. I thought it was all right till folks began to laugh."

"Well, Dick, if you'll only study well, you won't be liable to make such mistakes."

"I hope so," said Dick. "My friend Horace Greeley told me the other day that he'd get me to take his place now and then when he was off makin' speeches if my edication hadn't been neglected."

"I must find a good piece for you to begin on," said Fosdick, looking over the paper.

"Find an easy one," said Dick, "with words of one story."

Fosdick at length found a piece which he thought would answer. He discovered on trial that Dick had not exaggerated his deficiencies. Words of two syllables he seldom pronounced right, and was much surprised when he was told how "through" was sounded.

"Seems to me it's throwin' away letters to use all them," he said.

"How would you spell it?" asked his young teacher.

"T-h-r-u," said Dick.

"Well," said Fosdick, "there's a good many other words that are spelt with more letters than they need to have. But it's the fashion, and we must follow it."

But if Dick was ignorant, he was quick, and had an excellent capacity. Moreover he had perseverance, and was not easily discouraged. He had made up his mind he must know more, and was not disposed to complain of the difficulty of his task. Fosdick had occasion to laugh more than once at his ludicrous mistakes; but Dick laughed too, and on the whole both were quite interested in the lesson.

At the end of an hour and a half the boys stopped for the evening.

"You're learning fast, Dick," said Fosdick. "At this rate you will soon learn to read well."

"Will I?" asked Dick with an expression of satisfaction. "I'm glad of that. I don't want to be ignorant. I didn't use to care, but I do now. I want to grow up 'spectable."

"So do I, Dick. We will both help each other, and I am sure we can accomplish something. But I am beginning to feel sleepy."

---

1. Didn't shout out the headline correctly when selling papers.

"So am I," said Dick. "Them hard words make my head ache. I wonder who made 'em all?"

"That's more than I can tell. I suppose you've seen a dictionary."

"That's another of 'em. No, I can't say I have, though I may have seen him in the street without knowin' him."

"A dictionary is a book containing all the words in the language."

"How many are there?"

"I don't rightly know; but I think there are about fifty thousand."

"It's a pretty large family," said Dick. "Have I got to learn 'em all?"

"That will not be necessary. There are a large number which you would never find occasion to use."

"I'm glad of that," said Dick; "for I don't expect to live to be more'n a hundred, and by that time I wouldn't be more'n half through."

By this time the flickering lamp gave a decided hint to the boys that unless they made haste they would have to undress in the dark. They accordingly drew off their clothes, and Dick jumped into bed. But Fosdick, before doing so, knelt down by the side of the bed, and said a short prayer.

"What's that for?" asked Dick curiously.

"I was saying my prayers," said Fosdick, as he rose from his knees. "Don't you ever do it?"

"No," said Dick. "Nobody ever taught me."

"Then I'll teach you. Shall I?"

"I don't know," said Dick, dubiously. "What's the good?"

Fosdick explained as well as he could, and perhaps his simple explanation was better adapted to Dick's comprehension than one from an older person would have been. Dick felt more free to ask questions, and the example of his new friend, for whom he was beginning to feel a warm attachment, had considerable effect upon him. When, therefore, Fosdick asked again if he should teach him a prayer, Dick consented, and his young bedfellow did so. Dick was not naturally irreligious. If he had lived without a knowledge of God and of religious things, it was scarcely to be wondered at in a lad who, from an early age, had been thrown upon his own exertions for the means of living, with no one to care for him or give him good advice. But he was so far good that he could appreciate goodness in others, and this it was that had drawn him to Frank in the first place, and now to Henry Fosdick. He did not, therefore, attempt to ridicule his companion, as some boys better brought up might have done, but was willing to follow his example in what something told him was right. Our young hero had taken an important step towards securing that genuine respectability which he was ambitious to attain.

Weary with the day's work, and Dick perhaps still more fatigued by the unusual mental effort he had made, the boys soon sank into a deep and peaceful slumber, from which they did not awaken till six o'clock the next morning. Before going out Dick sought Mrs. Mooney, and spoke to her on the subject of taking Fosdick as a room-mate. He found that she had no objection, provided he would allow her twenty-five cents a week extra, in consideration of the extra trouble which his companion might be expected to make. To this Dick assented, and the arrangement was definitely concluded.

This over, the two boys went out and took stations near each other. Dick had more of a business turn than Henry, and less shrinking from publicity, so that his earnings were greater. But he had undertaken to pay the entire expenses of the room, and needed to earn more. Some-times, when two customers presented themselves at the same time, he was able to direct one to his friend. So at the end of the week both boys found themselves with surplus earnings. Dick had the satisfaction of adding two dollars and a half to his deposits in the Savings Bank, and Fosdick commenced an account by depositing seventy-five cents.

On Sunday morning Dick bethought himself of his promise to Mr. Greyson to come to the church on Fifth Avenue. To tell the truth, Dick recalled it with some regret. He had never been inside a church since he could remember, and he was not much attracted by the invi-tation he had received. But Henry, finding him wavering, urged him to go, and offered to go with him. Dick gladly accepted the offer, feel-ing that he required some one to lend him countenance under such unusual circumstances.

Dick dressed himself with scrupulous care, giving his shoes a "shine" so brilliant that it did him great credit in a professional point of view, and endeavored to clean his hands thoroughly; but, in spite of all he could do, they were not so white as if his business had been of a differ-ent character.

Having fully completed his preparations, he descended into the street, and, with Henry by his side, crossed over to Broadway.

The boys pursued their way up Broadway, which on Sunday pres-ents a striking contrast in its quietness to the noise and confusion of ordinary weekdays, as far as Union Square, then turned down Four-teenth Street, which brought them to Fifth Avenue.

"Suppose we dine at Delmonico's," said Fosdick, looking towards that famous restaurant.

"I'd have to sell some of my Erie shares," said Dick.

A short walk now brought them to the church of which mention has already been made. They stood outside, a little abashed, watch-ing the fashionably attired people who were entering, and were feel-ing a little undecided as to whether they had better enter also, when Dick felt a light touch upon his shoulder.

Turning round, he met the smiling glance of Mr. Greyson.

"So, my young friend, you have kept your promise," he said. "And whom have you brought with you?"

"A friend of mine," said Dick. "His name is Henry Fosdick."

"I am glad you have brought him. Now follow me, and I will give you seats."

Chapter 17

Dick's First Appearance in Society

It was the hour for morning service. The boys followed Mr. Greyson into the handsome church, and were assigned seats in his own pew.

There were two persons already seated in it,—a good-looking lady of middle age, and a pretty little girl of nine. They were Mrs. Greyson and her only daughter Ida. They looked pleasantly at the boys as they entered, smiling a welcome to them.

The morning service commenced. It must be acknowledged that Dick felt rather awkward. It was an unusual place for him, and it need not be wondered at that he felt like a cat in a strange garret. He would not have known when to rise if he had not taken notice of what the rest of the audience did, and followed their example. He was sitting next to Ida, and as it was the first time he had ever been near so well-dressed a young lady, he naturally felt bashful. When the hymns were announced, Ida found the place, and offered a hymn-book to our hero. Dick took it awkwardly, but his studies had not yet been pursued far enough for him to read the words readily. However, he resolved to keep up appearances, and kept his eyes fixed steadily on the hymn-book.

At length the service was over. The people began to file slowly out of church, and among them, of course, Mr. Greyson's family and the two boys. It seemed very strange to Dick to find himself in such different companionship from what he had been accustomed, and he could not help thinking, "Wonder what Johnny Nolan 'ould say if he could see me now!"

But Johnny's business engagements did not often summon him to Fifth Avenue, and Dick was not likely to be seen by any of his friends in the lower part of the city.

"We have our Sunday school in the afternoon," said Mr. Greyson. "I suppose you live at some distance from here?"

"In Mott Street, sir," answered Dick.

"That is too far to go and return. Suppose you and your friend come and dine with us, and then we can come here together in the afternoon."

Dick was as much astonished at this invitation as if he had really been invited by the Mayor to dine with him and the Board of Aldermen.

Mr. Greyson was evidently a rich man, and yet he had actually invited two boot-blacks to dine with him.

"I guess we'd better go home, sir," said Dick, hesitating.

"I don't think you can have any very pressing engagements to interfere with your accepting my invitation," said Mr. Greyson, good-humoredly, for he understood the reason of Dick's hesitation. "So I take it for granted that you both accept."

Before Dick fairly knew what he intended to do, he was walking down Fifth Avenue with his new friends.

Now, our young hero was not naturally bashful; but he certainly felt so now, especially as Miss Ida Greyson chose to walk by his side, leaving Henry Fosdick to walk with her father and mother.

"What is your name?" asked Ida, pleasantly.

Our hero was about to answer "Ragged Dick," when it occurred to him that in the present company he had better forget his old nickname.

"Dick Hunter," he answered.

"Dick!" repeated Ida. "That means Richard, doesn't it?"

"Everybody calls me Dick."

"I have a cousin Dick," said the young lady, sociably. "His name is Dick Wilson. I suppose you don't know him?"

"No," said Dick.

"I like the name of Dick," said the young lady, with charming frankness.

Without being able to tell why, Dick felt rather glad she did. He plucked up courage to ask her name.

"My name is Ida," answered the young lady. "Do you like it?"

"Yes," said Dick. "It's a bully name."

Dick turned red as soon as he had said it, for he felt that he had not used the right expression.

The little girl broke into a silvery laugh.

"What a funny boy you are!" she said.

"I didn't mean it," said Dick, stammering. "I meant it's a tip-top name."

Here Ida laughed again, and Dick wished himself back in Mott Street.

"How old are you?" inquired Ida, continuing her examination.

"I'm fourteen,—goin' on fifteen," said Dick.

"You're a big boy of your age," said Ida. "My cousin Dick is a year older than you, but he isn't as large."

Dick looked pleased. Boys generally like to be told that they are large of their age.

"How old be you?" asked Dick, beginning to feel more at his ease.

"I'm nine years old," said Ida. "I go to Miss Jarvis's school. I've just begun to learn French. Do you know French?"

"Not enough to hurt me," said Dick.

Ida laughed again, and told him that he was a droll boy.

"Do you like it?" asked Dick.

"I like it pretty well, except the verbs. I can't remember them well. Do you go to school?"

"I'm studying with a private tutor," said Dick.

"Are you? So is my cousin Dick. He's going to college this year. Are you going to college?"

"Not this year."

"Because, if you did, you know you'd be in the same class with my cousin. It would be funny to have two Dicks in one class."

They turned down Twenty-fourth Street, passing the Fifth Avenue Hotel on the left, and stopped before an elegant house with a brown stone front. The bell was rung, and the door being opened, the boys, somewhat abashed, followed Mr. Greyson into a handsome hall. They were told where to hang their hats, and a moment afterwards were ushered into a comfortable dining-room, where a table was spread for dinner.

Dick took his seat on the edge of a sofa, and was tempted to rub his eyes to make sure that he was really awake. He could hardly believe that he was a guest in so fine a mansion.

Ida helped to put the boys at their ease.

"Do you like pictures?" she asked.

"Very much," answered Henry.

The little girl brought a book of handsome engravings, and, seating herself beside Dick, to whom she seemed to have taken a decided fancy, commenced showing them to him.

"There are the Pyramids of Egypt," she said, pointing to one engraving.

"What are they for?" asked Dick, puzzled. "I don't see any winders."

"No," said Ida, "I don't believe anybody lives there. Do they, papa?"

"No, my dear. They were used for the burial of the dead. The largest of them is said to be the loftiest building in the world with one exception. The spire of the Cathedral of Strasburg[1] is twenty-four feet higher, if I remember rightly."

"Is Egypt near here?" asked Dick.

"Oh, no, it's ever so many miles off; about four or five hundred. Didn't you know?"

"No," said Dick. "I never heard."

"You don't appear to be very accurate in your information, Ida," said her mother. "Four or five thousand miles would be considerably nearer the truth."

After a little more conversation they sat down to dinner. Dick

---

1. One of the great Gothic cathedrals in the world. Its tower is 142 meters high.

seated himself in an embarrassed way. He was very much afraid of doing or saying something which would be considered an impropriety, and had the uncomfortable feeling that everybody was looking at him, and watching his behavior.

"Where do you live, Dick?" asked Ida, familiarly.

"In Mott Street."

"Where is that?"

"More than a mile off."

"Is it a nice street?"

"Not very," said Dick. "Only poor folks live there."

"Are you poor?"

"Little girls should be seen and not heard," said her mother, gently.

"If you are," said Ida, "I'll give you the five-dollar gold-piece aunt gave me for a birthday present."

"Dick cannot be called poor, my child," said Mrs. Greyson, "since he earns his living by his own exertions."

"Do you earn your living?" asked Ida, who was a very inquisitive young lady, and not easily silenced. "What do you do?"

Dick blushed violently. At such a table, and in presence of the servant who was standing at that moment behind his chair, he did not like to say that he was a shoe-black, although he well knew that there was nothing dishonorable in the occupation.

Mr. Greyson perceived his feelings, and to spare them, said, "You are too inquisitive, Ida. Some time Dick may tell you, but you know we don't talk of business on Sundays."

Dick in his embarrassment had swallowed a large spoonful of hot soup, which made him turn red in the face. For the second time, in spite of the prospect of the best dinner he had ever eaten, he wished himself back in Mott Street. Henry Fosdick was more easy and unembarrassed than Dick, not having led such a vagabond and neglected life. But it was to Dick that Ida chiefly directed her conversation, having apparently taken a fancy to his frank and handsome face. I believe I have already said that Dick was a very good-looking boy, especially now since he kept his face clean. He had a frank, honest expression, which generally won its way to the favor of those with whom he came in contact.

Dick got along pretty well at the table by dint of noticing how the rest acted, but there was one thing he could not manage, eating with his fork, which, by the way, he thought a very singular arrangement.

At length they arose from the table, somewhat to Dick's relief. Again Ida devoted herself to the boys, and exhibited a profusely illustrated Bible for their entertainment. Dick was interested in looking at the pictures, though he knew very little of their subjects. Henry Fosdick was much better informed, as might have been expected.

When the boys were about to leave the house with Mr. Greyson for

the Sunday school, Ida placed her hand in Dick's, and said persuasively. "You'll come again, Dick, won't you?"

"Thank you," said Dick, "I'd like to," and he could not help thinking Ida the nicest girl he had ever seen.

"Yes," said Mrs. Greyson, hospitably, "we shall be glad to see you
both here again."

"Thank you very much," said Henry Fosdick, gratefully. "We shall
like very much to come."

I will not dwell upon the hour spent in Sunday school, nor upon
the remarks of Mr. Greyson to his class. He found Dick's ignorance
of religious subjects so great that he was obliged to begin at the beginning with him. Dick was interested in hearing the children sing, and
readily promised to come again the next Sunday.

When the service was over Dick and Henry walked homewards.
Dick could not help letting his thoughts rest on the sweet little girl
who had given him so cordial a welcome, and hoping that he might
meet her again.

"Mr. Greyson is a nice man,—isn't he, Dick?" asked Henry, as they
were turning into Mott Street, and were already in sight of their
lodging-house.

"Aint he, though?" said Dick. "He treated us just as if we were
young gentlemen."

"Ida seemed to take a great fancy to you."

"She's a tip-top girl," said Dick, "but she asked so many questions
that I didn't know what to say."

He had scarcely finished speaking, when a stone whizzed by his
head, and, turning quickly, he saw Micky Maguire running round the
corner of the street which they had just passed.

Chapter 18

Micky Maguire's Second Defeat

Dick was no coward. Nor was he in the habit of submitting passively
to an insult. When, therefore, he recognized Micky Maguire as his
assailant, he instantly turned and gave chase. Micky anticipated pursuit, and ran at his utmost speed. It is doubtful if Dick would have
overtaken him, but Micky had the ill luck to trip just as he had
entered a narrow alley, and, falling with some violence, received a
sharp blow from the hard stones, which made him scream with pain.

"Ow!" he whined. "Don't you hit a feller when he's down."

"What made you fire that stone at me?" demanded our hero, looking down at the fallen bully.

"Just for fun," said Micky.

"It would have been a very agreeable s'prise if it had hit me," said Dick. "S'posin' I fire a rock at you jest for fun."

"Don't!" exclaimed Micky, in alarm.

"It seems you don't like agreeable s'prises," said Dick, "any more'n the man did what got hooked by a cow one mornin, before breakfast. It didn't improve his appetite much."

"I've most broke my arm," said Micky, ruefully, rubbing the affected limb.

"If it's broke you can't fire no more stones, which is a very cheerin' reflection," said Dick. "Ef you haven't money enough to buy a wooden one I'll lend you a quarter. There's one good thing about wooden ones, they aint liable to get cold in winter, which is another cheerin' reflection."

"I don't want none of yer cheerin' reflections," said Micky, sullenly. "Yer company aint wanted here."

"Thank you for your polite invitation to leave," said Dick, bowing ceremoniously. "I'm willin' to go, but ef you throw any more stones at me, Micky Maguire, I'll hurt you worse than the stones did."

The only answer made to this warning was a scowl from his fallen opponent. It was quite evident that Dick had the best of it, and he thought it prudent to say nothing.

"As I've got a friend waitin' outside, I shall have to tear myself away," said Dick. "You'd better not throw any more stones, Micky Maguire, for it don't seem to agree with your constitution."

Micky muttered something which Dick did not stay to hear. He backed out of the alley, keeping a watchful eye on his fallen foe, and rejoined Henry Fosdick, who was awaiting his return.

"Who was it, Dick?" he asked.

"A partic'lar friend of mine, Micky Maguire," said Dick. "He playfully fired a rock at my head as a mark of his 'fection. He loves me like a brother, Micky does."

"Rather a dangerous kind of a friend, I should think," said Fosdick. "He might have killed you."

"I've warned him not to be so 'fectionate another time," said Dick.

"I know him," said Henry Fosdick. "He's at the head of a gang of boys living at the Five-Points. He threatened to whip me once because a gentleman employed me to black his boots instead of him."

"He's been at the Island two or three times for stealing," said Dick. "I guess he won't touch me again. He'd rather get hold of small boys. If he ever does anything to you, Fosdick, just let me know, and I'll give him a thrashing."

Dick was right. Micky Maguire was a bully, and like most bullies did not fancy tackling boys whose strength was equal or superior to his own. Although he hated Dick more than ever, because he thought our hero was putting on airs, he had too lively a remembrance of his strength and courage to venture upon another open attack. He contented himself, therefore, whenever he met Dick, with scowling at him. Dick took this very philosophically, remarking that, "if it was soothin' to Micky's feelings, he might go ahead, as it didn't hurt him much."

It will not be necessary to chronicle the events of the next few weeks. A new life had commenced for Dick. He no longer haunted the gallery of the Old Bowery; and even Tony Pastor's hospitable doors had lost their old attractions. He spent two hours every evening in study. His progress was astonishingly rapid. He was gifted with a natural quickness; and he was stimulated by the desire to acquire a fair education as a means of "growin' up 'spectable," as he termed it. Much was due also to the patience and perseverance of Henry Fosdick, who made a capital teacher.

"You're improving wonderfully, Dick," said his friend, one evening, when Dick had read an entire paragraph without a mistake.

"Am I?" said Dick, with satisfaction.

"Yes. If you'll buy a writing-book to-morrow, we can begin writing to-morrow evening."

"What else do you know, Henry?" asked Dick.

"Arithmetic, and geography, and grammar."

"What a lot you know!" said Dick, admiringly.

"I don't *know* any of them," said Fosdick. "I've only studied them. I wish I knew a great deal more."

"I'll be satisfied when I know as much as you," said Dick.

"It seems a great deal to you now, Dick, but in a few months you'll think differently. The more you know, the more you'll want to know."

"Then there aint any end to learnin'?" said Dick.

"No."

"Well," said Dick, "I guess I'll be as much as sixty before I know everything."

"Yes; as old as that, probably," said Fosdick, laughing.

"Anyway, you know too much to be blackin' boots. Leave that to ignorant chaps like me."

"You won't be ignorant long, Dick."

"You'd ought to get into some office or countin'-room."

"I wish I could," said Fosdick, earnestly. "I don't succeed very well at blacking boots. You make a great deal more than I do."

"That's cause I aint troubled with bashfulness," said Dick. "Bashfulness aint as natural to me as it is to you. I'm always on hand, as the cat said to the milk. You'd better give up shines, Fosdick, and give your 'tention to mercantile pursuits."

"I've thought of trying to get a place," said Fosdick; "but no one would take me with these clothes;" and he directed his glance to his well-worn suit, which he kept as neat as he could, but which, in spite of all his care, began to show decided marks of use. There was also here and there a stain of blacking upon it, which, though an advertisement of his profession, scarcely added to its good appearance.

"I almost wanted to stay at home from Sunday school last Sunday," he continued, "because I thought everybody would notice how dirty and worn my clothes had got to be."

"If my clothes wasn't two sizes too big for you," said Dick, generously, "I'd change. You'd look as if you'd got into your great-uncle's suit by mistake."

"You're very kind, Dick, to think of changing," said Fosdick, "for your suit is much better than mine; but I don't think that mine would suit you very well. The pants would show a little more of your ankles than is the fashion, and you couldn't eat a very hearty dinner without bursting the buttons off the vest."

"That wouldn't be very convenient," said Dick. "I aint fond of lacin'[1] to show my elegant figger. But I say," he added with a sudden thought, "how much money have we got in the savings bank?"

Fosdick took a key from his pocket, and went to the drawer in which the bank-books were kept, and, opening it, brought them out for inspection.

It was found that Dick had the sum of eighteen dollars and ninety cents placed to his credit, while Fosdick had six dollars and forty-five cents. To explain the large difference, it must be remembered that Dick had deposited five dollars before Henry deposited anything, being the amount he had received as a gift from Mr. Whitney.

"How much does that make, the lot of it?" asked Dick. "I aint much on figgers yet, you know."

"It makes twenty-five dollars and thirty-five cents, Dick," said his companion, who did not understand the thought which suggested the question.

"Take it, and buy some clothes, Henry," said Dick, shortly.

"What, your money too?"

"In course."

"No, Dick; you are too generous. I couldn't think of it. Almost three-quarters of the money is yours. You must spend it on yourself."

"I don't need it," said Dick.

"You may not need it now, but you will some time."

"I shall have some more then."

"That may be; but it wouldn't be fair for me to use your money, Dick. I thank you all the same for your kindness."

"Well, I'll lend it to you, then," persisted Dick, "and you can pay me when you get to be a rich merchant."

---

1. Tying a corset tightly.

"But it isn't likely I ever shall be one."

"How d'you know? I went to a fortun' teller once, and she told me I was born under a lucky star with a hard name, and I should have a rich man for my particular friend, who would make my fortun'. I guess you are going to be the rich man."

Fosdick laughed, and steadily refused for some time to avail himself of Dick's generous proposal; but at length, perceiving that our hero seemed much disappointed, and would be really glad if his offer were accepted, he agreed to use as much as might be needful.

This at once brought back Dick's good-humor, and he entered with great enthusiasm into his friend's plans.

The next day they withdrew the money from the bank, and, when business got a little slack, in the afternoon, set out in search of a clothing store. Dick knew enough of the city to be able to find a place where a good bargain could be obtained. He was determined that Fosdick should have a good serviceable suit, even if it took all the money they had. The result of their search was that for twenty-three dollars Fosdick obtained a very neat outfit, including a couple of shirts, a hat, and a pair of shoes, besides a dark mixed suit, which appeared stout and of good quality.

"Shall I sent the bundle home?" asked the salesman, impressed by the off-hand manner in which Dick drew out the money in payment for the clothes.

"Thank you," said Dick, "you're very kind, but I'll take it home myself, and you can allow me something for my trouble."

"All right," said the clerk, laughing; "I'll allow it on your next purchase."

Proceeding to their apartment in Mott Street, Fosdick at once tried on his new suit, and it was found to be an excellent fit. Dick surveyed his new friend with much satisfaction.

"You look like a young gentleman of fortun'," he said, "and do credit to your governor."

"I suppose that means you, Dick," said Fosdick, laughing.

"In course it does."

"You should say *of* course," said Fosdick, who, in virtue of his position as Dick's tutor, ventured to correct his language from time to time.

"How dare you correct your gov'nor?" said Dick, with comic indignation. "I'll cut you off with a shillin', you young dog,' as the Markis says to his nephew in the play at the Old Bowery."

Chapter 19

Fosdick Changes His Business

Fosdick did not venture to wear his new clothes while engaged in his business. This he felt would have been wasteful extravagance. About ten o'clock in the morning, when business slackened, he went home, and, dressing himself, went to a hotel where he could see copies of the "Morning Herald" and "Sun," and, noting down the places where a boy was wanted, went on a round of applications. But he found it no easy thing to obtain a place. Swarms of boys seemed to be out of employment, and it was not unusual to find from fifty to a hundred applicants for a single place.

There was another difficulty. It was generally desired that the boy wanted should reside with his parents. When Fosdick, on being questioned, revealed the fact of his having no parents, and being a boy of the street, this was generally sufficient of itself to insure a refusal. Merchants were afraid to trust one who had led such a vagabond life. Dick, who was always ready for an emergency, suggested borrowing a white wig, and passing himself off for Fosdick's father or grandfather. But Henry thought this might be rather a difficult character for our hero to sustain. After fifty applications and as many failures, Fosdick began to get discouraged. There seemed to be no way out of his present business, for which he felt unfitted.

"I don't know but I shall have to black boots all my life," he said, one day, despondently, to Dick.

"Keep a stiff upper lip," said Dick. "By the time you get to be a gray-headed veteran, you may get a chance to run errands for some big firm on the Bowery, which is a very cheerin' reflection."

So Dick by his drollery and perpetual good spirits kept up Fosdick's courage.

"As for me," said Dick, "I expect by that time to lay up a colossal fortun' out of shines, and live in princely style on the Avenoo."

But one morning, Fosdick, straying into French's Hotel, discovered the following advertisement in the columns of "The Herald,"—

"WANTED—A smart, capable boy to run errands, and make himself generally useful in a hat and cap store. Salary three dollars a week at first. Inquire at No.—Broadway, after ten o'clock, A.M."

He determined to make application, and, as the City Hall clock just then struck the hour indicated, lost no time in proceeding to the store, which was only a few blocks distant from the Astor House. It was easy to find the store, as from a dozen to twenty boys were already assembled in front of it. They surveyed each other askance, feeling that they were rivals, and mentally calculating each other's chances.

"There isn't much chance for me," said Fosdick to Dick, who had accompanied him. "Look at all these boys. Most of them have good homes, I suppose, and good recommendations, while I have nobody to refer to."

"Go ahead," said Dick. "Your chance is as good as anybody's."

While this was passing between Dick and his companion, one of the boys, a rather supercilious looking young gentleman, genteelly dressed, and evidently having a very high opinion of his dress and himself, turned suddenly to Dick, and remarked,—

"I've seen you before."

"Oh, have you?" said Dick, whirling round; "then p'r'aps you'd like to see me behind."

At this unexpected answer all the boys burst into a laugh with the exception of the questioner, who, evidently considered that Dick had been disrespectful.

"I've seen you somewhere," he said, in a surly tone, correcting himself.

"Most likely you have," said Dick. "That's where I generally keep myself."

There was another laugh at the expense of Roswell Crawford, for that was the name of the young aristocrat. But he had his revenge ready. No boy relishes being an object of ridicule, and it was with a feeling of satisfaction that he retorted,—

"I know you for all your impudence. You're nothing but a boot-black."

This information took the boys who were standing around by surprise, for Dick was well-dressed, and had none of the implements of his profession with him.

"S'pose I be," said Dick. "Have you got any objection?"

"Not at all," said Roswell, curling his lip; "only you'd better stick to blacking boots, and not try to get into a store."

"Thank you for your kind advice," said Dick. "Is it gratooitous, or do you expect to be paid for it?"

"You're an impudent fellow."

"That's a very cheerin' reflection," said Dick, good-naturedly.

"Do you expect to get this place when there's gentlemen's sons applying for it? A boot-black in a store! That would be a good joke."

Boys as well as men are selfish, and, looking upon Dick as a possible rival, the boys who listened seemed disposed to take the same view of the situation.

"That's what I say," said one of them, taking sides with Roswell.

"Don't trouble yourselves," said Dick. "I aint agoin' to cut you out. I can't afford to give up a independent and loocrative purfession for a salary of three dollars a week."

"Hear him talk!" said Roswell Crawford, with an unpleasant sneer. "If you are not trying to get the place, what are you here for?"

"I came with a friend of mine," said Dick, indicating Fosdick, "who's goin' in for the situation."

"Is he a boot-black, too?" demanded Roswell, superciliously.

"He!" retorted Dick, loftily. "Didn't you know his father was a member of Congress, and intimately acquainted with all the biggest men in the State?"

The boys surveyed Fosdick as if they did not quite know whether to credit this statement, which, for the credit of Dick's veracity, it will be observed he did not assert, but only propounded in the form of a question. There was no time for comment, however, as just then the proprietor of the store came to the door, and, casting his eyes over the waiting group, singled out Roswell Crawford, and asked him to enter.

"Well, my lad, how old are you?"

"Fourteen years old," said Roswell, consequentially.

"Are your parents living?"

"Only my mother. My father is dead. He was a gentleman," he added, complacently.

"Oh, was he?" said the shop-keeper. "Do you live in the city?"

"Yes, sir. In Clinton Place."

"Have you ever been in a situation before?"

"Yes, sir," said Roswell, a little reluctantly.

"Where was it?"

"In an office on Dey Street."

"How long were you there?"

"A week."

"It seems to me that was a short time. Why did you not stay longer?"

"Because," said Roswell, loftily, "the man wanted me to get to the office at eight o'clock, and make the fire. I'm a gentleman's son, and am not used to such dirty work."

"Indeed!" said the shop-keeper. "Well, young gentleman, you may step aside a few minutes. I will speak with some of the other boys before making my selection."

Several other boys were called in and questioned. Roswell stood by and listened with an air of complacency. He could not help thinking his chances the best. "The man can see I'm a gentleman, and will do credit to his store," he thought.

At length it came to Fosdick's turn. He entered with no very sanguine anticipations of success. Unlike Roswell, he set a very low estimate upon his qualifications when compared with those of other applicants. But his modest bearing, and quiet, gentlemanly manner, entirely free from pretension, prepossessed the shop-keeper, who was a sensible man, in his favor.

"Do you reside in the city?" he asked.

"Yes, sir," said Henry.

"What is your age?"

"Twelve."[1]

"Have you ever been in any situation?"

"No, sir."

"I should like to see a specimen of your handwriting. Here, take the pen and write your name."

Henry Fosdick had a very handsome handwriting for a boy of his age, while Roswell, who had submitted to the same test, could do little more than scrawl.

"Do you reside with your parents?"

"No, sir, they are dead."

"Where do you live, then?"

"In Mott Street."

Roswell curled his lip when this name was pronounced, for Mott Street, as my New York readers know, is in the immediate neighborhood of the Five-Points, and very far from a fashionable locality.

"Have you any testimonials to present?" asked Mr. Henderson, for that was his name.

Fosdick hesitated. This was the question which he had foreseen would give him trouble.

But at this moment it happened most opportunely that Mr. Greyson entered the shop with the intention of buying a hat.

"Yes," said Fosdick, promptly; "I will refer to this gentleman."

"How do you do, Fosdick!" asked Mr. Greyson, noticing him for the first time. "How do you happen to be here?"

"I am applying for a place, sir," said Fosdick. "May I refer the gentleman to you?"

"Certainly, I shall be glad to speak a good word for you. Mr. Henderson, this is a member of my Sunday-school class, of whose good qualities and good abilities I can speak confidently."

"That will be sufficient," said the shop-keeper, who knew Mr. Greyson's high character and position. "He could have no better recommendation. You may come to the store to-morrow morning at half past seven o'clock. The pay will be three dollars a week for the first six months. If I am satisfied with you, I shall then raise it to five dollars."

The other boys looked disappointed, but none more so than Roswell Crawford. He would have cared less if any one else had obtained the situation; but for a boy who lived in Mott Street to be preferred to him, a gentleman's son, he considered indeed humiliating. In a spirit of petty spite, he was tempted to say, "He's a bootblack. Ask him if he isn't."

---

1. At the time, child labor was common; it was not unusual for children to start working at the age of twelve.

"He's an honest and intelligent lad," said Mr. Greyson. "As for you, young man, I only hope you have one-half his good qualities."

Roswell Crawford left the store in disgust, and the other unsuccessful applicants with him.

"What luck, Fosdick?" asked Dick, eagerly, as his friend came out of the store.

"I've got the place," said Fosdick, in accents of satisfaction; "but it was only because Mr. Greyson spoke up for me."

"He's a trump," said Dick, enthusiastically.

The gentleman, so denominated, came out before the boys went away, and spoke with them kindly.

Both Dick and Henry were highly pleased at the success of the application. The pay would indeed be small, but, expended economically, Fosdick thought he could get along on it, receiving his room-rent, as before, in return for his services as Dick's private tutor. Dick determined, as soon as his education would permit, to follow his companion's example.

"I don't know as you'll be willin' to room with a boot-black," he said, to Henry, "now you're goin' into business."

"I couldn't room with a better friend, Dick," said Fosdick, affectionately, throwing his arm round our hero. "When we part, it'll be because you wish it."

So Fosdick entered upon a new career.

Chapter 20

Nine Months Later

The next morning Fosdick rose early, put on his new suit, and, after getting breakfast, set out for the Broadway store in which he had obtained a position. He left his little blacking-box in the room.

"It'll do to brush my own shoes," he said. "Who knows but I may have to come back to it again?"

"No danger," said Dick; "I'll take care of the feet, and you'll have to look after the heads, now you're in a hat-store."

"I wish you had a place too," said Fosdick.

"I don't know enough yet," said Dick. "Wait till I've gradooated."

"And can put A.B. after your name."

"What's that?"

"It stands for Bachelor of Arts. It's a degree that students get when they graduate from college."

"Oh," said Dick, "I didn't know but it meant A Boot-black. I can put that after my name now. Wouldn't Dick Hunter, A.B., sound tip-top?"

"I must be going," said Fosdick. "It won't do for me to be late the very first morning."

"That's the difference between you and me," said Dick. "I'm my own boss, and there aint no one to find fault with me if I'm late. But I might as well be goin' too. There's a gent as comes down to his store pretty early that generally wants a shine."

The two boys parted at the Park. Fosdick crossed it, and proceeded to the hat-store, while Dick, hitching up his pants, began to look about him for a customer. It was seldom that Dick had to wait long. He was always on the alert, and if there was any business to do he was always sure to get his share of it. He had now a stronger inducement than ever to attend strictly to business; his little stock of money in the savings bank having been nearly exhausted by his liberality to his roommate. He determined to be as economical as possible, and moreover to study as hard as he could, that he might be able to follow Fosdick's example, and obtain a place in a store or counting-room. As there were no striking incidents occurring in our hero's history within the next nine months. I propose to pass over that period, and recount the progress he made in that time.

Fosdick was still at the hat-store, having succeeded in giving perfect satisfaction to Mr. Henderson. His wages had just been raised to five dollars a week. He and Dick still kept house together at Mrs. Mooney's lodging-house, and lived very frugally, so that both were able to save up money. Dick had been unusually successful in business. He had several regular patrons, who had been drawn to him by his ready wit, and quick humor, and from two of them he had received presents of clothing, which had saved him an expense on that score. His income had averaged quite seven dollars a week in addition to this. Of this amount he was now obliged to pay one dollar weekly for the room which he and Fosdick occupied, but he was still able to save half the remainder. At the end of nine months therefore, or thirty-nine weeks, it will be seen that he had accumulated no less a sum than one hundred and seventeen dollars. Dick may be excused for feeling like a capitalist when he looked at the long row of deposits in his little bank-book. There were other boys in the same business who had earned as much money, but they had had little care for the future, and spent as they went along, so that few could boast a bank-account, however small.

"You'll be a rich man some time, Dick," said Henry Fosdick, one evening.

"And live on Fifth Avenoo," said Dick.

"Perhaps so. Stranger things have happened."

"Well," said Dick, "if such a misfortin' should come upon me I should bear it like a man. When you see a Fifth Avenoo manshun for sale for a hundred and seventeen dollars, just let me know and I'll buy it as an investment."

"Two hundred and fifty years ago you might have bought one for that price, probably. Real estate wasn't very high among the Indians."

"Just my luck," said Dick; "I was born too late. I'd orter have been an Indian, and lived in splendor on my present capital."

"I'm afraid you'd have found your present business rather unprofitable at that time."

But Dick had gained something more valuable than money. He had studied regularly every evening, and his improvement had been marvellous. He could now read well, write a fair hand, and had studied arithmetic as far as Interest. Besides this he had obtained some knowledge of grammar and geography. If some of my boy readers, who have been studying for years, and got no farther than this, should think it incredible that Dick, in less than a year, and studying evenings only, should have accomplished it, they must remember that our hero was very much in earnest in his desire to improve. He knew that, in order to grow up respectable, he must be well advanced, and he was willing to work. But then the reader must not forget that Dick was naturally a smart boy. His street education had sharpened his faculties, and taught him to rely upon himself. He knew that it would take him a long time to reach the goal which he had set before him, and he had patience to keep on trying. He knew that he had only himself to depend upon, and he determined to make the most of himself,—a resolution which is the secret of success in nine cases out of ten.

"Dick," said Fosdick, one evening, after they had completed their studies, "I think you'll have to get another teacher soon."

"Why?" asked Dick, in some surprise. "Have you been offered a more loocrative position?"

"No," said Fosdick, "but I find I have taught you all I know myself. You are now as good a scholar as I am."

"Is that true?" said Dick, eagerly, a flush of gratification coloring his brown cheek.

"Yes," said Fosdick. "You've made wonderful progress. I propose, now that evening schools have begun, that we join one, and study together through the winter."

"All right," said Dick. "I'd be willin' to go now; but when I first began to study I was ashamed to have anybody know that I was so ignorant. Do you really mean, Fosdick, that I know as much as you?"

"Yes, Dick, it's true."

"Then I've got you to thank for it," said Dick, earnestly. "You've made me what I am."

"And haven't you paid me, Dick?"

"By payin' the room-rent," said Dick, impulsively. "What's that? It isn't half enough. I wish you'd take half my money; you deserve it."

"Thank you, Dick, but you're too generous. You've more than paid me. Who was it took my part when all the other boys imposed upon me? And who gave me money to buy clothes, and so got me my situation?"

"Oh, that's nothing!" said Dick.

"It's a great deal, Dick. I shall never forget it. But now it seems to me you might try to get a situation yourself."

"Do I know enough?"

"You know as much as I do."

"Then I'll try," said Dick, decidedly.

"I wish there was a place in our store," said Fosdick. "It would be pleasant for us to be together."

"Never mind," said Dick; "there'll be plenty of chances. P'r'aps A.T. Stewart might like a partner. I wouldn't ask more'n a quarter of the profits."

"Which would be a very liberal proposal on your part," said Fosdick, smiling. "But perhaps Mr. Stewart might object to a partner living on Mott Street."

"I'd just as lieves move to Fifth Avenoo," said Dick. "I aint got no prejudices in favor of Mott Street."

"Nor I," said Fosdick, "and in fact I have been thinking it might be a good plan for us to move as soon as we could afford. Mrs. Mooney doesn't keep the room quite so neat as she might."

"No," said Dick. "She aint got no prejudices against dirt. Look at that towel."

Dick held up the article indicated, which had now seen service nearly a week, and hard service at that,—Dick's avocation causing him to be rather hard on towels.

"Yes," said Fosdick, "I've got about tired of it. I guess we can find some better place without having to pay much more. When we move, you must let me pay my share of the rent."

"We'll see about that," said Dick. "Do you propose to move to Fifth Avenoo?"

"Not just at present, but to some more agreeable neighborhood than this. We'll wait till you get a situation, and then we can decide."

A few days later, as Dick was looking about for customers in the neighborhood of the Park, his attention was drawn to a fellow boot-black, a boy about a year younger than himself, who appeared to have been crying.

"What's the matter, Tom?" asked Dick. "Haven't you had luck to-day?"

"Pretty good," said the boy; "but we're havin' hard times at home. Mother fell last week and broke her arm, and to-morrow we've got to pay the rent, and if we don't the landlord says he'll turn us out."

"Haven't you got anything except what you earn?" asked Dick.

"No," said Tom, "not now. Mother used to earn three or four dollars a week; but she can't do nothin' now, and my little sister and brother are too young."

Dick had quick sympathies. He had been so poor himself, and obliged to submit to so many privations, that he knew from personal experience how hard it was. Tom Wilkins he knew as an excellent boy, who never squandered his money, but faithfully carried it home to his mother. In the days of his own extravagance and shiftlessness he had once or twice asked Tom to accompany him to the Old Bowery or Tony Pastor's, but Tom had always steadily refused.

"I'm sorry for you, Tom," he said. "How much do you owe for rent?"

"Two weeks now," said Tom.

"How much is it a week?"

"Two dollar a week—that makes four."

"Have you got anything towards it?"

"No; I've had to spend all my money for food for mother and the rest of us. I've had pretty hard work to do that. I don't know what we'll do. I haven't any place to go to, and I'm afraid mother'll get cold in her arm."

"Can't you borrow the money somewhere?" asked Dick.

Tom shook his head despondingly.

"All the people I know are as poor as I am," said he. "They'd help me if they could, but it's hard work for them to get along themselves."

"I'll tell you what, Tom," said Dick, impulsively, "I'll stand your friend."

"Have you got any money?" asked Tom, doubtfully.

"Got any money!" repeated Dick. "Don't you know that I run a bank on my own account? How much is it you need?"

"Four dollars," said Tom. "If we don't pay that before to-morrow night, out we go. You haven't got as much as that, have you?"

"Here are three dollars," said Dick, drawing out his pocket-book. "I'll let you have the rest to-morrow, and maybe a little more."

"You're a right down good fellow, Dick," said Tom; "but won't you want it yourself?"

"Oh, I've got some more," said Dick.

"Maybe I'll never be able to pay you."

"'Spose you don't," said Dick; "I guess I won't fail."

"I won't forget it, Dick. I hope I'll be able to do somethin' for you sometime."

"All right," said Dick. "I'd ought to help you. I haven't got no mother to look out for. I wish I had."

There was a tinge of sadness in his tone, as he pronounced the last four words; but Dick's temperament was sanguine, and he never gave way to unavailing sadness. Accordingly he began to whistle as he turned away, only adding, "I'll see you to-morrow, Tom."

The three dollars which Dick had handed to Tom Wilkins were his savings for the present week. It was now Thursday afternoon. His rent, which amounted to a dollar, he expected to save out of the earnings of Friday and Saturday. In order to give Tom the additional assistance he had promised, Dick would be obliged to have recourse to his bank-savings. He would not have ventured to trench upon it for any other reason but this. But he felt that it would be selfish to allow Tom and his mother to suffer when he had it in his power to relieve them. But Dick was destined to be surprised, and that in a disagreeable manner, when he reached home.

Chapter 21

Dick Loses His Bank-Book

It was hinted at the close of the last chapter that Dick was destined to be disagreeably surprised on reaching home.

Having agreed to give further assistance to Tom Wilkins, he was naturally led to go to the drawer where he and Fosdick kept their bank-books. To his surprise and uneasiness *the drawer proved to be empty!*

"Come here a minute, Fosdick," he said.

"What's the matter, Dick?"

"I can't find my bank-book, nor yours either. What's 'come of them?"

"I took mine with me this morning, thinking I might want to put in a little more money. I've got it in my pocket, now."

"But where's mine?" asked Dick, perplexed.

"I don't know. I saw it in the drawer when I took mine this morning."

"Are you sure?"

"Yes, positive, for I looked into it to see how much you had got."

"Did you lock it again?" asked Dick.

"Yes; didn't you have to unlock it just now?"

"So I did," said Dick. "But it's gone now. Somebody opened it with a key that fitted the lock, and then locked it ag'in."

"That must have been the way."

"It's rather hard on a feller," said Dick, who, for the first time since we became acquainted with him, began to feel down-hearted.

"Don't give it up, Dick. You haven't lost the money, only the bank-book."

"Aint that the same thing?"

"No. You can go to the bank to-morrow morning, as soon as it opens, and tell them you have lost the book, and ask them not to pay the money to any one except yourself."

"So I can," said Dick, brightening up. "That is, if the thief hasn't been to the bank to-day."

"If he has, they might detect him by his hand writing."

"I'd like to get hold of the one that stole it," said Dick, indignantly. "I'd give him a good lickin'."

"It must have been somebody in the house. Suppose we go and see Mrs. Mooney. She may know whether anybody came into our room to-day."

The two boys went downstairs, and knocked at the door of a little back sitting-room where Mrs. Mooney generally spent her evenings. It was a shabby little room, with a threadbare carpet on the floor, the walls covered with a certain large-figured paper, patches of which had been stripped off here and there, exposing the plaster, the remainder being defaced by dirt and grease. But Mrs. Mooney had one of those comfortable temperaments which are tolerant of dirt, and didn't mind it in the least. She was seated beside a small pine work-table, industriously engaged in mending stockings.

"Good-evening, Mrs. Mooney," said Fosdick, politely.

"Good-evening," said the landlady. "Sit down, if you can find chairs. I'm hard at work as you see, but a pore lone widder can't afford to be idle."

"We can't stop long, Mrs. Mooney, but my friend here has had something taken from his room to-day, and we thought we'd come and see you about it."

"What is it?" asked the landlady. "You don't think I'd take anything? If I am poor, it's an honest name I've always had, as all my lodgers can testify."

"Certainly not, Mrs. Mooney; but there are others in the house that may not be honest. My friend has lost his bank-book. It was safe in the drawer this morning, but to-night it is not to be found."

"How much money was there in it?" asked Mrs. Mooney.

"Over a hundred dollars," said Fosdick.

"It was my whole fortun'," said Dick. "I was goin' to buy a house next year."

Mrs. Mooney was evidently surprised to learn the extent of Dick's wealth, and was disposed to regard him with increased respect.

"Was the drawer locked?" she asked.

"Yes."

"Then it couldn't have been Bridget. I don't think she has any keys."

"She wouldn't know what a bank-book was," said Fosdick. "You didn't see any of the lodgers go into our room to-day, did you?"

"I shouldn't wonder if it was Jim Travis," said Mrs. Mooney, suddenly.

This James Travis was a bar-tender in a low groggery[1] in Mulberry Street, and had been for a few weeks an inmate of Mrs. Mooney's lodging-house. He was a coarse-looking fellow who, from his appearance, evidently patronized liberally the liquor he dealt out to others. He occupied a room opposite Dick's, and was often heard by the two boys reeling upstairs in a state of intoxication, uttering shocking oaths.

This Travis had made several friendly overtures to Dick and his room-mate, and had invited them to call round at the bar-room where he tended, and take something. But this invitation had never been accepted, partly because the boys were better engaged in the evening, and partly because neither of them had taken a fancy to Mr. Travis; which certainly was not strange, for nature had not gifted him with many charms, either of personal appearance or manners. The rejection of his friendly proffers had caused him to take a dislike to Dick and Henry, whom he considered stiff and unsocial.

"What makes you think it was Travis?" asked Fosdick. "He isn't at home in the daytime."

"But he was to-day. He said he had got a bad cold, and had to come home for a clean handkerchief."

"Did you see him?" asked Dick.

"Yes," said Mrs. Mooney. "Bridget was hanging out clothes, and I went to the door to let him in."

"I wonder if he had a key that would fit our drawer," said Fosdick.

"Yes," said Mrs. Mooney. "The bureaus in the two rooms are just alike. I got 'em at auction, and most likely the locks is the same."

"It must have been he," said Dick, looking towards Fosdick.

"Yes," said Fosdick, "it looks like it."

"What's to be done? That's what I'd like to know," said Dick. "Of course he'll say he hasn't got it; and he won't be such a fool as to leave it in his room."

"If he hasn't been to the bank, it's all right," said Fosdick. "You can go there the first thing to-morrow morning, and stop their paying any money on it."

"But I can't get any money on it myself," said Dick. "I told Tom Wilkins I'd let him have some more money to-morrow, or his sick mother'll have to turn out of their lodgin's."

"How much money were you going to give him?"

"I gave him three dollars to-day, and was goin' to give him two dollars to-morrow."

"I've got the money, Dick. I didn't go to the bank this morning."

"All right. I'll take it, and pay you back next week."

"No, Dick; if you've given three dollars, you must let me give two."

1. A grogshop, bar.

"No, Fosdick, I'd rather give the whole. You know I've got more money than you. No, I haven't, either," said Dick, the memory of his loss flashing upon him. "I thought I was rich this morning, but now I'm in destitoot circumstances."

"Cheer up, Dick; you'll get your money back."

"I hope so," said our hero, rather ruefully.

The fact was, that our friend Dick was beginning to feel what is so often experienced by men who do business of a more important character and on a larger scale than he, the bitterness of a reverse of circumstances. With one hundred dollars and over carefully laid away in the savings bank, he had felt quite independent. Wealth is comparative, and Dick probably felt as rich as many men who are worth a hundred thousand dollars. He was beginning to feel the advantages of his steady self-denial, and to experience the pleasures of property. Not that Dick was likely to be unduly attached to money. Let it be said to his credit that it had never given him so much satisfaction as when it enabled him to help Tom Wilkins in his trouble.

Besides this, there was another thought that troubled him. When he obtained a place he could not expect to receive as much as he was now making from blacking boots,—probably not more than three dollars a week,—while his expenses without clothing would amount to four dollars. To make up the deficiency he had confidently relied upon his savings, which would be sufficient to carry him along for a year, if necessary. If he should not recover his money, he would be compelled to continue a boot-black for at least six months longer; and this was rather a discouraging reflection. On the whole it is not to be wondered at that Dick felt unusually sober this evening, and that neither of the boys felt much like studying.

The two boys consulted as to whether it would be best to speak to Travis about it. It was not altogether easy to decide. Fosdick was opposed to it.

"It will only put him on his guard," said he, "and I don't see as it will do any good. Of course he will deny it. We'd better keep quiet, and watch him, and, by giving notice at the bank, we can make sure that he doesn't get any money on it. If he does present himself at the bank, they will know at once that he is a thief, and he can be arrested."

This view seemed reasonable, and Dick resolved to adopt it. On the whole, he began to think prospects were brighter than he had at first supposed, and his spirits rose a little.

"How'd he know I had any bank-book? That's what I can't make out," he said.

"Don't you remember?" said Fosdick, after a moment's thought, "we were speaking of our savings, two or three evenings since?"

"Yes," said Dick.

"Our door was a little open at the time, and I heard somebody come upstairs, and stop a minute in front of it. It must have been Jim Travis. In that way he probably found out about your money, and took the opportunity to-day to get hold of it."

This might or might not be the correct explanation. At all events it seemed probable.

The boys were just on the point of going to bed, later in the evening, when a knock was heard at the door, and, to their no little surprise, their neighbor, Jim Travis, proved to be the caller. He was a sallow-complexioned young man, with dark hair and bloodshot eyes.

He darted a quick glance from one to the other as he entered, which did not escape the boys' notice.

"How are ye, to-night?" he said, sinking into one of the two chairs with which the room was scantily furnished.

"Jolly," said Dick. "How are you?"

"Tired as a dog," was the reply. "Hard work and poor pay; that's the way with me. I wanted to go to the theatre, to-night, but I was hard up, and couldn't raise the cash."

Here he darted another quick glance at the boys; but neither betrayed anything.

"You don't go out much, do you?" he said.

"Not much," said Fosdick. "We spend our evenings in study."

"That's precious slow," said Travis, rather contemptuously. "What's the use of studying so much? You don't expect to be a lawyer, do you, or anything of that sort?"

"Maybe," said Dick. "I haven't made up my mind yet. If my feller-citizens should want me to go to Congress some time, I shouldn't want to disapp'int 'em; and then readin' and writin' might come handy."

"Well," said Travis, rather abruptly, "I'm tired, and I guess I'll turn in."

"Good-night," said Fosdick.

The boys looked at each other as their visitor left the room.

"He came in to see if we'd missed the bank-book," said Dick.

"And to turn off suspicion from himself, by letting us know he had no money," added Fosdick.

"That's so," said Dick. "I'd like to have searched them pockets of his."

Chapter 22

Tracking the Thief

Fosdick was right in supposing that Jim Travis had stolen his bank-book. He was also right in supposing that that worthy young man had come to the knowledge of Dick's savings by what he had accidentally overheard. Now, Travis, like a very large number of young men of his class, was able to dispose of a larger amount of money than he was able to earn. Moreover, he had no great fancy for work at all, and would have been glad to find some other way of obtaining money enough to pay his expenses. He had recently received a letter from an old companion, who had strayed out to California, and going at once to the mines had been lucky enough to get possession of a very remu-nerative claim. He wrote to Travis that he had already realized two thousand dollars from it, and expected to make his fortune within six months.

Two thousand dollars! This seemed to Travis a very large sum, and quite dazzled his imagination. He was at once inflamed with the desire to go out to California and try his luck. In his present situation he only received thirty dollars a month, which was probably all that his services were worth, but went a very little way towards gratifying his expensive tastes. Accordingly he determined to take the next steamer to the land of gold, if he could possibly manage to get money enough to pay the passage.

The price of a steerage passage at that time was seventy-five dollars,—not a large sum, certainly,—but it might as well have been seventy-five hundred for any chance James Travis had of raising the amount at present. His available funds consisted of precisely two dol-lars and a quarter; of which sum, one dollar and a half was due to his washerwoman. This, however, would not have troubled Travis much, and he would conveniently have forgotten all about it; but, even leav-ing this debt unpaid, the sum at his command would not help him materially towards paying his passage money.

Travis applied for help to two or three of his companions; but they were all of that kind who never keep an account with savings banks, but carry all their spare cash about with them. One of these friends offered to lend him thirty-seven cents, and another a dollar; but nei-ther of these offers seemed to encourage him much. He was about giving up his project in despair, when he learned, accidentally, as we have already said, the extent of Dick's savings.

One hundred and seventeen dollars! Why, that would not only pay his passage, but carry him up to the mines, after he had arrived in San Francisco. He could not help thinking it over, and the result of this thinking was that he determined to borrow it of Dick without leave.

Knowing that neither of the boys were in their room in the daytime, he came back in the course of the morning, and, being admitted by Mrs. Mooney herself, said, by way of accounting for his presence, that he had a cold, and had come back for a handkerchief. The landlady suspected nothing, and, returning at once to her work in the kitchen, left the coast clear.

Travis at once entered Dick's room, and, as there seemed to be no other place for depositing money, tried the bureau-drawers. They were all readily opened, except one, which proved to be locked. This he naturally concluded must contain the money, and going back to his own chamber for the key of the bureau, tried it on his return, and found to his satisfaction that it would fit. When he discovered the bank-book, his joy was mingled with disappointment. He had expected to find bank-bills instead. This would have saved all further trouble, and would have been immediately available. Obtaining money at the savings bank would involve fresh risk. Travis hesitated whether to take it or not; but finally decided that it would be worth the trouble and hazard.

He accordingly slipped the book into his pocket, locked the drawer again, and, forgetting all about the handkerchief for which he had come home, went down-stairs, and into the street.

There would have been time to go the savings bank that day, but Travis had already been absent from his place of business some time, and did not venture to take the additional time required. Besides, not being very much used to savings banks, never having had occasion to use them, he thought it would be more prudent to look over the rules and regulations, and see if he could not get some information as to the way he ought to proceed. So the day passed, and Dick's money was left in safety at the bank.

In the evening, it occurred to Travis that it might be well to find out whether Dick had discovered his loss. This reflection it was that induced the visit which is recorded at the close of the last chapter. The result was that he was misled by the boys' silence on the subject, and concluded that nothing had yet been discovered.

"Good!" thought Travis, with satisfaction. "If they don't find out for twenty-four hours, it'll be too late, then, and I shall be all right."

There being a possibility of the loss being discovered before the boys went out in the morning, Travis determined to see them at that time, and judge whether such was the case. He waited, therefore, until he heard the boys come out, and then opened his own door.

"Morning, gents," said he, sociably. "Going to business?"

"Yes," said Dick. "I'm afraid my clerks'll be lazy if I aint on hand."

"Good joke!" said Travis. "If you pay good wages, I'd like to speak for a place."

"I pay all I get myself," said Dick. "How's business with you?"

"So so. Why don't you call round, some time?"

"All my evenin's is devoted to literatoor and science," said Dick. "Thank you all the same."

"Where do you hang out?" inquired Travis, in choice language, addressing Fosdick.

"At Henderson's hat and cap store, on Broadway."

"I'll look in upon you some time when I want a tile,"[1] said Travis. "I suppose you sell cheaper to your friends."

"I'll be as reasonable as I can," said Fosdick, not very cordially; for he did not much fancy having it supposed by his employer that such a disreputable-looking person as Travis was a friend of his.

However, Travis had no idea of showing himself at the Broadway store, and only said this by way of making conversation, and encouraging the boys to be social.

"You haven't any of you gents seen a pearl-handled knife, have you?" he asked.

"No," said Fosdick; "have you lost one?"

"Yes," said Travis, with unblushing falsehood. "I left it on my bureau a day or two since. I've missed one or two other little matters. Bridget don't look to me any too honest. Likely she's got 'em."

"What are you goin' to do about it?" said Dick.

"I'll keep mum unless I lose something more, and then I'll kick up a row, and haul her over the coals. Have you missed anything?"

"No," said Fosdick, answering for himself, as he could do without violating the truth.

There was a gleam of satisfaction in the eyes of Travis, as he heard this.

"They haven't found it out yet," he thought. "I'll bag the money to-day, and then they may whistle for it."

Having no further object to serve in accompanying the boys, he bade them good-morning, and turned down another street.

"He's mighty friendly all of a sudden," said Dick.

"Yes," said Fosdick; "it's very evident what it all means. He wants to find out whether you have discovered your loss or not."

"But he didn't find out."

"No; we've put him on the wrong track. He means to get his money to-day, no doubt."

"My money," suggested Dick.

"I accept the correction," said Fosdick.

"Of course, Dick, you'll be on hand as soon as the bank opens."

"In course I shall. Jim Travis'll find he's walked into the wrong shop."

---

1. A stiff hat.

"The bank opens at ten o'clock, you know."

"I'll be there on time."

The two boys separated.

"Good luck, Dick," said Fosdick, as he parted from him. "It'll all come out right, I think."

"I hope 'twill," said Dick.

He had recovered from his temporary depression, and made up his mind that the money would be recovered. He had no idea of allowing himself to be outwitted by Jim Travis, and enjoyed already, in anticipation, the pleasure of defeating his rascality.

It wanted two hours and a half yet to ten o'clock, and this time to Dick was too precious to be wasted. It was the time of his greatest harvest. He accordingly repaired to his usual place of business, and succeeded in obtaining six customers, which yielded him sixty cents. He then went to a restaurant, and got some breakfast. It was now half-past nine, and Dick, feeling that it wouldn't do to be late, left his box in charge of Johnny Nolan, and made his way to the bank.

The officers had not yet arrived, and Dick lingered on the outside, waiting till they should come. He was not without a little uneasiness, fearing that Travis might be as prompt as himself, and finding him there, might suspect something, and so escape the snare. But, though looking cautiously up and down the street, he could discover no traces of the supposed thief. In due time ten o'clock struck, and immediately afterwards the doors of the bank were thrown open, and our hero entered.

As Dick had been in the habit of making a weekly visit for the last nine months, the cashier had come to know him by sight.

"You're early, this morning, my lad," he said, pleasantly. "Have you got some more money to deposit? You'll be getting rich, soon."

"I don't know about that," said Dick. "My bank-book's been stole."

"Stolen!" echoed the cashier. "That's unfortunate. Not so bad as it might be, though. The thief can't collect the money."

"That's what I came to see about," said Dick. "I was afraid he might have got it already."

"He hasn't been here yet. Even if he had, I remember you, and should have detected him. When was it taken?"

"Yesterday," said Dick. "I missed it in the evenin' when I got home."

"Have you any suspicion as to the person who took it?" asked the cashier.

Dick thereupon told all he knew as to the general character and suspicious conduct of Jim Travis, and the cashier agreed with him that he was probably the thief. Dick also gave his reason for thinking that he would visit the bank that morning, to withdraw the funds.

"Very good," said the cashier. "We'll be ready for him. What is the number of your book?"

"No. 5,678," said Dick.

"Now give me a little description of this Travis whom you suspect."

Dick accordingly furnished a brief outline sketch of Travis, not particularly complimentary to the latter.

"That will answer. I think I shall know him," said the cashier. "You may depend upon it that he shall receive no money on your account."

"Thank you," said Dick.

Considerably relieved in mind, our hero turned towards the door, thinking that there would be nothing gained by his remaining longer, while he would of course lose time.

He had just reached the doors, which were of glass, when through them he perceived James Travis himself just crossing the street, and apparently coming towards the bank. It would not do, of course, for him to be seen.

"Here he is," he exclaimed, hurrying back. "Can't you hide me somewhere? I don't want to be seen."

The cashier understood at once how the land lay. He quickly opened a little door, and admitted Dick behind the counter.

"Stoop down," he said, "so as not to be seen."

Dick had hardly done so when Jim Travis opened the outer door, and, looking about him in a little uncertainty, walked up to the cashier's desk.

Chapter 23

Travis Is Arrested

Jim Travis advanced into the bank with a doubtful step, knowing well that he was on a dishonest errand, and heartily wishing that he were well out of it. After a little hesitation, he approached the paying-teller, and, exhibiting the bank-book, said, "I want to get my money out."

The bank-officer took the book, and, after looking at it a moment, said, "How much do you want?"

"The whole of it," said Travis.

"You can draw out any part of it, but to draw out the whole requires a week's notice."

"Then I'll take a hundred dollars."

"Are you the person to whom the book belongs?"

"Yes, sir," said Travis, without hesitation.

"Your name is—"

"Hunter."

The bank-clerk went to a large folio volume, containing the names of depositors, and began to turn over the leaves. While he was doing this, he managed to send out a young man connected with the bank for a policeman. Travis did not perceive this, or did not suspect that it had anything to do with himself. Not being used to savings banks, he supposed the delay only what was usual. After a search, which was only intended to gain time that a policeman might be summoned, the cashier came back, and, sliding out a piece of paper to Travis, said, "It will be necessary for you to write an order for the money."

Travis took a pen, which he found on the ledge outside, and wrote the order, signing his name "Dick Hunter," having observed that name on the outside of the book.

"Your name is Dick Hunter, then?" said the cashier, taking the paper, and looking at the thief over his spectacles.

"Yes," said Travis, promptly.

"But," continued the cashier, "I find Hunter's age is put down on the bank-book as fourteen. Surely you must be more than that."

Travis would gladly have declared that he was only fourteen; but, being in reality twenty-three, and possessing a luxuriant pair of whiskers, this was not to be thought of. He began to feel uneasy.

"Dick Hunter's my younger brother," he said. "I'm getting out the money for him."

"I thought you said your own name was Dick Hunter," said the cashier.

"I said my name was Hunter," said Travis, ingeniously. "I didn't understand you."

"But you've signed the name of Dick Hunter to this order. How is that?" questioned the troublesome cashier.

Travis saw that he was getting himself into a tight place; but his self-possession did not desert him.

"I thought I must give my brother's name," he answered.

"What is your own name?"

"Henry Hunter."

"Can you bring any one to testify that the statement you are making is correct?"

"Yes, a dozen if you like," said Travis, boldly. "Give me the book, and I'll come back this afternoon. I didn't think there'd be such a fuss about getting out a little money."

"Wait a moment. Why don't your brother come himself?"

"Because he's sick. He's down with the measles," said Travis.

Here the cashier signed to Dick to rise and show himself. Our hero accordingly did so.

"You will be glad to find that he has recovered," said the cashier, pointing to Dick.

With an exclamation of anger and dismay, Travis, who saw the game was up, started for the door, feeling that safety made such a course prudent. But he was too late. He found himself confronted by a burly policeman, who seized him by the arm, saying, "Not so fast, my man. I want you."

"Let me go," exclaimed Travis, struggling to free himself.

"I'm sorry I can't oblige you," said the officer. "You'd better not make a fuss, or I may have to hurt you a little."

Travis sullenly resigned himself to his fate, darting a look of rage at Dick, whom he considered the author of his present misfortune.

"This is your book," said the cashier, handing back his rightful property to our hero. "Do you wish to draw out any money?"

"Two dollars," said Dick.

"Very well. Write an order for the amount."

Before doing so, Dick, who now that he saw Travis in the power of the law began to pity him, went up to the officer, and said,—

"Won't you let him go? I've got my bank-book back, and I don't want anything done to him."

"Sorry I can't oblige you," said the officer; "but I'm not allowed to do it. He'll have to stand his trial."

"I'm sorry for you, Travis," said Dick. "I didn't want you arrested. I only wanted my bank-book back."

"Curse you!" said Travis, scowling vindictively. "Wait till I get free. See if I don't fix you."

"You needn't pity him too much," said the officer. "I know him now. He's been to the Island[1] before."

"It's a lie," said Travis, violently.

"Don't be too noisy, my friend," said the officer. "If you've got no more business here, we'll be going."

He withdrew with the prisoner in charge, and Dick, having drawn his two dollars, left the bank. Notwithstanding the violent words the prisoner had used towards himself, and his attempted robbery, he could not help feeling sorry that he had been instrumental in causing his arrest.

"I'll keep my book a little safer hereafter," thought Dick. "Now I must go and see Tom Wilkins."

Before dismissing the subject of Travis and his theft, it may be remarked that he was duly tried, and, his guilt being clear, was sent to Blackwell's Island for nine months. At the end of that time, on his release, he got a chance to work his passage on a ship to San Francisco, where he probably arrived in due time. At any rate, nothing more has been heard of him, and probably his threat of vengeance against Dick will never be carried into effect.

Returning to the City Hall Park, Dick soon fell in with Tom Wilkins.

---

1. Reference to Blackwell's Island and its prison.

"How are you, Tom?" he said. "How's your mother?"

"She's better, Dick, thank you. She felt worried about bein' turned out into the street; but I gave her that money from you, and now she feels a good deal easier."

"I've got some more for you, Tom," said Dick, producing a two-dollar bill from his pocket.

"I ought not to take it from you, Dick."

"Oh, it's all right, Tom. Don't be afraid."

"But you may need it yourself."

"There's plenty more where that came from."

"Any way, one dollar will be enough. With that we can pay the rent."

"You'll want the other to buy something to eat."

"You're very kind, Dick."

"I'd ought to be. I've only got myself to take care of."

"Well, I'll take it for my mother's sake. When you want anything done just call on Tom Wilkins."

"All right. Next week, if your mother doesn't get better, I'll give you some more."

Tom thanked our hero very gratefully, and Dick walked away, feeling the self-approval which always accompanies a generous and disinterested action. He was generous by nature, and, before the period at which he is introduced to the reader's notice, he frequently treated his friends to cigars and oyster-stews. Sometimes he invited them to accompany him to the theatre at his expense. But he never derived from these acts of liberality the same degree of satisfaction as from this timely gift to Tom Wilkins. He felt that his money was well bestowed, and would save an entire family from privation and discomfort. Five dollars would, to be sure, make something of a difference in the amount of his savings. It was more than he was able to save up in a week. But Dick felt fully repaid for what he had done, and he felt prepared to give as much more, if Tom's mother should continue to be sick, and should appear to him to need it.

Besides all this, Dick felt a justifiable pride in his financial ability to afford so handsome a gift. A year before, however much he might have desired to give, it would have been quite out of his power to give five dollars. His cash balance never reached that amount. It was seldom, indeed, that it equalled one dollar. In more ways than one Dick was beginning to reap the advantage of his self-denial and judicious economy.

It will be remembered that when Mr. Whitney at parting with Dick presented him with five dollars, he told him that he might repay it to some other boy who was struggling upward. Dick thought of this, and it occurred to him that after all he was only paying up an old debt.

When Fosdick came home in the evening, Dick announced his

success in recovering his lost money, and described the manner in which it had been brought about.

"You're in luck, Dick," said Fosdick. "I guess we'd better not trust the bureau-drawer again."

"I mean to carry my book round with me," said Dick.

"So shall I, as long as we stay at Mrs. Mooney's. I wish we were in a better place."

"I must go down and tell her she needn't expect Travis back. Poor chap, I pity him!"

Travis was never more seen in Mrs. Mooney's establishment. He was owing that lady for a fortnight's rent of his room, which prevented her feeling much compassion for him. The room was soon after let to a more creditable tenant, who proved a less troublesome neighbor than his predecessor.

Chapter 24

Dick Receives a Letter

It was about a week after Dick's recovery of his bank-book, that Fosdick brought home with him in the evening a copy of the "Daily Sun."

"Would you like to see your name in print, Dick?" he asked.

"Yes," said Dick, who was busy at the wash-stand, endeavoring to efface the marks which his day's work had left upon his hands. "They haven't put me up for mayor, have they? 'Cause if they have, I shan't accept. It would interfere too much with my private business."

"No," said Fosdick, "they haven't put you up for office yet, though that may happen sometime. But if you want to see your name in print, here it is."

Dick was rather incredulous, but, having dried his hands on the towel, took the paper, and following the directions of Fosdick's finger, observed in the list of advertised letters the name of "Ragged Dick."

"By gracious, so it is," said he. "Do you s'pose it means me?"

"I don't know of any other Ragged Dick,—do you?"

"No," said Dick, reflectively; "it must be me. But I don't know of anybody that would be likely to write to me."

"Perhaps it is Frank Whitney," suggested Fosdick, after a little reflection. "Didn't he promise to write to you?"

"Yes," said Dick, "and he wanted me to write to him."

"Where is he now?"

"He was going to a boarding-school in Connecticut, he said. The name of the town was Barnton."

"Very likely the letter is from him."

"I hope it is. Frank was a tip-top boy, and he was the first that made me ashamed of bein' so ignorant and dirty."

"You had better go to the post-office to-morrow morning, and ask for the letter."

"P'r'aps they won't give it to me."

"Suppose you wear the old clothes you used to a year ago, when Frank first saw you? They won't have any doubt of your being Ragged Dick then."

"I guess I will. I'll be sort of ashamed to be seen in 'em though," said Dick, who had considerable more pride in a neat personal appearance than when we were first introduced to him.

"It will be only for one day, or one morning," said Fosdick.

"I'd do more'n that for the sake of gettin' a letter from Frank. I'd like to see him."

The next morning, in accordance with the suggestion of Fosdick, Dick arrayed himself in the long disused Washington coat and Napoleon pants, which he had carefully preserved, for what reason he could hardly explain.

When fairly equipped, Dick surveyed himself in the mirror,—if the little seven-by-nine-inch looking-glass, with which the room was furnished, deserved the name. The result of the survey was not on the whole a pleasing one. To tell the truth, Dick was quite ashamed of his appearance, and, on opening the chamber-door, looked around to see that the coast was clear, not being willing to have any of his fellow-boarders see him in his present attire.

He managed to slip out into the street unobserved, and, after attending to two or three regular customers who came down-town early in the morning, he made his way down Nassau Street to the post-office. He passed along until he came to a compartment on which he read ADVERTISED LETTERS, and, stepping up to the little window, said,—

"There's a letter for me. I saw it advertised in the 'Sun' yesterday."

"What name?" demanded the clerk.

"Ragged Dick," answered our hero.

"That's a queer name," said the clerk, surveying him a little curiously. "Are you Ragged Dick?"

"If you don't believe me, look at my clo'es," said Dick.

"That's pretty good proof, certainly," said the clerk, laughing. "If that isn't your name, it deserves to be."

"I believe in dressin' up to your name," said Dick.

"Do you know any one in Barnton, Connecticut?" asked the clerk, who had by this time found the letter.

"Yes," said Dick. "I know a chap that's at boardin'-school there."

"It appears to be in a boy's hand. I think it must be yours."

The letter was handed to Dick through the window. He received it eagerly, and drawing back so as not to be in the way of the throng who were constantly applying for letters, or slipping them into the boxes provided for them, hastily opened it, and began to read. As the reader may be interested in the contents of the letter as well as Dick, we transcribe it below.

It was dated Barnton, Conn., and commenced thus,—

"DEAR DICK,—You must excuse my addressing this letter to 'Ragged Dick;' but the fact is, I don't know what your last name is, nor where you live. I am afraid there is not much chance of your getting this letter; but I hope you will. I have thought of you very often, and wondered how you were getting along, and I should have written to you before if I had known where to direct.

"Let me tell you a little about myself. Barnton is a very pretty country town, only about six miles from Hartford. The boarding-school which I attend is under the charge of Ezekiel Munroe, A. M. He is a man of about fifty, a graduate of Yale College, and has always been a teacher. It is a large two-story house, with an addition containing a good many small bed-chambers for the boys. There are about twenty of us, and there is one assistant teacher who teaches the English branches. Mr. Munroe, or Old Zeke, as we call him behind his back, teaches Latin and Greek. I am studying both these languages, because father wants me to go to college.

"But you won't be interested in hearing about our studies. I will tell you how we amuse ourselves. There are about fifty acres of land belonging to Mr. Munroe; so that we have plenty of room for play. About a quarter of a mile from the house there is a good-sized pond. There is a large, round-bottomed boat, which is stout and strong. Every Wednesday and Saturday afternoon, when the weather is good, we go out rowing on the pond. Mr. Barton, the assistant teacher, goes with us, to look after us. In the summer we are allowed to go in bathing. In the winter there is splendid skating on the pond.

"Besides this, we play ball a good deal, and we have various other plays. So we have a pretty good time, although we study pretty hard too. I am getting on very well in my studies. Father has not decided yet where he will send me to college.

"I wish you were here, Dick. I should enjoy your company, and besides I should like to feel that you were getting an education. I think you are naturally a pretty smart boy; but I suppose, as you have to earn your own living, you don't get much chance to learn. I only wish I had a few hundred dollars of my own. I would have you come up here, and attend school with us. If I ever have a chance to help you in any way, you may be sure that I will.

"I shall have to wind up my letter now, as I have to hand in a composition to-morrow, on the life and character of Washington. I might say that I have a friend who wears a coat that once belonged to the general. But I suppose that coat must be worn out by this time. I don't

much like writing compositions. I would a good deal rather write letters.

"I have written a longer letter than I meant to. I hope you will get
it, though I am afraid not. If you do, you must be sure to answer it,
as soon as possible. You needn't mind if your writing does look like
'hens-tracks,' as you told me once.

"Good-by, Dick. You must always think of me, as your very true
friend,

"FRANK WHITNEY"

Dick read this letter with much satisfaction. It is always pleasant
to be remembered, and Dick had so few friends that it was more to
him than to boys who are better provided. Again, he felt a new sense
of importance in having a letter addressed to him. It was the first letter he had ever received. If it had been sent to him a year before, he
would not have been able to read it. But now, thanks to Fosdick's
instructions, he could not only read writing, but he could write a very
good hand himself.

There was one passage in the letter which pleased Dick. It was
where Frank said that if he had the money he would pay for his education himself.

"He's a tip-top feller," said Dick. "I wish I could see him ag'in."

There were two reasons why Dick would like to have seen Frank.
One was, the natural pleasure he would have in meeting a friend; but
he felt also that he would like to have Frank witness the improvement
he had made in his studies and mode of life.

"He'd find me a little more 'spectable than when he first saw me,"
thought Dick.

Dick had by this time got up to Printing House Square. Standing
on Spruce Street, near the "Tribune" office, was his old enemy, Micky
Maguire.

It has already been said that Micky felt a natural enmity towards
those in his own condition in life who wore better clothes than himself. For the last nine months, Dick's neat appearance had excited the
ire of the young Philistine.[1] To appear in neat attire and with a clean
face Micky felt was a piece of presumption, and an assumption of
superiority on the part of our hero, and he termed it "tryin' to be a
swell."

Now his astonished eyes rested on Dick in his ancient attire, which
was very similar to his own. It was a moment of triumph to him. He
felt that "pride had had a fall," and he could not forbear reminding
Dick of it.

1. Barbarian.

"Them's nice clo'es you've got on," said he, sarcastically, as Dick came up.

"Yes," said Dick, promptly. "I've been employin' your tailor. If my face was only dirty we'd be taken for twin brothers."

"So you've give up tryin' to be a swell?"

"Only for this partic'lar occasion," said Dick. "I wanted to make a fashionable call, so I put on my regimentals."

"I don't b'lieve you've got any better clo'es," said Micky.

"All right," said Dick, "I won't charge you nothin' for what you believe."

Here a customer presented himself for Micky, and Dick went back to his room to change his clothes, before resuming business.

Chapter 25

Dick Writes His First Letter

When Fosdick reached home in the evening, Dick displayed his letter with some pride.

"It's a nice letter," said Fosdick, after reading it. "I should like to know Frank."

"I'll bet you would," said Dick. "He's a trump."

"When are you going to answer it?"

"I don't know," said Dick, dubiously. "I never writ a letter."

"That's no reason why you shouldn't. There's always a first time, you know."

"I don't know what to say," said Dick.

"Get some paper and sit down to it, and you'll find enough to say. You can do that this evening instead of studying."

"If you'll look it over afterwards, and shine it up a little."

"Yes, if it needs it; but I rather think Frank would like it best just as you wrote it."

Dick decided to adopt Fosdick's suggestion. He had very serious doubts as to his ability to write a letter. Like a good many other boys, he looked upon it as a very serious job, not reflecting that, after all, letter-writing is nothing but talking upon paper. Still, in spite of his misgivings, he felt that the letter ought to be answered, and he wished Frank to hear from him. After various preparations, he at last got settled down to his task, and, before the evening was over, a letter was written. As the first letter which Dick had ever produced, and because it was characteristic of him, my readers may like to read it. Here it is,—

"DEAR FRANK,—I got your letter this mornin', and was very glad to hear you hadn't forgotten Ragged Dick. I aint so ragged as I was.

Openwork coats and trowsers has gone out of fashion. I put on the Washington coat and Napoleon pants to go to the post-office, for fear they wouldn't think I was the boy that was meant. On my way back I received the congratulations of my intimate friend, Micky Maguire, on my improved appearance.

"I've give up sleepin' in boxes, and old wagons, findin' it didn't agree with my constitution. I've hired a room in Mott Street, and have got a private tooter, who rooms with me and looks after my studies in the evenin'. Mott Street aint very fashionable; but my manshun on Fifth Avenoo isn't finished yet, and I'm afraid it won't be till I'm a gray-haired veteran. I've got a hundred dollars towards it, which I've saved up from my earnin's. I haven't forgot what you and your uncle said to me, and I'm tryin' to grow up 'spectable. I haven't been to Tony Pastor's, or the Old Bowery, for ever so long. I'd rather save up my money to support me in my old age. When my hair gets gray, I'm goin' to knock off blackin' boots, and go into some light, genteel employment, such as keepin' an apple-stand, or disseminatin' peanuts among the people.

"I've got so as to read pretty well, so my tooter says. I've been studyin' geography and grammar also. I've made such astonishin' progress that I can tell a noun from a conjunction as far away as I can see 'em. Tell Mr. Munroe that if he wants an accomplished teacher in his school, he can send for me, and I'll come on by the very next train. Or, if he wants to sell out for a hundred dollars, I'll buy the whole concern, and agree to teach the scholars all I know myself in less than six months. Is teachin' as good business, generally speakin', as blackin' boots? My private tooter combines both, and is makin' a fortun' with great rapidity. He'll be as rich as Astor some time, *if he only lives long enough.*

"I should think you'd have a bully time at your school. I should like to go out in the boat, or play ball with you. When are you comin' to the city? I wish you'd write and let me know when you do, and I'll call and see you. I'll leave my business in the hands of my numerous clerks, and go round with you. There's lots of things you didn't see when you was here before. They're getting on fast at the Central Park. It looks better than it did a year ago.

"I aint much used to writin' letters. As this is the first one I ever wrote, I hope you'll excuse the mistakes. I hope you'll write to me again soon. I can't write so good a letter as you; but I'll do my best, as the man said when he was asked if he could swim over to Brooklyn backwards. Good-by, Frank. Thank you for all your kindness. Direct your next letter to No. — Mott Street.

  "Your true friend,

              "DICK HUNTER."

When Dick had written the last word, he leaned back in his chair, and surveyed the letter with much satisfaction.

"I didn't think I could have wrote such a long letter, Fosdick," said he.

"Written would be more grammatical, Dick," suggested his friend.

"I guess there's plenty of mistakes in it," said Dick. "Just look at it, and see."

Fosdick took the letter, and read it over carefully.

"Yes, there are some mistakes," he said; "but it sounds so much like you that I think it would be better to let it go just as it is. It will be more likely to remind Frank of what you were when he first saw you."

"Is it good enough to send?" asked Dick, anxiously.

"Yes; it seems to me to be quite a good letter. It is written just as you talk. Nobody but you could have written such a letter, Dick. I think Frank will be amused at your proposal to come up there as teacher."

"P'r'aps it would be a good idea for us to open a seleck school here in Mott Street," said Dick, humorously. "We could call it 'Professor Fosdick and Hunter's Mott Street Seminary.' Boot-blackin' taught by Professor Hunter."

The evening was so far advanced that Dick decided to postpone copying his letter till the next evening. By this time he had come to have a very fair handwriting, so that when the letter was complete it really looked quite creditable, and no one would have suspected that it was Dick's first attempt in this line. Our hero surveyed it with no little complacency. In fact, he felt rather proud of it, since it reminded him of the great progress he had made. He carried it down to the post-office, and deposited it with his own hands in the proper box. Just on the steps of the building, as as he was coming out, he met Johnny Nolan, who had been sent on an errand to Wall Street by some gentleman, and was just returning.

"What are you doin' down here, Dick?" asked Johnny.

"I've been mailin' a letter."

"Who sent you?"

"Nobody."

"I mean, who writ the letter?"

"I wrote it myself."

"Can you write letters?" asked Johnny, in amazement.

"Why shouldn't I?"

"I didn't know you could write. I can't."

"Then you ought to learn."

"I went to school once; but it was too hard work, so I give it up."

"You're lazy, Johnny,—that's what's the matter. How'd you ever expect to know anything, if you don't try?"

"I can't learn."

"You can, if you want to."

Johnny Nolan was evidently of a different opinion. He was a good-natured boy, large of his age, with nothing particularly bad about him, but utterly lacking in that energy, ambition, and natural sharpness, for which Dick was distinguished. He was not adapted to succeed in the life which circumstances had forced upon him; for in the street life of the metropolis a boy needs to be on the alert, and have all his wits about him, or he will find himself wholly distanced by his more enterprising competitors for popular favor. To succeed in his profession, humble as it is, a boot-black must depend upon the same qualities which gain success in higher walks in life. It was easy to see that Johnny, unless very much favored by circumstances, would never rise much above his present level. For Dick, we cannot help hoping much better things.

Chapter 26

An Exciting Adventure

Dick now began to look about for a position in a store or counting-room. Until he should obtain one he determined to devote half the day to blacking boots, not being willing to break in upon his small capital. He found that he could earn enough in half a day to pay all his necessary expenses, including the entire rent of the room. Fosdick desired to pay his half; but Dick steadily refused, insisting upon paying so much as compensation for his friend's services as instructor.

It should be added that Dick's peculiar way of speaking and use of slang terms had been somewhat modified by his education and his intimacy with Henry Fosdick. Still he continued to indulge in them to some extent, especially when he felt like joking, and it was natural to Dick to joke, as my readers have probably found out by this time. Still his manners were considerably improved, so that he was more likely to obtain a situation than when first introduced to our notice.

Just now, however, business was very dull, and merchants, instead of hiring new assistants, were disposed to part with those already in their employ. After making several ineffectual applications, Dick began to think he should be obliged to stick to his profession until the next season. But about this time something occurred which considerably improved his chances of preferment.

This is the way it happened.

As Dick, with a balance of more than a hundred dollars in the savings bank, might fairly consider himself a young man of property, he thought himself justified in occasionally taking a half holiday from business, and going on an excursion. On Wednesday afternoon

Henry Fosdick was sent by his employer on an errand to that part of Brooklyn near Greenwood Cemetery. Dick hastily dressed himself in his best, and determined to accompany him.

The two boys walked down to the South Ferry,[1] and, paying their two cents each, entered the ferry-boat. They remained at the stern, and stood by the railing, watching the great city, with its crowded wharves, receding from view. Beside them was a gentleman with two children,—a girl of eight and a little boy of six. The children were talking gayly to their father. While he was pointing out some object of interest to the little girl, the boy managed to creep, unobserved, beneath the chain that extends across the boat, for the protection of passengers, and, stepping incautiously to the edge of the boat, fell over into the foaming water.

At the child's scream, the father looked up, and, with a cry of horror; sprang to the edge of the boat. He would have plunged in, but, being unable to swim, would only have endangered his own life, without being able to save his child.

"My child!" he exclaimed in anguish,—"who will save my child? A thousand—ten thousand dollars to any one who will save him!"

There chanced to be but few passengers on board at the time, and nearly all these were either in the cabins or standing forward. Among the few who saw the child fall was our hero.

Now Dick was an expert swimmer. It was an accomplishment which he had possessed for years, and he no sooner saw the boy fall than he resolved to rescue him. His determination was formed before he heard the liberal offer made by the boy's father. Indeed, I must do Dick the justice to say that, in the excitement of the moment, he did not hear it at all, nor would it have stimulated the alacrity with which he sprang to the rescue of the little boy.

Little Johnny had already risen once, and gone under for the second time, when our hero plunged in. He was obliged to strike out for the boy, and this took time. He reached him none too soon. Just as he was sinking for the third and last time, he caught him by the jacket. Dick was stout and strong, but Johnny clung to him so tightly, that it was with great difficulty he was able to sustain himself.

"Put your arms round my neck," said Dick.

The little boy mechanically obeyed, and clung with a grasp strengthened by his terror. In this position Dick could bear his weight better. But the ferry-boat was receding fast. It was quite impossible to reach it. The father, his face pale with terror and anguish, and his hands clasped in suspense, saw the brave boy's struggles, and prayed with agonizing fervor that he might be successful. But it is probable,

---

1. Travel between Brooklyn and Manhattan was revolutionized with the inauguration of Robert Fulton's steamboat ferry service in 1814.

for they were now midway of the river, that both Dick and the little boy whom he had bravely undertaken to rescue would have been drowned, had not a row-boat been fortunately near. The two men who were in it witnessed the accident, and hastened to the rescue of our hero.

"Keep up a little longer," they shouted, bending to their oars, "and we will save you."

Dick heard the shout, and it put fresh strength into him. He battled manfully with the treacherous sea, his eyes fixed longingly upon the approaching boat.

"Hold on tight, little boy," he said. "There's a boat coming."

The little boy did not see the boat. His eyes were closed to shut out the fearful water, but he clung the closer to his young preserver. Six long, steady strokes, and the boat dashed along side. Strong hands seized Dick and his youthful burden, and drew them into the boat, both dripping with water.

"God be thanked!" exclaimed the father, as from the steamer he saw the child's rescue. "That brave boy shall be rewarded, if I sacrifice my whole fortune to compass it."

"You've had a pretty narrow escape, young chap," said one of the boatmen to Dick. "It was a pretty tough job you undertook."

"Yes," said Dick. "That's what I thought when I was in the water. If it hadn't been for you, I don't know what would have 'come of us."

"Anyhow you're a plucky boy, or you wouldn't have dared to jump into the water after this little chap. It was a risky thing to do."

"I'm used to the water," said Dick, modestly. "I didn't stop to think of the danger, but I wasn't going to see that little fellow drown without tryin' to save him."

The boat at once headed for the ferry wharf on the Brooklyn side. The captain of the ferry-boat, seeing the rescue, did not think it necessary to stop his boat, but kept on his way. The whole occurrence took place in less time than I have occupied in telling it.

The father was waiting on the wharf to receive his little boy, with what feeling of gratitude and joy can be easily understood. With a burst of happy tears he clasped him to his arms. Dick was about to withdraw modestly, but the gentleman perceived the movement, and, putting down the child, came forward, and, clasping his hand, said with emotion, "My brave boy, I owe you a debt I can never repay. But for your timely service I should now be plunged into an anguish which I cannot think of without a shudder."

Our hero was ready enough to speak on most occasions, but always felt awkward when he was praised.

"It wasn't any trouble," he said, modestly. "I can swim like a top."

"But not many boys would have risked their lives for a stranger," said the gentleman. "But," he added with a sudden thought, as his glance rested on Dick's dripping garments, "both you and my little boy will-take cold in wet clothes. Fortunately I have a friend living close at hand, at whose house you will have an opportunity of taking off your clothes, and having them dried."

Dick protested that he never took cold; but Fosdick, who had now joined them, and who, it is needless to say, had been greatly alarmed at Dick's danger, joined in urging compliance with the gentleman's proposal, and in the end our hero had to yield. His new friend secured a hack, the driver of which agreed for extra recompense to receive the dripping boys into his carriage, and they were whirled rapidly to a pleasant house in a side street, where matters were quickly explained, and both boys were put to bed.

"I aint used to goin' to bed quite so early," thought Dick. "This is the queerest excursion I ever took."

Like most active boys Dick did not enjoy the prospect of spending half a day in bed; but his confinement did not last as long as he anticipated.

In about an hour the door of his chamber was opened, and a servant appeared, bringing a new and handsome suit of clothes throughout.

"You are to put on these," said the servant to Dick; "but you needn't get up till you feel like it."

"Whose clothes are they?" asked Dick.

"They are yours."

"Mine! Where did they come from?"

"Mr. Rockwell sent out and bought them for you. They are the same size as your wet ones."

"Is he here now?"

"No. He bought another suit for the little boy, and has gone back to New York. Here's a note he asked me to give you."

Dick opened the paper, and read as follows,—

"Please accept this outfit of clothes as the first instalment of a debt which I can never repay. I have asked to have your wet suit dried, when you can reclaim it. Will you oblige me by calling to-morrow at my counting room, No. —, Pearl Street.

"Your friend,

"JAMES ROCKWELL."

Chapter 27

Conclusion

When Dick was dressed in his new suit, he surveyed his figure with pardonable complacency. It was the best he had ever worn, and fitted him as well as if it had been made expressly for him.

"He's done the handsome thing," said Dick to himself; "but there wasn't no 'casion for his givin' me these clothes. My lucky stars are shinin' pretty bright now. Jumpin' into the water pays better than shinin' boots; but I don't think I'd like to try it more'n once a week."

About eleven o'clock the next morning Dick repaired to Mr. Rockwell's counting-room on Pearl Street. He found himself in front of a large and handsome warehouse. The counting-room was on the lower floor. Our hero entered, and found Mr. Rockwell sitting at a desk. No sooner did that gentleman see him than he arose, and, advancing, shook Dick by the hand in the most friendly manner.

"My young friend," he said, "you have done me so great a service that I wish to be of some service to you in return. Tell me about yourself, and what plans or wishes you have formed for the future."

Dick frankly related his past history, and told Mr. Rockwell of his desire to get into a store or counting-room, and of the failure of all his applications thus far. The merchant listened attentively to Dick's statement, and, when he had finished, placed a sheet of paper before him, and, handing him a pen, said, "Will you write your name on this piece of paper?"

Dick wrote, in a free, bold hand, the name Richard Hunter. He had very much improved his penmanship, as has already been mentioned, and now had no cause to be ashamed of it.

Mr. Rockwell surveyed it approvingly.

"How would you like to enter my counting-room as clerk, Richard?" he asked.

Dick was about to say "Bully," when he recollected himself, and answered, "Very much."

"I suppose you know something of arithmetic, do you not?"

"Yes, sir."

"Then you may consider yourself engaged at a salary of ten dollars a week. You may come next Monday morning."

"Ten dollars!" repeated Dick, thinking he must have misunderstood.

"Yes; will that be sufficient?"

"It's more than I can earn," said Dick, honestly.

"Perhaps it is at first," said Mr. Rockwell, smiling; "but I am willing to pay you that. I will besides advance you as fast as your progress will justify it."

Dick was so elated that he hardly restrained himself from some demonstration which would have astonished the merchant; but he exercised self-control, and only said, "I'll try to serve you so faithfully, sir, that you won't repent having taken me into your service."

"And I think you will succeed," said Mr. Rockwell, encouragingly. "I will not detain you any longer, for I have some important business to attend to. I shall expect to see you on Monday morning."

Dick left the counting-room, hardly knowing whether he stood on his head or his heels, so overjoyed was he at the sudden change in his fortunes. Ten dollars a week was to him a fortune, and three times as much as he had expected to obtain at first. Indeed he would have been glad, only the day before, to get a place at three dollars a week. He reflected that with the stock of clothes which he had now on hand, he could save up at least half of it, and even then live better than he had been accustomed to do; so that his little fund in the savings bank, instead of being diminished, would be steadily increasing. Then he was to be advanced if he deserved it. It was indeed a bright prospect for a boy who, only a year before, could neither read nor write, and depended for a night's lodging upon the chance hospitality of an alley-way or old wagon. Dick's great ambition to "grow up 'spectable" seemed likely to be accomplished after all.

"I wish Fosdick was as well off as I am," he thought generously. But he determined to help his less fortunate friend, and assist him up the ladder as he advanced himself.

When Dick entered his room on Mott Street, he discovered that some one else had been there before him, and two articles of wearing apparel had disappeared.

"By gracious!" he exclaimed; "somebody's stole my Washington coat and Napoleon pants. Maybe it's an agent of Barnum's, who expects to make a fortun' by exhibitin' the valooable wardrobe of a gentleman of fashion."

Dick did not shed many tears over his loss, as, in his present circumstances, he never expected to have any further use for the well-worn garments. It may be stated that he afterwards saw them adorning the figure of Micky Maguire; but whether that estimable young man stole them himself, he never ascertained. As to the loss, Dick was rather pleased that it had occurred. It seemed to cut him off from the old vagabond life which he hoped never to resume. Henceforward he meant to press onward, and rise as high as possible.

Although it was yet only noon, Dick did not go out again with his brush. He felt that it was time to retire from business. He would leave his share of the public patronage to other boys less fortunate than himself. That evening Dick and Fosdick had a long conversation. Fosdick rejoiced heartily in his friend's success, and on his side had the pleasant news to communicate that his pay had been advanced to six dollars a week.

"I think we can afford to leave Mott Street now," he continued. "This house isn't as neat as it might be, and I should like to live in a nicer quarter of the city."

"All right," said Dick. "We'll hunt up a new room tomorrow. I shall have plenty of time, having retired from business. I'll try to get my reg'lar customers to take Johnny Nolan in my place. That boy hasn't any enterprise. He needs somebody to look out for him."

"You might give him your box and brush, too, Dick."

"No," said Dick; "I'll give him some new ones, but mine I want to keep, to remind me of the hard times I've had, when I was an ignorant boot-black, and never expected to be anything better."

"When, in short, you were 'Ragged Dick.' You must drop that name, and think of yourself now as"—

"Richard Hunter, Esq.,"[1] said our hero, smiling.

"A young gentleman on the way to fame and fortune," added Fosdick.

---

1. Abbreviation for Esquire, an honorific title used primarily in writing instead of "Mr." Lawyers use this title frequently.

CONTEXTS

Illustration by Kinnersley. Frontispiece of First Book Edition.
(Boston: Loring Publisher, 1868).

HORATIO ALGER, JR.

Friar Anselmo†

Friar Anselmo (God's grace may he win!)
Committed one sad day a deadly sin;

Which being done he drew back, self-abhorred,
From the rebuking presence of the Lord,

And, kneeling down, besought, with bitter cry,
Since life was worthless grown, that he might die.

All night he knelt, and, when the morning broke,
In patience still he waits death's fatal stroke.

When all at once a cry of sharp distress
Aroused Anselmo from his wretchedness;

And, looking from the convent window high,
He saw a wounded traveller gasping lie

Just underneath, who, bruised and stricken sore,
Had crawled for aid unto the convent door.

The friar's heart with deep compassion stirred,
When the poor wretch's groans for help were heard

With gentle hands, and touched with love divine,
He bathed his wounds, and poured in oil and wine.

With tender foresight cared for all his needs,—
A blessed ministry of noble deeds.

† From *New York Weekly* (August 5, 1872).

In such devotion passed seven days. At length
The poor wayfarer gained his wonted strength.

With grateful thanks he left the convent walls,
And once again on death Anselmo calls.

When, lo! his cell was filled with sudden light,
And on the wall he saw an angel write,

(An angel in whose likeness he could trace,
More noble grown, the traveller's form and face),

"Courage, Anselmo, though thy sin be great,
God grants thee life that thou may'st expiate.

"Thy guilty stains shall be washed white again,
By noble service done thy fellow-men.

"His soul draws nearest unto God above,
Who to his brother ministers in love."

Meekly Anselmo rose, and, after prayer,
His soul was lighted of its past despair.

Henceforth he strove, obeying God's high will,
His heaven-appointed mission to fulfil.

And many a soul, oppressed with pain and grief,
Owed to the friar solace and relief.

HORATIO ALGER, JR.

Are My Boys Real?†

The idea is suggested that young people will be interested to learn whether the boy characters in my books are taken from real life. I answer in general terms that I have always preferred to introduce real boys into my stories, and have done so in many instances where it has been possible for me to find a character suited to a plot.

The first street boy with whom I became acquainted in New York was Johnny Nolan, a young boot-black, who made daily calls at the office of one of my friends whose office, in 1867, was on Spruce

† From *Ladies Home Journal* (November 1890).

street, on the site now occupied by the "Tribune" building. My conversations with him gave me my first knowledge of New York street-
boys and their mode of life. My interest was excited, and led me a few
months later to undertake the story of "Ragged Dick," in which
Johnny figures. I have described him as he was a good-natured but
lazy boy, without enterprise or ambition. I gave Johnny a copy of the
book when it appeared, and he was quite proud at figuring in print.
The original of "Micky Maguire" was Paddy Shea, a tough character,
who lived not far from the City Hall, and generally passed the summer at "the island." "Ragged Dick" was a real name, but I never knew
the boy who bore it.

I met the hero of "Rough and Ready" at the Newsboys' Lodge, in the
upper part of the old "Sun" building. "Ben, the Luggage Boy." I met
at the same place, and the story of that name substantially accords
with his. The boys who made for themselves a home beneath one of
the piers, were known to Superintendent O'Connor, and he arranged
for me an interview with one of them. I had conversations with many
street boys while writing "Ragged Dick" and "Tattered Tom" series,
and derived from many of them sketches of character and incidents.

When I was preparing to write "The District Telegraph Boy," I sent
for a boy who had served in that capacity for nearly two years, and
used some of the incidents he supplied to me. "Phil the Fiddler," was
a real Italian boy. I obtained the picture which appears in the book,
from a Broadway photographer, to whom he sat for it. Mr. Casale,
then editor of an Italian semi-weekly paper in New York, furnished
me with many of the incidents.

Some of the characters in "The Young Circus Rider" are still living,
in particular Charlie Davis, who left home at an early age and accompanied a circus to Australia. In "Frank's Campaign," the boys forming the military company commanded by Frank Frost, were all real
boys, and all, with one exception, are living to-day. The colored boy,
little Pomp, in the same story, was intended as a male counterpart to
Mrs. Stowe's "Topsy."

I have, by request, given to many of my characters the real names
of young friends and acquaintances without necessarily making them
portraits. Some of my books and serial stories were suggested in part
by incidents in the lives of young persons whom I knew. I am now
writing for a juvenile publication a story called "The Evil Train Boy."
Fred, the hero, served in that capacity last summer, securing the position through me.

I am often indebted for characters and incidents to paragraphs in
the daily press. Whenever I find one that seems available, I follow the
example of Charles Reade,[1] and cut it out for future reference. I have

1. English novelist and dramatist (1814–1884).

probably written seventy-five juvenile books and serials, and I have no hesitation in saying that it would have been quite impossible for me to write half the number if I had not drawn in large part my characters and material from real life. The story of "Joe's Luck," located in California, was written in San Francisco. Years afterwards the name of the book was given to a mine in Southern Africa, of which a picture appeared in the "London Illustrated News." In like manner I went to Chicago in October, 1887, to obtain material for a story just published in book-form, called "Luke Walton; or, The Chicago Newsboy."

I have, of course, introduced a large number of adult characters in my various stories. Many of these are special studies from life. I hold that a novelist, or writer of fiction, is best situated in a large city, where he has an opportunity to study life in many phases, and come in contact with a large variety of types of character. The experience of prominent American and foreign novelists, notably of Charles Dickens, will bear me out in this statement.

EDWARD G. ALCORN

Advice from Horatio Alger, Jr.†

Many young literary aspirants ask what they must read to become "a writer." Horatio Alger, Jr., who is always willing to give a word of encouragement to young authors, in reply to a short note which I wrote him some time ago, sent me the following letter, which he has given me permission to publish:—

NATICK, Mass., Aug. 11, 1891.
MY DEAR SIR: Your letter has been forwarded to me at my summer home.

Your question is rather difficult to answer. I think, perhaps, it may be well for you to read carefully and critically the books of successful juvenile authors. This will enable you to learn what has contributed to their success. When I commenced writing for young people my publisher recommended me to read "Optic's"[1] books (he had been in the field ten or a dozen years) and judge for myself what made the boys like his books. I did so, but retained my own individuality, so that there are marked differences between my books and his. My present taste inclines me to prefer the juvenile books of J. T. Trowbridge[2] to any

---

† From *The Writer* (January 1892).
1. Oliver Optic, pseudonym for William Taylor Adams (1822–1897), American writer of juvenile fiction and editor of *Student and Schoolmate*.
2. Writer of children's books and magazine fiction (1827–1916).

other. Let me add that I have always made a close study of boys in order that my characters might seem to be drawn from life. I have a natural liking for boys, which has made it easy for me to win their confidence and become intimately acquainted with them. It would be well, I think, for you to write short juvenile stories first. I did so, and it was the success of one in particular that led me to think I had found my vocation. It was copied in hundreds of papers.

I don't know whether you will find these suggestions of any service. I hope you may, and wish you success in any work you may undertake.

Yours truly,
HORATIO ALGER, JR.

The success of Mr. Alger's books make his suggestions valuable to all writers of books for boys.

HORATIO ALGER, JR.

Writing Stories for Boys†

When I began to write for publication it was far from my expectation that I should devote my life to writing stories for boys. I was ambitious, rather, to write for adults, and for a few years I contributed to such periodicals as *Harper's Magazine, Harper's Weekly, Putnam's Magazine,* and a variety of literary weeklies. I achieved fair success, but I could see that I had so many competitors that it would take a long time to acquire a reputation. One day I selected a plot for a two-column sketch for the Harpers. It was during the war. Thinking the matter over, it occurred to me that it would be a good plot for a juvenile book. I sat down at once and wrote to A. K. Loring, of Boston, at that time a publisher in only a small way, detailing the plot and asking if he would encourage me to write a juvenile book. He answered: "Go ahead, and if I don't publish it, some other publisher will." In three months I put in his hands the manuscript of "Frank's Campaign." This story was well received, but it was not till I removed to New York and wrote "Ragged Dick" that I scored a decided success.

I don't intend to weary the reader with a detailed account of my books and the circumstances under which they were written. It is enough to say that I soon found reason to believe that I was much more likely to achieve success as a writer for boys than as a writer for adults. I therefore confined myself to juvenile writing, and am at

† From *The Writer* (March 1896).

present the author of more than sixty boys' stories, besides a considerable number of serials, which may eventually appear in book form.

As may be supposed, I have some idea in regard to the qualifications that are needed in an author who would succeed in this line of work, and will set them down briefly, at the request of the editor of THE WRITER.

A writer for boys should have an abundant sympathy with them. He should be able to enter into their plans, hopes, and aspirations. He should learn to look upon life as they do. Such books as "Sandford and Merton"[1] would no longer achieve success. Boys object to be written down to. Even the Rollo books,[2] popular as they were in their time, do not suit the boys of to-day. A boy's heart opens to the man or writer who understands him. There are teachers and writers who delight to lecture the young. They are provided with a little hoard of maxims preaching down a schoolboy's heart, if I may adapt a well-known line of Tennyson's.[3] Those parents who understand and sympathize with their boys have the strongest hold upon them. I call to mind one writer for boys (he wrote but a single book) whose hero talked like a preacher and was a perfect prig. He seemed to have none of the imperfections of boyhood, and none of the qualities that make boys attractive. Boys soon learn whether a writer understands and sympathizes with them. I have sometimes wondered whether there ever was a boy like Jonas in the Rollo books. If so, I think that while probably an instructive, he must have been a very unpleasant companion for a young boy like Rollo.

A writer for boys should remember his responsibility and exert a wholesome influence on his young readers. Honesty, industry, frugality, and a worthy ambition he can preach through the medium of a story much more effectively than a lecturer or a preacher. I have tried to make my heroes manly boys, bright, cheerful, hopeful, and plucky. Goody-goody boys never win life's prizes. Strong and yet gentle, ready to defend those that are weak, willing to work for their families if called upon to do so, ready to ease the burden that may have fallen upon a widowed mother, or dependent brothers and sisters, such boys are sure to succeed, and deserve success.

It should not be forgotten that boys like adventure. There is no objection to healthy excitement. Sensational stories, such as are found in the dime and half-dime libraries, do much harm, and are very objectionable. Many a boy has been tempted to crime by them. Such

1. *The History of Sandford and Merton* (1783) by Thomas Day (1748–1789) is one of the earliest novels written for children. It is an anti-slavery book, and Day expanded it into a series with two other volumes appearing in 1787 and 1789.
2. Juvenile series written by Jacob Abbott (1803–1879), American theologian and writer of children's books, including the *Rollo Series* (1835–58) and the *Jonas Series* (1839–41).
3. Line 94 of "Locksley Hall" by British poet Alfred Tennyson (1809–1892).

stories as "The Boy Highwayman," "The Boy Pirate,"[4] and books of that class, do incalculable mischief. Better that a boy's life should be humdrum than filled with such dangerous excitement.

Some writers have the art of blending instruction with an interesting story. One of the best, known   perhaps the best known of juvenile writers   excels in this department. Carrying his boy heroes to foreign lands, he manages to impart a large amount of information respecting them without detracting from the interest of the story. I have never attempted this, because it requires a special gift, which I do not possess.

One thing more, and the last I shall mention—a story should be interesting. A young reader will not tolerate dullness. If there are dull passages which he is tempted to skip, he is likely to throw the book aside. The interest should never flag. If a writer finds his own interest in the story he is writing failing, he may be sure that the same effect will be produced on the mind of the reader. It seems to me that no writer should undertake to write for boys who does not feel that he has been called to that particular work. If he finds himself able to entertain and influence boys, he should realize that upon him rests a great responsibility. In the formation period of youth he is able to exert a powerful and salutary influence. The influence of no writer for adults can compare with his. If, as the years pass, he is permitted to see that he has helped even a few of his boy readers to grow into a worthy and noble manhood, he can ask no better reward.

4. Possibly an allusion to *The Pirate Boy, or, Adventures of Henry Warrington: A Story of the Sea* (1844) by Maturin Ballou Murray (1820–1895).

F. J. OTTARSON

New York and Its People†

Pausing a moment, on the opening day of the present year, to glance at what remained of the Stuyvesant pear tree[1] in the Third Avenue, and looking up and down the long streets almost in vain for signs of the pleasant Knickerbocker[2] custom of making New Year's calls, I was forcibly reminded of the rapid growth and even more rapid ethnological changes that have occurred since old hard-koppig[3] Peter spitefully turned his back upon the intruding English, and stumped off up the rude path that led to his "Bouerie," where he puffed his pipe, nursed his wooden leg, and swore in genuine Hollandisch at all Britons and Yankees, until death ended alike his swearing and his smoking.

In the increasing whirl and excitement of the now acknowledged Metropolis of the Western Hemisphere, we find little time and perhaps little inclination to inquire who and what we are, and where we came from; some may perhaps occasionally wonder where they are going to, but, indeed, hardly a tithe of us are likely to waste time on that subject until the moment of departure is at hand; we are literally too closely occupied in trying to live to make preparation for dying. In truth, there is no city in the world where men have so little leisure or spare time as in New York. While its million of intramural and suburban residents are made up of many nations and every variety of the human family, the motive power that keeps up the whirl and the strife of business is almost entirely American—and intensified American at that; for the native, who is a restless worker everywhere, works nowhere so hard as in New York; it is the heart of his country, and as the human heart is the centre of physical force—the

---

† From *The Galaxy. A Magazine of Entertaining Reading* (May 1, 1867): 58–64.
1. Located at East 13th Street and 3rd Avenue, it was believed to be the oldest tree in New York City, planted in 1647 by Peter Stuyvesant, the former Dutch governor of New Amsterdam, who had brought it from Holland. The tree was killed in 1857 by two colliding horse carriages.
2. Dutch.
3. Hard-headed, stubborn.

particular spot where the life-sustaining blood is most active and efficient—so in this national heart the force that has made us a great people, and our country a great power—I mean the force of hard work—is ever at its maximum intensity. Like all other vast aggregations of people, we have among us the lazy and the thriftless, but very few such are of native birth; on the contrary, the native example operates powerfully upon the non-native element, and transforms a generous proportion of that material from idleness and servility to thrift and independence. There is no bee-hive without its drones; ours is not an exception, though the workers are chiefly native, and the drones, for the most part, refugees from stranger hives.

* * *

The total population of the city in 1855 was 629,904; in 1865 it was 726,386—an increase in ten years of about 17 per cent. For the preceding ten years, by State enumeration, the increase was nearly 70 per cent. Such an increase on the Federal census of 1860 would have given us a round million in '65. The native-born population was 303,721 in '55 and 407,312 in '65—the first being 42 ¼ and the last 56 per cent. of the whole. This shows a considerable gain upon the rapidly-increasing proportion of foreigners, which may be accounted for probably by the great stampede of aliens in 1862—'63, who feared they might be forced into the army.

* * *

Therefore, while I use the census figures as they are for comparisons, it would be well to suppose that the round numbers for 1865 probably ought to be: of native-born, 420,000; of foreign-born, 530,000—a total of 950,000.

Of the native-born in 1865, there were 312,210 born in the city, 3,087 in Kings County, 3,390 in Westchester, and 15,980 in other parts of the State. Of those born in other States, there were 7,190 from Massachusetts, 6,262 from Connecticut, 4,404 from other Eastern States, in all, 17,856 from Yankee Land. In common with the natives of New York, these Down Easters are the wide-awake, go-ahead element in our daily life, and for their numbers they yield an amount of propelling force unequalled by any other people. They are emphatically workers, and make their energy felt, if not always respected, wherever they may be. The 22,500 natives of New York (born out of the city) are another element of great power; less aggressive and less venturesome than the unadulterated Yankee, they are equally firm of conviction and persistent in effort, with the additional virtue of more steadiness of purpose and greater strength of will under discouragements. A great portion of the responsible business of our city is controlled by these men. New Jersey sends us 9,741 of her children, a majority of whom are dealers in something to eat. The Jerseymen, and the 5,500 Pennsylvanians who come with them, are strongly tinctured with Dutch cautiousness or slowness, and seldom undertake extensive business or great risks; but they are generally prudent and safe, with a constant reference to "number one" that would do honor to a Connecticut trader. All the Southern or slaveholding States gave us 1,304 in 1865 against 3,289 in 1855. There are not enough (or were not) of this class to make any particular impress upon the city, and since the war the little influence they might have had is quite gone. The days of their vast political importance have passed away, and the disgraceful spirit of toadying to the few hundreds of rich planters who gave us their society in the hot months, has also vanished. From the great West we receive but little— only 2,282 in all, of whom half are from Ohio. California sends back 207, and Oregon not one. The human current of course sets that way, and New York (the whole State) has done her share, as for instance: In 1860 there were 191,128 New Yorkers in Michigan, 121,508 in Illinois, 75,550 in Ohio, 21,574 in Minnesota, 46,053 in Iowa, and so on; nearly 30,000 in California, and 10,000 in the Territories, or, to sum up, the State of New York had furnished to other parts of the Union 867,000 of her children, and received from all the States only 275,000. By the census of 1850 we had sent out 750,000, and received 290,000; so it appears that in ten years we had increased our contributions by 117,000, and decreased receipts by 15,000. I believe census compilers seldom take notice of these movements, but if they undertake to record nativities they should do so; the New Yorker in California is as much a New Yorker as an Irishman in Boston is an Irishman. The human production of a State are those who were born in it, not those who emigrate to it. Of the United States born population of our own city, 65,102 were born beyond its borders. Probably more than 45,000 of these are men, and were adults when they came here. It is safe, therefore, to say that as an element of business and moral force, they represent a city population of five times as many, including women and children—say 225,000, or more than half the native total. It is no disparagement to city-born people, but nevertheless true, that the greater portion of its moneyed, trading and manufacturing business is managed by those who were once "greenhorns" from the country. Instance the great medium of intelligence—the press: Raymond, Greeley, Brooks, Bryant, Marble, are Eastern or New York State men, all born in rural districts; Bennett[4] is a Scotchman; and the same is

4. See note 1, p. 33; *Raymond*: Henry Javis Raymon (1820–1869), founder, editor, and chief proprietor of the *New York Times*; *Greeley*: see note 1, p. 20; *Brooks*: possibly Charles William Shirley Brooks (1816–1874), journalist and novelist, born in London; *Bryant*: William Cullen Bryant (1794–1878), poet and journalist, worked for the *New York Review* and then the *New York Evening Post*, of which he became editor in 1829; *Marble*: Manton Marble (1834–1917), journalist, editor, and publisher of the *New York World*.

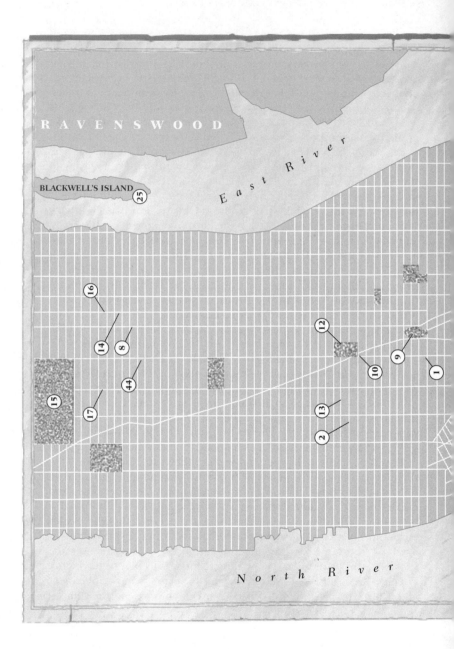

RAVENSWOOD

East River

BLACKWELL'S ISLAND 25

North River

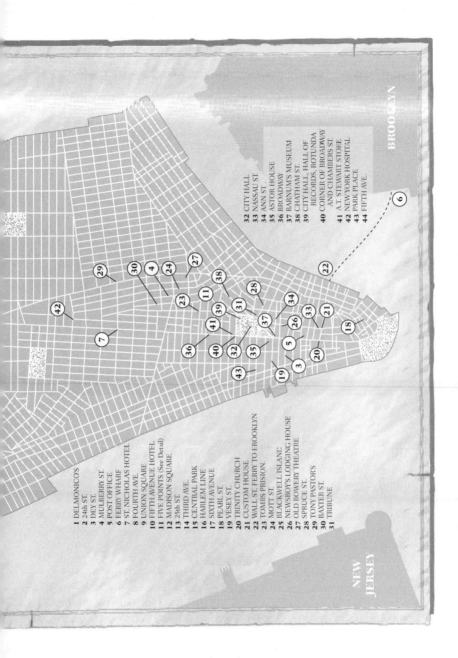

1 DELMONICO'S
2 24th ST.
3 DEY ST.
4 MULBERRY ST.
5 FERRY WHARF
6 FERRY WHARF
7 ST. NICHOLAS HOTEL
8 FOURTH AVE.
9 UNION SQUARE
10 FIFTH AVENUE HOTEL
11 FIVE POINTS (See Detail)
12 MADISON SQUARE
13 25th ST.
14 THIRD AVE.
15 CENTRAL PARK
16 HARLEM LINE
17 SIXTH AVENUE
18 PEARL ST.
19 VESEY ST.
20 TRINITY CHURCH
21 CUSTOM HOUSE
22 WALL ST. FERRY TO BROOKLYN
23 TOMBS PRISION
24 MOTT ST.
25 BLACKWELL ISLAND
26 NEWSBOY'S LODGING HOUSE
27 OLD BOWERY THEATRE
28 SPRUCE ST.
29 TONY PASTOR'S
30 BAXTER ST.
31 TRIBUNE

32 CITY HALL
33 NASSAU ST.
34 ANN ST.
35 ASTOR HOUSE
36 BROADWAY
37 BARNUM'S MUSEUM
38 CHATHAM ST.
39 CITY HALL, HALL OF
    RECORDS, ROTUNDA
40 CORNER OF BROADWAY
    AND CHAMBERS ST.
41 A.T. STEWART STORE
42 NEW YORK HOSPITAL
43 PARK PLACE
44 FIFTH AVE.

NEW JERSEY

BROOKLYN

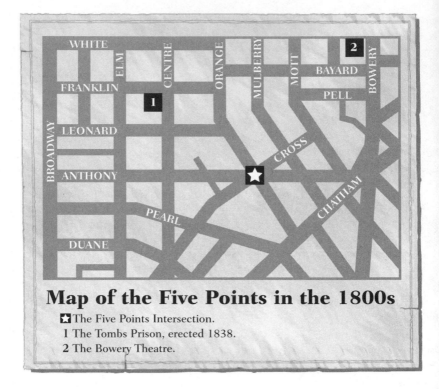

Map of the Five Points in the 1800s

★ The Five Points Intersection.
1 The Tombs Prison, erected 1838.
2 The Bowery Theatre.

true of their publishers and the principal assistant editors, with scarcely exceptions enough to prove the rule. Thus much for origin and influence of our driving native-born population.

The foreign element is very different material. New York, by her situation as the port of ingress of two-thirds of the foreign commerce of the nation and a much greater proportion of all the emigration from the Eastern Hemisphere, is very naturally a city of many peoples and many tongues; a polylingual, cosmopolitan capital—a half-way house for gregarious races. It is not more than forty years since the great human current first started across the ocean, then merely a little rill, but steadily increasing until the revolutions and attempted revolutions of 1848 in Germany and Ireland raised the stream into a rushing river. The political impetus was more than equalled (in Ireland) by the great famine. Before that time we had received a large number of Irish, and but very few Germans; after that they came in floods from both countries, and it was not unusual to have from three to six thousand foreigners landed at Castle Garden in a single day.

From 1847 to 1860 inclusive the number of aliens landed in this city
was 2,671,819; in 1854 alone the number was nearly 320,000. During the first part of the late war the tide slackened very materially, but
increased again from 1864. The whole number received by the Commissioners of Emigration in twenty years ending last December, was
3,583,184, equivalent to the population of more than twelve of the
smaller States of the Union in 1860. The immigration last year was
233,410. But I will not confuse the reader with figures—all remember the overwhelming tide, and we were thankful for the national and
individual prosperity that enabled us to receive millions of the persecuted and the destitute without perceptible diminution of our
resources or danger to our Government. Of these emigrants the Irish
were the most numerous and the poorest; thousands were paupers in
fact, and had not even a change of clothing. This grievance became
so great that Congress enacted laws to prevent or mitigate the evil,
by securing from shippers certain head-money that could be used to
support the helpless. Unfitted for venture in the Western prairies, the
Irish mostly remained in or near the city, crowding into whatever
place of shelter they could find, seeking the commonest and poorest
paid work when they sought any, setting up little dirty liquor shops,
a great portion of them falling naturally into an unhealthy and
degraded way of life. There were many notable exceptions; I speak of
the mass of the indigent classes. Of the Germans, nearly all who were
heads of families brought a little money, and more than half of them
wisely pushed on to the prairies. But the figures will best illustrate
this point. The census of 1860 shows in all the States 1,611,304 Irish
and 1,301,136 Germans; New York, Pennsylvania and Massachusetts—
each having large cities—retained 885,445, or more than half of all the
Irish; while the new States of the Northwest got 655,427, or more
than half the German influx. Still there were a great many Germans
who preferred the city and lager-beer peddling to the country. The
Germans seized upon the wooden tenements in the Tenth and Sev-
enteenth Wards, and crowded out the natives; the Irish were partial
to the Fourth, Sixth and Fourteenth, and made their stronghold in
the rookeries of those localities. Whenever these classes have
intruded in force, the native New Yorker has fled before them. Little
by little they may have assimilated with us, and there has been some
intermarrying; but there seems to be an antagonism too strong to
expect anything like a general fusion. On one hand difference of language, on the other difference of religion, stands in the way.

These classes constitute the great bulk of our foreign-born population, but by no means the extent of foreign influence upon the
city. The children of these people, though born here and technically called Americans, are as much foreigners in instinct, education and behavior as their parents. Now, when we remember that

the increase by Irish mothers is to Americans as three to one, and by Germans at least two to one; further, that the majority of immigrants are adults upon arrival, we find a powerful addition to the foreign element not set down in the census. As proof of the remarkable difference in the fecundity of these classes, look at the mortality tables, where the number of children deceased in 1865 was 14,804, of whom 13,158 were born of foreign mothers, and only 1,646 of native mothers—showing the astonishing proportion of eight to one! From a partial record of births, I find that, of 3,151 children, 2,756 were of foreign, and but 570 of native parentage. Notwithstanding the greater mortality in ratio of children of foreign parents, as many of them as of Americans come to maturity. Adding, then, these children to the foreign side, we shall get, as a low estimate, this result: Natives, 33 per cent., foreign-born and their children, 67 per cent., of the whole population. The numbers of immigrants other than Irish and German are insignificant, except English, of whom we have 19,700. There are 6,617 Scotch, 572 Welsh, 3,541 British Americans, 5,800 French, 955 Italian, 350 Spanish, etc. The number of Irish by the census in 1865 was 161,334, nearly 15,000 less than in 1855; the Germans (including Scandinavians, Poles, Belgians and other Germanic people) were 113,833, against 102,235 ten years before. As the actual immigration from 1855 to 1865 was more than a million and a quarter, we are again reminded that the enumerators of the last census must have omitted a very large portion of the alien residents.

The influence of the foreign element upon our business interests has been almost insignificant, in view of its great preponderance of numbers. We have a number of wealthy English, French and German merchants and bankers, and too many foreign speculators, such as gold gamblers and general money brokers; yet these do not weigh conspicuously in the aggregate of business, except, perhaps, the Hebrews of the gold room.[5] There is a great deal of foreign capital here, but most of it is worked through native hands. The foreign element, even when wealthy, is not notable for enterprise in business ventures, and incoming capitalists look with astonishment upon the daring of our financial lions. There are two or three rich and wide-awake natives in New York who could—and, had they undertaken it, would—have laid the Atlantic Cable in less time than it took the British directors to cipher out the length of the wire. With few exceptions, our foreign residents of means take the world easily and do a moderate business in a quiet way, with little of the slap-dash and hurry-skurry that mark

---

5. Anti-semitic remark, exemplifying the anxiety felt by some about Jews gaining economic power and control; the relation to gold taps into a tradition of anti-semitic images of Jews hoarding gold.

our own people under similar conditions. As for politics, the wealthy foreigner remains aloof and manifests very little interest in parties or party questions. He comes here to make money; perhaps returns after a few years of profitable effort; if he remains, it is an even chance that he will not become legally naturalized unless it be desirable to do so for the furtherance of his business operations. Socially, this class mingle freely with native society, and exert a wide influence in that direction.

The second or middle class of imported residents, comprising those of some means and tolerable education, take to politics as naturally as ducks to water. They expand under the inspiration of an atmosphere where every man is a sovereign; they secure the right of franchise at the earliest moment, and seldom fail to use it upon the slightest provocation. From voting to holding office is their natural proclivity, and our frequent elections give ample opportunity for the gratification of their ambition. For any ordinary office, say alderman, councilman or school trustee, there are forty naturalized to ten native aspirants. While their votes were a minority, they were the allies of this or that party as the chances of preferment inclined to the one or the other. Within four years, however, they have risen to a decisive majority of all the voters, and the question now is not how many offices ought the foreign element to ask for, but how many shall it permit native Americans to retain. But I am verging upon party grounds and must beware. The business and social influence of this middle class is on the whole healthy. They are generally strong and hearty men, good workers and tolerable managers; and those who choose to work are pretty sure to find employment, often where Americans would meet with refusal. The children of this class are usually bright, and grow up to be as good citizens as we can expect in such a town.

The third, and unfortunately the largest class of immigrants is to be considered. This class embraces the very poorest and most ignorant and debased of the millions that pour upon us from the old world; it comprises the criminals and paupers of Great Britain, Ireland and the Continent, and with them an immense throng who are not criminals, but so poor that American paupers look like princes beside them. These wretched creatures find shelter as best they may in cellars and garrets, work as little as possible, preferring to send their ragged children into the streets to beg and steal; they indulge freely in the atrocious liquors sold in low rum-shops, repel all healthy influences—such as schools and missions, and soon become scarcely less dangerous to society than so many wild beasts. These are the squalid wretches who burrow in the worst class of tenement houses and in the old worm-eaten sheds of the dirtiest portions of the town. To give an idea of the manner in which this division of our foreign element exists, I quote, from a careful report by a city missionary of unimpeachable veracity, the following facts:

> In the Fourth Ward, human beings are packed in some places at the rate of 240,000 to the square mile. There are 465 places where intoxicating liquor is sold, or one grog-shop for 47 souls. In a single block, there are 59 miserable buildings, occupied by 382 families, the individuals in which are 812 Irish, 218 Germans, 186 Italians, 189 Polanders, 12 French, 9 English, 7 Portuguese, 2 Welsh, 39 negroes and 10 Americans; total, 1,520. Of these, 113 are Protestants, 287 Jews, and 1,062 Catholics. Of the 613 children, but 166 attend any school. Of the 900 adults, 605 can neither read nor write. There are 50 degraded women, but not one of them an American. In this block are 33 underground tenements, the most of which are from eight to ten feet below the sidewalk. There are 20 grog-shops. One Sabbath a gentleman counted for five hours the number of persons who went into two of them. There were 450 men, 445 women, 82 boys and 68 girls; total, 1,045.

It is scarcely necessary to add that from this vile sub-stratum of mortality come crimes of all descriptions, offences of every grade—except those requiring shrewdness and intelligence; and murder, burglary, theft, prostitution, assaults, and preëminently drunkenness and disorderly behavior spring mainly from these miserable people. Hence it happens that of all our paupers, over seventy per cent. are foreign-born, and four-fifths of those are Irish; of vagrants, ninety per cent. are foreigners; of convicts in State and other prisons, seventy per cent.; of prostitutes of the lower sort, at least eighty per cent.; of applicants for dispensary and other charitable relief, about eighty per cent.; of police arrests for all manner of offences, seventy-five per cent., while of cholera, small-pox, typhus fever, and other virulent and dangerous diseases, they are the natural breeders, nurses and disseminators. As for influence, of course this class has none, unless it be to embitter the native mind against all foreigners whatsoever.

Errors excepted, such is a fair view of the origin and present composition of the denizens of this Metropolis. The data are as nearly accurate as possible; the deductions are intended to express a candid and liberal judgment. Our active, vital, energetic, propelling force, is of Dutch and English descent, but now purely American; it is not mainly of city-born men, but of those who have come in from the State and the Eastern States. Our laboring force is made up of city-born, country-born, and the middle class or the best of the foreign increment. The foreign-born element preponderates in numbers, but is entirely subjective to the native element and under its control, especially in a moral sense; but politically—where numbers are looked to and morals too often ignored—the foreign element holds and wields the power. Socially, we are distinctively American, with the largest catholicity of toleration. The New Yorker is certainly proud of his noble city; but he feels that its greatness is manifest and everywhere known; that to doubt such greatness would be to doubt the daylight with the sun at meridian; and he is quite content that his city and her people should manifest and approve themselves in what they have done and will yet do for this country and the world.

JAMES D. McCABE, JR.

Street Children†

In spite of the labors of the Missions and the Reformatory Institutions, there are ten thousand children living on the streets of New York, gaining their bread by blacking boots, by selling newspapers, watches, pins, etc., and by stealing. Some are thrust into the streets by dissolute parents, some are orphans, some are voluntary outcasts, and others drift here from the surrounding country. Wherever they may come from, or however they may get here, they are here, and they are nearly all leading a vagrant life which will ripen into crime or pauperism.

* * *

The Bootblacks rank next to the newsboys. They are generally older, being from ten to sixteen years of age. Some are both newsboys and bootblacks, carrying on these pursuits at different hours of the day.

They provide themselves with the usual bootblack's "kit," of box and brushes. They are sharp, quick-witted boys, with any number of bad habits, and are always ready to fall into criminal practices when enticed into them by older hands. Burglars make constant use of them to enter dwellings and stores and open the doors from the inside. Sometimes these little fellows undertake burglaries on their own account, but they are generally caught by the police.

* * *

A large part of the earnings of the bootblacks is spent for tobacco and liquors. These children are regular patrons of the Bowery Theatre and the low-class concert halls. Their course of life leads to miserable results. Upon reaching the age of seventeen or eighteen the bootblack generally abandons his calling, and as he is unfit for any

---

† From *Light and Shadows of New York Life; or, The Sights and Sensations of the Great City.* A Facsimile Edition (New York: Farrar, Straus and Giroux, 1970).

other employment by reason of his laziness and want of skill, he becomes a loafer, a bummer, or a criminal.

For the purpose of helping these and other outcasts, the Children's Aid Society was organized nineteen years ago. Since then it has labored actively among them, and has saved many from their wretched lives, and has enabled them to become respectable and useful members of society.

The Children's Aid Society extends its labors to every class of poor and needy children that can be reached, but makes the street children the especial objects of its care. It conducts five lodging houses, in which shelter and food are furnished at nominal prices to boys and girls, and carries on nineteen day and eleven evening Industrial Schools in various parts of the city. The success of the society is greatly, if not chiefly, due to the labors and management of Charles Loring Brace, its secretary, who has been the good genius of the New York street children for nearly twenty years.[1]

The best known, and one of the most interesting establishments of the Children's Aid Society, is the *Newsboys' Lodging House*, in Park Place, near Broadway. It was organized in March, 1854, and, after many hard struggles, has now reached a position of assured success. It is not a charity in any sense that could offend the selfrespect and independence of its inmates. Indeed, it relies for its success mainly in cultivating these qualities in them. It is in charge of Mr. Charles O'Connor, who is assisted in its management by his wife. Its hospitality is not confined to newsboys. Bootblacks, street venders, and juvenile vagrants of all kinds are welcomed, and every effort is made to induce them to come regularly that they may profit by the influences and instruction of the house. Boys pay five cents for supper (and they get an excellent meal), five cents for lodging, and five cents for breakfast. Those who are found unable to pay are given shelter and food without charge, and if they are willing to work for themselves are assisted in doing so.

The boys come in toward nightfall, in time for supper, which is served between six and seven o'clock. Many, however, do not come until after the theatres close. If they are strangers, their names and a description of them are recorded in the register. "Boys have come in," says Mr. Brace, "who did not know their own names. They are generally known to one another by slang names, such as the following: 'Mickety,' 'Round Hearts,' 'Horace Greeley,' 'Wandering Jew,' 'Fat Jack,' 'Pickle Nose,' 'Cranky Jim,' 'Dodge-me-John,' 'Tickle-me-foot,' 'Know-Nothing Mike,' 'O'Neill the Great,' 'Professor,' and innumerable others. They have also a slang dialect."

* * *

1. Charles Loring Brace (1826–1890) established the Children's Aid Society in 1853.

The officers of the Lodging House use their influence to induce the boys, who are the most notoriously improvident creatures in the city, to save their earnings. They have met with considerable success. There is now a Newsboys' Savings Bank, which began in this way: A former superintendent, Mr. Tracy, caused a large table to be provided and placed in the Lodging House. This table contained "a drawer divided into separate compartments; each with a slit in the lid, into which the boys dropped their pennies, each box being numbered and reserved for a depositor. The drawer was carefully locked, and, after an experience of one or two forays on it from petty thieves who crept in with the others, it was fastened to the floor, and the under part lined with tin. The Superintendent called the lads together, told them the object of the Bank, which was to make them save their money, and put it to vote how long it should be kept locked. They voted for two months, and thus, for all this time, the depositors could not get at their savings. Some repented, and wanted their money, but the rule was rigid. At the end of the period, the Bank was opened in the presence of all the lodgers, with much ceremony, and the separate deposits were made known, amid an immense deal of 'chaffing' from one another. The depositors were amazed at the amount of their savings; the increase seemed to awaken in them the instinct of property, and they at once determined to deposit the amounts in the city savings banks, or to buy clothes with them. Very little was spent foolishly. This simple contrivance has done more to break up the gambling and extravagant habits of the class than any other one influence. The Superintendent now pays a large interest on deposits, and the Trustees have offered prizes to the lads who save the most." The deposits of the boys now foot up an aggregate of about $1800.

* * *

EDWARD CRAPSEY

Outcast Children†

Ten thousand human beings under the age of fourteen years are adrift in the streets of New York. Four-fifths of them are confirmed vagrants, and the majority are growing up in ignorance of everything but the depravity which is gleaned from the city slums, and all of them are being pushed by the relentless force of untoward circumstances into the criminal practices in which many have become

† From *The Nether Side of New York; or the Vice, Crime and Poverty of the Great Metropolis* (Montclair, N.J.: Patterson Smith, 1969).

adepts in the dawn of their blighted lives. The major portion are boys rapidly preparing for the almshouses, prisons, and gallows; but hundreds are girls, who have before them the darker horror of prostitution as well as those appliances of civilization for the care or repression of the pauperism and lawlessness which it creates. It is this juvenile army of vagabondage and crime hanging upon the flanks of society, and occasionally startling it from its propriety by manifestations of an immeasurable capacity for mischief, which is a prominent peril and the most sorrowful of the nether aspects of the city.

* * *

Akin to the newsboys in many respects are the bootblacks, who are, however, a much smaller class, as their calling has of late years greatly decreased as a street pursuit. It has now become a common thing for a boy to have a number of customers whom he serves every morning at their places of business, at a fixed rate per week; and some of them make more money than unskilled adults, as their gains amount to $12 or $15 per week. But these are not common cases, and the average is about $8 per week for those having regular customers. The nomads who roam the streets or lounge in the public parks, depending upon chance patrons, do not average more than $5, and many of them glean much less from the many hours of the day and night which they devote to their calling. Nor is the meagreness of its rewards the only hardship of their avocation. Of all street children seeking an honest livelihood, the bootblacks are most liable to temptation. Necessarily having much time unemployed by their trade, they use it in penny-pitching or other methods of petty gambling. They learn to chew tobacco and to smoke by picking up the ends of cigars which have been cast into the gutters. They become more proficient in profanity than the Water street[1] roughs, and rival the most degraded in obscenity. The rivalry of an over-done trade makes them adepts in lying. Brought in contact with all classes of men, they are reached by the burglars, who so often need a "kid" in their nefarious enterprises, and thus lead these hapless boys to deadly familiarity with crime. Keeping in mind these general facts, I have not been surprised to find so many of the bootblacks passing so readily into criminal practices. In their homes these Arabs of the street[2] are no better and no worse off than their comrades of all classes of outcast children. When their hours of seeking for labor are brought to a close by the thoroughfares becoming solitudes, they must kennel like dogs in some area, must go to the foulness of some tenement, or must

1. Street running north from Battery Park on the Lower East Side.
2. Commonly used term for urban, homeless children.

seek some one of the lodging houses which the charity of New York has
provided for the little wanderers in its streets.

*   *   *

CHARLES LORING BRACE

Homeless Boys†

The Newsboys' Lodging-House

The spectacle which earliest and most painfully arrested my attention
in this work, were the *houseless boys* in various portions of the city.

There seemed to be a very considerable class of lads in New York
who bore to the busy, wealthy world about them something of the
same relation which Indians bear to the civilized Western settlers.
They had no settled home, and lived on the outskirts of society, their
hand against every man's pocket, and every man looking on them as
natural enemies; their wits sharpened like those of a savage, and their
principles often no better. Christianity reared its temples over them,
and Civilization was carrying on its great work, while they—a happy
race of little heathens and barbarians—plundered, or frolicked, or led
their roving life, far beneath. Sometimes they seemed to me, like what
the police call them, "street-rats," who gnawed at the foundations of
society, and scampered away when light was brought near them. Their
life was, of course, a painfully hard one. To sleep in boxes, or under
stairways, or in hay-barges on the coldest winter-nights, for a mere
child, was hard enough; but often to have no food, to be kicked and
cuffed by the older ruffians, and shoved about by the police, standing
barefooted and in rags under doorways as the winter-storm raged, and
to know that in all the great city there was not a single door open with
welcome to the little rover—this was harder.

Yet, with all this, a more light-hearted youngster than the street-
boy is not to be found. He is always ready to make fun of his own sufferings, and to "chaff" others. His face is old from exposure and his
sharp "struggle for existence;" his clothes flutter in the breeze; and
his bare feet peep out from the broken boots. Yet he is merry as a
clown, and always ready for the smallest joke, and quick to take "a
point" or to return a repartee. * * * [H]is more ideal pictures of the
world about him, and his literary education, come from the low the-

---

† From *The Dangerous Classes of New York and Twenty Years' Work Among Them* (Montclair,
N.J.: Patterson Smith, 1967).

atres, to which he is passionately attached. His morals are, of course, not of a high order, living, as he does, in a fighting, swearing, stealing, and gambling set. * * *

* * *

Extracts from the journal of a visitor from the country:

A Visit to the Newboys

"It requires a peculiar person to manage and talk to these boys. Bullet-headed, short-haired, bright-eyed, shirt-sleeved, go-ahead boys. Boys who sell papers, black boots, run on errands, hold horses, pitch pennies, sleep in barrels, and steal their bread. Boys who know at the age of twelve more than the children of ordinary men would have learned at twenty; boys who can cheat you out of your eye-teeth, and are as smart as a steel-trap. They will stand no fooling; they are accustomed to gammon, they live by it. No audience that ever we saw could compare in attitudinizing with this. Heads generally up; eyes full on the speaker; mouths, almost without an exception, closed tightly; hands in pockets; legs stretched out; no sleepers, all wide-awake, keenly alive for a pun, a point, or a slangism. Winding up, Mr. Brace said: 'Well, boys, I want my friends here to see that you have the material for talkers amongst yourselves; whom do you choose for your orator?'

" 'Paddy, Paddy,' shouted one and all. 'Come out, Paddy. Why don't you show yourself?' and so on.

"Presently Paddy came forward, and stood upon a stool. He is a youngster, not more than twelve, with a little round eye, a short nose, a lithe form, and chuck-full of fun.

" 'Bummers,' said he, 'snoozers, and citizens, I've come down here among ye to talk to yer a little! Me and my friend Brace have come to see how ye'r gittin' along, and to advise yer. You fellers what stands at the shops with yer noses over the railin', smellin' ov the roast beef and the hash—you fellers who's got no home—think of it how we are to encourage ye. [Derisive laughter, "Ha-ha's," and various ironical kinds of applause.] I say, bummers—for you're *all* bummers (in a tone of kind patronage)—*I was a bummer once* [great laughter]—I hate to see you spendin' your money on penny ice-creams and bad cigars. Why don't you save your money? You feller without no boots, how would you like a new pair, eh? [Laughter from all the boys but the one addressed.] Well, I hope you may get 'em, but I rayther think you won't. I have hopes for you all. I want you to grow up to be rich men—citizens, Government men, lawyers, generals, and influence men. Well, boys, I'll tell you a story. My dad was a hard 'un. One beautiful day he went on a spree, and he came home and told me where's yer mother? and I axed him I didn't know, and he clipt me over the head with an iron pot, and knocked me down, and me mither drapped in on him, and at it they went. [Hi-hi's, and demonstrative applause.] Ah! at it they went, and at it they kept   ye should have seen 'em—and whilst they were fightin', I slipped meself out the back door, and away I went like a scart dog. [Oh, dry up! Bag your head! Simmer down!] Well, boys, I wint on till I kim to the 'Home' [great laughter among the boys], and they took me in [renewed laughter], and did for me, without a cap to me head or shoes to me feet, and thin I ran away, and here I am. Now boys [with mock solemnity], be good, mind yer manners, copy me, and see what you'll become.'

* * *

CLARK KIDDER

From Orphan Trains and Their Precious Cargo†

An organization called the Children's Aid Society was formed in New York City in 1853 by a theologian turned reformer named Charles Loring Brace. It was to become an early child welfare program for America and was formed because of a pressing need to deal with the many thousands of homeless, abandoned and orphaned children that roamed the streets of New York City. Many of these were the children of the masses of immigrants that flowed into Ellis Island from primarily European countries. Many of the immigrants arrived penniless, hungry, and confused which resulted in children being separated from their parents or relatives in the midst of the mass chaos of the crowds. In its infant stages the Society placed children in homes in the New York City area. In time, the practice branched out to include New York State and some of the surrounding states. The practice became known as "placing out."

As the American West grew there became a severe shortage of workers for the factories and farms that sprang up at a record pace on America's frontier. During the mid and late 1800s, the area we now know as the Midwest was referred to as the West and Northwest, as it was the western-most point to which settlers in any numbers had reached. These were the days long before child labor laws were even heard of and when it was really expected that children, beginning at very young ages, would work right alongside their peers. After all, it was quite often a matter of survival.

The Children's Aid Society would gather up the children from various asylums, orphanages and street corners and promise them a new

† From *Orphan Trains and Their Precious Cargo* (Bowie, MD: Heritage Books, 2001). Reprinted by permission of the author.

THE WORK OF THE CHILDREN'S AID SOCIETY

Illustration commonly used as a frontispiece in Children's Aid Society annual reports between 1873 and 1890. From Stephen O'Connor, *Orphan Trains: The Story of Charles Loring Brace and the Children He Saved and Failed* (New York: Houghton Mifflin, 2001).

Jacob Riis, "Didn't live nowhere." From *How the Other Half Lives* (New York: Scribner's, 1890). By permission of the Granger Collection, New York.

Jacob Riis, "Street arabs in sleeping quarters." From *How the Other Half Lives* (New York: Scribner's, 1890). © Bettmann/CORBIS.

A cartoon from an 1874 edition of the *Irish World* newspaper, showing a widely held Catholic vision that the the true nature of the "work of the Children's Aid Society" is the selling and conversion of Irish boys. From Stephen O'Connor, *Orphan Trains: The Story of Charles Loring Brace and the Children He Saved and Failed* (New York: Houghton Mifflin, 2001).

life on the farms of America's new frontier. While this sounded exciting to some of the children, others were terrified of leaving their siblings or parents, regardless of how deprived their little lives were. Not all of the children sent West were true orphans. Many had either one or both parents who were still living, but unable to provide adequate care for them. As the streets of New York City filled to overflowing with such children, the crime rate began to escalate as the children were forced to grow up seemingly overnight and fend for themselves. Many became thieves, gamblers, and prostitutes and slept on the street. Some became newsboys, delivering papers to earn money for food and clothing, much of which was squandered away nonetheless. It was clear that something had to be done and Mr. Brace was convincing in his arguments on sending the children West to alleviate both the city's crime problems and the country's labor force deficiencies.

The mode of transport for the children was the train. Groups ranging from six to upwards of one hundred children were loaded on the train, along with the Society's agents and were sent on a two or three day trip to a pre-arranged destination. The very first distribution by the Society took place in Dowagiac, Michigan in March of 1854. A notice would be placed in the town newspaper a few weeks ahead of the impending arrival and a local committee would be established to coordinate the placing of the children. Farmers from miles around would attend the distribution, which often took place at an opera house or courthouse. The children would be lined up and inspected, not unlike cattle, and would be chosen (or not) by the various farmers. Often, the children would be asked to perform for the audience and would sing or dance. The lucky ones (relatively speaking) were chosen by a farmer or his wife, or both, and were taken to their new homes in the country. The unlucky children were left standing on the stage or steps, often feeling abandoned once again. Some were painfully separated from their siblings and would shed rivers of tears. In fact, the policy of the Aid Society was to not place siblings together, believing sibling rivalry was a potential problem in the new homes. These rejected children would be loaded on the train and taken to the next stop, and hopefully would be chosen there. Yet others were never chosen and would be returned to New York City. The Society's agents would follow up on the children and make occasional visits to the farms they were placed on. If the new homes were found unsuitable for one reason or another, the children would be removed and placed once again. Some children were placed in as many as eight or more homes before finally finding one that was suitable. A handful were eventually adopted by their new foster parents.

The children would be asked to write the Society at least twice a year and report on their new lives in the country and their hopes for the future. The Author's Grandmother, Emily (Reese) Kidder (orphan train rider) wrote one such letter from Waukon, Iowa the day after Christmas in 1906. She was fourteen years old. It reads (verbatim),

"Dear Sir—

   I received your letter quite a while ago but did not answer. I go to school with the children that I live with. I stay at home and help with the work. I have not any photograph to sent. We live 2 1/2 miles south east of Waukon. I do not know of the future years what I am going to do. I think I will be a dressmaker. I believed I will start to sew next summer. Well, I will close this time.

Your Truly,
Emily Reese."

   This quaint letter was on file at the Children's Aid Society, which is still active to this day, though it ceased sending children on the trains in about 1929. Between 1854 and 1929, it is estimated that around two hundred thousand children, and even some adults, were sent to new homes on what we now refer to as "orphan trains." It is a chapter in America's history that thus far has not been significantly addressed in history books.

CRITICISM

Tangled Threads†

Nov. 1866

We have so far completed our arrangements for the next volume as to announce that a spirited story, of six chapters, will commence with the January number, and be continued till July.

This story is drawn from life as it actually exists in the great metropolis, and will be sketched with that fidelity which actual observation on the spot affords. It will be amply illustrated, and prepared expressly for our readers. Both young and old will be interested to know something of a large class of boys whose life is full of remarkable incidents, and consequently the first pages of *Ragged Dick, or Street Life in New York,* will be looked for with eagerness.

We make this announcement thus early, as those who accept our liberal terms for forming clubs may have opportunity to promise an instructive and entertaining story as one of our many attractions for the coming season.

* * *

Dec. 1866

The leading story in the next volume, which, growing in interest as it progresses, will necessarily be continued through more than six chapters, is to be finely illustrated, and in the January number, by a full page drawing of "Ragged Dick," drawn from life, and foreshadowing the future hero. We are confident that this story will prove to be more interesting than any of its predecessors.

* * *

Feb. 1867

Ragged Dick has created no little excitement among our numerous readers, as we supposed it would. Everybody is delighted, and the full

---

† In *The Student and Schoolmate*, a juvenile magazine that published the first serialized edition of *Ragged Dick.*

length portrait of the "distinguished individual" which we gave last month, is pronounced "first rate."

* * *

Jan. 1868

With the advance pay for the present year came many encouraging words, and we should like to give a specimen to our readers, were it in good taste. But one, having a word of suggestion as well as encouragement, deserves notice. Walter S. says, "We are always in great commotion to get your magazine, and the only fault we find, is, that Ragged Dick is too short in each number."—What say you, Mr. Alger?

* * *

Mar. 1868

Yes, we reply to the many inquiries, "Ragged Dick" *is* to be published in book form. The story has been carefully re-written and enlarged by Mr. Alger, new and beautiful illustrations are in preparation, and it is our expectation to announce the publication of the volume in the April number of the SCHOOLMATE, when we shall be ready to answer orders. We are glad that Mr. Alger's engagements permit him thus to gratify an increasing demand to possess this interesting story, in a permanent and attractive form. Probably no magazine story has ever excited so much attention as this, not only among the juveniles, but by its naturalness and vigor it has equally interested their parents and adult friends. It cannot fail to place Mr. Alger at the head of successful writers for the young, and the book will undoubtedly have a large sale. It will be sent postage pre-paid, on receipt of retail price, $1.25.

* * *

May 1868

Ragged Dick, or Street Life in New York. By Horatio Alger, Jr., is now before us, brought out in beautiful style by Loring, whose "Up Town Bookstore" is so well known to Bostonians. The readers of the SCHOOLMATE looked with too much eagerness for the monthly chapters in our magazine, not to feel a desire to own a book of so much interest, in which *five* entirely new chapters appear. We thank Mr. Alger for so kindly and unexpectedly connecting our name with this exceedingly interesting work, and accept the position he assigns us with due appreciation of its great worth.

* * *

June 1868

We were disappointed in not receiving "Ragged Dick" before May 5th, and on that day we mailed every copy ordered or bestowed as a prize for new subscribers. Mr. Loring has got it up with admirable taste and every body is delighted with it. We are prepared to answer all orders for this and Mr. Alger's previous volumes.

* * *

July 1868

The first edition of "Ragged Dick" is well nigh exhausted, and the demand is increasing for this, and also for Mr. Alger's previous works. We had no doubt that such would be the case, for these books need but be better known to place Mr. Alger in advance of all other writers for the young.

* * *

Aug. 1868

We regret the delay which has attended several orders for "Ragged Dick," and can assure those of our readers who have been impatiently waiting, that it has been owing to the fact that the first edition was exhausted, and consequently a second edition must be issued at once.

It is gratifying to perceive the great demand for this excellent book, and we shall now be able, from the new issue, to answer orders more promptly.

* * *

Nov. 1869

As we had anticipated, the offer we made of an excellent photograph likeness of Mr. Alger, whose contributions to our pages have given so unqualified satisfaction, and made him a universal favorite, has induced many to forward their subscriptions at even this early date. A subscriber who had the opportunity to meet Mr. Alger during one of his visits here, writes us that the likeness is excellent, and he prizes it highly as representing one who has done so much for the New York newsboys.

* * *

The manager of the Newsboy's Home in St. Louis, writes, "When on East last year, I got a copy of Ragged Dick and the boys have enjoyed it so much, that it will not last much longer, and are continually asking for the second volume. You will oblige us very much by sending us a copy of both Ragged Dick, and Fame and Fortune."

* * *

Putnam's Magazine†

"*Ragged Dick,*" by HORATIO ALGER, Jr., published by A. K. Loring, Boston, is a well-told story of street-life in New York, that will, we should judge, be well received by the boy-readers, for whom it is intended.

The hero is a boot-black, who, by sharpness, industry, and honesty, makes his way in the world, and is, perhaps, somewhat more immaculate in character and manners than could naturally have been expected from his origin and training.

We find in this, as in many books for boys, a certain monotony in the inculcation of the principle that honesty is the best policy, a proposition that, as far as mere temporal success is concerned, we believe to be only partially true. However, the book is very readable, and we should consider it a much more valuable addition to the Sunday-school library than the tales of Inebriates, and treatises on the nature of sin, that so often find place there.

† This review was published in the issue of July 7, 1868.

Who Should Read Alger?
Alger and the Public Library

CHARLES C. CUTTER

The Public Library, and Its Choice of Books†

"Six months ago the Boston public library was severely censured for buying books that would interest scholars alone, as if scholars were not part of the public which it was founded to serve. Lately an attack came from the opposite quarter." Objection was made in strong terms to the quality of the fiction supplied, and a list of suspicious titles published. C. remarks of some of them that the "first five, however, can hardly have any other demerit than that of inanity, for they are by Mrs. Southworth and Mrs. Stephens. Their titles are evidently their worst part. The two authors named, Alger and Optic, are also rather hardly treated. Alger is commonplace, if you like, and occasionally dull, but not often. And as to 'demoralizing,' there is no fear of that. Alger, so far as we know him, is obtrusively moral, with a morality of the Benjamin Franklin type. Perhaps that is one secret of his popularity."

* * *

* * * We should not include any of [his or of] Alger's works in a 'Best reading,' but neither do they belong in an *Index expurgatorius*. The characters are certainly not very good company for well-educated boys and girls; but they are of as good tone as the associates of those who read the books, and as the public library is for all the citizens, and not merely for the well educated, the trustees may properly believe themselves justified in providing a kind of reading which is sought for by a large class; gives them pleasure; does them at least no harm; and, being suited to them, brings them a certain amount of intellectual profit and a kind of moral instruction; and finally, that

† From *Boston Advertiser* (February 12, 1878).

attracts them to the library, where there is a chance that something better may get hold of them.

S. S. GREEN

Sensational Fiction in Public Libraries†

The question to which good men who have studied library economy give different answers is, whether such books as those of which the writings of William T. Adams ("Oliver Optic"), and Horatio Alger, Jr., are examples among books provided for the young, and of Mrs. Southworth and Mrs. Hentz, among works wished for by older persons, ought to find a place in public libraries.

I reserve my own answer to this question until I have discussed the subject. Books of the kind referred to depend for their power to interest the reader upon the presence in them of accounts of startling incidents and not upon a description of the processes by which interesting conjunctions in life grow out of character, or upon narration replete with fine imagination or delicate humor.

These books are not condemned, however, because they have an interesting plot, but because the incidents are startling and unnatural, and the sole reliance of the writer for attracting readers. They have little literary merit, and give us incorrect pictures of life.

This is a correct description of sensational novels and stories. They are poor books. Poor as they are, however, they have a work to do in the world. Many persons need them. They have been written by men who mean well. * * *

* * * Mr. Alger is a son of a clergyman, and himself a graduate of Harvard College and the Divinity School at Cambridge. * * *

* * * There are many uneducated boys who need sensational stories. There are many unintellectual men and women who need sensational novels. Intellectual men like this kind of reading when they are tired or sick.

* * *

There are classes in the community of grown-up persons and of children who require exciting stories if they are to read at all, and there are times in every man's life when he craves such books, and when it is well for him to read them.

Such exciting stories as are found in the circulating departments

† From *Library Journal* (September–October 1879). Samuel Swett Green (1837–1918), director of the Worcester Free Public Library, is generally regarded as a pioneer in library practices; he emphasized relations with the library's visitors and particularly cared about the relation of librarians with schoolchildren and factory workers.

of our libraries do good in two ways. They keep men and women and boys from worse reading.

* * * Now, I felt very sure that if these boys had not been considered too young to take books from the public library, but had been allowed to read the stories of Messrs. Alger and Adams, that they would have been contented with these books, and not have sought worse reading.

* * * But sensational books in the circulating departments of our public libraries do good in another way. They give young persons a taste for reading. It is certainly better for certain classes of persons to read exciting stories than to be doing what they would be doing if not reading.

* * *

* * * A boy begins by reading Alger's books. He goes to school. His mind matures. He outgrows the books that pleased him as a boy. If boys and girls grow up with a dislike of reading, or without feeling attracted towards this occupation, they will not read anything. But if a love of reading has been cultivated by giving them when young such books as they enjoy reading, then they will turn naturally to reading as an employment of their leisure, and will read such books as correspond to the grade of culture and the stage of intellectual development reached by them. They will thus be saved from idleness and vice.

* * * Perhaps there is no book that the average Irish boy likes better than one of Mr. Alger's stories. Now such a boy is likely to learn that his powers are subject to limitations, and not be led by these books to feel an overweening self-reliance.

* * *

When called upon recently to select a few hundred dollars' worth of books for young persons in such a town, I did not put on the list a single book by Adams, Alger, Kellogg, Mayne Reid, Fosdick ("Castlemon")[1] or any other sensational writer for the young. Had there been a great shoe-shop or cotton factory in the town for whose people I was providing books, and sensational works of a good quality had not been elsewhere accessible to operatives, I should have put a small supply of the books of the authors just mentioned into the library.

The best thing to do in such a case, however, is, it seems to me, to have a branch library, supplied with a considerable proportion of exciting stories, in the factory itself, or in the part of the town where the operatives live, and keep the main library almost free from sensational literature. * * *

1. Fosdick: see p. 64, n. 1, above; *Adams:* see n. 1, p. 124; *Kellogg:* Elijah Kellogg (1873–1901), Maine Clergyman and author of juvenile books; *Mayne Reid:* Thomas Mayne Reid (1818–1883), Irish-American novelist writing mostly about the West.

PECCATOR

As to Novel-reading—A Confession†

* * *

I have noticed that, throughout the entire discussion, Irish boys and the poor are branded as being the only people who read bad novels, and the proposition of Mr. S. S. Green to stock the branches of the library which are located in the meaner parts of the city with sensational novels—with novels that are not only sensational but vicious— struck me as being the surest way to keep these people on a low intellectual level forever. Are Irish boys sinners above all others in this matter, and do the poor always read bad novels from choice? I trow[1] not. People who are poor in worldly possessions are often rich in intellectual gifts, and the children of factory hands should not be forced to read the vile stuff which they would find in their branch of the library, while the good, wholesome novels, which they perhaps would rather read, are away off in the main library, where they have not time to go and get them. * * *

Boys of all classes read novels, and, whether it is owing to original sin or not, if left to themselves, seem more inclined to bad novels than good ones. But this does not always continue so, and after a while a time comes with most of them when they desire better intellectual food, and if they are rightly directed at this period they are saved from future mental debasement.

I confess to have been an Irish boy, and to have been tolerably poor. * * *

I am now an officer in a public library where only the best novels find a place, and I can say, as the result of my daily experience, that young people, whether they be the children of the street or the children of the college professor, will read healthful novels, if a little tact is used at first, and they are properly directed to them.

† From *Library Journal* (March 1880).
1. Believe or think.

S. S. GREEN

Class Adaptation in the Selection of Books: The Fiction Question†

FREE PUBLIC LIBRARY,
WORCESTER, MASS., May 9, 1880.

I have been very much interested in reading the confession of "Peccator" as to novel reading, recorded in the number of the JOURNAL for April. Such a recital awakens sympathy and stimulates to philanthropic effort.

* * *

I said, it is true, that the average Irish boy relished very much the stories of Horatio Alger, Jr., but meant to bring him forward as a typical example of boys of all nationalities who have a somewhat hard time in life on account of their poverty, introducing the example only to show that such boys were likely to have fancies regarding the facts of existence, imbibed from reading Mr. Alger's books, knocked out of them by the somewhat rough experiences which they necessarily have in actual life. I know that there are very great differences in capacity and training among the children of the poor, and am not likely to place a low estimate upon the intellectual power or attainments of Irish boys, brought, as I am daily, into close contact with the pupils of the High School in Worcester, where boys of foreign parentage often take the highest places in their classes, and with students of the College of the Holy Cross, also situated in this city.

* * * I did not mean to suggest such a course. There is nothing here about introducing "vicious" books into such branches. To do such a thing as this would be repugnant to my whole moral nature.

While I am not aware of having national or class prejudices, it does seem to me obvious that there are differences among men and boys, occasioned by the opportunities for culture which they have enjoyed, and that it is the part of wisdom in establishing libraries and branches to consider carefully what opportunities of this kind the constituencies have enjoyed, as a suggestion in regard to the kind of books to be put into these institutions.

† From *Library Journal* (May 1880).

FLETCHER FREE LIBRARY, BURLINGTON, VERMONT

Annual Report†

Added, 908 v.; total, 12,785; issued, 29.132. Fiction 66 per cent.— "a point never before reached by this library, and, I believe, not exceeded by any public circulating library in the country. The wise innovation made by the Trustees two years ago, in withdrawing from the shelves such books as those written by 'Oliver Optic,' Horatio Alger, jr., and 'Harry Castlemon,' has, without doubt, contributed to this satisfactory result. This library was, so far as I know, the first one to make the experiment."

YOUNG MEN'S ASSOCIATION, BUFFALO

Annual Report‡

Urges that the library should be assumed or assisted by the city. On the "novel" question says: "It is not to be questioned, I think, that such a library as this must set up, in the field of romance literature, some kind of a standard of quality, both literary and moral, below which it will not go in furnishing books to its patrons, young or old. In fact, that has always been done, since there are certain writers and certain classes of books which have never been represented on our shelves. But if it is our right and our duty to establish that standard at once, may we not with propriety, and ought we not, in fulfilment of the educational functions of a public library, to raise it considerably higher than we do? If we decline to become the distributer of 'dime novels,' why consent to be an agent for distribution for novels that are just a poor degree higher in literary rank and nothing better in morality? It can hardly be a presumptuous censorship that would condemn and expel from our shelves the whole works of a full score of the popular romancers of the day, on one or all of these several grounds: First, as being without one genuine touch of art, or nature, or wisdom, or wit, or knowledge, or any valuable quality whatsoever; or, secondly, as cultivating unwholesome falsities of sentiment and mischievously misrepresenting the honest realities of life; or, thirdly,

---

† From *Library Journal* (May 1881).
‡ From *Library Journal* (March 1882)

as putting villainies and vices into the foreground of every picture, to make them the conspicuous subjects of interest and the too familiar objects of contemplation. If we make three categories of such novels, I am not sure that those falling in the division last named are worse in influence than the rest. Perhaps we cannot altogether banish this wretched stuff from our catalogues; but can we not make some beginning toward that end by refusing place any longer to the works of such writers, for example, as Mrs. Southworth, Mrs. Stevens, Mrs. Wartield, Mrs. Holmes, Mrs. Hentz, Mrs. Forrester. Miss Braddon. Rhoda Broughton, Helen Mathers, Bertha Clay, May Agnes Fleming, Cecil Hay, Eliza A. Dupuy, Ouida, Gaboriau, Mayne Reid, Ballantine, Alger, Oliver Optic, Harry Castlemon, and their like?"

UNSIGNED REVIEW

Books for Young People†

An attempt has been made by the conductors of *The Christian Union* to secure what may be termed, in the slang of the day, "a consensus of opinion" as to the qualities and characteristics of the best literature for young people. The authors whose opinions are evoked at the invitation of the editors of *The Christian Union* are Horatio Alger, Jr., Frank H. Converse, Eliot McCormick, Charles Barnard, and J. T. Trowbridge. * * *

Mr. Horatio Alger, Jr., appears to believe that young people should be allowed large liberty in choosing their own reading, and should not be kept in leading-strings too long. He does not approve of the arbitrary repression of a boy's natural taste. If the young reader thirsts for tales of gore, rapine, and crime gilded with heroism, then his taste should not be arbitrarily repressed by those who consider the "Memoir of Harriet Newell," or the "Guide to the thoughtful" superior to all other publications intended for the young. Mr. Alger very justly says that "a young man ought not to be satisfied with the same class of books which he enjoyed when a boy." This is a safe saying, but it throws no light whatever upon the theme submitted to the symposiasts. * * *

Alger's Legacy:
Parodies and Responses

STEPHEN CRANE

A Self-Made Man†

An Example of Success That Any One Can Follow

Tom had a hole in his shoe. It was very round and very uncomfortable, particularly when he went on wet pavements. Rainy days made him feel that he was walking on frozen dollars, although he had only to think for a moment to discover he was not.

He used up almost two packs of playing cards by means of putting four cards at a time inside his shoe as a sort of temporary sole, which usually lasted about half a day. Once hE PUT IN FOUR ACES FOR LUCK. HE WENT DOWN TOWN THAT MORNING AND GOT refused work. He thought it wasn't a very extraordinary performance for a young man of ability, and he was not sorry that night to find his packs were entirely out of aces.

One day, Tom was strolling down Broadway. He was in pursuit of work, although his pace was slow. He had found that he must take the matter coolly. So he puffed tenderly at a cigarette and walked as if he owned stock. He imitated success so successfully that if it wasn't for the constant reminder (king, queen, deuce, and tray) in his shoe, he would have gone into a store and bought something.

He had borrowed five cents that morning of his landlady, for his mouth craved tobacco. Although he owed her much for board, she had unlimited confidence in him, because his stock of self-assurance was very large indeed. And as it increased in a proper ratio with the amount of his bills, his relations with her seemed on a firm basis. So he strolled along and smoked, with his confidence in fortune in nowise impaired by his financial condition.

† From *Cornhill Magazine* (March 1899): 324–29.

Of a sudden he perceived an old man seated upon a railing and smoking a clay pipe.

He stopped to look because he wasn't in a hurry, and because it was an unusual thing on Broadway to see old men seated upon railings and smoking clay pipes.

And to his surprise the old man regarded him very intently in return. He stared, with a wistful expression, into Tom's face, and he clasped his hands in trembling excitement.

Tom was filled with astonishment at the old man's strange demeanour. He stood, puffing at his cigarette, and tried to understand matters. Failing, he threw his cigarette away, took a fresh one from his pocket, and approached the old man.

'Got a match?' he inquired pleasantly.

The old man, much agitated, nearly fell from the railing as he leaned dangerously forward.

'Sonny, can you read?' he demanded, in a quavering voice.

'Certainly I can,' said Tom encouragingly. He waived the affair of the match.

The old man fumbled in his pocket. 'You look honest, sonny. I've been lookin' fer an honest feller fur a'most a week. I've set on this railing fur six days,' he cried plaintively.

He drew forth a letter and handed it to Tom. 'Read it fur me, sonny, read it;' he said coaxingly.

Tom took the letter and leaned back against the railings. As he opened it and prepared to read, the old man wriggled like a child at a forbidden feast.

Thundering trucks made frequent interruptions and seven men in a hurry jogged Tom's elbow, but he succeeded in reading what follows:

> 'Office of Ketchum R. Jones, Attorney-at-Law.
> 'Tin Can, Nevada, May 19, 18—.

'Rufus Wilkins, Esq.

'Dear Sir,—I have as yet received no acknowledgment of the draft from the sale of the north section lots, which I forwarded to you on June 25. I would request an immediate reply concerning it.

'Since my last I have sold the three corner lots at five thousand each. The city grew so rapidly in that direction that they were surrounded by brick stores almost before you would know it. I have also sold for four thousand dollars the ten acres of outlying sage-bush which you once foolishly tried to give away. Mr. Simpson, of Boston, bought the tract. He is very shrewd, no doubt, but he hasn't been in the West long. Still, I think if he holds it for about a thousand years he may come out all right.

'I worked him with the projected-horse-car-line gag. Inform me of the address of your New York attorneys and I will send on the papers. Pray do not neglect to write me concerning the draft sent on June 25.

'In conclusion I might say that if you have any eastern friends who are after good western investments, inform them of the glorious future of Tin Can. We now have three railroads, a bank, an electric-light plant, a projected horse car line, and an art society. Also, a saw manufactory, a patent car-wheel mill, and a Methodist church. Tin Can is marching forward to take her proud stand as the metropolis of the West. The rose-hued future holds no glories to which Tin Can does not——' Tom stopped abruptly. 'I guess the important part of the letter came first,' he said.

'Yes,' cried the old man, 'I've heard enough. It is just as I thought. George has robbed his dad.'

The old man's frail body quivered with grief. Two tears trickled slowly down the furrows of his face.

'Come, come, now,' said Tom, patting him tenderly on the back. 'Brace up, old feller. What you want to do is to get a lawyer and go put the screws on George.'

'Is it really?' asked the old man eagerly.

'Certainly it is,' said Tom.

'All right,' cried the old man, with enthusiasm; 'tell me where to get one.' He slid down from the railing and prepared to start off.

Tom reflected. 'Well,' he said finally, 'I might do for one myself.'

'What!' shouted the old man in a voice of admiration, 'are you a lawyer as well as a reader?'

'Well,' said Tom again, 'I might appear to advantage as one. All you need is a big front,' he added slowly. He was a profane young man.

The old man seized him by the arm. 'Come on, then,' he cried, 'and we'll go put the screws on George.'

Tom permitted himself to be dragged by the weak arms of his companion around a corner and along a side-street. As they proceeded, he was internally bracing himself for a struggle, and putting large bales of self-assurance around where they would be likely to obstruct the advance of discovery and defeat.

By the time they reached a brown stone house, hidden away in a street of shops and warehouses, his mental balance was so admirable that he seemed to be in possession of enough information and brains to ruin half the city, and he was no more concerned about the king, queen, deuce and tray than if they had been discards that didn't fit his draw. Too, he infused so much confidence and courage into his companion, that the old man went along the street breathing war, like a decrepit hound on the scent of new blood.

He ambled up the steps of the brown stone house as if he were charging earthworks. He unlocked the door, and they passed along a dark hall-way. In a rear room they found a man seated at table engaged with a very late breakfast. He had a diamond in his shirt front, and a bit of egg on his cuff.

'George,' said the old man in a fierce voice that came from his aged throat with a sound like the crackle of burning twigs, 'here's my lawyer, Mr.—er—ah—Smith, and we want to know what you did with the draft that was sent on June 25th.'

The old man delivered the words as if each one was a musket shot. George's coffee spilled softly upon the table-cover, and his fingers worked convulsively upon a slice of bread. He turned a white, astonished face toward the old man and the intrepid Thomas.

The latter, straight and tall, with a highly legal air, stood at the old man's side. His glowing eyes were fixed upon the face of the man at the table. They seemed like two little detective cameras taking pictures of the other man's thoughts.

'Father, what d-do you mean?' faltered George, totally unable to withstand the two cameras and the highly legal air.

'What do I mean?' said the old man with a feeble roar, as from an ancient lion; 'I mean that draft—that's what I mean. Give it up, or we'll—we'll——' he paused to gain courage by a glance at the formidable figure at his side, 'we'll put the screws on you.'

'Well, I was—I was only borrowin' it for 'bout a month,' said George.

'Ah,' said Tom.

George started, glared at Tom, and then began to shiver like an animal with a broken back.

There were a few moments of silence. The old man was fumbling about in his mind for more imprecations. George was wilting and turning limp before the glittering orbs of the valiant attorney. The latter, content with the exalted advantage he had gained by the use of the expression, 'Ah,' spoke no more, but continued to stare.

'Well,' said George finally, in a weak voice, 'I s'pose I can give you a check for it, though I was only borrowin' it for 'bout a month. I don't think you have treated me fairly, father, with your lawyers, and your threats, and all that. But I'll give you the check.'

The old man turned to his attorney. 'Well?' he asked. Tom looked at the son and held an impressive debate with himself. 'I think we may accept the check,' he said coldly, after a time.

George arose and tottered across the room. He drew a check that made the attorney's heart come privately into his mouth. As he and his client passed triumphantly out, he turned a last highly legal glare upon George that reduced that individual to a mere paste.

On the sidewalk the old man went into a spasm of delight and called his attorney all the admiring and endearing names there were to be had.

'Lord, how you settled him!' he cried ecstatically. They walked slowly back toward Broadway. 'The scoundrel,' murmured the old man. 'I'll never see 'im again. I'll desert 'im. I'll find a nice quiet boarding-place, and——'

'That's all right,' said Tom. 'I know one. I'll take you right up,' which he did.

He came near being happy ever after. The old man lived at advanced rates in the front room at Tom's boarding-house. And the latter basked in the proprietress's smiles, which had a commercial value and were a great improvement on many we see.

The old man, with his quantities of sage-bush, thought Thomas owned all the virtues mentioned in high-class literature, and his opinion, too, was of commercial value. Also, he knew a man who knew another man who received an impetus which made him engage Thomas on terms that were highly satisfactory. Then it was that the latter learned he had not succeeded sooner because he did not know a man who knew another man.

So it came to pass that Tom grew to be Thomas G. Somebody. He achieved that position in life from which he could hold out for good wines when he went to poor restaurants. His name became entangled with the name of Wilkins in the ownership of vast and valuable tracts of sage-bush in Tin Can, Nevada.

At the present day he is so great that he lunches frugally at high prices. His fame has spread through the land as a man who carved his way to fortune with no help but his undaunted pluck, his tireless energy, and his sterling integrity.

Newspapers apply to him now, and he writes long signed articles to struggling young men, in which he gives the best possible advice as to how to become wealthy. In these articles he, in a burst of glorification, cites the king, queen, deuce, and tray, the four aces, and all that. He alludes tenderly to the nickel he borrowed and spent for cigarettes as the foundation of his fortune.

'To succeed in life,' he writes, 'the youth of America have only to see an old man seated upon a railing and smoking a clay pipe. Then go up and ask him for a match.'

GILBERT W. GABRIEL

The Alger Complex†

Into all things that bear the marks, "Made in U. S. A.," has been woven, hammered or distilled a curious, imperative, hyperbolical idealism. None of the ten thousand products of which America is proud

† Originally published in *The New Yorker* (August 8, 1925).

would be what they are if idealism were not mixed into their manufacture. There must be a moral even for shaving soaps, and an ethical justification for Fords and insecticides. All is gangway for the ghost of Horatio Alger.

Perhaps, across the counter of a lifetime, you can buy nothing with idealism. Here in the United States you can buy nothing without it. It is the bleat inside the mama-doll in every nursery. It is the worshipful wind around our hugest architecture. It is the code, of our home morals, of our diplomatic dealings. It is the sob in each Congressman's throat, and the starch in the collar that holds every little stock clerk's head higher. All things are said and unsaid, done or demolished, in a desperate idealism's name.

Lugging Horatio Alger's name into it is no wild misadventure. You must remember those brave, sanctimonious books for juveniles which Alger wrote. They were shovelled by tons into all the best homes—and the worst, too—of a generation ago. They told with sweet, glamorous simplicity the histories of little bootblacks and newsboys, and they made romance of the one great American discovery that sobriety is the best policy. We who were urchins thirty years ago, and now are either millionaires or ash can experts, know that our success or failure can be traced to the seriousness with which we did or did not assimilate the morals of Horatio Alger.

Of course the psychiatrists will go further back and blame it all on the Puritans. But then, nothing baffling happens in modern American affairs which is not sooner or later traced back to the heel-marks on Plymouth Rock—and, as a gentleman with such a name as Tannenbaum" was overheard to remark between acts of "Desire Under the Elms,"[1] "This is certainly a terrible indictment of our New England ancestors!"

But from the Puritans (our guides into the subconscious tell us) the American inherited a need to be always self-reliant and superior. From the attitude of the godly he has switched only to the attitude of the superlatively and righteously successful. No author managed to instill idealism into street corner existence as nicely as Horatio Alger did. It is thanks to "Ragged Dick" and "Tom the Bootblack" that the firecracker of our dream has been tied to the tail of our daily business. Each of us, willy-nilly, is a character unto himself from out of Alger.

Those were the days before the *Saturday Evening Post* discovered the possibility of turning a good-looking young shoe salesman into a pickle magnate overnight. Industry admitted of no paradoxes in the Alger days. If you found ten cents on the sidewalk, then, you never

1. Play (1924) by American playwright Eugene O'Neill.

could dream of investing it in radio stock and opening a cabaret in
Havana within a fortnight. No, you learned from Horatio that the
canny thing to do was to hunt the city over until you discovered the
rightful owner of that dime and delivered him back his property.

He would not let you keep it, of course, because it was, after all, his
dime. But he was invariably a merchant with a kindly eye and a glossy
shirt front and a pretty little daughter about six years your junior. Your
career would be made from then on, but it would be a slow and pure
and uprighteous career. You would go to work for the merchant as an
office boy, and you might happen to rescue his little daughter when
she fell off a ferry-boat, and the grateful family might give you a gold
watch, and you would work harder, and be purer and more righteous
than ever, and in time—in good and decent time, mind you—you
would become the husband of the pretty daughter, and papa's partner,
and have a kindly eye and a glossy shirt front of your own.

Well, that was your ideal at the age of ten. Probably it still is.
Because at ten we have laid in our stock of ideals, and must spend the
rest of our lives giving them away. Or rather, here in America, trading
them off.

Almost a century ago the most theoretic Brahmin[2] in America,
Emerson, had already complained to his diary that Americans "always
idealize!" Of everything and everybody, he wrote in a sad huff, "we
tinge them with the glories of that Idea in whose light they are seen."

Yesterday, deep in the heart of another great American institution,
the Sunday Paper, (itself an idealistic means of helping Americans to
dodge their horror of leisure and meditative thought) there was an
interview with a real estate operator. "Has another Era of wonderful
Metropolitan expansion started?" he was asked. Oddly enough, he
answered that it had. And that "changing conditions are making every
man in every walk of life a realtor, and Real Estate is King." This is
no cruel, delusive highfalutin. It is simply the ability and the necessity of every American to tinge his semi-detached life in Floral Flats
with "the glories of that Idea."

Foreigners think they are forever finding us out. Time and again
you will have to read them remarking on the American romantic.
Nothing happens naturally over here, they claim. What they smile at,
wonder at, what awes and angers them most, is this wardrobe of ethical optimism in which we clothe our commonest, most obligatory
acts.

All requirements of our daily life, stockyards to skyscrapers, have
in them the crow of godly triumph, the consecration of sober and
great intentions. Had Horatio Alger been translated more frequently

---

2. Variant of Braham, a member of a cultural and social elite, especially a descendant of an
   old New England family.

into other languages, these foreign critics would know the why and the how-much of American philosophy. For Elbert Hubbard[3] was only Alger dipped in caramel, and Dr. Crane[4] is only Alger pickled in syndicate.

No people in the history of civilization has blown the dream so passionately in business, nor had so much business blown back at them from out the dream. England may be a nation of shopkeepers, but America is a sanatorium of sufferers from the Alger complex. We have founded our future on the lives of his little, industrious, abstemious, joyless boys, who never could leap out of the page and scream at him: "There are more things in heaven and earth, Horatio. . . ."

JAMES THURBER

Tom the Young Kidnapper, or, Pay Up and Live†

A KIND OF HORATIO ALGER STORY BASED ON THE SUCCESSFUL $30,000
KIDNAPPING IN KANSAS CITY OF MISS MARY MCELROY,[1]
WHO HAD A LOVELY TIME, WHOSE ABDUCTORS GAVE HER ROSES
AND WEPT WHEN SHE LEFT, AND WHOSE FATHER SAID HE DID NOT
WANT THE YOUNG MEN TO GO TO THE PENITENTIARY

"I would admire to walk with youse to a small, dark cellar and manacle you to a damp wall."

The speaker was a young American, of perhaps twenty-five years, with a frank, open countenance. Betty Spencer, daughter of old Joab Spencer, the irate banker and the richest man in town, flushed prettily. Her would-be abductor flushed, too, and stood twisting his hat in his hands. He was neatly, if flashily, dressed.

"I am sorry," she said, in a voice which was sweet and low, an excellent thing in woman, "I am sorry, but I am on my way to church, for my faith is as that of a little child."

"But I must have sixty or a hundred thousand dollars from your irate father tonight—or tomorrow night at the latest," said Tom McGirt, for it was he. "It is not so much for me as for the 'gang.'"

"Do you belong to a gang?" cried Betty, flushing prettily, a look of admiration in her eyes. In his adoring embarrassment, the young kidnapper tore his hat into five pieces and ate them.

---

3. American author and publisher (1856–1915).
4. Dr. Frank Crane, American inspirational writer.
† From *The New Yorker* (June 10, 1933). Copyright © 1933 by James Thurber. Copyright © renewed 1961 by Helen Thurber and Rosemary A. Thurber. Reprinted by arrangement with the Barbara Hogenson Agency. All rights reserved.
1. At age twenty five Mary McElroy, daughter of City Manager H. F. McElroy, was kidnapped on Saturday May 27, 1933, and held hostage for more than thirty hours. She began to sympathize with her captors and persuaded the judge to commute the death sentence of one of her captors.

"My, but you must have a strong stomach!" cried the young lady.

"That was nothing," said Tom, modestly. "Anybody would of done the same thing. You know what I wisht? I wisht it had been me stopping a horse which was running away with you at the risk of my life instead of eating a hat." He looked so forlorn and unhappy because no horse was running away with her that she pitied him.

"Does your gang really need the money?" she cried. "For if it really does, I should be proud to have you kidnap me and subject me to a most humiliating but broadening experience."

"The gang don't work, see?" said the young man, haltingly, for he hated to make this confession. "They're too young and strong to work—I mean there is so much to see and do and drink, and if they was working in a factory, say, or an old stuffy office all day, why—"

She began to cry, tears welling up into her eyes.

"I shall come with you," she said, "for I believe that young men should be given hundreds of thousands of dollars that they may enjoy life. I wear a five-and-a-half glove, so I hope your manacles fit me, else I could easily escape from those which were too large."

"If we ain't got ones your size," he said, earnestly, drawing himself up to his full height, "I'll go through smoke and flame to git some for you. Because I—well, you see, I—"

"Yes?" she encouraged him, gently.

"Aw, I won't tell youse now," he said. "Some day when I have made myself worthy, I'll tell youse."

"I have faith in you," she said, softly. "I know you will pull this job off. You can do it, and you *will* do it."

"Thanks, Betty," he said. "I appreciate your interest in me. You shall be proud some day of Tom the Young Kidnapper, or Pay Up and Live." He spoke the subtitle proudly.

"I'll go with you," she said. "No matter where."

"It ain't much of a basement," he said, reddening, and twisting an automatic between his fingers. "It's dark and the walls are damp, but me old mother ain't there, and that's something. She's no good," he added.

"I know," she said, softly. They walked on slowly down the street to a nasty part of town where an automobile drew up alongside the curb, and they got in. Four young men with frank, open countenances were inside, their faces freshly scrubbed, their dark hair moistened and slicked down. Tom introduced them all, and they put away their automatics, and took off their hats, and grinned and were very polite. "I am quite happy," Betty told them.

The cellar in which the young gang manacled Betty to a wall was, as Tom had promised, dark and damp, but the chains which fitted around her wrists were very nice and new and quite snug, so she was quite content. Two of the boys played tiddlywinks with her, while the

others went out to mail a letter which she had written at the gang's
dictation. It read: "Dear Father—Put a hundred thousand berries in
an old tin box and drop it out of your car when you see a red light on
the old Post Road tonight, or your daughter will never come home. If
you tell the police we will bite her ears off." "That's nice," said Betty,
reading it over, "for it will afford Father an opportunity, now that I am
in mortal danger, to realize how much he loves me and of how little
worth money is, and it will show him also that the young men of this
town are out to win!"

Betty was kept in the cellar all night, but in the morning Tom
brought her chocolate and marmalade on an ivory-colored breakfast
tray, and also a copy of Keats'[2] poems, and a fluffy little kitty with a
pink ribbon around its neck. One of the other boys brought her a
table badminton set, and a third, named Thad the Slasher, or Knife
Them and Run, brought her a swell Welsh pony named Rowdy. "Oh,"
said Betty, "I am so happy I could cry," and she jangled her manacles.
Several of the boys did cry, she looked so uncomfortable and so
happy, and then Betty cried, and they all laughed, and put a record
on the Victrola.[3]

That night, Betty was still chained to the wall because her old
father had not "come through." "He's holding out for only forty
grand," explained Tom, reluctantly, for he did not wish her to know
that her father was stingy. "I don't guess your father realizes that we
really will make away with you if he don't kick in. He thinks mebbe
it's a bluff, but we mean business!" His eyes flashed darkly, and
Betty's eyes snapped brightly.

"I know you do!" she cried. "Why, it's been worth forty thousand
just the experience I've had. I *do* hope he gives you the hundred, for
I should like to go back alive and tell everybody how sweet you have
been and how lovely it is to be kidnapped!"

On the second morning, Betty was sitting on the damp cellar floor
playing Guess Where I Am with Tom and Ned and Dick and Sluggy,
when Thad came in, toying with his frank, open clasp knife, his
genial countenance clouded by a frown.

"What is wrong, Thad," asked Betty, "for I perceive that something
is wrong?" Thad stood silent, kicking the moist dirt of the floor with
the toe of his shoe. He rubbed a sleeve against his eye.

"The old man come across with all the dough," he said. "We—we
gotta let you go now." He began to cry openly. Tom paled. One of the
boys took Betty's chains off. Betty gathered up her presents, the kitty,
and the table badminton set, and the poems. "Rowdy is saddled an'
waitin' outside," said Thad, brokenly, handing tens and twenties, one
at a time, to his pals.

2. John Keats (1795–1821), English Romantic poet.
3. Phonograph.

"Goodbyeee," said Betty. She turned to Tom. "Goodbyeee, Tom," she said.

"Goo—" said Tom, and stopped, all choked up.

When Betty arrived at her house, it was full of policemen and relatives. She dropped her presents and ran up to her father, kindly old Judge Spencer, for he had become a kindly old judge while she was in the cellar, and was no longer the irate old banker and no longer, indeed, the town's richest man, for he only had about seven hundred dollars left.

"My child!" he cried. "I wish to reward those young men for teaching us all a lesson. I have become a poorer but a less irate man, and even Chief of Police Jenkins here has profited by this abduction, for he has been unable to apprehend the culprits and it has taken some of the cockiness out of him, I'll be bound."

"That is true, Joab," said the Chief of Police, wiping away a tear. "Those young fellows have shown us all the error of our ways."

"Have they skipped out, Betty?" asked her father.

"Yes, Father," said Betty, and a tear welled up into her eye.

"Ha, ha!" said old Judge Spencer. "I'll wager there was one young man whom you liked better than the rest, eh, my chick? Well, I should like to give him a position and invite him to Sunday dinner. His rescuing you from the flames of that burning shack for only a hundred thous—"

"I didn't do *that*, sir," said a modest voice, and they all turned and looked at the speaker, Tom the Kidnapper, for it was he. "I simply left her loose from the cellar after we got the dough."

"It's the same thing," said her father, in mock sternness. "Young man, we have all been watching you these past two days—that is to say, we have been wondering where you were. You have outwitted us all and been charming to my daughter. You deserve your fondest wish. What will you have?"

"I'll have Scotch-and-soda, sir," said Tom. "And your daughter's hand."

"Ha, ha!" said the kindly old Judge. "There's enterprise for you, Jenkins!" He nudged Jenkins in the ribs and the Chief nudged back, and laughed. So they all had a Scotch-and-soda and then the Judge married his blushing daughter, right then and there, to Tom the Young Kidnapper, or If You Yell We'll Cut Your Throat.

AMIRI BARAKA

The Death of Horatio Alger†

The cold red building burned my eyes. The bricks hung together, like
the city, the nation, under the dubious cement of rationalism and need.
A need so controlled, it only erupted out of the used-car lots, or sat
parked, Saturdays, in front of our orange house, for Orlando, or Algernon, or Danny, or J.D. to polish. There was silence, or summers, noise.
But this was a few days after Christmas, and the ice melted from the
roofs and the almost frozen water knocked lethargically against windows, tar roofs and slow dogs moping through the yards. The building
was Central Avenue School. And its tired red sat on the corner of Central Avenue and Dey (pronounced *die* by the natives, *day* by the teachers, or any non-resident whites) Street. Then, on Dey, halfway up the
block, the playground took over. A tarred-over yard, though once there
had been gravel, surrounded by cement and a wire metal fence.

The snow was dirty as it sat dull and melting near the Greek restaurants, and the dimly lit "grocey" stores of the Negroes. The rich boys
had metal wagons, the poor rode in. The poor made up games, the
rich played them. The poor won the games, or as an emergency measure, the fights. No one thought of the snow except Mr. Feld, the
playground director, who was in charge of it, or Miss Martin, the
husky gym teacher Matthew Stodges had pushed into the cloakroom,
who had no chains on her car. Grey slush ran over the curbs, and our
dogs drank it out of boredom, shaking their heads and snorting.

I had said something about J.D.'s father, as to who he was, or had
he ever been. And J., usually a confederate, and private strong arm,
broke bad because Augie, Norman, and white Johnny were there, and
laughed, misunderstanding simple "dozens" with ugly insult, in that
curious scholarship the white man affects when he suspects a
stronger link than sociology, or the tired cultural lies of Harcourt,
Brace sixth-grade histories. And under their naïveté he grabbed my
shirt and pushed me in the snow. I got up, brushing dead ice from my
ears, and he pushed me down again, this time dumping a couple
pounds of cold dirty slush down my neck, calmly hysterical at his act.

J. moved away and stood on an icy garbage hamper, sullenly throwing wet snow at the trucks on Central Avenue. I pushed myself into
a sitting position, shaking my head. Tears full in my eyes, and the cold
slicing minutes from my life. I wasn't making a sound. I wasn't thinking any thought I could make someone else understand. Just the rush

† From *Tales* (New York: Grove Press, 1967) Reprinted by permission of Sterling Lord Liter-
istic Ltd.

of young fear and anger and disgust. I could have murdered God, in that simple practical way we kick dogs off the bottom step.

Augie (my best white friend), fat Norman, whose hook shots usually hit the rim, and were good for easy tip-ins by our big men, and useless white Johnny who had some weird disease that made him grimy, even in the middle of a game, he'd freeze, and sometimes like drives almost knocked his head off while he shuddered slightly, cracking and recracking his huge knuckles. They were howling and hopping, they thought it was so funny that J. and I had come to blows. And especially, I guess, that I had got my lumps. "Hey, wiseass, somebody's gonna break your nose!" fat Norman would say over and over whenever I did something to him. Hold his pants when he tried his jump shot; spike him sliding into home (he was a lousy catcher); talk about his brother who hung out under the El and got naked in alleyways.

(The clucks of Autumn could have, right at that moment, easily seduced me. Away, and into school. To masquerade as a half-rich nigra with shiny feet. Back through the clean station, and up the street. Stopping to talk on the way. One beer gets you drunk and you stand in an empty corridor, lined with Italian paintings, talking about the glamours of sodomy.)

Rise and Slay.

I hurt so bad, and inside without bleeding I realized the filthy grey scratches my blood would carry to my heart. John walked off staring, and Augie and Norman disappeared, so easily there in the snow. And J.D. too, my first love, drifted against the easy sky. Weeping at what he'd done. No one there but me. THE SHORT SKINNY BOY WITH THE BUBBLE EYES.

Could leap up and slay them. Could hammer my fist and misery through their faces. Could strangle and bake them in the crude jungle of my feeling. Could stuff them in the sewie hole with the collected garbage of children's guilt. Could elevate them into heroic images of my own despair. A righteous messenger from the wrong side of the tracks. Gym teachers, cutthroats, aging pickets, ease by in the cold. The same lyric chart, exchange of particulars, that held me in my minutes, the time "Brownie" rammed the glass door down and ate up my suit. Even my mother, in a desperate fit of rhythm, was not equal to the task. Which was simple economics. I.e., a white man's dog cannot bite your son if he has been taught that something very ugly will happen to him if he does. He might pace stupidly in his ugly fur, but he will never never bite.

But what really stays to be found completely out, except stupid enterprises like art? The word on the page, the paint on the canvas (Marzette dragging in used-up canvases to revive their hopeless correspondence with the times), stone clinging to air, as if it were real. Or something a Deacon would admit was beautiful. The conscience rules against ideas. The point was to be where you wanted to, and do what you wanted to. After all is "said and done," what is left but those sheepish constructions. "I've got to go to the toilet" is no less pressing than the Puritans taking off for Massachusetts, and dragging their devils with them. (There is in those parts, even now, the peculiar smell of roasted sex organs. And when a good New Englander leaves his house in the earnestly moral sub-towns to go into the smoking hells of soon to be destroyed Yankee Gomorrahs,[1] you watch him pull very firmly at his tie, or strapping on very tightly his evil watch.) The penitence there. The masochism. So complete and conscious a phenomenon. Like a standard of beauty; for instance, the bespectacled, soft-breasted, gently pigeon-toed maidens of America. Neither rich nor poor, with intelligent smiles and straight lovely noses. No one would think of them as beautiful but these mysterious scions of the puritans. They value health and devotion, and their good women, the lefty power of all our nation, are unpresuming subtle beauties, who could even live with poets (if they are from the right stock), if pushed to that. But mostly they are where they should be, reading good books and opening windows to air out their bedrooms. And it is a useful memory here, because such things as these were the vague images that had even so early, helped shape me. Light freckles, sandy hair, narrow clean bodies. Though none lived where I lived then. And I don't remember a direct look at them even, with clear knowledge of my desire, until one afternoon I gave a speech at East Orange High, as sports editor of our high school paper, which should have been printed in Italian, and I saw there, in the auditorium, young American girls, for the first time. And have loved them as flesh things emanating from real life, that is, in contrast to my own, a scraping and floating through the last three red and blue stripes of the flag, that settles the hash of the lower middle class. So that even sprawled there in the snow, with my blood and pompous isolation, I vaguely knew of a glamorous world and was mistaken into thinking it could be gotten from books. Negroes and Italians beat and shaped me, and my allegiance is there. But the triumph of romanticism was parquet floors, yellow dresses, gardens and sandy hair. I must have felt the loss and could not rise against a cardboard world of dark hair and linoleum. Reality was something I was convinced I could not have.

           And thus to be flogged or put to the rack. For all our secret energies. The first leap over the barrier: when the victim finds he can no longer stomach his own "group." Politics whinnies, but is still correct, and asleep in a windy

---

1. Biblical: Sodom and Gomorrah were cities destroyed by fire from heaven because of their moral failings.

barn. The beautiful statue of victory, whose arms were called duty. And they curdle in her snatch thrust there by angry minorities, along with their own consciences. Poets climb, briefly, off their motorcycles, to find out who owns their words. We are named by all the things we will never understand. Whether we can fight or not, or even at the moment of our biggest triumph we stare off into space remembering the snow melting in our cuts, and all the pimps of reason who've ever conquered us. It is the harshest form of love.

I could not see when I "chased" Norman and Augie. Chased in quotes because, they really did not have to run. They could have turned, and myth aside, calmly whipped my ass. But they ran, laughing and keeping warm. And J.D. kicked snow from around a fire hydrant flatly into the gutter. Smiling and broken, with his head hung just slanted towards the yellow dog ice running down a hole. I took six or seven long running steps and tripped. I couldn't have been less interested, but the whole project had gotten out of hand. I was crying, and my hands were freezing, and the two white boys leaned against the pointed metal fence and laughed and slapped their knees. I threw snow stupidly in their direction. It fell short and was not even noticed as it dropped.

(All of it rings in your ears for a long time. But the payback . . . in simple terms against such actual sin as supposing quite confidently that the big sweating purple whore staring from her peed up hall very casually at your whipping has *never* been loved . . . is hard. We used to say.)

Then I pushed to my knees and could only see J. leaning there against the hydrant looking just over my head. I called to him, for help really. But the words rang full of dead venom. I screamed his mother a purple nigger with alligator titties. His father a bilious white man with sores on his jowls. I was screaming for help in my hatred and loss, and only the hatred would show. And he came over shouting for me to shut up. Shut Up skinny bastard. I'll break your ass if you don't. Norman had both hands on his stomach, his laugh was getting so violent, and he danced awkwardly toward us howling to agitate J. to beat me some more. But J. whirled on him perfectly and rapped him hard under his second chin. Norman was going to say, "Hey me-an," in that hated twist of our speech, and J. hit him again, between his shoulder and chest, and almost dropped him to his knees. Augie cooled his howl to a giggle of concern and backed up until Norman turned and they both went shouting up the street.

I got to my feet, wiping my freezing hands on my jacket. J. was looking at me hard, like country boys do, when their language, or the new tone they need to take on once they come to this cold climate (1940's New Jersey) fails, and they are left with only the old Southern tongue, which cruel farts like me

used to deride their lack of interest in America. I turned to walk away.
Both my eyes were nothing but water, though it held at their rims, sto-
ically refusing to blink and thus begin to sob uncontrollably. And to
keep from breaking down I wheeled and hid the weeping by screaming at that boy. You nigger without a father. You eat your mother's
pussy. And he wheeled me around and started to hit me again.

Someone called my house and my mother and father and grandmother and sister were strung along Dey street, in some odd order.
(They couldn't have come out of the house "together.") And I was conscious first of my father saying, "Go on Mickey, hit him. Fight back."
And for a few seconds, under the weight of that plea for my dignity, I
tried. I feinted and danced, but I couldn't even roll up my fists. The
whole street was blurred and hot as my eyes. I swung and swung, but
J.D. bashed me when he wanted to.

My mother stopped the fight
finally, shuddering at the thing she'd made. "His hands are frozen,
Michael. His hands are frozen." And my father looks at me even now,
wondering if they'll ever thaw.

VICTOR WILSON

Legendary Alger Was a Homosexual†

Horatio Alger Jr., whose 100-odd books urged millions of boy readers
to live clean and work hard if they wanted to be successful, was a
homosexual—and he preferred young boys.

Alger was forced out as minister of a Unitarian church at Brewster
on Massachusetts' Cape Cod when his "gross immorality" with boys
was uncovered.

He quit the ministry, headed for New York City, and embarked on
a writing career that brought him wealth—and made him an American legend.

The long-hidden story was unearthed in church records by a
scholar doing research for a book on how success is achieved in the
United States.

Dr. Richard M. Huber needed background on Alger for his book,
"The American Idea of Success" (McGraw-Hill. $10), recently pub-
lished. The trail led to the Cape Cod church, and then to a bank vault
where 100-year-old church records revealed the story.

Huber, an eminent historian, quotes this section of a report by a
church committee which investigated the Rev. Alger:

† From the *Miami Herald* (January 23, 1972).

"We learn from (two boys) that Horatio Alger Jr. has been practicing on them at different times deeds that are too revolting to relate.
"Such charges were put to Alger and he did not deny them. He
admitted that he had been imprudent, and considered his connection
with the Unitarian Society of Brewster dissolved."

Thulu i il lati s tliat aiiidlu i i iiiiiiiiiili i tlu ii iiiiili Uiiitai iaii li ail-
quarters in Boston, "communicating the feelings of an 'outraged
community.'"

The committee's communication continued:

> "That Horatio Alger Jr., who has officiated as our minister for
> about 15 months past has recently been charged with gross
> immorality and a most heinous crime, a crime of no less magni-
> tude than the abominable and revolting crime of unnatural
> familiarity with boys . . . whereupon the committee sent for
> Alger, and to him specified the charges and evidence of his guilt,
> which he neither denied or attempted to extenuate but received
> it with apparent calmness of an old offender—and hastily left
> town on the very next train for parts unknown."

"Parts unknown" was New York City, where Alger began grinding
out Inspirational novels for young boys bearing such titles as,
"Ragged Dick." "Phil the Fiddler." and "Luck and Pluck." His fictional heroes usually started poor and became rich.

A typical one was a New York City bootblack. He rescued a small
girl who tumbled from a ferryboat, winning the everlasting gratitude
of her father. The man employed the lad in his brokerage house, from
where the step to riches was easy.

The books began appearing in the late 1860s and were an instant
success. Publishers apparently competed for Alger's manuscripts.
Before he died in 1899 some 60 publishing houses had issued his
novels. Alger could produce as many as four a year.

They remained successful during the first third of this century,
then lost their appeal in the depression.

But the name Alger remained associated with the American ethos
for success. As late as 1947, the American Schools and Colleges
Association set up annual Horatio Alger awards.

They have been won by such successful Americans as Walter S.
Mack Jr. (Pepsi-Cola); Bernard Baruch (adviser to presidents), and
Grover Whalen (who served several terms as New York City's official
greeter of visiting famous personalities).

Huber comments on Alger's books: "Luck, in a good many of
Alger's novels, is a stranger whom the young hero helps in some
manner, a stranger, fortunately, who is in some position to recipro-
cate with funds or a promising job."

A more pungent comment came from the biographical writing team of Henry and Katherine Pringle, who said, "No Alger hero was so silly as to rescue anybody with less than an AAA rating in Dun and Bradstreet."[1]

GARY SCHARNHORST

Demythologizing Alger†

When Horatio Alger, Jr., died in 1899, one brief obituary reported that this American writer of juvenile stories had been "perhaps better known to the boys of thirty years ago than to the present generation."[1] Available sales statistics tend to support this assertion. Alger's only best-sellers had been published between 1868 and 1871,[2] and his early modest popularity had so waned by 1881 that he had been surprised by the sale of 20,000 copies of his biography of James Garfield, the President assassinated that year.[3] A prolific writer, Alger completed over a hundred juvenile books during his career, yet by his own estimate in 1897 his aggregate sales totaled only about 800,000 volumes.[4] Sales of the six volumes comprising the early "Ragged Dick series" (1868–70) accounted for about one-fifth of this total.[5] After his death, however, Alger's popularity soared. By 1910, his juvenile novels were enjoying estimated *annual* sales of over one million[6]— that is, more Alger novels than were sold in total during his life. His books, of which an estimated seventeen to twenty million copies were sold in all,[7] remained popular until about 1920, when sales plummeted. By 1926, the circle of Alger's middle-class readers had so shrunk[8] that the leading publisher of his books stopped printing them. By 1932, less than twenty per cent of seven thousand surveyed New York boys recognized Alger's name and only about fourteen per cent admitted to having read even one of his books.[9] He was

1. Dun and Bradstreet Corporation was founded in 1841 as a commercial credit service.
†. From *Markham Review* 10 (Fall 1980–Winter 1981): 20–27. Copyright © 1980 Gary Scharnhorst. Reprinted by permission of the author.
1. E. S. Martin, "This Busy World," *Harper's Weekly*, 5 Aug. 1899, p. 761.
2. Frank Luther Mott, *Golden Multitudes* (New York: Macmillan, 1947), pp. 309, 321, 322.
3. Alger to Mr. Elderkin, 2 Aug. 1844. Used by permission of Yale University.
4. *Who's Who in America 1899–1900* (Chicago: Marquis, 1899), p. 10. In a letter owned by the Huntington Library dated 25 Mar. 1897, Alger mentioned receiving the form to be completed and returned to the editor of this volume.
5. Alger to R. A. Alger, 2 May 1888. Used by permission of the University of Michigan.
6. Everett T. Tomlinson, "The Perpetual 'Best-Sellers,' " *World's Work*, 20 (June 1910), 13045.
7. Mott, p. 159.
8. Arthur M. Jordan, *Children's Interests in Reading* (Chapel Hill: University of North Carolina Press, 1926), *passim*.
9. "The Cynical Youngest Generation," *Nation*, 17 Feb. 1932, p. 186.

described that year in the pages of one mass-circulation periodical as "forgotten" and two years later in the pages of another as "extinct."[1] In 1947, a poll of twenty thousand New York children revealed that ninety-two per cent of them "had never heard of Alger. Less than one per cent had read any of his books."[2]

On the crests and troughs of this sales curve may be graphed two questions I wish to address in this essay: If Alger's didactic tales were more popular in 1869 than in 1899 why did he enjoy such astounding posthumous popularity? And, more importantly, if Alger was virtually forgotten by the late 1920s, how did he acquire renown as a success ideologue? As Malcolm Cowley has complained, "I cannot understand how [Alger] should come to be regarded as the prophet of business enterprise; nor why the family melodrama that he wrote and rewrote for boys should be confused with the American dream of success."[3] As long ago as 1945, Cowley noted this discrepancy between what Alger is believed to have written and what he actually wrote. He observed that the original Alger hero was not a poor boy who became a millionaire by dint of honesty, enterprise, and patience, but a poor boy who rose to middle-class respectability as a reward for his filial piety.[4] Alger's unearned reputation as a success mythmaker was institutionalized only two years later with the inauguration, in 1947, of the Horatio Alger Awards for meritorious service to the causes of political or religious conservatism and economic orthodoxy. By tracing apparent transformations in the image of success associated with Alger in the mass media, including literature, between the Civil War and World War II, the network of assumptions governing the American idea of success over several generations may be silhouetted.

I

During that era of the late-nineteenth century known in America as the Gilded Age, Alger was viewed, much as he wished to be viewed,[5] simply as a writer of didactic juvenile stories. His tales were invariably evaluated according to the standard of moral influence—for good or ill—which they exerted on impressionable young minds. Particularly during the late 1860s and 1870s, critical opinion of Alger's fiction, expressed in such prestigious periodicals as the *North American Review*, *Putnam's*, and the *Nation*, generally was favorable.[6] Thomas

1. "A Forgotten Boy's Classic," *Literary Digest*, 30 Jan. 1932, p. 20; Winifred King Rugg, "A Library Exile," *Christian Science Monitor*, 19 Nov. 1934, p. 7, col. 1.
2. "Horatio Alger is an Unknown to 92% of Boys and Girls in Seven Clubs in City," *New York Times*, 13 Jan. 1947, p. 23, col. 2–3.
3. "Horatio Alger: Failure," *Horizon*, 12 (Summer 1970), p. 65.
4. "Holy Horatio," *Time*, 13 Aug. 1945, p. 98.
5. Alger, "Writing Stories for Boys," *Writer*, 9 (Feb. 1896), 36.
6. See, for example, "Literature," *Putnam's*, NS 2 (July 1868), 120; and "Children's Holiday Books," *Nation*, 3 Dec. 1874, p. 368.

Wentworth Higginson commended *Frank's Campaign* (1864) as "a good story of home life,"[7] for example, and Lyman Abbott similarly praised *Tattered Tom* (1871).[8] Even late in his career, Alger's defenders insisted that a "fine vein of high morality . . . pervades everything from his pen."[9] However, these defenders gradually were overwhelmed by the superior forces of those who complained about the potentially nefarious effect of his unrealistic and sensational fiction. As early as 1869, parents were warned to beware of Alger's crippling influence on children by a review for the *Nation*, one of the first American magazines to promote literary realism.[1] This complaint, echoed in a variety of forums, crescendoed through the 1870s and 1880s. For example, a reviewer for *St. Nicholas* charged that Alger's *Brave and Bold* (1872) contained characters "such as we do not meet in real life—and we are very glad that we don't meet them."[2] In 1877, a Boston minister condemned the "endless reams" of "drivel poured forth" by Alger and other decadent *fin de siécle* juvenile writers and asked why "young and growing minds" should be polluted with "books which can only weaken and demoralize them."[3] These criticisms tended to undermine Alger's modest initial popularity, and their appearance coincided with the first precipitous decline in sales of his books. The volumes even were removed from some library shelves during this period. Still, whether defenders or detractors, all applied the same critical standard to Alger's fiction: Does it improve and instruct its readers?

This common view of Alger as an aspiring, if misguided, moralist was shared by literary artists of the Gilded Age. At least three late-nineteenth century authors criticized the sensational and unrealistic characteristics of his didactic fiction. In her novel *Eight Cousins* (1875), Louisa May Alcott expressed her conviction that juvenile literature like Alger's damaged its young readers, even though, as she admitted, "The writers of these popular stories intend to do good."[4] W.D. Howells, in *The Minister's Charge* (1887), satirized Alger's juvenile stories by writing a realistic version of the country-boy myth. Rather than ridiculing the Alger tradition, Howells in this novel "preserved the tradition in all its essentials, altering only the surface heroics and popular gilding by which Alger sentimentalized it for his juvenile readers."[5] Although composed of many original elements,

---

7. "Children's Books of the Year," *North American Review*, 102 (Jan. 1866), 242.
8. "Editor's Literary Record," *Harper's Monthly*, 43 (Aug. 1871), 459.
9. "Horatio Alger, Jr.," *Golden Argosy*, 17 Oct. 1885, p. 364.
1. "The Last of the Children's Books," *Nation*, 30 Dec. 1869, p. 587.
2. "Books for Boys and Girls," *St. Nicholas*, 2 (Jan. 1875), 190.
3. Quoted in *Library Journal*, 2 (1878), 299.
4. *Eight, Cousins* (New York: Grosset & Dunlap, 1973), p. 187. See also Thomas Beer, *The Mauve Decade* (New York: Knopf, 1926), p. 24.
5. Robert Falk, *The Victorian Mode in American Fiction, 1865–1885* (East Lansing: Michigan State University Press, 1965), p. 132. See also Scharnhorst, "Howell's *The Minister's Charge*: A Satire of Alger's Country-Boy Myth," forthcoming in *Mark Twain Journal*.

Howells's novel bears a strong resemblance to Alger's two-part story about Sam Barker, *The Young Outlaw* (1875) and *Sam's Chance* (1876). Each author described his subsequent misadventures there, and each set at least part of the story in Boston. In Howells's realistic version, Lemuel Barker leaves his home in a New England village to seek success in the city. In quick succession, like a victimized country boy from an Alger novel, he is mistaken for a criminal, cheated of his money by a clever confidence man, robbed by tramps of his few remaining possessions, and jailed for a night after being falsely accused of purse-snatching. Though acquitted and released, he spends a second night in a charity flophouse before, gradually, he begins to rise to respectability. Even the conclusion to the novel realistically revises the conventional Alger ending: Lem indefinitely postpones his marriage and returns to his hometown sadder, wiser, and alone. Similarly, Stephen Crane a few years later satirized Alger's unrealistic plots in one of his comic sketches, entitled "A Self-Made Man; An Example of Success That Anyone Can Follow" (1899), by exaggerating their defects to the point of absurdity.[6] In short, Alcott, Howells, and Crane shared the view common during this period that Alger, though well-intentioned, failed to write ennobling fiction for boys.

II

During the heyday of his popularity early in this century, Alger acquired a reputation as a champion of Uplift whose formulaic fiction blended moral heroism with economic success. As early as 1898, he was praised in a religious magazine for his "clever trick of turning incidents to account," a new twist on the old complaint about his unrealistic plots; and his latest hero was commended as "an admirable boy with wonderful ability to take care of himself."[7] Three years later, Carolyn Wells publicly celebrated Alger for teaching "bravery, courage, and pluck through the medium of such characters as newsboys, shoe-blacks, match-sellers and luggage boys, who almost invariably rise to fame and fortune by their own persevering efforts."[8] Similarly, in 1906, the ambitious hero of Alger's *The Young Musician* was praised in the pages of the *New York Times*.[9] Such comments indicate that Alger's original reputation as a writer of simple moral tales for boys had begun to be blurred. When he was criticized, he was less liable to be charged with writing unwholesome fiction

---

6. R.W. Stallman, *Stephen Crane: A Biography* (New York: Braziller, 1968), p. 209; Eric Solomon, *Stephen Crane: From Parody to Realism* (Cambridge: Harvard University Press, 1966), p. 50.
7. *The Independent*, 20 Oct. 1898, p. 1128.
8. "Writers of Juvenile Fiction," *Bookman*, 14 (Dec. 1901), 352.
9. "Found: A Hero," *New York Times Saturday Review of Books*, 8 Dec. 1906, p. 846.

than reprimanded for emphasizing the accretion of material rewards. [1]Whatever the personal taste of the reader, when read according to the canons of taste which were observed early in this century his moral tracts seemed to praise entrepreneurs who earned and spent their wealth honestly. His books were popular during this Progressive era, a period of intense nostalgia for an imaginary olden time of equal opportunity and equitable trade, because they satisfied the popular desire to reform the institutions of business and government through a "return to fundamental morality."[2] As Richard Weiss has noted, Alger became "a nostalgic spokesman of a dying order. Of middle-class rural origins, he was always an alien in the industrially dominated society of his adulthood. . . . Alger's work reflects an attempt to re-create the more harmonious society in which he was raised."[3] Because he idealized in his juvenile fiction the moral certainties of a pre-industrial economy, Alger ironically enhanced his appeal among a later generation of readers for whom he was reinvented as a kind of Progressive prophet. Significantly, some of his books even were packaged for sale as Progressive reform tracts. At least two editions of his novels issued during the first decade of the new century—a New York Book Company edition of *Joe's Luck* and the Street and Smith edition of *Tom Brace*—pictured President Theodore Roosevelt on the cover, though Alger had died before the Great Trustbuster assumed the Presidency and had not referred to him in his fiction. Unlike the more arcane preachments of Edward Ellis, Oliver Optic, and other long-forgotten juvenile writers of the nineteenth century, Alger's moral fables apparently could be adapted to the exigencies of a new age.

Moreover, modern opinions of Alger, undoubtedly have been influenced by the confusing mass republication of the books early in this century. Cheap editions of Alger's novels were published by approximately forty firms between his death in 1899 and 1920. However, many of his earliest novels which conclude as the moral hero grasps the bottom rung on the ladder of respectability were rarely reprinted, and some publishers abridged others by deleting as many as seven of the original chapters, often those in which the hero performs virtuous deeds for which he later is rewarded. Thus the most popular editions of Alger's novels garbled the moral message of the original editions. In effect, Alger's work was editorially reinvented to appeal to Progressive era readers. Whereas in his own time Alger was credited with inventing a moral hero who became modestly successful, during the early years of this century he seemed to have invented a

1. *Public Libraries*, 16 (1911), 454.
2. Robert H. Wiebe, *The Search for Order 1877–1920* (New York: Hill and Wang, 1967), p. 8.
3. *The Myth of American Success* (New York: Basic Books, 1969), pp. 49, 59–60.

successful hero who was modestly moral. The moral uses of money, not moral behavior *per se*, seemed to have been the focus of the stories.

Still, many writers popular during this era adapted Alger's fictional formula, at least as it had been slightly skewed, to their own versions of the success story. Alger's most direct successor, Edward Stratemeyer, who dominated the juvenile market for over two decades before his death in 1930, blended moral heroism and economic success in his fiction. Alger himself wrote to Stratemeyer that "of all the juvenile writers you can write most like me,"[4] so he arranged for his friend to inherit some of his literary remains. Between 1900 and 1910, Stratemeyer published a total of eleven "completions" under Alger's name. His own works, including the Tom Swift and Rover Boys series, likewise testify to the popularity of the Alger model. As early as 1902, he was praised for writing "the sort of book that used to come from the pen of Horatio Alger, Jr."[5] One of the most popular novels for adults published during this era, Owen Wister's *The Virginian* (1902), of which were sold an estimated two million copies, owed at least part of its sales success to its assimilation of the Alger pattern. Like an adult Alger hero, the Virginian begins as a poor cowboy, becomes the ranch foreman, invests his wages in land, and by the end of the novel is destined to become one of Wyoming's chief citizens.[6] Similarly, Gene Stratton-Porter in her best-selling novel *Michael O'Halloran* (1915) tapped the wellsprings of Progressive sentiment by copying "the Horatio Alger formula, taking a little newsboy up the success ladder on the wings of determination and pluck."[7] Her novel might well have been entitled "Ragged Dick Redux."

Alger's new-won popularity as a champion of Uplift also influenced so-called "serious" authors during this period. Theodore Dreiser, who later acknowledged that he had read Alger novels avidly as a Hoosier farm boy,[8] probably modeled a chapter of *Sister Carrie* (1900) on an episode in Alger's *Helen Ford*.[9] Moreover, Dreiser apparently meant the middle name of his protagist Frank Algernon Cowperwood, a robber-baron who first appeared in *The Financier* (1910), to be read quite literally: not an Alger hero.[1] Except for the fact that both earn money, Cowperwood and Alger's scrupulously moral hero have little in common. Dorothy Parker years later would chastise Dreiser for

4. Alger to Stratemeyer, 26 Oct. 1898. Quoted by permission of the Stratemeyer Syndicate.
5. Tudor Jenks, "High Tide in Juvenile Literature," *Book Buyer*, 25 (Dec. 1902), 495.
6. John G. Cawelti, *Adventure, Mystery, and Romance* (Chicago and London: University of Chicago Press, 1976), p. 224.
7. Roderick Nash, *The Nervous Generation* (Chicago: Rand McNally, 1970), p. 138.
8. *Dawn* (New York: Liveright, 1931), pp. 122, 125.
9. Scharnhorst, "A Possible Source for *Sister Carrie*," *Dreiser Newsletter*, 9 (Spring 1978) 1–4.
1. Amiri Baraka (Leroi Jones) uses the same device in "The Death of Horatio Alger," on p. 176 of this volume [*Editor*].

"approximating" Alger's style; ironically, her comment evinced his success in adopting the deliquescent Alger formula for his own purposes.[2] Similarly, Sherwood Anderson satirized the Progressive view of Alger in *Windy McPherson's Son* (1916), in which he described the hollow success won by an Iowa newsboy who goes to Chicago, becomes rich, and marries his boss's daughter. As long ago as 1916, Waldo Frank discerned "the faint footprints of Horatio Alger" in the novel,[3] and Wright Morris again has claimed recently that the "strain of experience" in it "is closer to Horatio Alger" than to Anderson's own.[4] Sinclair Lewis also adapted "the tradition of Horatio Alger" to the expectations of Progressive era readers by depicting "the mystique of mechanics, rather than the formula of hard work and brave honesty, as the key to economic success" in his early novel *The Trail of the Hawk* (1915).[5] Like Wister and Porter, Anderson and Lewis were indebted to Alger although they did not acknowledge that debt. It seems that, whereas the Alger formula was frequently employed in the fiction of the period, Alger himself had not yet acquired symbolic status as the progenitor of an American success myth. Wister, Porter, Anderson, and Lewis did not explicitly confess their debt to Alger partly because, despite the increased sales of his books, his name had not yet acquired widespread cash value in the popular culture.

III

The most radical transformations in Alger's reputation, his canonization as an American success mythmaker, occurred largely after 1920 as his books declined in popularity and lapsed from print. Much as his novels seemed to endorse Progressive reform when read in the benign spirit of the Progressive age, a generation later these same novels, no longer submitted for correction either to current readers or the bar of critical opinion, were recollected in the acquisitive spirit of the prosperous 1920s. Just as Bruce Barton reinvented Jesus of Nazareth as a business leader in *The Man Nobody Knows* (1924), Alger's hero was reinvented during this decade as a business tycoon. According to a *Time* magazine article published in 1928, "Ragged Dick, Phil the Fiddler, and the heroes of every one of his 119 books survived adversity, invariably achieved fame and fortune at the end of the last chapter."[6] Simply stated, Alger's moral tracts, unlike the less

2. "Words, Words, Words," *New Yorker*, 30 May 1931, p. 66.
3. "Emerging Greatness," *Seven Arts*, Nov. 1916; rpt. in Walter Rideout, ed., *Sherwood Anderson: A Collection of Critical Essays*, Twentieth Century Views (Englewood Cliffs: Prentice-Hall, 1974), pp. 14, 15.
4. "*Windy McPherson's Son*: the Storyteller's Story," in *Windy McPherson's Son*, by Sherwood Anderson (Chicago: University of Chicago Press, 1965), pp. x, xiii.
5. Mark Schorer *Sinclair Lewis* (New York: McGraw-Hill, 1961), p. 225.
6. "Alger," *Time*, 7 May 1928, p. 47.

adaptable novels by Ellis, Optic, and other nineteenth-century writers for boys, acquired new meanings in each new cultural context.
Alger himself was transformed into a popular symbol of economic
triumph. No longer considered merely a writer for didactic fiction, he
became, in the words of the *New York Times*, a mythologizer who had
created "successful protagonists, ambitious boys who, through one
variation or another of an ever-efficient formula, found their way up
the ladder of achievement."[7] The phrase "Horatio Alger hero" also
obtained popular currency in the language during the 1920s—its first
appearance in print may have occurred as late as 1926,[8] even as more
libraries were removing his books from their shelves. By 1928, only
the common invocation of Alger's name reminded people of his earlier popularity. As one commentator asked rhetorically that year,
"Everyone knows Alger—and yet, do they? To most people Alger is
just a name."[9]

The first biography of Alger, published in 1928, also serviced this
popular impression of Alger as a successful ideologue. The author
assigned the task of writing it for a commercial press, Herbert R.
Mayes, later director of the *Saturday Review* and editor of *Good
Housekeeping*, portrayed his subject as the victim of a tyrannical
father who forbade his son's marriage to a childhood sweetheart and
bullied him into the Unitarian ministry. As a result of his tragic adolescence, according to Mayes, Alger became neurotically obsessed
with success. That the work would not be recognized as potboiling
histrionics seems hardly possible today, yet not until 1972 did Mayes
finally admit publicly that his biography had been a hoax. "Not
merely was my Alger biography partly fictional, it was practically *all*
fictional," he wrote. "Unfortunately—how unfortunately!—the book
when it appeared was accepted pretty much as gospel. Why it was not
recognized for what it was supposed to be baffled the publisher and
me."[1] The best explanation for the uncritical acceptance of Mayes'
fictionalized biography is that its representation of Alger as a success-
worshipper was wholly compatible with the view of Alger popular
during the prosperous 1920s. "Nobody bothered to do any digging,"
as Mayes later observed,[2] because his work seemed to satisfy the need
for a usable past about Alger. Ironically, it is valuable as a source of
information, not about Alger's life, but about Alger's utility as a symbol of success. The desperate achievement of his heroes, according

---

7. Halsey Raines, "Horatio Alger Created 119 Synthetic Heroes," *New York Times Book Review*, 22 April 1928, p. 2.
8. "Frank A. Munsey as a Horatio Alger Hero," *Literary Digest*, 9 Jan. 1926, p. 48.
9. Milton Byron, "New Biography," *Outlook*, 11 April 1928, p. 598.
1. Herbert R. Mayes to William Henderson, 3 July 1972. Quoted by permission of the Horatio Alger Society. Excerpts of this letter appear in "A Few Words about Horatio Alger, Jr.," *Publishers' Weekly*, 23 April 1973, p. 33.
2. "Holy Horatio!" *Time*, 10 June 1974, p. 18.

to Mayes, was less a reward for faithful service and moral behavior than the psychological compensation of a writer who suffered with an inferiority complex and sought emotional catharsis in his fiction. "All of Horatio Alger's heroes started poor and ended up well-to-do. All of them were in search of money," Mayes wrote.[3] Thirty years later, students of Alger were still psychoanalytically interpreting his stories on the basis of the Mayes biography. For example, Kenneth S. Lynn claimed that by "Sublimating a lifetime which Alger himself judged to be ignominiously unheroic, he created the 'Alger hero,' and thereby became one of the great mythmakers of the modern world."[4] Obviously, Mayes's admission of hoax undermines this too-tidy interpretation; still, it is significant that the seed which produced this hybrid Alger was planted during the boom years of the 1920s.

During this decade, too, Alger's name and supposed authority as a popular proponent of business success began to be invoked by some *literati* whose adolescence had coincided with the heyday of Alger's popularity early in the century. In 1923, Thomas Wolfe, still a struggling young playwright in New York, complained that "I feel like Horatio Alger's boy hero: alone in the cit-ee—which has no pit-ee. . . . Unfortunately I have not the money-making penchant which all of Horatio's boy-heroes seemed to have."[5] Wolfe's identification with the Alger hero of economic myth acquires even greater significance in light of his allusions to Alger as a success ideologue in *Look Homeward, Angel* (1929). In that autobiographical novel, he described his hero reading "through all the infinite monotony of the Algers—*Pluck and Luck, Sink or Swim, Grit, Jack's Ward, Jed the Poor-House Boy*— and dozens more. He gloated over the fat money-making of these books . . . reckoning up the amount of income, if it were not given, or if it were, dividing the annual sum into monthly and weekly portions, and dreaming on its purchasing power. His desires were not modest—no fortune under $250,000 satisfied him."[6] Wolfe's reminiscence vividly illustrates how easily the message of the original Alger books could be misappropriated, for Alger's heroes rarely won a reward so large as this.

Alger's symbolic status among writers of the 1920s is most apparent in the works of F. Scott Fitzgerald, whose satires of the Alger stories popular in his childhood became a vehicle for his condemnation of the crass materialism rampant in his adulthood.[7] For example, in his little-known play *The Vegetable, or From President to Postman*

3. *Alger: A Biography Without a Hero* (New York: Macy-Masius; 1928), p. 220.
4. *The Dream of Success* (Boston: Little, Brown, 1955), p. 6.
5. Elizabeth Nowell, ed., *The Letters of Thomas Wolfe* (New York: Scribner's, 1956), p. 53.
6. *Look Homeward, Angel* (New York: Scribner's, 1929), p. 85.
7. Scharnhorst, "Scribbling Upward: Fitzgerald's Debt of Honor to Horatio Alger," *Fitzgerald/Hemingway Annual* (1978), 162–169.

(1922), the title of which burlesques such Alger titles as *From Canal Boy to President*, Fitzgerald parodied popular success literature in general and Alger's work in particular. The protagonist is an ironic Alger hero whose father, a doddering old fool named Horatio, is a caricature of Alger himself. Fitzgerald's failure with this play was one of execution, not intention, for on it he discovered the rich parodic vein profitably mined earlier by Crane and later by Nathanael West. Notably in *The Great Gatsby*(1925), he again paid curled-lip service to the popular image of success by satirizing Alger. While it has become a critical commonplace to observe that this novel "is a contemporary variation of an old American success pattern, the rags-to-riches story exalted by American legend,"[8] the extent to which Fitzgerald assimilated Alger specifically in it has not been fully appreciated. Rather than "an inverted Horatio Alger novel,"[9] it may be more acccurately described as a sequel to an ironic Alger fable. Indeed, Fitzgerald probably parodied Alger's *Jed the Poor-House Boy* in chapter VI, in which he treated Gatsby's adolescent apprenticeship to a patron named Dan Cody. Like Alger's hero Jed Gilman, young James Gatz (who shares his initials) meets his patron aboard a luxurious yacht and is given a job and a new suit of clothes. Moreover, in both novels the hero changes his name "at the specific moment that witnessed the beginning of his career."[1] However, whereas Jed's patron is a neat and mannerly young gentleman, Dan Cody is a "pioneer debauchee." Whereas at the end of Alger's story the hero moves into his ancestral mansion and lives happily-ever-after on an annual bequest of $25,000, Gatsby is cheated of his $25,000 legacy and must survive by his wits. Fitzgerald's story is, in effect, a sequel to that ironic version of Alger. For yet another satire of Alger, his story "Forging Ahead" (1929), originally published in the *Saturday Evening Post*, Fitzgerald borrowed the title of an Alger novel about the rise of a poor but virtuous sixteen-year-old hero who is designated the heir of a rich uncle and thereby wins his way to Yale College. In Fitzgerald's parody, sixteen-year-old Basil Lee's plan to attend Yale is threatened when his family suffers financial reverses. Rather than abandoning his dream, Basil resolves to work his way through school and immediately begins to read "half a dozen dusty volumes of Horatio Alger, unopened for years."[2] Through a friend he eventually finds employ-

8. Edwin Fussell, "Fitzgerald's Brave New World," *ELH*, 19 (Dec. 1952), rpt. in Arthur Mizener, ed., *F. Scott Fitzgerald: A Collection of Critical Essays*, Twentieth Century Views (Englewood Cliffs: Prentice-Hall, 1963), p. 48.
9. Richard Lehan, "The Nowhere Hero," in David Madden, ed., *American Dreams, American Nightmares* (Carbondale and Edwardsville: Southern Illinois University Press, 1970), p. 110.
1. *The Great Gatsby* (New York: Scribner's, 1953), p. 98.
2. Jackson R. Bryer and John Kuehl, eds., *The Basil and Josephine Stories*, by F. Scott Fitzgerald (New York: Scribner's, 1973), pp. 145–164.

ment in the shops of the Great Northern Railroad but learns his first morning there that, alas, life does not imitate Horatio Alger novels: "The president's little daughter had not come by, dragged by a runaway horse; not even a superintendent had walked through the yard and singled him out with an approving eye."[3] Instead, he is reprimanded for loafing and soon fired. As a last resort, he visits a cantankerous great-undle who has feuded with the rest of the family for twenty years and is hired as an escort for his square-chinned cousin, but he soon loses even this sinecure. Despite his ill-success at holding a job, Basil triumphs at the end of the story when his mother sells family property for four hundred thousand dollars—a plot machination reminiscent of Alger. In all, these satires of the economic myth associated with Alger are another indication that by the 1920s he had acquired symbolic status.

IV

Alger ultimately was transformed from an economic mythmaker, a reputation he acquired during the prosperous 1920s, into a patriotic defender of the social and political *status quo* and erstwhile proponent of *laissez-faire* capitalism. During the Great Depression of the 1930s and the world war that followed, Alger's name became a shibboleth used to identify Americans who affirmed traditional verities and values. The characteristics which had come to be associated with the Alger hero—the potential greatness of the common man, rugged individualism, economic triumph in a fabled land of opportunity—seemingly summarized the American way of life threatened by the Depression and preserved by the war. Significantly, whereas Samuel Eliot Morison and Henry Steele Commager, in the original edition of *The Growth of the American Republic*, published in 1930, did not mention Alger at all, in the second and third editions of this standard history text, published in 1937 and 1942, they asserted that Alger probably had exerted greater influence on the American character than any other writer except perhaps Mark Twain.[4] Moreover, the *Reader's Guide to Periodical Literature*, an index of articles published in popular magazines since 1892, finally catalogued its first article about Alger in 1932, the centenary of his birth—a telling symptom of his enshrinement as a culture hero after his sales popularity had waned. As one writer observed in the *New York Times* that year, "It is difficult for an adult to appraise the Alger books unless he has read them during his boyhood. If this is the case he is likely to be lost in a

---

3. *Ibid.*
4. *The Growth of the American Republic*, 2nd and 3rd eds. (New York: Oxford University Press, 1937 and 1942), pp. 287–288.

glamour of pleasant memories."[5] Read or selectively remembered during the Depression and the war, the novels seemed to be neither moral tracts nor simple success stories, but popular political propaganda. As the national economy collapsed, Alger's presumed celebration of the merits of free enterprise won popular acclaim. In 1932, on the hundredth anniversary of his birth, both the *New York Times* and the *Herald Tribune* editorially praised him for propagating a philosophy of self-help.[6] In 1934, a writer for the *Christian Science Monitor* assured his readers that despite hard times "the Alger pattern still persists."[7] A popular biography of Frank Munsey published in 1935 celebrated that publishing entrepreneur as "an Alger hero."[8] Over the next few years, Alger enjoyed a steady crescendo of popular praise. In 1938, Frederick Lewis Allen repeated the by-then common opinion that Alger had "had a far-reaching influence upon the economic and social thought of America" and had helped "to determine the trend and tradition of American business life."[9] In 1939, on the fortieth anniversary of his death, Alger was eulogized in the *New York Times Magazine*: "His imprint on American life is still clear after forty years; the papers almost every week report the success of some typical Alger hero' of the present."[1] The following year, Street and Smith published a comic-book version of Alger's *Mark the Match Boy* and NBC radio broadcast a dramatization of his *From Farm Boy to Senator*. During this program, the governor of New York, Herbert Lehman, declared that as a boy he had been an Alger fan and that "I was particularly interested because he showed in his books that the United States was a country of great opportunity for all and he was always a steadfast advocate of the democratic principles on which our nation was created and which have made it great." Rather than despair during the Depression, Lehman adjured his listeners to affirm that, as in Alger's time, "Broad and unrestricted opportunities for success exist for those who have the vision, the equipment, the industry and the courage to seize them."[2] A week later, the *New York Times* editorially commended Lehman for "rallying to the defense of Horatio Alger, and confessing without shame that he was 'an Alger fan when a boy.' It was Alger's comforting thesis that virtue and industry are always rewarded. . . . Hard times come and go, but America is not going to

5. David Ferris Kirby, "The Author of the Alger Books for Boys," *New York Times Magazine*, 10 Jan. 1932, p. 5.
6. "The Newsboys' Hero," *New York Times*, 13 Jan. 1932, p. 22, col. 4.
7. Rugg, p. 7, col. 2.
8. George Britt, *Forty Years—Forty Millions* (New York: Farrar & Rinehart, 1935), pp. 56 and *passim*.
9. "Horatio Alger, Jr.," *Saturday Review of Literature*, 17 Sept. 1938, pp. 3, 17. This article was reprinted in *Reader's Digest*.
1. L.H. Robbin, "Alger: No Alger Hero," *New York Times Magazine*, 16 July 1939, p. 11.
2. "Lehman Speaks as Old Alger Fan in Acclaiming Our Opportunities," *New York Times*, 30 Mar. 1940, p. 9, col. 2.

shut up shop. We expect the country to prosper."[3] Symbolically,
Lehman had prescribed Alger as a home-remedy for the economic ills
afflicting the nation, reassuring a patient with a strong constitution
of her eventual complete recovery.

With the advent of world war, Alger's symbolic importance was
enhanced. Hardly a month after the bombing of Pearl Harbor, Alger's
birthday was celebrated by the Children's Aid Society of New York—
an annual event by this time, after the date had been ignored for
decades—and the ceremony was reported and editorially praised in
the *New York Times*.[4] In the popular motion picture *Yankee Doodle
Dandy* (1942), a wartime biography of the patriotic playwright
George M. Cohan, the protagonist describes his life to President
Franklin Roosevelt as a Horatio Alger story.[5] In 1943, the *Atlantic
Monthly*, a magazine which had not even reviewed an Alger book during the author's life, featured an article about Alger's contemporary
influence entitled "They Made Me What I Am Today." Its author suggested that because "the generation that grew up . . . before the last
war" had, as boys, been inspired by Alger, their "faith in *laissez-faire*,
in the best of all possible worlds, in the inevitability of rags to riches"
served the nation well in the prosecution of the new war.[6] In 1944,
Stewart Holbrook discussed Alger's influence in still more grandiose
terms:

> With "Ragged Dick" Alger founded a new school of American lit-
> erature, the Work and Win, Upward and Onward story; and no
> matter that today he is unread, Alger was a man of destiny. At
> exactly the right moment he put into simple words and a stan-
> dard plot the hopes and beliefs of a nation, and by the sheer
> power of reiteration caused them to congeal into a national char-
> acter, the Horatio Alger hero. . . . For the next half century and
> more nearly everyone in the U.S. believed that every bootblack
> was a potential capitalist with plug hat and gold-headed cane.[7]

As a wartime patriotic gesture in 1945, a publisher reissued four
Alger novels that had been out-of-print for a generation.[8] Copies of
this volume still were available for purchase in 1970, however, so it
would seem that Alger's books were hardly more popular in-than out-
of-print. Still, the impression that Alger was enjoying a revival and that
his novels remained influential was indelible. Among the periodicals

3. "An Alger Fan," *New York Times*, 6 April 1940, p. 16, col. 3.
4. "Alger's Birthday Marked," *New York Times*, 14 Jan. 1942, p. 12, col. 4.
5. *Yankee Doodle Dandy*, with James Cagney, Warner Bros., 1942.
6. Newman Levy, "They Made Me What I Am Today," *Atlantic Monthly*, 172 (Nov. 1943), 117.
7. "Horatio Alger, Jr., and Ragged Dick," *New York Times Book Review*, 2 July 1944, p. 9.
8. *Struggling Upward and Other Works* (New York: Bonanza Books, 1945). The other works were *Ragged Dick, Phil the Fiddler,* and *Jed the Poor-House Boy.*

which reviewed the omnibus favorably were the *New Yorker, Time,* the *New York Times, Commonweal, New Republic,* and *Saturday Review;* and the title of the review written by William Rose Benet for the latter magazine, "A Monument to Free Enterprise," suggests the slant adopted by all.

After the war, as the rest of the country demobilized, Alger retained his appointive political office. In 1947, the *New York Times* again praised him on its editorial pages, contending that only disillusioned historians "who wrote, or may still be writing, in strong disapproval of America as a whole" dared to criticize Alger and his legendary success story,[9] and *Advertising Age* called for a new Alger to inspire contemporary American youth with the self-reliance of their father's and to counteract "government interference" in business.[1] Meanwhile, Holbrook suggested that the original Alger had "put free and untramelled competition on the side of the angels. . . . Though the 1870s and the eighties and nineties saw dismal and widespread poverty in the United States, and though anarchists and socialists fomented strikes and riots, the Red Dawn never came up over the horizon. Too many Americans held the vision of Upward and Onward."[2] No longer perceived as merely moral fables, Alger's novels seemed more like tools of social control wielded by an entrenched ruling class. Basking in popular esteem like a decorated war hero, he lent his name and reputation to the Horatio Alger Awards, a merchandising vehicle for political and economic orthodoxy also inaugurated in 1947. Sponsored by the American Schools and Colleges Association, Inc., which had become "concerned about the trend among young people towards the mind-poisoning belief that equal opportunity was a thing of the past," the Alger Awards Committee decided to select annually "living individuals who by their own efforts had pulled themselves up by their bootstraps in the American tradition."[3] Past winners include Dwight Eisenhower, Ronald Reagan, Billy Graham, W. Clement Stone, and Ray Kroc. Clearly, during this final phase of Alger's transformation into a maker of American myth his books were no longer considered as simple literary documents, but were evaluated according to the social and political ends they seemed to serve. Alger was viewed in a new light which distorted his original moral intention.

Richard Wright, the American novelist, shared this popular perspective, on Alger for, in 1945, soon after leaving the Communist

---

9. "Topics of the Times," *New York Times,* 16 Jan. 1947, p. 24, col. 4.
1. John G. Cawelti, *Apostles of the Self-Made Man* (Chicago and London: University of Chicago Press, 1965), p. 102.
2. *Lost Men of American History* (New York: Macmillan, 1946), pp. 228, 238.
3. *Opportunity Still Knocks,* Jubilee ed. (New York: Horatio Alger Awards Committee, 1971), p. 3.

Party, he argued in print that the juvenile writer had been "perhaps American capitalism's greatest and most effective propagandist."[4] Still, the most notorious invocation of Alger as a capitalist myth-maker in the literature of this period appeared in Nathanael West's caustic parody, *A Cool Million* (1934). Shortly before his death in 1940, West would write in an unproduced screenplay of *A Cool Million* that "Only fools laugh at Horatio Alger, and his poor boys who make good. The wise man who thinks twice about that sterling author will realize that Alger is to America what Homer was to the Greeks."[5] In his novel, he turned this American Homer on his head and satirized the facile optimism of Americans in their collective epic-dream. His absurd hero, Lemuel Pitkin, who is exploited throughout the work by an ironic patron, ex-President Nathan "Shagpoke" Whipple, loses his money, teeth, right eye, left thumb, a leg, his scalp, and finally his life in a *tour de force* of misadventures. In the grotesque *tableau* that ends the novel, Whipple eulogizes the martyred all-American boy and inaugurates the fascist millennium. Unfortunately, the novel has been generally unappreciated or disregarded since its publication. Its style has been the special object of condemnation. Ironically, however, the complaint that its prose "is as flat as the Alger series itself"[6] may underscore the extent to which West succeeded in mocking the writer he considered a type of American Homer, "the Bulfinch of American fable and the Marx of the American Revolution."[7] Selecting a style designed to serve his thematic purpose, West constructed his work from altered and rearranged fragments of at least six Alger books. In all, over a fifth of his finished novel is vintage Alger only slightly revised.[8] Whereas Alger had written in *Tom Temple's Career*, for example, "Tom beheld a stout young fellow, about two years older than himself, with a face in which the animal seemed to predominate," West wrote, "Lem beheld a stout fellow about three years older than himself, with a face in which the animal seemed to predominate."[9] This systematic plagiarism went unrecognized until recently because, much as Mayes had assimilated the popular image of Alger as a success-worshipper in his biography, West assimilated

---

4. "Alger Revisited, or My Stars! Did We Read That Stuff?" *PM*, 16 Sept. 1945, magazine section, p. 13.
5. Quoted in Jay Martin, *Nathanael West: The Art of His Life* (New York: Farrar, Straus and Giroux, 1970), p. 219.
6. David G. Galloway, "A Picaresque Apprenticeship: Nathanael West's *The Dream Life of Balso Snell* and *A Cool Million*," in Jay Martin, ed., *Nathanael West: A Collection of Critical Essays*, Twentieth Century Views (Englewood Cliffs: Prentice-Hall, 1971), p. 47.
7. Quoted in Martin, *Nathanael West: The Art of His Life*, p. 218.
8. For a more detailed description of West's plagiarisms, see Douglas Shepard, "Nathanael West Rewrites Horatio Alger, Jr.," *Satire Newsletter*, 3 (Fall 1965), 13–28; and Scharnhorst; "Good Fortune in America" (Ph D. diss., Purdue University, 1978), app. D.
9. *Tom Temple's Career* (Racine: Whitman, n.d.), pp. 50–52; *A Cool Million* (New York: Avon, 1973), pp. 15–17.

the image of Alger as a political ideologue in his parody. Significantly, however, West invented all polemical passages that appear in his novel, for he found no political manifesto in the actual Alger stories from which he copied. He had to reinvent Alger to serve his literary purpose and to appeal to the readers of his generation.

Recent invocations of the Alger myth, as in the annual ceremonies of the Alger Awards Committee, Garry Wills's *Nixon Agonistes* (1970), and John Seelye's novel *Dirty Tricks, or Nick Noxin's Natural Nobility* (1974), indicate that Alger's reputation crystallized with his institutionalization in 1947 and that his utility as a political symbol has remained essentially unchanged since the Depression. Each succeeding generation between the Civil War and World War II, however, discovered its own usable past in Alger by reinventing him according to the spirit and values of the particular moment. The transformations which his reputation underwent—from didactic writer for boys, to Progressive moralist, economic mythmaker, and finally political ideologue—seem to have been dictated less by the content of his books than by the cultural context in which the books were read or remembered. Unlike other juvenile writers, Alger's thematic concerns were peculiarly adaptable to popular contemporary concerns long after his death. An economic and political symbol of success today more by accident of birth than by deliberate design, "it was not until 1947 that anyone got around to exploiting him into an organized symbol."[1] More than ever, Alger had become, with the features of his mutation complete, the victim of mistaken identity.

In his juvenile novels, to be sure, Alger influenced a generation of young readers early in this century. As one familiar only with his modern reputation as an apologist for industrial capitalism might expect, many of these readers, such as Benjamin Fairless of U.S. Steel and James A. Farley of Coca Cola,[2] became real-life counterparts to the mythic Alger heroes. But to consider Alger simply as an apologist for business is to distort grossly his basic humanitarian impulse. As one familiar only with his modern reputation might *not* expect, many well-known American writers on the political left, including not only Dreiser and Wright, but Jack London and Upton Sinclair,[3] read Alger's books as youngsters and were not stirred to embrace capitalism as adults. As John Cawelti has concluded, "Judging from the prominence of his themes, there is as much evidence that Alger was an important influence on future reformers as a popular model for

1. Richard Huber, *The American Idea of Success* (New York: McGraw-Hill, 1971), p. 43.
2. *Opportunity Still Knocks, passim.*
3. Jack London, *John Barleycorn* (New York: Century, 1913), p. 133; Upton Sinclair, *Autobiography* (New York: Harcourt, Brace, 1962), p. 9.

incipient robber barons."[4] Alger himself hardly could have imagined that he would be so long remembered, much less celebrated as an American mythologizer of success a half-century after his death. As he wrote to a friend in 1897, "If I could come back 50 years from now probably I should feel bewildered in reading the New York *Tribune* of 1947."[5] He wrote this with a soothsayer's foresight, for one of the items in the news that year which undoubtedly would have perplexed him beyond his wildest flights of fancy publicized the inauguration of the annual Horatio Alger Awards. After fifty years, Alger could not have recognized his progeny.

4. Cawelti, *Apostles of the Self-Made Man*, p. 117.
5. Alger to Irving Blake, 12 May 1897. Quoted by permission of the Henry E. Huntington Library.

Critical Essays

MARY ROTH WALSH

Selling the Self-Made Woman†

Chroniclers of the American dream of success have limited their investigations to changing interpretations of male opportunities for social mobility. Whether or not "self-made women" harbored any such dreams seems to have been of little interest to historians. While they may differ in emphasis or interpretation, historians appear to agree on at least one point: success is clearly a male prerogative.[1]

Richard Huber, author of *The American Idea of Success,* and the only writer to even acknowledge the existence of female achievement, dismisses it in a single paragraph in which he notes: "The cultural definition of success was the same for a woman as a man in American society if the woman competed with the man in a world of work."[2]

Huber, in fact, is mistaken; definitions of male and female success have differed markedly in the past and continue to do so even today. For women, success in business or the professions has traditionally meant failure as a woman.

It is little wonder that in 1964 when Matina Horner administered a projective test measuring attitudes toward achievement among male and female college students, the women's responses revealed a high degree of fear of success. While the male stories were filled with traditional Horatio Alger images of accomplishment, the female responses revealed an anxious awareness that femininity and individual achievement are desirable, but mutually exclusive goals.[3]

† From *Journal of American Culture* 2 (Spring 1979): 52–60. Copyright © 1979 Blackwell Publishing. Reprinted with permission from Blackwell Publishing

1. Rex Burns, *Success in America* (Amherst, Mass.: Univ. of Mass. Press, 1976); John Cawelti, *Apostles of the Self-Made Man* (Chicago: Univ. of Chicago Press, 1965); Lawrence Chenoweth, *The American Dream of Success* (N. Scituate, Mass.: Duxbury Press, 1974).
2. Richard Huber, *The American Idea of Success* (New York: McGraw Hill Book Co., 1971), pp. 5, 9.
3. Matina Horner and Mary Roth Walsh, "Psychological Barriers to Success in Women," in Ruth Kundsin, *Women and Success* (New York: William Morrow & Co., Inc., 1974), pp. 138–44. There is a voluminous psychological literature extending Horner's original

Other studies have demonstrated that the females' fear of being censured for their success is well founded. Identical credentials or professional products are evaluated lower when a woman's name, rather than a man's, is attached to them.[4] Male subjects have also been shown to react negatively to female success, just as some women fear. In an extension of the classic thematic apperception test used to collect data on this, men were provided with a description of a successful female medical student and were asked to write a story. The typical response explained away the student's success as compensation for her social inadequacy and usually concluded with a description of some physical catastrophe that ended her career or her life.[5]

Although psychologists and sociologists have devoted a great deal of attention to the contemporary issues surrounding female achievement, little effort has been made to gain an understanding of the socio-historical forces that have shaped our definitions of success for women.

It is first necessary to define what is meant by success. Success in America has traditionally meant making money and translating it into status, or becoming famous. Richard Huber has pointed out that success "was not earned by being a loyal friend or good husband."[6] He could have added that neither was it earned by being a loyal mother or good wife. Success was the reward for performance in the public world of work.

How women were excluded from or relegated to the periphery of that world is a story that is an integral part of American social history. This article focuses on the years between 1880 and 1920 because I believe this period was a crucial one in the history of women's efforts to expand their opportunities for achievement.

The rates of expansion of the work force during the 1880s and the first decade of the twentieth century have never been surpassed in any census interval. The huge demand for labor drew an increasing percentage of women into the labor force. Thus, between 1880 and

---

hypotheses and summarizing the numerous empirical studies which have been done to replicate her work. See David Ward Tresemer, *Fear of Success* (New York: Plenum Press, 1977); Donnah Canavan-Gumpert, Katherine Garner, Peter Gumpert, *The Success-Fearing Personality*, (Lexington, Mass: D.C. Heath and Company, Lexington Books, 1978); Leon Tec, M.D., *The Fear of Success* (New York: Reader's Digest Press, 1976); Janet T. Spence and Robert L. Helmreich, *Masculinity & Feminity: Their Psychological Dimensions, Correlates and Antecedents* (Austin, Tex.: Univ. of Texas Press, 1978).

4. P. Goldberg, "Are Some Women Prejudiced Against Women?" *Trans-Action*, 1968, 5 (5), 28–30. The debate on this continues. See Michael Moore, "Discrimination or Favoritism: Sex Bias in Book Reviews," *American Psychologist* (Oct., 1978) 33 (10), pp. 936–38.

5. L. Monahan, D. Kuhn, P. Shaver, "Intrapsychic versus Cultural Explanations of the 'Fear of Success' motive." *Journal of Personality and Social Psychology*, 1974, pp. 29, 60–64; and N.T. Feather and Alfred C. Raphelson, "Fear of Success in Australian and American Student Groups: Motive or Sex-Role Stereotype?" *Journal of Personality*, 1974, pp. 42, 190–201.

6. Huber, 1.

1910 the proportion of working women increased from 14.7% to 24.8%.[7]

During these years, a growing number of women advocated their right to pursue a career on an equal footing with men. Although their hopes were eventually dashed, women did experience significant progress in the latter part of the nineteenth century. So much so, that they touched off a male backlash in the years before World War I.

One measure of women's growing interest in success was the proliferation of books on this topic between the 1880s and 1910. One has only to look at Frances E. Willard's book, *Occupations for Women*, published in 1897 to understand why she wrote it. Emblazoned on the cover is a banner with the word "SUCCESS" boldly printed on it. The point is further reinforced by the notation that the book had been published by The Success Company of Cooper Union, New York. Other books dealing with the same subject included Sara Bolton's *Successful Women* (1888); M. L. Rayne's *What Can a Woman Do: Or Her Position in the Business and Literary World* (1893); and Florence Wenderoth Saunders' *Letters to a Business Girl* (1908).

The female success writers were motivated by the belief, as Frances Willard put it, that "nowadays a girl may be anything from a college president to a seamstress." All of these authors were as eager as their male counterparts to celebrate the glories of work. Juliet Wilbor Tompkins writing in *Success* magazine informed her readers that participation in the workforce would put them "in company with the universal law, which says, 'Produce! Create!' "[8]

Their objective was to convince women that they too could experience success. Two steps seemed necessary to guarantee the realization of their goal: career training for women and the restructuring of marriage so that women could play an equal role in supporting the family.

As Tompkins put it, "The only hope is to catch girls young enough and begin practical training for a career in school and college days, so that such preparation becomes the matter of course to them that it does to a boy."[9] Equally important was the necessity to avoid the temptation to become dependent on one's marriage partner. Juliet Tompkins cited the example of two women who had entered the antique business; one who became a rich woman and one who failed. "The significant difference between them," wrote Tompkins, "is that

7. W. Elliot and Mary M. Brownlee, *Women in the American Economy* (New Haven: Yale Univ. Press, 1976). p. 23.
8. Juliet Wilbor Tompkins, "Five Million Women New Workers," *Success* (March, 1906), p. 158.
9. Ibid., pp. 158, 201.

the one who failed was married. That is, she could fail; there was someone for her to go home to and rest on."[1]

Quite clearly, these authors viewed marriage in less roseate terms than women of a previous generation. When Annie Nathan Meyer was asked why she had omitted a chapter on women in marriage from her book on women's work, she responded dryly: "my answer was that so far as I knew women had never been denied that privilege, and so it could have no legitimate place in my book."[2]

Advocates of female achievement had undertaken a monumental task: the reversal of the Victorian definition of what constituted a woman's work. Horatio Alger's stories represent a popular view of mobility during this period. His contrasting pictures of heroes and heroines clearly demonstrated the sex role divisions of the day. The young heroes of his stories are usually rewarded with a step up the career ladder and money for some action which crowns a period of hard work and some luck. Alger's heroines, however, live a much more circumscribed life.

One of Alger's first books, and one of his few that feature a female protagonist, is *Helen Ford,* published in 1866, two years before his initial success, *Ragged Dick.*

Helen lives in a boarding house in New York with her father who had been cheated out of his inheritance. Forced to work to support the two of them (her father is a dreamer who is trying to invent a flying machine), Helen secures a position as a singer in a theater. Although she is clearly on the road to fame and fortune, Helen gives up her career when her father's wealth is restored.

A further contrast to the typical Alger hero is Helen's disinterest in money. Ragged Dick's eyes sparkle, Luke Walton's face flushes when they first learn of their own good fortune—reactions with which the reader could readily identify. Helen's reaction, however, differs sharply as revealed in her response to the question of how much money her father had inherited. "'It will be a few hundred thousand dollars,' said Helen in a monotone. There was not the least trace of exultation in her tone."[3] At this point one almost hopes that her father will adopt an appropriately appreciative Mark the Matchboy or Phil the Fiddler who could exult in their new found fortune.

At first glance, Alger's second experiment with a story featuring a young girl appeared to offer a more promising type of heroine. Tattered Tom seems to be a typical, Alger street arab, and as it develops, something of a prototype of the assertive woman. Consequently, when asked by a stranger who is uncertain about her sex, she

1. Ibid., p. 158.
2. Annie Nathan Meyer, ed., *Woman's Work in America* (Henry Holt & Co., 1891), p. iii.
3. Horatio Alger, *Helen Ford* (Boston: Loring, Publisher, 1866), pp. 72, 286, 287.

responds, "I'm a girl, but I wish I was a boy. . . . Cause boys are stronger than girls and can fight better." Nevertheless, gender doesn't appear to be too much of a handicap for Tom. At one point, she threatens to punch a girl's head in, and, in fact, does defeat a boy who is the schoolyard bully.[4]

There is further hope for Tom when we learn that she has what it usually takes for other Alger heroes to become successes. As her patron notes, "What a self-reliant spirit the little chit has. . . . I've known plenty of young men, who had less faith in their ability to cope with the world, and gain a livelihood, than she."[5]

Nevertheless, despite Tom's self-reliance, she is, in fact, much more a passive heroine than the initiator of her own success, as is usually the case in other Alger books.

When her true identity is revealed at the end of the novel, Tom is transformed into the wealthy Jane Lindsay and is reunited with her mother. In the final scene, Jane, although now properly attired in a dress, still displays a lingering trace of independence "produced by the strange life she had led as a street arab." But, Alger added, "No doubt, her new life would soften and refine her manners, and make her more like girls of her own age."[6] Meaning, we assume, that last trace of independence would soon be erased.

Nonetheless, Tattered Tom, of all Alger's female characters, comes closest to escaping her sexual destiny. Other young women, such as Florence Linden in *Adrift in New York,* must wait for some young man—Tom Dodger in this case—to rescue them. The title is, in fact, somewhat imprecise since only Florence is adrift; Tom ably swims against the tides of adversity to restore her to her rightful place in society.

To Alger, there appeared to be no attractive alternatives for women other than a life of secure dependency. Women in his book usually fall into four categories: wealthy women who are either mean-spirited or who have had their only child abducted; widowed mothers who can only be saved by hardworking sons; poorer women who take in boarders or sell apples; and younger women who either work in sweatshops, or who must wait for a young man to restore their fortune.

The character of Florence Linden in *Adrift in New York* combines the latter two roles. Forced to work she sews vests and "grew pale and thin, and her face was habitually sad." Faced with such a future, it is little wonder that she is ecstatic when Tom reappears at the end of

---

4. Horatio Alger, *Tattered Tom* (Phila.: The John C. Winston Co., 1871), pp. 16–17.
5. Ibid., p. 85.
6. Ibid., p. 273.

the book. "I've come back to restore you to your rights," says Tom, "I've struck luck, Florence, and you're going to share it."[7]

But there were more and more women who were becoming increasingly reluctant to wait to share the fruits of someone else's work. As Juliet Wilbor Tompkins pointed out in 1906, "Thirty years ago Harriet Martineau, while visiting America, declared that she found here but seven occupations for women. . . . Now there are scarcely seven occupations closed to them." While Tompkins was overly sanguine, the 1900 census revealed a surprising number of women in male dominated occupations. The figures included 7,387 doctors and surgeons, 1,010 lawyers, 807 dentists, 1,041 architects, 293 bankers and brokers, and 2,193 journalists.[8]

One of the subjects that attracted the attention of a number of writers in the late nineteenth century was the emerging female physician. As the census figures demonstrate, the last quarter of the century witnessed a major breakthrough for women in medicine. This period stands as a "golden age" in the history of American medical women. For example, women accounted for a higher percentage of physicans in many cities at the turn of the century than they do today.[9]

Thus, it is no coincidence that during the 1880s, the woman doctor as heroine made her debut in American popular fiction. At least three novels featured women physicians during the decade: William Dean Howells' *Doctor Breen's Practice* (1882); Elizabeth Stuart Phelps' *Doctor Zay* (1882); and Sarah Orne Jewett's *A Country Doctor* (1884).

Reflecting an era that still viewed with suspicion any female achievement outside the home, all three dealt with the question: were women capable of practicing medicine? Howells' novel, true to the temper of the times, testified to his conviction that they they were not. As a matter of fact, in his story, Dr. Breen is as much in need of help as she is capable of offering it.

Sarah Orne Jewett's *A Country Doctor* presents a more favorable view of a woman physician. The heroine of the story, Nan Prince, flaunts tradition and enters medical school. While on a break from her studies, she visits her aunt's home where she meets George Gerry, a young lawyer, who becomes her constant companion during her holiday.

Unlike Howells' Dr. Breen, Prince is the embodiment of self-confidence. For example, one day while she and George are out walking, they are asked to go for help for a man who had been hurt.

---

7. Horatio Alger, *Adrift in New York* (New York: A.L. Burt Co., 1904), pp. 243, 246.
8. Tompkins, p. 156.
9. Mary Roth Walsh, *Doctors Wanted No Women Need Apply* (New Haven: Yale Univ. Press, 1977).

Prince, however, examines the man, and then to George's astonishment, calmly removes her boot, "planted her foot on the damaged shoulder and caught up the hand and gave it a quick pull. . . . There was an unpleasant cluck as the bone went back into its socket."[1]

And as quickly as the victim's pain was ended, George's began. George had been nurturing the hope that Nan would eventually give up her foolish notion of becoming a doctor and settle down as the wife of a small town lawyer. Nan's quick action becomes all the more disconcerting to George because "all his manliness was at stake, and his natural rights would be degraded and lost, if he could not show his power to be greater than her own."[2]

Nevertheless, George does propose. Nan's thoughts as she muses over his offer strike a remarkably familiar note for the modern reader. Contemplating a future as Mrs. George Gerry, she reflects, "I can look forward and see something a thousand times better than being his wife and keeping his house and trying to forget all that nature fitted me to do." In the last scene, Nan, having successfully escaped a life sentence in Gerry's prison, stands alone "and suddenly she reached her hands upward in an ecstasy of life and strength and gladness. 'O God,' she said, 'I thank thee for my future'."[3]

It is not until Elizabeth Stuart Phelps' Dr. Zay that we arrive at the nineteenth-century feminist ideal of the successful achiever. Zay is, in fact, something of a nineteenth-century wonder woman. The novel focuses on her relationship with a male patient, a wealthy young man named Waldo Yorke. Yorke is an attractive and charming playboy who seems to spend most of his time attending Boston's society dances and parties.

He is presented in the novel as weak and sickly. His recovery from an accident is slow, leaving him weak and tired. The result is a complete role reversal with a dominant woman treating a male patient who is suffering from a common female malady in the nineteenth century, "nervous strain." Compared to Waldo's exhausted state, Dr. Zay is in splendid health, relying on "her own physical strength, as another woman might lean upon a man's."[4] Waldo is a replica of the helpless, clinging female so popular in nineteenth-century literature. When Dr. Zay must leave to attend her other patients, Waldo is described as receiving a slowly-lessening strength from the doctor's departing figure. . . ." He feels slighted by her inattention and interprets her departure as a "cruel thing that she should not permit him to see her for twenty-four hours more."[5]

---

1. Sarah Orne Jewett, A Country Doctor (Boston, 1884), p. 265.
2. Ibid., p. 295.
3. Ibid., pp. 317, 351.
4. Elizabeth Stuart Phelps, Doctor Zay (Boston, 1882), p. 111.
5. Ibid., p. 99.

Eventually he recovers his strength sufficiently to accompany her on a visit to a patient, a young unmarried woman who is pregnant. After Dr. Zay has completed her house call and has returned to the carriage, they hear a call from a nearby stream. Zay's leadership skill is immediately apparent. She delegates Waldo to be the messenger who obtains help. The stress of the situation is too much for Waldo, however, and he faints (just like a woman). Meanwhile, Dr. Zay runs to the stream to pull out the drowning man.

When Waldo comes to, Zay is laboring to resuscitate the man whom onlookers have given up as dead. "Give him up, doctor," they yell. "Give him up? No!" she asserts with vigor. Watching Zay's strength and dominance, "Yorke quivered with the pride he felt in her."[6]

Finally she revives the victim, who, it turns out, is the unwed father. Zay loses no time. She reminds him that he owes his life to her and has a moral obligation to the pregnant woman. "Do you suppose you were worth touching," she asks, "except that you had it in your miserable power to right a poor wronged girl? Come! Do you?" A marriage ceremony takes place despite the fact that there is no license. Zay overrides all objections, pronounces the marriage legal, and promises to pay any fines. A "greatly exhausted" Waldo is sent home to bed by Zay, who then goes off on her afternoon rounds.[7]

The role reversal is completed with the realization that Zay has the power to save Waldo, but he has nothing to offer her except love and devotion. Moreover, like a nineteenth-century woman, he suffers from the debilitating psychological effects of enforced passivity. As Phelps notes, "The terrible leisure of invalidism gaped, a gulf—if he could have risen like a man, and bridged it, or like a hero, and leaped into it, she would never, he said to himself doggedly, have the exquisite advantage over him. He lay there like a woman, reduced from activity to endurance, from resolve to patience."[8]

Unfortunately medical women would have needed several Dr. Zay's to withstand the pressures they experienced in the early twentieth century. As I have demonstrated elsewhere, progress for women physicians was short-lived. By 1910, medical schools had established a quota system sharply limiting the number of female admissions.[9]

Similarly the growing success of women at the undergraduate level touched off a corresponding attempt at retrenchment. During the last quarter of the nineteenth century women were entering hitherto male colleges in increasing numbers. By 1900 there were more

6. Ibid., pp. 137–43.
7. Ibid., pp. 144–49.
8. Ibid., pp. 119.
9. Walsh, Ch. 6.

women enrolled in coeducational schools than in separate women's colleges. Moreover, the number of women attending coeducational institutions was expanding twice as fast as male enrollment.[1]

Even more threatening was the fact that despite earlier predictions that women were incapable of complex thinking, they were walking off with a disproportionate share of honors. College presidents and other educational leaders quickly became alarmed over the possibility that women would drive men out of the classroom. Even if men were able to hang on, it was argued, they would be demasculinized, and experience as Theodore Roosevelt put it, a "general softening of fiber."[2]

Professor Armstrong in the 1905 *Commissioners of Education Report* summed up the fear of many men over the fruits of creeping feminization: "The boy in America is not being brought up to punch in another's head, or to stand having his own punched in a healthy and proper manner; there is a strange and indefinable feminine air coming over the men; a tendency toward a common, if I may so call it, sexless tone of thought."[3]

The result of these fears was an all-out campaign in the early years of the twentieth century to stem the female invasion of higher education. The battle was not limited to one geographical area. Among others Stanford and the University of Washington on the west coast, the universities of Chicago, Wisconsin, Kansas and Western Reserve College in the midwest, and the University of Rochester, Tufts and Wesleyan in the east, all sought in one way or another to put an end to their rising female enrollments.

Some schools established quotas while others simply refused to accept any more women. A number of colleges, unwilling to risk a frontal attack, decided to segregate their female students, either by enrolling them in separate courses or classes or by herding them into separate women's colleges.

William Chafe has noted that "the spirit of the first generation of college women did not carry over into the post-suffrage era."[4] Clearly the women's experience both at the undergraduate and graduate school levels in the decade before the vote did much to destroy that spirit.

A poem by Alice Duer Miller in 1915 must have summed up the experience of many college women:

1. Thomas Woody, *A History of Women's Education in the United States*, II (New York: Octagon Books, Inc., 1929, 1966 reprint), p. 252.
2. Julius Sachs, "Coeducation in the United States," *Education Review*, 33 (March, 1907), 300–301; Barrett Wendell, "The Relations of Radcliffe with Harvard," *The Harvard Monthly* (Oct.,1899), p. 7.
3. Report of the Commissioner of Education (1905), I, 7.
4. William Chafe, *Women and Equality* (New York: Oxford Univ. Press, 1977), pp. 29, 30.

There, little girl, don't read.
You're fond of your books, I know
But Brother might mope
If he had no hope
Of getting ahead of you.
It's dull for a boy who cannot lead.
There, little girl, don't read.

To some women the solution appeared to be to leave the field of battle. Many turned to the rapidly developing field of home economics which it was hoped would "eliminate competition between the sexes." By 1927, 249 colleges had established degree programs in domestic science or home economics while 243 other colleges and 168 normal schools offered it as an elective.[5]

In 1919 historian Arthur Calhoun reassured his readers that college education for women was not a threat to the status quo. "Her sense of maternal and connubial responsibility," he asserted, "is quickened and strengthened and her reverence for that true meaning of the relationship is exalted." If there was any question about what Calhoun meant by the "true meaning of the relationship" it was quickly cleared up by his conclusion that "College women make cheery, efficient homes."[6]

The hopes of the female success writers of the 1890s to learn, achieve, produce and create were not enough to overcome the opposition. There was little change in the next two decades. In 1920, for example, approximately 12% of women workers were professionals; in 1940 they numbered 12.3%. One can argue that the flappers' flaunting of manners and morals demonstrated that it was easier to overturn Victorian prudery than Victorian views on women's "place."

In 1898 Charlotte Perkins Gilman had argued in *Women and Economics* that the major source of women's inferior status was their economic dependence on men. Equality between the sexes, she asserted, could only be achieved if women could earn their own living. In this sense, college-educated Carol Kennicott in Sinclair Lewis' *Main Street,* published in 1920, "a woman with a working brain and no work," forced to beg household expenses from her husband, is the fulfillment of Gilman's warning.

5. Roberta Wein, "Women's Colleges and Domesticity, 1875–1918," *History of Education Quarterly* (Spring, 1974), pp. 31–47.
6. Arthur Calhoun, *A Social History of the American Family*, III (Boston: Barnes and Noble, 1919), p. 95.

MICHAEL MOON

"The Gentle Boy from the Dangerous Classes": Pederasty, Domesticity, and Capitalism in Horatio Alger†

Throngs of ragged children bent on earning or cadging small sums of money filled the streets of mid-nineteenth-century New York, if we are to credit the testimony of a large number of chroniclers of city life of the period. These genteel observers—journalists, novelists, social reformers, early criminologists—professed to be alternately appalled and enchanted by the spectacle of street children noisily and energetically playing, begging, and hawking a multitude of services and goods—shoeshines, matches, newspapers, fruit. In considering the accounts of this scene made by those who first concerned themselves with it, one soon becomes aware that a significant number of writers respond to it with strong ambivalence. For many of them, there is an undeniable charm or beauty, strongly tinged with pathos, in the spectacle of the pauper children: the high style with which they collectively wage their struggle for subsistence exerts a powerful appeal. For some of the same observers, though, the charm of the street urchins is a siren song: beneath their affecting exteriors many of them are prematurely criminal, expert manipulators of the responses of naive and sentimental adults.

George Matsell, New York's first chief of police, initiated the vogue for writing "sketches" of the city's street children with his sensationalistic and strongly unfavorable report of 1849 on "the constantly increasing number of vagrants, idle and vicious children of both sexes, who infest our public thoroughfares."[1] The extensive testimony of minister and reformer Charles Loring Brace, who devoted a long career to "saving" street children, is more ambiguous, and consequently more representative of genteel response in general. While professing to detest the criminal tendencies that he believes street life encourages in poor children—indeed, the "philanthropic" plans for them that he and his colleagues in the Children's Aid Society (founded in 1853) framed and enacted involved systematically removing them from the city—Brace nevertheless often confesses to

† From *Representations* 19 (Summer 1987): 87–110. Copyright © 1987 University of California Press. Used by permission of University of California Press.
1. Quoted in Christine Stansell, *City of Women: Sex and Class in New York, 1789–1860* (New York, 1986), 194. I have depended on the chapter of Stansell's book in which this report is quoted ("The Use of the Streets," 193–216) for my brief opening account in this essay of genteel response to street children in New York City in the years just before Alger's arrival on the scene.

feeling a powerful attraction toward the children themselves, especially the boys. Brace seems to have possessed a remarkable capacity for "activat[ing] male sympathies," to borrow a phrase historian Christine Stansell has used to characterize his program: both the middle-class, reform-minded men who funded and worked in his programs and many of the ragged boys whom they housed, counseled, educated and sent away to work seem to have found compelling the particular version of male community institutionalized in his charities.[2]

One often hears in the language Brace and his colleagues directed toward their boy charges the familiar intensities of evangelical piety, hortatory and emotionally charged. Unsurprisingly to readers familiar with the rhetoric of nineteenth-century American Protestant revivalism, Brace's language frequently exhibits a markedly homoerotic character, as when in one of his *Sermons to News Boys* he appeals to his boy auditors' longings for an "older and wiser" male friend who would love and support them unreservedly:

> Though you are half men in some ways, you are mere children in others. You hunger as much as other children for affection, but you would never tell of it, and hardly understand it yourselves.
>
> You miss a friend; somebody to care for you. It is true you are becoming rapidly toughened to friendlessness; still you would be very, very glad, if you could have one true and warm friend.[3]

Although the "friendship" Brace is urging the street boys to accept here is ostensibly that of Christ, one can readily see how closely congruent a rhetoric of seduction could be with discourses of middle-class philanthropy like his, as when the adult male avows his willingness to recognize and respond (in various institutionally mediated ways) to adolescent male desires for dependency on an older, more powerful man for affection and support. The genteel gaze of Gilded Age New Yorkers seems always to descry disturbingly mixed qualities in pauper children, and the boundaries these imputed mixtures disturb are often ones of age and gender, as witness the ambiguous "half men" (adult males)/"mere children" (minors of indeterminate gender) to whom Brace addresses his exhortations.

Despite the pederastic overtones of some of their discourse, Brace and his fellow reformers seem to have been primarily interested in seducing poor children away from their underclass environments rather than actually engaging in sexual activity with them. However, at least one man who long associated himself with Brace's boy

---

2. Ibid., 212.
3. Charles Loring Brace, *Short Sermons to News Boys* (1866), 140–41.

charities—Horatio Alger, Jr.—is known to have seduced boys sexually during at least one period of his career as well as to have actively participated in the reform movement to "seduce" New York street boys away from their milieu into an at least minimally genteel way of life. Alger has long been recognized as (in Hugh Kenner's phrase) "the laureate of the paradigms of ascent" in early corporate capitalist America; since 1971, his expulsion from the Unitarian ministry for pederasty in 1866 has been a matter of public record.[4]

In this essay I propose to explore how Alger's reformulation of domestic fiction as a particular brand of male homoerotic romance functions as a support for capitalism. Alger's writing provides a program cast in moralistic and didactic terms for maximizing a narrow but powerfully appealing range of specifically male pleasures; certain forms of social respectability and domesticity, the accumulation of modest wealth, and the practice of a similarly modest philanthropy toward younger needy boys. As a number of critics have noted, Alger's tales generally prove on inspection to be quite different from what the "Alger myth"—"rags to riches" for industrious poor boys—has prepared readers to expect. Rather than promising riches to boy readers, they hold out merely the prospect of respectability; also, rather than presenting an example of "rugged" and competitive individualism, they show boys "rising" through a combination of genteel patronage and sheer luck. As Michael Zuckerman perceptively observed, "beneath [Alger's] paeans to manly vigor" one can discern "a lust for effeminate indulgence; beneath his celebrations of self-reliance, a craving to be taken care of and a yearning to surrender the terrible burden of independence."[5] Alongside the apparent support of such capitalist ideals of the period as the self-made man and the cult of success, notions to which Alger's writing pays lip service but fails to narrativize or thematize effectively, another agenda inconspicuously plays itself out in tale after tale—one that would appear to be the antithesis of the idea commonly associated with Alger that any reasonably bright boy can rely on his own hard work and "pluck" to catapult him to a place near the top of the Gilded heap. Actually, Alger's tales hold out a considerably less grandiose prospect for boy readers: that any boy who is reasonably willing to please his potential employers can attain a life of modest comfort. Only a character as programmatically resistant to this prospect as Bartleby the Scrivener stands to lose out entirely in the new modest-demand, modest-reward ethos

4. Hugh Kenner's phrase occurs in his "The Promised Land," in *A Homemade World: The American Modernist Writers* (New York, 1975), 20. Richard Huber rediscovered the documentary material on Alger's pederasty and discussed it in his book *The American Idea of Success* (New York, 1971).

5. Michael Zuckerman, "The Nursery Tales of Horatio Alger," *American Quarterly* 24, no. 2 (May 1972): 209.

of the rapidly expanding corporate/clerical workplace. A characteristic authorial aside in Alger's 1873 *Bound to Rise; or, Up the Ladder*
makes apparent in unmistakable terms the large part patient passivity, rather than competitive aggression, plays in the scheme of his
stories:

> Waiting passively for something to turn up is bad policy and
> likely to lead to disappointment; but waiting actively, ready to
> seize any chance that may offer, is quite different. The world is
> full of chances, and from such chances so seized has been based
> many a prosperous career.[6]

"Rising" for Alger's heroes always remains a waiting game; within this
pervasive passivity, there is an active and a passive position, but there
is no way for a boy to take a more direct approach to the world of work
and achievement in Alger's books.

   How does one explain the gap that yawns between the reputation
of Alger's books as heroic fables of ascents from the gutter to the pin-
nacle of power and wealth with their actual narrative contents: the
achievement—with the benefit of considerable "luck" and patronage—
of a mild form of white-collar respectability that releases the boy hero
from the competitive struggle he has had to wage on the street? I propose that the answer lies not in some quirk in Alger's personality but
in some basic contradictions in his culture that the tales engage.
Alger's books can be read—and were by generations of young readers, albeit probably largely unwittingly—as primers in some of the
prevailing modes of relationship between males in corporate/capital-
ist culture. I will argue further that the pederastic character of much
of the "philanthropic" discourse about boys in this period is particularly marked in Alger's texts, and that what this sexual undercurrent
reveals is not so much that the leading proponents of this discourse
were motivated in large part by conscious or unconscious pederastic
impulses—some, like Alger, no doubt were; perhaps others were
not—but that there are determinate relations between social forms
engendered by the emergent Gilded Age culture and some of the quasisexual ties and domestic arrangements between males that impel
Alger's fiction.[7]

---

6. Horatio Alger, Jr., *Bound to Rise; or, Up the Ladder* (New York, 1909), 101, in a chapter significantly entitled "The Coming of the Magician."
7. My thinking about homoeroticism, homophobia, social class, and capitalism in this essay is
indebted to Eve Kosofsky Sedgwick, *Between Men: English Literature and Male Homosocial
Desire* (New York, 1985), especially her chapter "Homophobia, Misogyny, and Capital: The
Example of *Our Mutual Friend*," 161–79. I am also indebted to Luce Irigaray, "Commodities
Among Themselves," in *This Sex Which Is Not One*, trans. Catherine Porter with Carolyn
Burke (Ithaca, N.Y., 1985), for her analysis of the determinate relation between homophobia and the foundations of patriarchal economics: "Why is masculine homosexuality consid-
ered exceptional, then, when in fact the economy as a whole is based upon it? Why are
homosexuals ostracized, when society postulates homosexuality?" (192). In considering

"Gentle-but-Dangerous" Horatio Alger

Alger arrived in New York City in 1866, eager to put his disgrace in Brewster, Massachusetts, behind him and to establish himself as a professional writer for boys (he had combined careers as a divinity student and fledgling juvenile author for a few years before his exposure). In one of the first pieces he published after moving to New York, Alger expresses the kind of fascination with the precocity of street boys familiar from other genteel writing:

> The boys looked bright and intelligent; their faces were marked by a certain sharpness produced by the circumstances of their condition. Thrown upon the world almost in infancy, compelled to depend upon their own energy for a living, there was about them an air of self-reliance and calculation which usually comes much later. But this advantage had been gained at the expense of exposure to temptations of various kinds.[8]

Struggling to establish himself as a popular writer in a competitive and demanding market, Alger may well have envied the ragged boys of Brace's Newsboys' Lodging House the "self-reliance" they had acquired not from reading Emerson (who is said to have once visited the home of Alger's parents) but from premature and extensive "exposure to temptations." The element of glamour he attributes to the street boy heroes of the books that followed *Ragged Dick; or, Street Life in New York* (1867) for a decade or so after is a quality that arises (as I shall try to show) from the way the figure embodies certain sexual and class tensions that were markedly present in the culture of Alger's period, tensions that had forcefully asserted themselves at critical points in his own life. Unlike most of his genteel contemporaries, Alger shared with the street boys he began writing about in New York the experience of having been deemed outcast and "dangerous" to the community. That the boy ideal in his fiction should magically combine both "gentle" (genteel) and "dangerous" (underclass) qualities is the generative contradiction in Alger's work, but it bears closely on significant contradictions in his culture. Gentility and public disgrace, respectability and criminality were states that were not supposed to interact closely in mid-nineteenth-century America, but they did so with notable violence at several points for

the profound effects of the requirements of the forms of corporate capitalism emergent in Alger's time on his culture, I have also profited from Alan Trachtenberg's treatment of this matter in *The Incorporation, of America: Culture and Society in the Gilded Age* (New York, 1982).

8. Alger's sketch of the boy residents of the Newsboys' Lodging House of the Children's Aid Society (Brace's organization) originally appeared in the pages of the *Liberal Christian*. It is reprinted in Gary Scharnhorst with Jack Bales, *The Lost Life of Horatio Alger, Jr.* (Bloomington, Ind., 1985), 79. The appearance at long last of a factually reliable biography of Alger like this one makes writing about his work substantially easier.

Alger, as when his Unitarian minister father, plagued with debt throughout the author's childhood, was forced to declare bankruptcy in 1844, or when Alger himself was ejected from the ministry for (in the words of the report of the church's committee of inquiry) "the abominable and revolting crime of unnatural familiarity with *boys.*"[9]

The Discourse of the "Dangerous Classes"

Alger's pederasty was an act that simultaneously transgressed a number of fundamental proscriptions in his culture: its object was male rather than female, and a child rather than an adult. Although apparently the boys with whom he was sexually involved during his days as a Unitarian minister were themselves middle class, Alger may have added a third form of transgression—sex across class lines—to his offenses against the dominant morality with some of the numerous underclass boys he fostered during his thirty years' residence in New York.[1]

Although there is no lack of documentary evidence to support the assertion that feelings of guilt and anxiety over real and imaginary wrongdoing were felt by many of Alger's middle-class contemporaries, a considerable amount of literary energy in America as well as in Europe in the two decades before he began producing his books was devoted to representing the actual states of being deemed outcast or criminal as conditions that properly happened only to the denizens of a segment of the urban world somehow fundamentally disjunct from the one middle-class readers inhabited—despite the physical proximity of the two worlds. Some of the most popular writing of the day served to provide these readers with a vicarious experience of the supposed color and romance of underclass life while reassuring them not only that the "honest" or "deserving" poor could readily transcend the worst effects of poverty but also that the squalor and violence of their lives could be readily contained—in slums, workhouses, charity wards, and prisons. Such experiences were likewise contained (and placed on exhibit, as it were) on the fictive level in such voluminous and widely read works as Eugène Sue's *Les Mystères de Paris* (1842), G. W. M. Reynolds's *Mysteries of London* (1845–48), George Lippard's *The Quaker City* (1845), and Ned

---

9. I quote this formulation from Scharnhorst, ibid., 67.

1. The boys involved were apparently all members of Alger's Unitarian congregation in the small Cape Cod community of Brewster. If Alger did cross class lines "for sex" in his later years in New York, where, according to Scharnhorst, he entertained hundreds of street-boy friends in his rooms (*Lost Life*, 77) and semi-officially adopted three of them (124–25), it was of course only the official version of the morality of his time and place that he was violating: the casual sexual exploitation of the poor by those economically and socially "better off" than they was of course a pervasive feature of nineteenth-century urban life. For the example of New York City in the decade before the Civil War, see Christine Stansell, "Women on the Town: Sexual Exchange and Prostitution," in *City of Women*, 171–92.

Buntline's *Mysteries and Miseries of New York* (1848). In the late 1850s, *Godey's Lady's Book* opined that the vogue for books like these, which depicted the lives of "rag-pickers, lamp-lighters, foundlings, beggars . . . murderers, etc.," was having what it saw as the undesirable effect of "widen[ing] the social breach between honest wealth and honest poverty." In 1867 Alger would begin pursuing his own literary method of bringing the "gentle" and the "dangerous" back into touch with one another—by locating these supposedly mutually exclusive qualities in the person of the same boy character.

An abundance of stimulating scholarship published in recent years has established the interdependence of the discourse of "the dangerous classes" in mid- to late-nineteenth-century fiction with the forensic forms of the same discourse, in government reports, police dossiers, and sociological studies.[3] One of the most notable characteristics of this massive body of discourse is its frequent placement of the figure of the child in the foreground. From its inception, writing of all kinds about "the dangerous classes" took as its special concern the peril to the social order that the children of the urban poor allegedly posed.[4] Writing about the children of "the dangerous classes" frequently exceeded the ostensible purpose of alerting its readership to the minatory aspects of these "dangerous" children to celebrate their beauty or charm. This conflicting tendency reaches a culmination of sorts in the heroes of Alger's street-boy fictions, in which the child of "the dangerous classes" is presented as being an estimable and even desirable figure.

2. Quoted in Nina Baym, *Novels, Readers, and Reviewers: Responses to Fiction in Antebellum America* (Ithaca, N.Y., 1984), 210–11.
3. Stansell gives a brief and useful history of the "sketch" of scenes, especially street scenes, of urban poverty in New York in the three decades before the Civil War in *City of Women*, 195–97, demonstrating as she does so how much what genteel observers of the time "saw" depended on expectations that writing about "the problem" had helped form. Stansell writes, "Although the *problems* of the streets—the fights, the crowds, the crime, the children—were nothing new, the 'problem' itself represented altered bourgeois perception and a broadened political initiative." She goes on to say, "Matsell's report and the writing Brace undertook in the 1850s distilled the particular way the genteel had designated themselves arbiters of the city's everyday life" (197). Louis Chevalier, *Laboring Classes and Dangerous Classes in Paris During the First Half of the Nineteenth Century,* trans. Frank Jellinek (New York, 1973), gives extensive documentation of the interdependence of the depictions of the urban poor to be found in Sue, Balzac, and Hugo with contemporary forensic writing. D. A. Miller has analyzed similar interdependences between contemporary "policing" techniques and the fiction of Wilkie Collins, Dickens, and Trollope in such articles as "From *Roman policier* to *Roman-police*: Wilkie Collins's *The Moon-stone*," *Novel* 13 (Winter 1980): 153–70; "The Novel and the Police," *Glyph* 8 (1981): 127–47; "Discipline in Different Voices: Bureaucracy, Police, Family, and *Bleak House*," *Representations* 1 (February 1983): 59–89; and "The Novel as Usual: Trollope's *Barchester Towers*," in Ruth Bernard Yeazell, ed., *Sex, Politics, and Science in the Nineteenth-Century Novel*, Selected Papers from the English Institute, 1983–84 (Baltimore, 1986), 1–38. Mark Seltzer has explored the relation of the forensic discourse of surveillance to Henry James's writing in "*The Princess Casamassima*: Realism and the Fantasy of Surveillance," in Eric J. Sundquist, ed., *American Realism: New Essays* (Baltimore, 1982), 95–118.
4. M. A. Frégier's influential 1840 study *Des Classes dangereuses de la population dans les grandes villes* has been called "a close study of the process by which the course of the lower-class child's life was shaped toward crime" by Louis Chevalier, *Laboring Classes*, 120.

The Discourse of the "Gentle Boy"

The particular means by which the boy of the "dangerous classes" is idealized in Alger's texts involves his being conflated with another, older writerly construction, the "gentle boy." This figure was itself a hybrid, two of its principal antecedents being the exemplary "good little boy" (sometimes middle-class, sometimes not) of evangelical tract literature for children and (coming out of a quite different discursive formation) the boy version of the "natural aristocrat" central to Jeffersonian social mythology. This latter figure, the "natural little gentleman," the boy of lowly origins who manifests from early childhood the virtues and graces associated with "true gentility," was a staple of "democratic" writing for children. Alger's boy heroes are both a belated and an extreme version of him.[5]

One need not look far in the discourse of the "gentle boy" in nineteenth-century America to appreciate that the terms *gentle* and *gentleman* were extremely unstable markers of a broad spectrum of attributes ranging from purely moral qualities like chivalrousness and benevolence to purely economic ones like the source of one's income. Given the constantly shifting meanings that *gentleman* is given in the nineteenth century, one of the few generalizations about its usage it seems to me safe to hazard is that the term's exclusionary powers are usually more important than its inclusionary ones. That is, establishing who *is* a gentleman is usually secondary in importance to establishing who is *not*; a *gentleman* often is not so much a description of a type of person as an attempt to draw a line between two levels of social status. This yields widely various definitions of *gentle* and *gentleman*, such as (for example) the "high" or "aristocratic" sense of the the term, "a man of 'good' family and independent financial means who does not engage in any occupation or profession for gain"—a sense of the term quite different from what one might call the "bourgeois" one, "a man who does not engage in a menial occupation or in manual labor to earn his living." By the first definition, to be a "true" gentleman one must be rich, leisured, and a member of an upperclass family; by the second, one need only not be a working man to qualify—that is, it excludes from its compass only lower-class men.[6]

Besides signifying rigid divisions and invidious distinctions between social classes, *gentle* and *gentleman* bore a number of other meanings.

5. John G. Cawelti traces the lines of descent of this "democratic" boy hero in his chapter on Alger in *Apostles of the Self-Made Man: Changing Concepts of Success in America* (Chicago, 1965). See also in the same volume, "Natural Aristocracy and the New Republic: The Idea of Mobility in the Thought of Franklin and Jefferson," 1–36.
6. For comparative purposes, see the discussions of the shifting parameters of gentility in nineteenth-century England in the respective introductory chapters of the following two works: Robin Gilmour, *The Idea of the Gentleman in the English Novel* (London, 1981), 1–15; and Shirley Robin Letwin, *The Gentleman in Trollope: Individuality and Moral Conduct* (Cambridge, Mass., 1982), 3–21.

"Soft" definitions of *gentleman* were based not on the source of his income or on the lowest level of work that it was necessary for him to do, but on an unstable set of moral qualities that commonly included courtesy, chivalry, benevolence to "inferiors," and a lively sense of personal "honor." The range was even wider (and must have been even more confusing) for boys who aspired to be "gentlemen": to be considered "gentle," boys, besides possessing various combinations of the foregoing qualities, were also expected to be (in certain relations) tractable, docile, and mild—types of behavior neither required of nor even particularly admired in adult males. At the extreme of the "soft" end of the spectrum, we arrive at a stretch of potentially hazardous meanings for males living in a society in which gender roles were becoming ever more polarized, elaborated, and rigidly prescribed: "sweet," "delicate," "tender," "fond," "loving," "affectionate." Embodying such qualities, even when they were part of behaving in a "gentle" or "gentlemanly" manner, could be a treacherous business for nineteenth-century boys, especially if these qualities came into play not between the boy and an infant or female family member, where they might seem appropriate, but between one boy and another or between a boy and a man. At the "soft" end of the "gentle" spectrum, disgrace by (alleged) feminization threatened the unwary boy.[7] Social constructions of such matters as what success and security, manliness and "gentle" behavior are, as well as what is truly "dangerous" about the urban poor, are some of the basic elements of which Alger's tales are composed. His attempts to stabilize in didactic narratives the volatile field of meanings these terms represented in his culture remain instructive in ways he could not have anticipated.

Ragged Dick and Tattered Tom

Perhaps the master trope, insofar as there is one, for nineteenth-century attitudes toward the urban poor is the figure common to pictorial representations of the proletarian uprisings in Paris in 1830: that of the young or mature man, usually depicted half naked, who is possessed of a beautiful, muscular torso and a bestial face.[8] Middle-class facial beauty, lower-class muscle; middle-class mentality, lower-class bodiliness; middle-class refinement, lower-class brutality; lower-class vigor and middle-class malaise; an overbred middle class

---

7. All these senses of the term, and all these potential occasions of social unease ranging from simple embarrassment to disgrace and persecution, are alive in American Renaissance writing about the "gentle" and "gentlemen." The figure of the "gentle boy" reached an apogee of sorts in Hawthorne's 1832 tale of that name. A second key text for this figure as it appears in American Renaissance writing is Thoreau's poem, "Lately, alas, I knew a gentle boy . . . ," which he published in the "Wednesday" section of *A Week on the Concord and Merrimack Rivers* (1849).

8. See Chevalier, *Laboring Classes*, 414.

and an overbreeding lower class—these are some of the constants in
the shifting spectrum of stereotypical paradigms of social class in
which nineteenth-century sociologists, journalists, novelists, and
illustrators traded. Ragged Dick, the prototypical Alger hero, is not
composed of ugly face and muscular torso as a thoroughly "dangerous" youth in popular representation might be: other qualities are
mixed in him. As the hero-to-be of Alger's particular brand of male
homoerotic domestic romance, he conspicuously combines, to begin
with, the qualities of appearing both dirty and handsome:[9]

> But in spite of his dirt and rags there was something about Dick
> that was attractive. It was easy to see if he had been clean and
> well dressed he would have been decidedly good looking.
> (*Ragged Dick*, 40)

Sexual attractiveness is the one characteristic Alger's heroes all have
in common. "Luck" comes to them, and "pluck" they exhibit when it
is required, but their really defining attribute is good looks. Statements like the following occur ritualistically on the opening pages of
the books:

> Both [boys] had bright and attractive faces. . . . [Dick] had a
> fresh color which spoke of good health, and was well-formed and
> strong. (*Fame and Fortune*, 53)

> In spite of the dirt, his face was strikingly handsome. (*Phil the
> Fiddler*, 283)

> He was a strongly-made and well-knit boy of nearly sixteen, but
> he was poorly dressed. . . . Yet his face was attractive. (*Jed the
> Poorhouse Boy*, 401)

The narrators of Alger's tales are fierce discriminators of good looks
in boys, which they suggest might be obscured for other spectators
by shabbiness and grime. The boy's initially mixed appearance, the
good looks revealing themselves despite the physical evidence of
poverty—dirt and rags—is the infallible sign that one of Alger's boy
characters is likely to emerge from his outcast condition to become
a "gentle/dangerous" boy.

Besides the handsome faces and comely bodies visible despite their
shabby coverings, another strikingly homoerotic characteristic of
Alger's writing is the element of seduction involved in the first steps

---

9. References to Alger's novels will be given by short titles in the text. The editions cited are:
Ragged Dick (New York, 1962); *Fame and Fortune* (Boston, 1868); *Phil the Fiddler*, in
Struggling Upwards and Other Works (New York, 1945); *Jed the Poorhouse Boy*, in *Struggling Upwards*; *Tattered Tom* (Boston, 1871); *Mark the Match Boy* (New York, 1962); *Risen
from the Ranks* (Boston, 1874); *Sam's Chance, and How He Improved It* (Chicago, n.d.);
Paul the Peddler: The Fortunes of a Young Street Merchant (New York, n.d.); *Bound to Rise;
or, Up the Ladder* (New York, 1909).

of the ragged hero's conversion to respectability through his chance street encounters with genteel boys and men. Here the mixing is not figured on the hero's person (handsome/dirty) but on the social level: "dangerous" (street boy) and "gentle" (genteel boy or man) not only meet but make lasting impressions on one another. This impression making, taking of the form of a mutual seduction of sorts, as in the following representative episode from early on in *Ragged Dick*. When Dick puts himself forward for hire as a guide for a rich boy who is visiting the city, the boy's businessman uncle hesitates to entrust his nephew to him. After a moment's reflection the older man decides to take the risk: "He isn't exactly the sort of guide I would have picked out for you," the man says. "Still, he looks honest. He has an open face, and I think he can be depended upon" (55). The man's quick physiognomic assessment of Dick is amply borne out by the rest of the story: the ragged boy is not only honest, open, and dependable; his contact with Frank (the rich boy) is decisive in his transformation from "street pigeon" to young gentleman. It is Ragged Dick's looks that initially allay the older man's anxieties about him; on the rich boy's side, young Frank does some seducing of his own. Amidst the plethora of advice and encouragement Dick receives from Frank and his uncle in the course of the single day of their acquaintance, it is possible to overlook the significance that direct physical contact has in Frank's ability to convince Dick that he is capable of "rising." The first instance of this occurs when Dick lapses for a short time from his usual jocular tone to tell Frank about his occasional "blue spells" over the hard and lonely life he lives on the street. Frank replies, "'Don't say you have no one to care for you, Dick,' . . . lightly laying his hand on Dick's shoulder. 'I will care for you'" (99). There is another laying on of hands by Frank when the two boys part and Frank persuades Dick to give up his unthrifty (and, by Frank's lights, immoral) street-boy amusements: "'You won't gamble any more,— will you, Dick?' said Frank, laying his hand persuasively on his companion's shoulder" (110). "A feeling of loneliness" is said to overwhelm Dick after Frank leaves the city, as a result of the "strong attachment" he has rapidly formed for the rich boy, but this feeling of loneliness soon gives way to Dick's overriding desire to be fully "gentle" (genteel), rather than merely Frank's "gentle" (sweet, fond, affectionate) ragamuffin.

A modest suit of new clothes is almost always the symbolic gift that enables the Alger hero to begin rising (Dick's is a "hand-me-down" from Frank), just as the gift of a pocket watch is often ritually made at a later point in his ascent. It is as a part of the ritual of donning his first suit that the matter of the boy's still mixed nature frequently arises for a second time: "He now looked quite handsome," the narrator says of Dick when he has put on Frank's gift, "and might readily have been taken for a young gentleman, except that his hands were red and grimy" (58). Alger's hero's face can simply be washed clean, and most of his body encased in suit and shoes, but his hands are the last part of his person to be divested of signs of hard toil and "dangerous" living.

A particularly interesting example of the mixed Alger hero is Tattered Tom, hero of a book of that title (1871) that inaugurated the Tattered Tom series, which soon followed the successful Ragged Dick series. The appropriately named Tom, a girl who has taken to living on the streets disguised as a boy, is the only "girl hero" in all of Alger's books for boys. She competes on an equal basis with other boys selling newspapers and carrying heavy luggage for nickels. Although the narrator makes passing gestures toward women's rights ("There seemed a popular sentiment in favor of employing boys, and Tom, like others of her sex, found herself shut out from an employment for which she considered herself fitted"; 71), the book, far from being a feminist fable, thoroughly endorses the privileging of the figure of the attractive boy that impels all of Alger's books. Of all of his heroes, only Tom does not "rise" as a consequence of her demonstrably enterprising and honest behavior: she is finally rescued from her plight on the street and restored to her mother, a rich Philadelphia lady from whom she had been abducted years earlier, whereupon she resumes her long-lost genteel, feminine identity as "Jane Lindsay."

Alongside this conventional story of a tomboy who attempts to live as a street boy but is rescued and reclaimed for genteel femininity it is possible to perceive a highly unconventional story of a partially feminized street boy who is drawn upward into genteel femininity by the irresistible magnetic force of Alger's model. This tale represents a twist on the standard one because its hero ends up becoming entirely feminine, instead of the mixed composite of putatively masculine and feminine qualities that Alger's heroes usually represent. *Tattered Tom* can be read not as a story of a literal sex change but of the "rise" from the street to the parlor usual in Alger combined with an unusually complete reversal of gender roles from street boy to young lady.

While it might be difficult to support such a reading of *Tattered Tom* on the basis of that text alone, it is possible to do so by interpreting the tale in the context of the series it follows (the Ragged Dick series, and the first three volumes of the Luck and Pluck series) and the one it introduces and to which it gives its name. One of the characteristics of a proliferating multiple series like Alger's street-boy stories is that repetitions and variations in the writing from volume to volume can produce meanings that are not readily available to the reader of any single volume in the series. The unique degree to which *Tattered Tom* in its course completely refigures Alger's typical boy hero as a genteel young lady provides a good example of the way formulaic and apparently tautological and repetitious writing like that in Alger's serials can generate unexpected meanings. By inaugurating a major series of boys' books with the story of a "female street boy" and by frequently employing gender-related formulae from the other stories of the series with the gender-signifier reversed, tattered Tom represents a point in Alger's writing where the dynamic interactions of the relative age, gender, and class positions of child and adult characters are revealed with particular clarity. When, for example, the narrator says that Tattered Tom's face is dirty but that if it were clean, "Tom would certainly have been considered pretty" (80), his use of the normative feminine-gender term *pretty* recalls at the same time that it momentarily reverses other descriptions of the boy heroes of the previous tales in the series who have been said to have dirty but *handsome* faces. Similarly, when the narrator says of the benevolent gentleman who takes an interest in Tattered Tom, "There was something in this strange creature—half boy in appearance—that excited his interest and curiosity" (42–43), the text exhibits with exceptional directness the primary role that ambiguities of age and gender play in the appeal of Alger's heroes (one thinks of Brace's "half men"/"mere children") to their genteel benefactors.

"The Fashionable Newsboy at Home": Alger's Reformulation of the Domestic Ideal

"The idea of a fashionable newsboy! It's ridiculous!"
—Alger, *Herbert Carter's Legacy* (1875)

Having attracted the attention and favor of a genteel man with his unmistakable good looks, and having in turn been "seduced" by the warm concern of a rich boy into embracing genteel aspirations, Alger's prototypical hero begins his transformation from "dangerous" child/vagrant into "gentle" youth. That Alger's books are not only homoerotic romances but also represent a genuine reformulation of popular domestic fiction is made evident by the regularity and narrative intensity with which the tales highlight the boy hero's moving from the street or from a transitional charity shelter into his own modest little home (usually a boardinghouse room).[1] That this transition is perhaps the most crucial in the boy's development is manifested in the elaborate care that Alger expends on discriminating the fine points of comparative domestic amenities at this point in his narratives. Once his boy hero reaches the point of setting up a little home of his own, Alger, otherwise often vague about "realistic" detail,

1. Nina Baym briefly but perspicaciously classifies Alger as a domestic writer in *Woman's Fiction: A Guide to Novels by and About Women in America, 1820–1870* (Ithaca, N.Y., 1978), 261.

shows himself to be as astute a recorder of the differences between the four or five lowest grades of boardinghouses as Balzac could have wished to be.

Having negotiated shifting one type of social construction of themselves ("dangerous") for another ("gentle"), Alger's heroes, in their culminating move into private lodgings, undertake the project of shifting another set of social constructions—those of gender identity and family role. As I have discussed above, gender confusion is thematized extensively in the street phases of Alger's tales only in the case of the female street boy, Tattered Tom. As long as he remains a poor boy on the streets, the Alger hero's behavior remains fairly conventionally gender bound. But once the "gentle boy" is removed from the street and street occupations and is placed in a private, at least minimally genteel domestic setting, he and his boy friends begin to differentiate themselves along (for boys of Alger's day, or of our own) highly unconventional gender-role lines. For example, as soon as fifteen-year-old (formerly Ragged) Dick can manage it, he moves his twelve-year-old friend Henry Fosdick (their very names suggesting they somehow belong together) into his lodgings with him. The two boys share a cult of domestic comfort and respectability that in many ways conforms to the standards of simplicity, cleanliness, and efficiency set in Alger's time by ideologues of "scientific" domesticity like Catharine Beecher.[2] As it is in her work, the Alger hero's first real home, like the poor but decent lodgings Dick and Fosdick take on Mott St., is a man's refuge from the demands of the marketplace and an appropriately ordered decor in which for him to pursue self-improvement.[3]

Dick and his friend and roommate Fosdick inaugurate the second major phase of their joint ascent by moving from their extremely modest digs in Mott St. to a more pleasant place uptown on Bleecker St. These are the opening lines of the sequel to *Ragged Dick*:

> "Well, Fosdick, this is a little better than our old room in Mott St.," said Richard Hunter, looking complacently about him.
>
> "You're right, Dick," said his friend. "This carpet's rather nicer than the ragged one Mrs. Mooney supplied us with. The beds are neat and comfortable, and I feel better satisfied, even if we do have to pay twice as much for it."
>
> The room which yielded so much satisfaction to the two boys was on the fourth floor of a boarding-house in Bleecker St. No

---

2. For an informative account of Beecher's theory of domesticity, see Kathryn Kish Sklar, *Catharine Beecher: A Study in American Domesticity* (New Haven, 1973), 158ff.
3. See Mary Ryan, "Varieties of Social Retreat: Domesticity, Privacy, and the Self-Made Man," in *Cradle of the Middle Class: The Family in Oneida County, New York, 1790–1865* (Cambridge, 1981), 146–55, for Ryan's discussion of the compatibility and indeed the congruence of the cult of the "self-made man" with the cult of (feminine) domesticity.

doubt many of my young readers, who are accustomed to elegant homes, would think it very plain; but neither Richard nor his friend had been used to anything as good. They had been thrown upon their own exertions at an early age, and [had] had a hard battle to fight with poverty and ignorance. Those of my readers who are familiar with Richard Hunter's experiences when he was "Ragged Dick" will easily understand what a great rise in the world it was for him to have a really respectable home. (*Fame and Fortune*, 9–10)

The Bleecker St. boardinghouse that is the boys' second home together is relatively luxurious; the narrator contrasts it with the minimal, unfastidious amenities that have been available to them back on Mott St.: "There once a fortnight was thought sufficient to change the sheets, while both boys were expected to use the same towel, and make that last a week" (52).

The practical, quotidian ideals of the domestic ideology in its "scientific" and privatizing aspect (a clean and comfortable home that serves as both a haven from the world and a suitable environment for continuous self-improvement) seem entirely congenial to Alger. Other aspects of the conventional domestic ideal that had come into being in the two or three decades preceding, such as its rigid polarization of gender roles, seem considerably less congenial to him. In order to consider how Alger represents these matters, one must attend not to those attitudes that Dick and Fosdick share, like their desire to live as "respectably" as they possibly can afford to, but those characteristics of either boy by means of which the text differentiates, and indeed to some degree dichotomizes (although not nearly as far as other domestic definers of gender roles would have done), their respective personalities.

Alger characterizes the younger boy, Fosdick, as a sweet, timid, quiet, and clever boy, obviously the stereotypically feminine version of the "gentle boy" type, in contrast with the stereotypically masculine Dick, who is thoroughly "gentle" in Alger's ambiguous sense (handsome, kind, nurturant, and, to all appearances, born with embryonic genteel values despite his actual origins in poverty) but is also self-confident, "handy," and generally competent in the realm of what Alger's culture defined as masculine affairs. The significant twist on the gender-role stereotypes in this representative tale of Alger's is that it is Dick, the "dominant" type of these two gentle boys, who plays the maternal role in Alger's version of domesticity and not, as one might expect, the "feminine" character Fosdick.

The relationship between the dominant boy in the maternal role and his partner (for example, Dick and Fosdick, respectively, in the first three volumes of the Ragged Dick series) is thoroughly familial; so much so, in fact, that Alger specifies (another significant example of his uncharacteristic precision about detail) that nine months after the two boys move in together ("at the end of nine months, therefore, or thirty-nine weeks"; chapter 20, "Nine Months Later," *Ragged Dick*, 166), Dick is said to bring forth a little bundle—a nest egg of $117 that has accumulated in his new savings account. But fascinating as the nursing of this nest egg is depicted as being for both boys, they eventually acquire a real human child: in the third volume of the series they adopt a small beggar boy to round out their family, and they make available to him in his turn the experiences—primarily domestic ones—that have aided their own earlier transformations from "dangerous but gentle" street boys to young gentlemen and members of an ideal, genteel, all-boy family.

This fantasmatic family serves as a lingering ideal in Alger's books, but, as he depicts it, it is a far from stable unit.[4] For example, Mark the Match Boy, the adopted "son" of Dick and Fosdick, is revealed at novel's end to be the missing and long-sought-for grandson of a rich merchant from Milwaukee. The old man rewards Dick and Fosdick handsomely for fostering the boy, who is then removed to Milwaukee to enjoy the life of the grandson of a rich gentleman. Dick and Fosdick revert to nursing a now considerably enlarged nest egg. Dick's intermittent maternity toward his "nest egg" and his temporary ward Mark, and the essential interchangeability of "baby" and capital in this scheme—the last in the series of transformations I have been describing—requires consideration in relation to one final aspect of domesticity in Alger, and that is the all-important habit of "saving." Good looks combined with other virtures—honesty, enterprise, male homosociability—are all qualifications for "good fortune" in the forms this takes in Alger. But once the hero begins to "rise" and achieves a modicum of domestic stability, the activity or habit that is represented as being indispensable to maintaining his personal ascendancy is that of "saving." It is by saving, i.e., thriftily and systematically accumulating bits of capital, that Dick produces his nest egg; it is by virtue of these habits that he shows himself to be a fit parent (mother) for Mark; and it is his "saving"—by rescuing from dead-end poverty—first Fosdick and then Mark that the cycle of ascent is renewed in the series. Just as Dick has been saved in order to learn to "save" himself,

---

4. Fredric Jameson, *The Political Unconscious: Narrative as a Socially Symbolic Act* (Ithaca, N.Y., 1981), employs the term *fantasm* to denote "the traces and symptoms of a fundamental family situation which is at one and the same time a fantasy master narrative" that "is an unstable and contradictory structure, whose persistent actantial functions and events . . . demand repetition, permutation, and the ceaseless generation of various structural 'resolutions'" (180). If, as Jameson suggests, a residue of fantasmatic thinking about "a fundamental family situation" is characteristic of all bourgeois narratives, then it becomes possible to perceive many more narratives as being fundamentally "domestic"— or antidomestic—in their emphases than most of us are probably used to doing.

so will he save younger boys and provide them a model of "saving" both money and still more boys. This religion of accumulating (saving) both money and other boys is ubiquitous in Alger:

> The disposition to save is generally the first encouraging symptom in a street boy and shows that he has really a desire to rise above his circumstances, and gain a respectable position in the world. (*Mark the Match Boy*, 293)

> Of greater value than the [monetary] sum . . . was the habit of self-denial and saving which our hero had formed. (*Risen from the Ranks*, 141)

> Boys who have formed so good a habit of saving can be depended upon. (*Fame and Fortune*, 11)

> "All labor is respectable, my lad, and you have no cause to be ashamed of any honest business; yet when you can get something to do that promises better for your future prospects, I advise you to do so. Till then earn your living in the way you are accustomed to, avoid extravagance, and save up a little money if you can." (*Ragged Dick*, 109)

It is in the "saving" (i.e., salvific) habit of "saving" money and other boys that Alger's work represents its cycle of transformations—street boy into "gentle" boy, newly "gentle" boy into domestic partner and foster parent (mother), capital into baby and baby back into further capital—reaching a state of equilibrium: at the end of the narrative, there lies ahead for Alger's heroes a static future of endlessly pursuing the two "saving" projects (i.e., of money and other boys). I want now to consider the question of what is being "saved" in Alger's fantasmatic no-loss chain of transformations and exchanges, the process that begins at the lowest end of his society—at an isolated ragged boy—and extracts from this supposedly unpromising figure the particular combination of virtues and powers normally ascribed to his remote social superiors—gentility, domesticity, wealth, philanthropy.

"Taking an Interest": The Art of Saving Boys

As became apparent in the last section, the salvaging operation ongoing in Alger's writing is a complex one. In each book, a boy is "saved from ruin," from possibly becoming a criminal or a derelict, by being fostered as a candidate for recruitment into the petty bourgeoisie. Furthermore, an outmoded model of virtue (thrift, probity, self-restraint, ambition, hard work—"the Protestant work ethic") is reformulated to correspond more closely to the requirements of changed social and economic conditions: aspiring to and finally reaching the kind of low-level clerical position that brings "respectable" social status as well as access to a modest array of consumer "goodies" to its holder is presented as being a high moral achievement. What is ultimately being saved or recuperated in Alger's writing, though, is something more primal than the notion of the worldly efficacy of a certain combination of virtues: it is a belief that a kind of "magic" acts to secure his boy heroes in the corporate/capitalist network. As I have discussed earlier in this essay, critics of Alger have often decried the regularity with which an experience of sheer "luck" sets his boy heroes on their way, rather than some experience like a recognition of the workings in their world of some consistent notion of "character" or "self-making." It is crucial to notice in this regard that the ritualistic "lucky break" that initiates the boy's rising usually takes the form of his attracting the attention of a well-to-do male patron, usually through some spontaneous exhibition of his physical strength and daring. The "magic trick" that the Alger text ultimately performs is to recuperate the possibility of a man's taking an intense interest in an attractive boy without risking being vilified or persecuted for doing so—indeed, this "interest" is taken in a manner that is made thoroughly congruent with the social requirements of corporate capitalism on the sides of both parties: boy and potential employer alike "profit" from it.

Alger's 1876 *Sam's Chance; and How He Improved It*, in the second Tattered Tom series, provides a representative example of this in the interactions of fifteen-year-old Henry, a clerk in a shipping company, and his employer, James Hamilton. Although Henry is said not to be aware that Hamilton favors him or is even aware of his presence in the firm, the narrator relates that the older man has been "observing him [Henry] carefully, fully determined to serve him in the future if he should deserve it" (89). One day, after four years in the firm, Henry is called into Hamilton's office, where his employer interviews him about how he manages his life and his small income, and then, pleased with what he learns, invites the boy to make a substantial investment in a shipping venture the firm is about to undertake:

> Henry stared at his employer in surprise. How could he, a boy with thirty-five dollars capital, join in such an enterprise?
> "I don't see how I can," he replied. "I am afraid you take me for a capitalist."
> "So you are," said his employer. "Have you not money in the bank?"
> Henry smiled. (93)

Hamilton encourages Henry to participate in the venture, saying he will take the boy's savings bank book (with thirty-five dollars in the account) as security. "Thirty-five dollars will pay a year's interest on the five hundred dollars I lend you; so my interest is secure," Hamilton tells him. "I am willing to take the risk," the older man tells him (twice) to counter Henry's anxieties about becoming his "partner" (94–95). Henry finally happily agrees to the transaction and rises to leave Hamilton's office with the words, "Thank you, sir I am very grateful to you for your kind interest in me."

With Hamilton's "interest" in Henry thus firmly secured, three months come and go, during which period nothing passes between man and boy except frequent "pleasant word[s] or smile[s]" (107). Henry is then called back into Hamilton's office, and their talk immediately turns to their mutual "interest": "I have just received a statement of [the outcome of the shipping venture]," Hamilton tells Henry, "and as you are interested, I have called you in to let you know how it has turned out." Henry is delighted to learn his investment has earned him a hundred dollars. The following conversation ensues:

> "I shall charge you interest on the five hundred dollars you borrowed of me, at the rate of seven per cent. You have had the use of the money for three months."
> "Then the interest will amount to eight dollars and three quarters," said Henry, promptly.
> "Quite right; you are very quick at reckoning," said Mr. Hamilton, looking pleased.
> "That is not a difficult sum," answered Henry, modestly.
> "I did not suppose you knew much about computing interest. You left school very young, did you not?"
> "At twelve, sir."
> "You had not studied interest then, had you?"
> "No, sir; I have studied it since."
> "At evening school?"
> "No, sir; I study by myself in the evening."
> "How long have you done that?"
> "For two years."
> "And you keep it up regularly?"
> "Yes, sir; occasionally I take an evening for myself, but I average five evenings a week at studying."
> "You are a remarkable boy," said the merchant, looking surprised.
> "If you flatter me, sir, I may grow self-conceited," said Henry, smiling. (108–9)

Once again, a mutually "profitable" encounter leaves Henry "smiling" and Hamilton looking "surprised" and "pleased," their "partnership" fulfilled. The boy has proven himself to be as quick and expert a computer of "interest" as his merchant employer; with a little further education in calculating "risk," one suspects, he will have little more to learn from Hamilton. (In their crucial first nine months together,

Ragged Dick is said to learn everything from Fosdick that he has to teach, which includes reading, writing, and "arithmetic as far as Interest"; 167.)

The recognition and avowal of "interest"—one's own in other men and theirs in oneself—and the close study of calculation and risk in pursuing these "interests" are matters that have figured as highly problematic and emotionally charged concerns in male homosexual behavior in homophobic capitalist culture. As Michael Pollak has written of the institutions of the "sexual market" of the gay ghetto (bars, baths, cinemas, and so on), as these functioned between the time of the emergence of gay liberation in Western metropolises at the beginning of the 1970s and the decline of "casual sex" practices among many gay men in recent years in response to the AIDS epidemic: "Of all the different types of masculine sexual behavior, homosexuality is undoubtedly the one whose functioning is most strongly suggestive of a market, in which in the last analysis one orgasm is bartered for another."[5]

As is evident from passages like the dialogue from *Sam's Chance* quoted above, the network of calculation, risk, and interest that binds males together in Alger's work is a complex one; the economic workings of the quasisexual marketplace of these "boys' books" leaves the crude barter system described by Pollak far behind. At a representative moment in an earlier entry in the Tattered Tom series, *Paul the Peddler*, distinctions between the boy hero or his body and corporate economic forms vanish; as Paul considers how to come up with thirty-five dollars to buy out another boy's necktie stand, the narrator observes:

> If Paul had been a railroad corporation, he might have issued first mortgage bonds at a high rate of interest, payable in gold, and negotiated them through some leading banker. But he was not much versed in financial schemes, and therefore was at a loss. (164)

Paul's being "at a loss" is a circumstance that "gets worse before it gets better"; his case provides a typical example of the way in which the networks of interest between males in Alger's fiction can be disrupted by the incursion of the feminine—a quality that is frequently represented in these stories as being equivalent to (in readily recognizable infantile-fantasy form) the quality of anality. Paul becomes involved in a series of misadventures when he attempts to sell a valuable "ring" his mother has found and given him to provide the capi-

---

5. Michael Pollak, "Male Homosexuality; or, Happiness in the Ghetto," in Philippe Ariès and André Béjin, eds., *Western Sexuality: Practice and Precept in Past and Present Times,* trans. Anthony Foster (Oxford, 1985), 44.

tal for his "rise." A con man named Montgomery who poses as "a jew-eler from Syracuse" is said to overhear "with evident interest" a con-versation between Paul and another boy about this ring. The man steps forward and avows his "interest in examining" and possibly buy-ing Paul's ring; permitted to do so, he pronounces it "handsome" and valuable, and invites the boy to his hotel room to complete the trans-action (199–200). Once at the hotel (called "Lovejoy's"), Mont-gomery grabs Paul and applies a sponge soaked in chloroform to his nose until the boy passes out. "Eyeing the insensible boy with satis-faction," he seizes the ring and flees (208–9).

Alger's fictions never allow such disruptions of the networks of male interest by the incursion of what it represents as the feminine/anal—a position of jeopardy into which every "gentle boy" can at least potentially be forced—to become more than temporary: Paul recov-ers his ring and completes his sale of it, then deposits most of the pro-ceeds with his gentleman patron, who promises him "interest" on it (295). When the con man is sent off to Sing Sing after being con-victed of assaulting and robbing Paul, according to the narrative, even the man's wife is said to be indifferent: "As the compact between her and her husband was one of interest rather than of affection, her grief at his confinement is not very deep" (304). Compacts of inter-est between man and wife, the narrative leads us to assume, are igno-ble, but between man and boy "on the market," there is no comparably invidious distinction to be drawn between mutual "inter-est" and "affection": they come to the same thing, and both qualities are estimable.

Older men who might (but actually do not) stand in relation to Alger's boy heroes as fathers may "take an interest" in them that may eventuate (as we have seen) in actions as various as respectful advancement or rape, but none of these interactions with older men on the boys' part leaves any permanent trace in the lives of the boy characters except in the form of yet another accession of capital. Domestic arrangements are formed between boy and boy, but rela-tions between man and boy remain casual, intermittent, and extrado-mestic: the "rise" of Alger's hero is fostered by "interested" older patrons, but (the informing, contradictory fantasy runs) the boy remains entirely self-fathering.

Alger's particular version of the "self-made man" takes the form of this "self-made" all-boy family that the boy protagonist generates with his money. This version of domesticity, as I have suggested above, derives from the infantile-fantasy equivalence that the stories pro-pose between femininity and anality. Drawing on the succinct psy-choanalysis of the "magic-dirt" complex that Norman O. Brown makes in *Life Against Death*, I would argue that Alger's writing denies sexual difference—and privileges the figure of the formerly "dirty" boy-turned-gentle over figures of other age, gender, and class positions—"in the interest" of promoting this particular notion of self-making, of simultaneous self-mothering and self-fathering, that it takes over from capitalist culture:

> The infantile fantasy of becoming father of oneself first moves out to make magic use of objects instead of its own body when it gets attached to that object which both is and is not part of its own body, the feces. Money inherits the infantile magic of excrement and then is able to breed and have children: interest is an increment.[6]

Alger's all-boy families merely imitate the extraordinary propensities for self-reproduction, for apparently asexual breeding, that they are represented as discovering already ongoing in their first accumulations of capital. The chain of "magical" transformations I have charted in Alger's writing from ragged to gentle boy by way of a series of negotiations of capital into baby and then back into capital conforms entirely to Brown's Freudian reading of the fantasy of transformation of bodily excrement into capital increment by way of the metamorphosis of feces into baby and subsequently into "magical," self-engendering money.

Alger's tales sometimes manifest a modicum of self-awareness on the author's part with regard to his role of purveyor of a "magical thinking" that effectively links infantile fantasies of self-fathering with some of the fundamental formations of capitalist culture. In his recent study of forms of popular narrative in nineteenth-century America, Michael Denning has likened the function of Alger's street-boy heroes—"dangerous" figures drawn from contemporary popular, nongenteel fiction (story papers, dime novels) who enact what Denning (correctly) reads as unequivocally genteel moralistic fables—to the use of "a ventriloquist's dummy to recapture and reorganize working class culture."[7] I would supplement Denning's characterization of Alger as a ventriloquist across class lines (as well as, I would add, across lines of prohibited sexuality between man and boy) with a brief analysis of Alger's representation of himself in the figure of Professor Henderson, a magician/ventriloquist who figures as a patron/employer of the boy hero of *Bound to Rise*. Henderson first deceives the boy Harry Walton, who has come to work as his assistant, by throwing his voice into a trunk, from which emerges a child's voice pathetically pleading, "Oh, let me out! Don't keep me locked up in here!" Harry is said merely to "smile" when he realizes Henderson has tricked him with ventriloquism (102).

6. Norman O. Brown, *Life Against Death: The Psychoanalytical Meaning of History* (Middletown, Conn., 1959), 279.
7. Michael Denning, "Cheap Stories: Notes on Popular Fiction and Working-Class Culture in Nineteenth-Century America," *History Workshop* 22 (Autumn 1986): 6.

Shortly thereafter, Henderson repeats the trick in the boy's presence, this time at the expense of an elderly woman character; Henderson and Harry have a good laugh at her chagrin. The trick is more elaborate the second time: Henderson throws his voice into the boy's body and increases their mirth by making Harry seem to lie to the woman to the effect that the professor does indeed have someone locked away in the trunk; this time Henderson specifies (ventriloquially) that the child is female—in fact, his little daughter. The climax of the trick comes when the professor throws open the trunk and shows the woman that there is no one there (114–15).

The reader may share some of the woman character's discomfort over the "little girl in the trunk" trick that at a critical point in the episode turns into the "vanishing daughter" trick. Not much imagination is required to produce the biographical speculation that the little girl locked in the trunk, crying to be released, is a figure from Alger's psychological past who survived in encrypted and rejected form in his unconscious and whose ultimate fate was to be pressed into service as comic relief in texts like *Bound to Rise*. Even more thoroughly than the ambiguously feminine Tattered Tom, this fantasmatic "little girl" vanishes almost without a trace from the magical network of male interests through which she is passed in this text—leaving the reader to suspect, at this and other points in the Alger corpus, that the "dangerous" figures in his writing are not really at any point the ragged street boys whose labile qualities it celebrates but the little girls it almost totally excludes—along with the femininity they embody, a "threatening" quality insofar as it might permanently disrupt the smooth unfolding in the America of the time of the exclusively male homosocial institutions of corporate capitalism.

It was in the decade or so after Alger's death in 1899 that Lewis Hine began to produce his extraordinary photographs of the new, turn-of-the-century generation of urban street boys at their work of peddling, shining shoes, selling newspapers, and delivering parcels. What is striking about Hine's photographs is their self-conscious refusal to "gentle" their underclass subjects in the way that Alger and his philanthropist colleagues had done: Hine's boy subjects are not represented as picturesque ragamuffins or charming but dangerous "animals" or "savages," some of whom will inevitably make their way to affluence and respectability. Rather, his images of these boys reveal their sufferings as real, lasting deformations rather than as transient experiential way stations on the road to untroubled security and success: the child subjects of Hine's photographs characteristically look weary, depressed, and even bitter. In association with the Progressivist reform organization the National Child Labor Committee (NCLC), Hine wrote and lectured extensively on the need for legislation prohibiting the exploitation of poor children as laborers by either their parents or their employers: his photographs, he insisted, were his incontrovertible documentary evidence that children forced to support themselves by full-time employment at low-paying labor were generally destroyed physically and morally in the process. Hine supplemented his photographic record of street-boy life with his own antisentimental testimony about their plight: for example, a propos of his 1909 photograph of a Hartford, Connecticut newsboy named Tony Casale, Hine records that the boy had recently shown his boss the marks on his arm where his father had bitten him "for not selling more papers"; Hine also mentions that the boy said he disliked being the object of verbal abuse from the drunken men with whom he constantly came in contact on the city streets.[8]

Hine and the NCLC encountered strong popular resistance to their movement; politicians and other members of their audiences vociferously denied that conditions for street-child laborers were as grim and brutalizing as Hine represented them as being. Hine's street boys, his opponents often argued, were Horatio Alger heroes, toiling their way up from paupery to comfortable, respectable lives.

It was during these years, between the turn of the century and the beginning of World War I, at the height of the Progressive Era, that Alger's books, republished in cheap reprints that suppressed substantial amounts of the books' didactic moralizing, sold in the millions of copies.[9] During his lifetime, Alger had had only one genuine bestseller, the early *Ragged Dick*; only posthumously did he achieve true mass popularity. It was also during the early years of the twentieth century that the term "a Horatio Alger story" became fixed in the language to mean a tale of a man's "rise" from boyhood poverty to a position of great wealth and power. The myth that Alger's are male-capitalist Cinderella tales has had an astonishing success of its own. How can one account for the ubiquity of this inaccurate characterization of the content of Alger's stories? With the benefit of hindsight, we can see that one thing that was being "saved" in Alger's writing was a notion of "virtuous poverty rewarded" that was already archaic when his first street-boy series appeared in the decade after the Civil War. The Alger mania of readers in the first fifteen years of this century might be said to have served as a reinoculation of American readers with the myth of "virtuous poverty rewarded," an article of faith that was being vociferously combatted from Progressivist, socialist, and organized-labor quarters during those years. I would attribute some of the popularity of Alger's

---

8. Quoted in the catalog entry for Lewis Hine's photograph entitled *Bologna, Hartford, Connecticut, 1909,* in Julie R. Myers, et al., *Of Time and Place: American Figurative Art from the Corcoran Gallery* (Washington, D.C., 1981), 92.

9. Scharnhorst, *Lost Life,* 149–56, provides an illuminating account of the "editorial reinvention" of Alger's work (often by silent abridgement) in the years after his death (149–56).

stories with boy readers during and after his lifetime to their propensity for combining a not inaccurate representation of the conditions, requirements, and mild rewards to be expected on the extensive lower reaches of the corporate workplace with a version of boy life—idyllic, domestic, self-perpetuating, untroubled by direct intervention from parents or other adult figures of authority or by the "threat" (to male supremacy) of female enfranchisement—that may strike us as highly unrealistic at first glance but that is (again) a not inaccurate version of some of corporate culture's favorite modes of self-presentation (i.e., as fraternal, financially rewarding, benevolently hierarchical, open to individual talent or "merit").

I would attribute the extraordinary tenacity of the "rags-to-riches" misreading of Alger to corporate/capitalist culture's need for a serviceable mythology of "success" like Alger's—but one which entirely represses (as Alger's does not) the determinate relations perceptible in his stories between the achievement and maintenance of white-collar "lifestyles" and particular, exclusive modes of relationship between males. I first began to read Alger's writing out of an interest in thinking about ways in which his pederasty might have determined it, but I have come to think that the far more interesting way his work manifests male homosexuality is not as indirect autobiographical data for a single figure (i.e., Alger) but as an encapsulation of corporate/capitalist America's long-cherished myth, its male homoerotic foundations fiercely repressed, that the white males who control wealth and power have their eye out for that exceptional, "deserving," "attractive" underclass youth who defies his statistical fate to become (with the benefit of limited paternalistic "interest") yet another "gentle boy from the dangerous classes."

GLENN HENDLER

Pandering in the Public Sphere:
Masculinity and the Market in Horatio Alger†

Early in Horatio Alger's *Ragged Dick*, the title character takes his wealthy new friend, Frank Whitney, to see Central Park. When, six chapters later, the boys finally arrive at their destination, Frank is disappointed to find that it is still under construction. "It had not been long since work had been commenced upon it," Alger writes, "and it was still very rough and unfinished." What had been the

† From *American Quarterly* 48.3 (1996): 415–38. Copyright © 1996 The American Studies Association. Reprinted with permission of The Johns Hopkins University Press.

goal of the tour, however, turns out to be only a detour; the boys decide not to enter the park. After gazing briefly at the unattractive, broken landscape, they return downtown to see the financial district.[1]

In this scene, two boys from opposite ends of the economic spectrum glimpse the construction of a new kind of public place. Designed to be simultaneously didactic and pleasurable, Frederick Law Olmsted's Central Park was an attempt to construct a cultural public sphere for the masses, instilling in "the dangerous classes" norms of gentility and civility and allowing the "middling classes" to display their own adherence to such norms.[2] Contemporary celebrations of Central Park often compared its functions to those of other relatively new institutions like public libraries and public schools, calling it "a great free school for the people . . . a magnetic charm of decent behavior, giving salutary lessons in order, discipline, comeliness, culminating in mutual good will."[3] Such public spaces were to be neither domestic nor commercial; rather, they were differentiated from the parlor and especially the marketplace. Olmsted declared that Central Park should display "the greatest possible contrast with the streets and the shops."[4] The official regulations prohibited the "display [of] any sign, placard, flag, banner, target transparency, advertisement or device of business . . . nor shall any hawking or peddling be allowed on the Central Park."[5] Olmsted's intransigent opposition to the park's commercialization was one of the factors that in 1878 led to his dismissal from his position as Central Park's landscape architect.[6] Conceiving of a public sphere

---

1. Horatio Alger, Jr., *Ragged Dick; or, Street Life in New York*, in *Ragged Dick and Struggling Upward* (1868; New York, 1985), 48. All further references to the novel will be from the 1985 edition and will be cited parenthetically in the text.
2. See Frederick Law Olmsted, *Central Park as a Work of Art and as a Great Municipal Enterprise, 1853–1895*, vol. 2 of *Forty Years of Landscape Architecture: Being the Professional Papers of Frederick Law Olmsted, Senior*, ed. Frederick Law Olmsted, Jr. and Theodora Kimball (New York, 1928); and Olmsted, *Landscape into Cityscape: Frederick Law Olmsted's Plans for a Greater New York City*, ed. Albert Fein (Ithaca, N.Y., 1968). A useful account of Olmsted's conflicts with commercial and political interests is Elizabeth Barlow, *Frederick Law Olmsted's New York* (New York, 1972). The analyses I draw on most extensively here are those in Alan Trachtenberg, *The Incorporation of America: Culture and Society in the Gilded Age* (New York, 1982), 101–47; Lawrence W. Levine, *Highbrow/Lowbrow: The Emergence of Cultural Hierarchy in America* (Cambridge, Mass., 1988), 200–219; Thomas Bender, *Toward an Urban Vision: Ideas and Institutions in Nineteenth-Century America* (Lexington, Ky., 1975); and Roy Rosenzweig, *The Park and the People: A History of Central Park* (Ithaca, N.Y., 1992).
3. Cited in Trachtenberg, *The Incorporation of America*, 147.
4. Cited in Levine, *Highbrow/Lowbrow*, 202.
5. Olmsted, *Central Park*, 464, 410. Olmsted's ideal was continually threatened by plans to add to the park such structures as "auditoriums, restaurants, burial grounds, trotting tracks, playgrounds, athletic fields, zoos, statues, even museums." Levine, *Highbrow/Lowbrow*, 202–3; Olmsted, *Central Park*, 247–48.
6. Olmsted fought another such battle at the 1893 Columbian Exposition, trying unsuccessfully to keep his "Wooded Island" free of commercial activity: see Neil Harris, *Cultural Excursions: Marketing Appetites and Cultural Tastes in Modern America* (Chicago, 1990), 121–22.

distinguishable from the market was apparently not a simple or uncontroversial project.[7]

In this article, I read Horatio Alger's novels and the responses they provoked, like the controversies over Olmsted's plans for Central Park, as moments in the struggle to shape the American public sphere, in particular to define the roles men and boys were to play in the economic market and the mass-cultural public.[8] Alger's narrative formula is designed to enlist his readers in the construction of a literary counterpart to the ideal realm of leisure, discipline, and genteel performance Olmsted envisioned. Alger's stories were reformulations of the traditional association of masculinity with the public sphere, ways of interpellating boys as virtuous, "manly" individuals destined to play a role in an especially homosocial version of that sphere.[9] Like Olmsted, Alger tried to imagine a public realm distinct from overtly commercial values and linked to an older model of republican virtue. Despite his best efforts, though, his novels also provoked controversies about the possibility of distinguishing between the public sphere and the realm of economic exchange, controversies that were articulated as anxieties about masculinity and the market. What males bought, what they read, and what they were, all were intimately intertwined with contemporary notions of the public sphere. To some of his adult readers, Alger's form of address to a reading public comprising boys and young men was a morally dubious form of "pandering" to his audience's basest desires and pleasures, a further step in the regrettable and ongoing commodification of the reading public. Because, to use Linda Kerber's words, masculinity and the public sphere were "reciprocal social constructions,"[1] anything that seemed

---

7. Thomas Bender, in *Intellect and Public Life: Essays on the Social History of Academic Intellectuals in the United States* (Baltimore, Md., 1993), see esp. chap. 3, "The Erosion of Public Culture: Cities, Discouses, and Professional Disciplines," 30–46; and William R. Taylor, *In Pursuit of Gotham: Culture and Commerce in New York* (New York, 1992), esp. chap. 3, "The Evolution of Public Space: The Commercial City as Showcase," 35–50; and chap. 5, "Launching a Commercial Culture: Newspaper, Magazine, and Popular Novel as Urban Baedekers," 69–92. Both books provide useful historical accounts of shifting definitions of the public in the United States.
8. For an analysis of the way Alger negotiated the public/private split in his writing career, see Carol Nackenoff, *The Fictional Republic: Horatio Alger and American Political Discourse* (New York, 1994).
9. *Interpellation* is a term used by Louis Althusser to describe the way that ideology "hails" a subject, constituting identity through the very process of addressing the individual. Thus a genre that addresses its audiences as gendered subjects helps to reinscribe in each reader's subjectivity, virtually tautologically, his or her status as a gendered subject. "Ideology and Ideological State Apparatuses (Notes towards an Investigation)," in *Lenin and Philosophy*, trans. Ben Brewster (New York, 1971), 127–86.
1. In an important revisionary analysis of the use in women's history of the notion of separate spheres, Kerber writes that "political systems and systems of gender relations are reciprocal social constructions." "Separate Spheres, Female Worlds, Women's Place: The Rhetoric of Women's History," *Journal of American History* 75 (June 1988): 39.

to debase the contemporary public sphere put the meaning and stability of masculinity into question, and vice versa.

This article is also meant to intervene in an ongoing redefinition of
the public sphere in the study of gender in nineteenth-century American culture. For differentiating the public sphere from the market is
also something that has not been easy to do in American studies. For
two decades now discussions of the nineteenth-century division
between public and private have been framed by variations on the
notion of gendered separate spheres.[2] To be somewhat reductive about
what has proven to be a powerful and useful conceptualization, the
theory of separate spheres maps a set of binary oppositions onto one
another: Masculine is to feminine as reason is to sentiment as the economic market is to the domestic sphere as the political is to the personal as the public is to the private. Historians and literary scholars use
phrases like "the cult of true womanhood," "separate spheres," and
"domestic ideology" to divide and describe nineteenth-century culture,
just as in the nineteenth century a set of opposed values and assumptions could be conjured by reference to "the street" and "the hearth."

This framework has been useful in recovering the ideological con-
straints faced by middle-class white women, as well as in analyzing the
way such women rearticulated this discourse to grant themselves
social, cultural, and protopolitical power.[3] More recently, however,
work by Mary Ryan, Lauren Berlant, Michael Warner, Nancy Fraser,
Linda Kerber, and others has complicated our understanding of the
development of the public-private split, first by pointing out that the
doctrine of separate spheres was always more bourgeois ideology than
national reality, then by beginning the more difficult work of reading
the contradictions that structure and destructure that ideology.[4]
Although each does so quite differently, all of these historians, literary scholars, and political theorists use as their starting points Jürgen

2. Among the key critical and historical texts to have developed and institutionalized the
   domestic-public opposition as central to an understanding of nineteenth-century American culture, especially "women's sphere" and sentimental fiction, are: Ann Douglas, *The
   Feminization of American Culture* (New York, 1977); Nancy F. Cott, *The Bonds of Womanhood: "Women's Sphere" in New England, 1780–1835* (New Haven, Conn., 1977); Nina
   Baym, *Women's Fiction: A Guide to Novels by and about Women in America, 1820–1870*
   (Ithaca, N.Y., 1978); and Mary Kelley, *Private Woman, Public Stage: Literary Domesticity
   in Nineteenth-Century America* (New York, 1984).
3. The literary analyses that set the terms for discussion of these issues are Douglas's *The
   Feminization of American Culture* and Jane Tompkins's *Sensational Designs: The Cultural
   Work of American Fiction, 1790–1860* (New York, 1985). The essays in Shirley Samuels's
   *The Culture of Sentiment: Race, Gender, and Sentimentality in Nineteenth-Century Amer-
   ica* (New York, 1992) are framed as developments in this debate, as is my "The Limits of
   Sympathy: Louisa May Alcott and the Sentimental Novel," *American Literary History* 3
   (winter 1991): 685–706.
4. See Mary P. Ryan, *Women in Public: Between Banners and Ballots, 1825–1880* (Baltimore,
   Md., 1990); Lauren Berlant, *The Anatomy of National Fantasy: Hawthorne, Utopia, and
   Everyday Life* (Chicago, 1991); Michael Warner, *The Letters of the Republic: Publication
   and the Public Sphere in Eighteenth-Century America* (Cambridge, Mass., 1990); Nancy

Habermas's *Structural Transformation of the Public Sphere*.[5] One thing Habermas offers is a way of understanding how market capitalism, even as it provides the economic base for the bourgeois public sphere, also destabilizes that sphere. To oversimplify once again, the problem is exactly the one that Olmsted tried to avoid: Even though the market is supposed to be neither domestic nor political, it still has to be simultaneously private and public, to mediate the contradictions within possessive individualism's founding distinction between the two spheres.[6] Before looking at Alger's imaginary resolution to these contradictions, it will be helpful to understand Habermas's theoretical and historical account of the bourgeois public sphere and especially the roles played by both literature and the market in what he calls the "idea and ideology" of the public.

Habermas argues that the capitalist market and the bourgeois public sphere were from the start closely intertwined but importantly distinguishable. Property ownership was often a prerequisite for political participation; such limits to the public were legitimated by the assertion of a "fictitious identity of the two roles assumed by the privatized individuals who came together to form a public: the role of property owners and the role of human beings pure and simple."[7] Those who were most able socially and psychologically to construct their subjectivity as private were deemed best equipped to participate in the cultural and political world. The bourgeois public sphere thus resolved its potential contradictions by defining the public as made up of privatized individuals gathered together for social ends.

Habermas attributes to literature, and to the novel in particular, a central role in the development of the bourgeois public, which "from the outset was a reading public."[8] The novel mediates between private personality and public sociality because it enacts the division of public and private in each reader merely by evoking his or her identification:

Fraser, "Rethinking the Public Sphere: A Contribution to the Critique of Actually Existing Democracy," in *Habermas and the Public Sphere*, ed., Craig Calhoun (Cambridge, Mass., 1992), 109–42; Linda K. Kerber, *Women of the Republic: Intellect and Ideology in Revolutionary America*, 1980 (New York, 1986).

5. Jürgen Habermas, *The Structural Transformation of the Public Sphere: An Inquiry into a Category of Bourgeois Society*, trans. Thomas Burger with the assistance of Frederick Lawrence (Cambridge, Mass., 1989). The following explanation draws on Craig Calhoun's admirably clear account of Habermas in his Introduction to *Habermas and the Public Sphere*, 1–48.

6. Self-possession is in liberal political theory a prerequisite for entrance into liberal political activity and a capitalist market economy. Both of these connotations exist in Alger's model of subjectivity, placing him in the tradition of possessive individualism. See C. B. Macpherson, *The Political Theory of Possessive Individualism: Hobbes to Locke* (Oxford, 1962).

7. Habermas. *Structural Transformation*, 56. This portion of Habermas's argument is essentially that of Karl Marx. "On the Jewish Question," in *Early Writings* (New York, 1975), 212–41.

8. Habermas, *Structural Transformation*, 23.

[U]s[ing] the relationships between the figures, between the author, the character, and the reader as substitute relationships for reality . . . , the empathetic reader repeated within himself [*sic*] the private relationships displayed before him in literature; from his experience of real familiarity (*Intimität*) he gave life to the fictional one, and in the latter he prepared himself for the former.[9]

The novel, then, prepared its readers for participation in the public realm by inscribing at the psychological level the political division between public and private. And the literary market played an enabling role in this process by making this form of experience available, at least in theory, to anyone who had access to books. It also inspired the establishment of a whole set of institutions in civil society that Habermas, here following Tocqueville, sees as the foundation of the bourgeois public sphere: coffeehouses, reading clubs, subscription libraries, and in some countries newspapers. Books and other cultural texts, as commodities that pretend to exist for their own sakes—or, perhaps more importantly, that exist for the purpose of being interpreted—can instantiate the public sphere in much the same way as one of these institutions. Inasmuch as literature is designed to be openly criticized and actively interpreted, it exemplifies the openness and the rational-critical basis of the political public.[1]

The act of reading, in Habermas's account, both psychologically and materially positions the private subject to participate in public discourse. The same is true in Horatio Alger's public sphere. Alger typically foregrounds his protagonist's illiterate status early in his stories. "I ain't much on readin'," says Ragged Dick early in the novel, "'It makes my head ache'" (28). Along with the acquisition of property—a bank account, a gold watch, and a new suit of clothes—the Alger boy's success is marked by his learning to read.[2] But literacy is not just the means to an economic end one might expect it to

---

9. Habermas, *Structural Transformation*, 50–51. The fact that in this section of his argument Habermas doesn't discuss women—who, at least in the United States, likely made up the majority of novel readers—is indicative of the general gender blindness that Nancy Fraser points out in his work in "What's Critical About Critical Theory?: The Case of Habermas and Gender," in *Unruly Practices: Power, Discourse and Gender in Contemporary Social Theory* (Minneapolis, Minn., 1989), 113–43.
1. For an historical evaluation of the applicability of Habermas's framework to the American case, see Michael Schudson, "Was there Ever a Public Sphere? If So, When? Reflections on the American Case," in Calhoun, *Habermas and the Public Sphere*, 143–63.
2. As historians of literacy have shown, literacy is always more than a statistical fact or practical skill; it has cultural meanings that shift geographically and historically. See Harvey J. Graff, ed., *Literacy and Social Development in the West: A Reader* (Cambridge, England, 1981); Harvey J. Graff, *The Legacies of Literacy: Continuities and Contradictions in Western Culture and Society* (Bloomington, Ind., 1987); Harvey J. Graff, *The Literacy Myth: Literacy and Social Structure in the Nineteenth-Century City* (New York, 1979); Warner's *The Letters of the Republic*; and several of the essays in Cathy N. Davidson, ed., *Reading in America: Literature and Social History* (Baltimore, Md., 1989).

be in an Alger novel, even though it is usually accompanied by the
hero's upward mobility. More importantly, the boys develop a relation
to books that makes reading a significantly public act. The path to
economic success in the Alger novel runs parallel with a path toward
a closer connection to the public sphere.

To be sure, few of Alger's characters enter public life in the conventional sense; the hero never really comes to be or even know the
president or the mayor, although he jokingly claims both. When
asked "What's the use of studying so much," Dick responds, "If my
feller-citizens should want me to go to Congress some time, I
shouldn't want to disapp'int 'em; and then readin' and writin' might
come handy" (107). Alger's publicity—and here I am using the
somewhat awkward translation of Habermas's word *Offentlichkeit*,
which might more literally be translated as "publicness"[3]—is not
overtly social or political; it is a characteristic an individual boy can
cultivate in himself.[4] All of the positive adjectives Alger repeatedly
uses to introduce his protagonists—"frank," "honest," "bold,"
"attractive," and "manly"—refer to some degree to an ideal of
transparent legibility. The prerequisite of virtuous publicity is simply that the boy's interiority and surface appearance are identical.
In Alger's public sphere, the moral character of things and especially people is immediately legible to anyone trained in sympathetic observation.[5] One can recognize an honest boy, whether by
means of his outward actions or his physiognomy, and he will recognize you in turn. Some such scene occurs in virtually every novel;
the Alger hero meets a businessman, usually in a public space like
a street or a train car, and each judges the other in an instant.
Dick's "open face," along with his claim to "know all about the public buildings," convinces Mr. Whitney that the boy is a suitable tour
guide for his son. "I may be rash in trusting a boy of whom I know
nothing," the man says, "but I like your looks" (17). Even when one
Alger character, tricked into assisting in a robbery, is caught in the

---

3. See Thomas Burger, Translator's Note, in Habermas, *Structural Transformation*, xv–xvi.
4. The telling exception to this rule is *Phil, the Fiddler,* which Alger claimed exposed and
thereby ended the exploitation of Italian street musicians by their *padrones.* Gary Scharnhorst and Jack Bales claim that "in *Phil* more than in any other novel Alger wrote, his altru-
istic impulses were at war with his formula," because "his angry story had to end happily."
The Lost Life of Horatio Alger, Jr. (Bloomington, Ind., 1985), 96–97. This is only true if we
see his "formula" as a set of narrative conventions, rather than as a mechanism for character formation that works through publicity. Alger makes explicit in *Phil* his notion of the
function of literature as socially ameliorative and asserts that it fulfills that function precisely by publicizing the problem it is meant to address. Even the musicians' exploitation
is framed as a problem in the transparency of language rather than power or economics;
their inability to communicate their own situation is clearly the source of their oppression.
Until he masters English, Phil cannot even "analyze his own emotions." Horatio Alger,
Phil, the Fiddler; or, The Young Street Musician (1872; New York, 1945), 301.
5. For a discussion of transparency of character as an ideal of sincerity, see Karen Halttunen,
Confidence Men and Painted Women: A Study of Middle-Class Culture (New Haven, Conn.,
1982), 33–55.

act, the victim can see the boy's innocence immediately: " 'You have an innocent face' responded the young man kindly. 'I am sure you are a good boy.' "[6] This ability to be read as attractively virtuous is at the origin of the Alger hero's success. As another boy's benefactor puts it with disarming ambiguity: "He is a very good looking boy, and he looks *good*, which is still better."[7]

Literacy and personal legibility are tied in the Alger novel to another set of meanings: They are prerequisites for honest and profitable participation in the market. It is this association that links the world of the street boy to the world of business, for "Street boys . . . are by their circumstances made preternaturally sharp" and "Wall Street men are good judges of human nature."[8] The boy's "sharpness" and his "active sympathy" are signs of and means toward his moral and financial rise. This assumption links Alger's ostensible moral cause—the construction of a public sphere of linguistic and economic exchange based in confidence, active sympathy, and transparency of communication—with his hero's personal quest for success. Alger's analogy between personal and social publicity relies for its legitimacy on a corresponding connection between literacy and legibility, between reading well and looking good.

The Alger boy's virtuousness, an older male observer remarks in *The Store Boy*, "is of the old-fashioned kind. It is not the kind now in vogue."[9] His combination of literacy and legibility is not "in vogue" because it derives from an older model of public masculinity; the representation of literature as public disclosure of hidden wrongs and the association of literacy with public virtue were characteristic of the republican rhetoric that Alger appropriated.[1] As historians of the early Republic have pointed out, early American writers and politicians alike represented the political public and the reading public as analogous and even identical. The act of reading was, David Paul Nord argues, "a form of participation in the new social order of

---

6. Horatio Alger, Jr., *Jed, the Poorhouse Boy*, in *Struggling Upward and Other Works* (1892; 1899; New York, 1945), 522.

7. Horatio Alger, Jr., *Silas Snobden's Office Boy* (1889–1890; Garden City, N.Y., 1973), 91.

8. Horatio Alger, Jr., *Julius; or, The Street Boy Out West*, in *Strive and Succeed: Two Novels by Horatio Alger* (1874; New York, 1967), 35–36; Horatio Alger, Jr., *The World Before Him*, in *Adrift in New York and The World Before Him* (1880, ed. William Coyle; New York, 1966), 229.

9. Horatio Alger. Jr., *The Store Boy; or, The Fortunes of Ben Barclay*, in *Strive and Succeed: Two Novels by Horatio Alger* (1887; New York, 1967), 140.

1. Alger's affinity with eighteenth-century ideals has been well documented in John Cawelti, *Apostles of the Self-Made Man: Changing Concepts of Success in America* (Chicago, 1965). This nostalgia provides another rhetorical parallel between Alger and Olmsted. Olmsted's earliest writings were published under the Jeffersonian pseudonyms of Yeoman and An American Farmer and made recourse to an agrarian republican model of the public sphere predicated on a separation between the cultural and the commercial. See Barlow, *Frederick Law Olmsted's New York*, 7.

postrevolutionary America."[2] When Dick describes himself as having "diffused intelligence among the masses"—meaning that he has sold newspapers—his phrasing is classical republican rhetoric, a phrase used since the eighteenth century to describe the public function of print (38).[3]

An it to made a a one this association, the boy's apparent virtue often becomes public reality when he is put into print himself. When Dick is told that a newspaper is advertising an unaddressed letter under the name of RAGGED DICK, his pride in having received a letter— in itself an act that signifies access to a protopublic sphere of literate exchange—is doubled by his excitement over seeing his name in print.[4] This is the first moment in the book in which Dick's openness to being read is equaled by his ability to read. It marks a turning point in the novel, a confirmation that the boy is on the road from rags to respectability. Upward economic mobility and the moral development of character are figured in Alger novels as a kind of publication, a chain of publicity that begins within the novel, where an experience like seeing his name in the newspaper is enough to motivate the boy to further good deeds, through each series of novels, where the spectacle of the hero's actions influences his "ward" for the better,[5] to the reader, who is subject to a discourse of moral suasion that assumes he will be improved by his identification with the character in print. Reading Alger's books, like entering Olmsted's parks, puts one in a public place distinguishable from and immune to the deception characteristic of the market.

Although the boy's combination of literacy and publicity establishes an apparently stable, proper, and legible character that he and his readers can build upon, it can also produce in Alger's heroes a crisis of identity, evidence of one contradiction in Alger's construction of masculine publicity. For there is a disjunction between print and persons, between publicity and subjectivity, that makes the boy

2. David Paul Nord, "A Republican Literature: Magazine Reading and Readers in Late Eighteenth-Century New York" in Davidson, Reading in America: Literature and Social History, 115. For a discussion of the meaning of this association for women, see Kerber, Women of the Republic, 235–64.

3. As Michael Warner points out, George Washington argued in his farewell address that "a general diffusion of knowledge" was one of the prerequisites for the continued survival of the republic. Warner also notes the continuity between Washington's rhetoric and Alger's (The Letters of the Republic, 123). Dick's claim that his ragged coat had been owned by Washington, who "wore it all through the Revolution" and then "told his widder to give it to some smart young feller" shows that Alger was intent on making his hero's ideological ancestry clear (5).

4. For more on the relationship between letter writing and the public sphere, see Habermas, The Structural Transformation of the Public Sphere. On pleasure at seeing one's name in print, see Gilles Deleuze and Félix Guattari, A Thousand Plateaus: Capitalism and Schizophrenia, trans. Brian Massumi (Minneapolis, Minn., 1987), xviii.

5. Beginning with Ragged Dick, Alger's publishing contracts were usually for series of four or five novels; hence the Ragged Dick series was followed by the Tattered Tom series, and so on.

uncomfortable, threatening to reveal his "manliness" as a masquerade. In short, the Alger hero's ability to "look *good*" is a potentially dangerous quality because it risks making his performance of virtue look like a confidence game.[6] Publicity, Alger warns his readers, may undermine the very virtue it is meant to guarantee.

Even Dick, among the most self-assured of Alger's heroes, is unnerved by having to match his identity to his printed name when he goes to pick up the advertised letter. He fears that the postal officials will not give him the letter, because he no longer fits the advertised description of Ragged Dick, but at his friend Fosdick's suggestion he dons his old clothes, disapprovingly surveys himself in a mirror, and sneaks out (118). The discomfort Dick shows when forced to assume his former identity threatens to reveal both roles—the street urchin and the respectable working boy—as fictions. "I believe in dressin' up to your name," Dick says to the postal clerk who questions his identity, and that assertion and the boy's raggedness are enough to convince the clerk that the letter is indeed for him (119). The boy's statement is humorous in part because it goes against the grain of the narrative as a whole, in which Ragged Dick changes his name to Dick and then to Richard Hunter. It would be more accurate to say that Dick believes in changing his name to match his dress.[7] The changes in identity that are so central to the Alger narrative come to seem a kind of theatrical performance, a willed assumption of a role.

The fact that boys can take on and dispose of names and identities at will is a source of hope that their lives and fortunes may be concomitantly changed; it is an essential part of the fantasy of upward mobility and personal mutability that made Alger's novels so popular and pleasurable. Karen Halttunen has argued that the Alger hero's manipulation of appearance marks a decisive shift in the moral connotations of theatricality in middle-class culture. Whereas earlier in the nineteenth century, the figure of the confidence man was a threat to the bourgeois system of economic and symbolic exchange, in Alger's novels and the advice books published for young men in the

---

6. Nathaniel West's vicious parody-pastiche of Alger, *A Cool Million* (New York, 1934), is based on the idea that Alger's formula universalizes the con game, that it makes the world into a big con.

7. Names and identities are even more flexible in Alger's *Adrift in New York; or, Tom and Florence Braving the World*, in *Adrift in New York and The World Before Him* (1889, ed. William Coyle; New York, 1966). When the novel's protagonist, known as Tom Dodger, wakes up after being kidnapped, drugged, and put on a slow boat to California, he is mistakenly addressed by the captain as Arthur Grant. Dodger's renaming makes him strangely happy: "He had recently felt the need of a name," he says to himself, "and didn't see why this wouldn't answer his purpose as well as any other." And, like Ragged Dick's recognition of himself in the newspaper, the writing of this new name stabilizes his identity: "'I must write it down so as not to forget it,' he resolved. 'It would seem queer if I forgot my own name'" (81). Grant/Dodger's later transformation into the heir to a fortune is paralleled by his assumption of yet another name, Harvey Linden (144).

latter decades of the century, the confidence man becomes a figure to emulate. "[T]he manipulation of others through artifice was coming to be accepted as a necessary executive skill," and as evidence Halttunen cites an advice book writer who extolled "the arts by which we read the hearts of men, and artifices by which we mould them to our purposes . . . it is not enough for us to do, we must also seem. . . ."[8]

This positive valuation of conscious manipulation had been latent in American narratives of success since Benjamin Franklin's *Autobiography*, and it is an important element in Alger's formula. However, it is also in tension with the model of virtue, legibility, and literacy that just as certainly structures Alger's narratives. The very idea of the confidence man militates against his fantasy of a transparent publicity, undermining both its individual and its social manifestations. Thus Alger insists that his heroes do not "calculate" on success; a supposedly instinctive or inadvertent performance is virtually the only form of agency allowed to the boy in his trek to publicity. The Alger hero must constantly be waiting for an opportunity to attract the attention of a wealthy male observer, whose daughter must coincidentally fall off the ferryboat when the boy is the only person watching. The often-noted passivity of the Alger hero is fundamental to his virtuousness; although his preferred path to success is recognition from an affluent observer, anything consciously designed to attract such notice would be a morally ambiguous theatrical manipulation of an audience, a performance of masculinity. Virtuous publicity and active agency—both of which are seen as constitutive of masculinity—are thus placed in tension with one another.

Alger's public sphere is, again, an attempt to mediate these contradictions. For the boy's actions always takes place on a public stage, whether he means them to or not. Male actions in Alger novels are inherently public, performed for an audience larger than the boy's intimate circle of friends. No matter where the boy is, the books lead us to expect that someone he does not know is always watching and waiting to reward virtue or even the appearance of virtue. A contrast with two of the very few cases in which Alger creates female protagonists illustrates his interdependent definitions of masculinity and the public sphere. While Mabel, the adult woman who is the heroine of Alger's *A Fancy of Hers*, gains a husband as a reward for her performance of virtue—a performance that is never revealed to anyone but this man—the Alger boy never escapes the notice of benefactors, even if his virtue is hidden beneath a veneer of filth, because the publicity in which he exists makes him immediately legible. And in Alger's only attempt to place a girl at the center of his standard formula, *Tattered*

8. Halttunen, *Confidence Men and Painted Women*, 204.

Tom, he starts the novel with his heroine seemingly on the standard path to the public sphere—she is dressed as a newsboy—but by the end she is firmly ensconced in respectable domesticity. Both Mabel and Tom are reinscribed in a feminine privacy, whereas the telos of the male protagonist's performance of virtue is publicity.[9]

Alger's ambivalent representation of masculinity lies at the center of his formula's appeal, marking for readers both the pleasures and the dangers of his fiction. Toward the end of *Ragged Dick*, Alger describes the change that the title character has undergone in the following terms: "He was beginning to feel the advantages of his steady self-denial, and to experience the pleasures of property" (105). This sentence in part supports the most standard interpretation of Alger's moral stance: Work hard and save and you will become rich. But the phrase "the pleasures of property" sweetens its offer of financial success with a promise of something more seductive, a reward more affective than economic. Given that Dick's "steady self-denial" has included giving up the activities he found pleasurable in his former life—the Old Bowery theater and Barnum's museum—what new pleasures accrue to a boy who still owns little more than a single suit of clothing and a small bank account?

In place of the mass-cultural theatricality available at Barnum's and the Old Bowery, *Ragged Dick* offers its protagonist and audience the pleasures, again, of *reading*. Of course, reading is presented not as a pleasure but as a virtue. Yet it quite literally replaces the theater in Dick's schedule as well as in his affections; at Frank Whitney's behest, he stops spending his nights at plays and instead gives his friend Fosdick a space in his bed in exchange for reading lessons. At the same time, reading is represented as a property relation. Frank's father advises Dick to "'Save your money, my lad, buy books, and determine to be somebody, and you may yet fill an honorable position'" (56). Reading is essential to the virtuous respectability toward which the Alger hero aspires, and buying books is a form of consumerism in which it is virtuous to take pleasure, even the intimately homosocial pleasure of reading in bed with a friend. Alger thus offers

---

9. Horatio Alger, Jr., *A Fancy of Hers*, in *A Fancy of Hers/The Disagreeable Woman* (1892; New York, 1981). *Tattered Tom; or, The Story of a Street Arab* (Boston, 1871). Michael Moon discusses the latter tale briefly, arguing that Tom's restoration to her rich mother and "her long-lost genteel, feminine identity" is the only example of an Alger protagonist who "does not 'rise' as a consequence of her demonstrably enterprising and honest behavior." See Michael Moon, "'The Gentle Boy from the Dangerous Classes': Pederasty, Domesticity, and Capitalism in Horatio Alger," *Representations* 19 (summer 1987): 95–97. In fact, several of Alger's books culminate in the hero's succeeding because of the discovery that he is of genteel or even noble descent, rather than because of his behavior; what differentiates Tom's rise is that, like Mabel in *A Fancy of Hers*, she rises to a place *out* of the public eye.

his readers an affective lure—rather than a narrowly political or economic one—to accept their interpellation into the public sphere.

Alger was not the only writer of his time to represent reading as a virtuous property relation that comes with an affective bonus. Essays and books, aimed at young men and boys who were aspiring to middle-class respectability, counseled their readers not only to read more, but to purchase and collect books. It is perhaps not surprising that a volume commissioned by Appleton's Home Books, purveyors of atlases and moral guidebooks, argued that "A book that is really worth reading is worth owning," especially since this advice is closely followed by a sales pitch for several of the company's other publications.[1] But similar advice came from less overtly interested sources as well. For instance, Noah Porter, then president of Yale University, argues in his *Books and Reading* that "Readers of books desire to become the owners of books . . . Hence, books like everything else which is desirable come to be sought for and valued as property."[2] Books are commodities which it is virtuous not only to possess but also to enjoy.

Writers like Porter praise young men's "desire to become the owners of books," and yet they condemn works of "cheap literature" that are "simply a reflex of the commonplace aims and the vulgar feelings of the mass of readers for whom they are written. They are made to *take* and made to *sell*, and they both *take* and *sell*, because they humor what their readers like."[3] These authors' aversion to "selling" is not rooted in any antipathy toward market capitalism; many of the literary advice books are bound with advertisements not only for other books but also for other commodities. Moreover, most include a list of books deemed necessary to comprise a respectable library, thus blurring the distinction between moral advice and advertisement.[4] The counsel they offer is thus somewhat contradictory: The most virtuous "pleasures of property" derive from buying things that are not "made to sell."

All of these advice books and articles demand that young men and boys ask themselves the questions in Porter's subtitle: *What Books Shall I Read and How Shall I Read Them?* The two questions are linked quite deliberately; what matters is how a book asks to be read,

---

1. Arthur Penn, *The Home Library*, Appleton's Home Books (New York, 1883), 15.
2. Noah Porter, *Books and Reading; or, What Books Shall I Read and How Shall I Read Them?* (1870; New York, 1882), 360.
3. Porter, *Books and Reading*, 97–98.
4. The copy of the Appleton's guide I examined includes promotions for stained glass and gas fixtures as well as *Webster's Unabridged* and a book of reminiscences of great authors. Those volumes that include a section on "some choice books for boys" seldom if ever place any of Alger's fiction on their lists, although one recommends Alger's biography of James Garfield, *From Canal Boy to President, or, The Boyhood and Manhood of James A. Garfield* (New York, 1881) and praises him as "another sympathetic writer for boys." Mary Alice Caller, *A Literary Guide for Home and School* (New York, 1892), 131.

the kind of response it provokes in its audience. Porter answers his question in revealingly contradictory ways. On the one hand, one should only read what is made to be read in the proper way. He approvingly cites Robert Southey's rules for distinguishing "whether the tendency of a book is good or evil," which advises readers to "examine in what state of mind you lay it down": If the book has made you "dissatisfied and impatient under the control of others" or weakened your "self-government, without which both the laws of God and man tell us there can be no virtue and consequently no happiness," then "throw the book into the fire, young man, though it should have been the gift of a friend!"[5] According to this statement, one can immediately apprehend the intention and effect of a book and can judge it accordingly. In other words, the book itself predetermines its reader's responses, and books exist in the same sphere of transparent legibility that Alger creates for his boys. Yet elsewhere in *Books and Reading*, the Yale president argues that how one reads is at least as important as the content or intention of the book itself, that the same book might be read in different ways. "*Passive* reading is the evil habit against which most readers need to be guarded, and to overcome which, when formed, requires the most manful and persevering efforts."[6] Novels—Porter's examples are women's sentimental novels and boy-books—are the kinds of literature that are most likely to elicit this seductively passive response, for the novel reader "often becomes for the time an unconscious imitator or a passive reflex of his author."[7]

Porter distinguishes between two kinds of reading: one manly and virtuous, the other passive, feminizing, and "dangerous." The reader of mass-cultural trash, especially boy-books and sentimental novels, risks becoming "almost an intellectual idiot or an effeminate weakling by living exclusively upon the enfeebling swash or the poisoned stimulants that are sold so readily under the title of tales and novels." In contrast, the virtuous reader "will find in himself . . . the manhood that he has and which he is bound to think of and care for."[8] Protecting and cultivating this manhood is, finally, the purpose of reading.[9]

Even virtuous reading, however, requires a degree of readerly passivity, or at least a tentative acquiescence to the author's power. At

5. Porter, *Books and Reading*, 72–73.
6. Ibid., 33.
7. Ibid., 230.
8. Ibid., 232, 41.
9. Here I am drawing on recent historical scholarship on the construction and reproduction of masculinity and manliness in the nineteenth century, much of which is ably synthesized in the opening chapter of Gail Bederman, *Manliness and Civilization: A Cultural History of Gender and Race in the United States, 1880–1917* (Chicago, 1995).

times this passivity is figured as an intersubjective relation of sympathy between author and reader; the reader "sympathize[s] with the feelings which [the author] experienced . . . ," Porter writes, and throughout his text he reiterates that when we read we must "widen and make yielding our sympathies" to the point where we "yield our feelings to his control by that pliant sympathy which is requisite for our enjoyment of his enthusiasm."[1] Sympathy in this context designates a communication of affect; as Theodore Parker concisely defined the term in an essay on how men can encourage manly character: "Feeling, he must make others feel."[2] Alger conceived of his fiction as evoking a similar communication of affect between reader, character, and author: "A writer for boys should have an abundant sympathy with them. . . . A boy's heart opens to the man or writer who understands him."[3] But while Porter and Alger share the concept of sympathy, their conceptions differ in their intended result. Alger seeks not the critical reflection Porter advocates, but imitation. "Perhaps," he says of Dick, "although he was only a bootblack, [readers] may find something in him to imitate" (44). As didactic fiction, Alger's novels depend on his readers' acceptance of precisely the role that Porter warns them against: becoming "an unconscious imitator or passive reflex of his author," just as his model of success necessitates a degree of patience and passivity, at least until the opportunity arises to save a rich man's daughter from drowning or to unmask a pickpocket.

In its motivations and mechanisms, this description of sympathy recalls the sympathetic identification valorized above all in the women's sentimental novel, which entails a potentially self-negating surrender to the emotions of a suffering heroine.[4] But it is important to resist the temptation to see in this discourse a straightforward feminization of the male reader. Such an interpretation is certainly invited by Porter's image of the novel reader as an "effeminate weakling" and the statement by Charles Francis Adams, Jr., that "insipid or sensational fiction . . . simply and certainly emasculates and destroys the intelligent reading power."[5] But Porter insists that this passivity can be a form of masculinity, for male sympathy allows the reader to find "the manhood that he has." Alger as well argues that his "abundant sympathy" is most evident in the fact that his heroes

---

1. Porter, *Books and Reading*, 20, 51, 235, 51.
2. Theodore Parker, *Lessons from the World of Matter and the World of Man.* Selected from notes of unpublished sermons by Rufus Leighton. *The Collected Works of Theodore Parker* (London, 1872), 108–9.
3. Horatio Alger, Jr., "Writing Stories for Boys.—IV," *The Writer* 9 (Mar. 1896): 37.
4. For an account of sympathy's self negation, see Hendler, "The Limits of Sympathy," 690–94.
5. Charles Francis Adams, Jr., "Fiction in Public Libraries and Educational Catalogues," *Library Journal* 4 (Sept.–Oct. 1879): 334.

are "manly boys," because boy readers are unwilling to identify with "goody-goody boys."[6]

What guarantees that male sympathy is not feminizing is, simply if circularly, that it is a relation between males. Porter advises that "when a man reads he should put himself in the most intimate intercourse with his author, so that all his energies of apprehension, judgment and feeling may be occupied with and aroused by what his author furnishes. . . ."[7] Perhaps to contain the feminizing potential of sympathetic male reading, the writers of literary advice books consistently represent the relation between readers and authors and between readers and books as an affectively charged form of homosocial companionship. As Charles Thwing writes in his 1883 text, *The Reading of Books: Its Pleasures, Profits, and Perils,* "The book is a friend who never fails to respond to every emotion."[8]

The metaphor of books as companions is not peculiar to the second half of the nineteenth century, but in that period the metaphor acquired new, economic connotations. Thwing writes that "the reader buys books gradually. He gains them, as he gains friends, one by one."[9] Here Thwing, like Alger, blurs the distinction between an affective relation and a economic one; two pages earlier he has described books as a kind of decorative furniture, while here they are figured as friends.[1] While the advice books claim to differentiate the public virtue enacted in male reading from the commercialism of the market, ultimately the public and the economic come to be instances of the same "pleasures of property." In other words, these books work through some of the same tensions between the public and the market, the affective and the economic, as does Alger's fiction, offering readers a vision of an affectively charged, male homosocial public sphere made up of literate, virtuous, possessive individuals.

Late in Alger's career, the tensions underlying his formula became more visible, provoking a critical revaluation of his fiction. Appropriately enough, the ambivalence about Alger played itself out as a controversy over whether public funds should be used to supply public libraries with Alger's books and other popular fiction.[2] The debate, which motivated a conference at the Boston Public Library and filled the November 1879 issue of *The Library Journal,* raises the same issues of gender, the market, publicity, and reading that traverse

---

6. Alger, "Writing Stories for Boys," 37.
7. Porter, *Books and Reading,* 47.
8. Charles Thwing, *The Reading of Books: Its Pleasures, Profits, and Perils* (Boston, 1883), 2.
9. Ibid., 124.
1. "[Books] are in a sense the 'fixtures' of a home." Ibid., 121.
2. For a useful account of this and similar controversies, see Esther Jane Carrier, *Fiction in Public Libraries,* 1876–1900 (New York, 1965).

Alger's narratives. It represents another move in the struggle to artic-
ulate the shape of the cultural public sphere.

The *Library Journal* reprinted papers by several professional librarians, as well as professors like William T. Atkinson and luminaries
like the Reverends James Freeman Clarke and Thomas W. Higginson,[2] The issue at hand was succinctly delineated by the librarian of
Worcester, Massachusetts, when he asserted that while "no librarian
would think of putting an immoral book into a library," a more difficult problem is raised by those books whose morality is ambiguous,
"written by men who mean well" like Alger and his mentor, Oliver
Optic. Should such books, he asks, "find a place in public libraries?"[4]

The debate revolved around two related questions: What effect did
morally ambiguous fiction like that written by Alger and Optic have
on its audience, and what does the word "public" mean in the phrase,
public library? The first question provoked strongly gendered rhetoric, as some believed that "Oliver Opticism" damages the "limp mind
of the ordinary boy," while others argued that it promotes a virtuously
imperialistic masculinity:

> It is not a bad impulse but a good one which makes the child
> seek the reading you call sensational. The motive that sends him
> to Oliver Optic is just that love of adventure which has made the
> Anglo-American race spread itself across a continent, taking
> possession of it in spite of forests, rivers, deserts, wild Indians
> and grizzly bears. . . . [5]

On the meaning of the word "public," the participants were almost
as starkly divided. Most agreed that libraries, like Olmsted's parks,
should carve out a space between "instruction" and "rational entertainment." What was more problematic, though, was the relation
between the public library and the market. Again discussing Alger
and Optic, James Freeman Clarke asserted that

> the Public library is for the same purpose as the Public Garden,
> Public Baths, music on the Common provided by the city, or fire-
> works on the Fourth of July. Why do we provide these things at
> the public expense? Because they tend to refine and elevate the

3. Higginson in 1864 wrote one of the earliest positive reviews of Alger's first full novel,
   Frank's Campaign, or, The Farm and the Camp (1864; New York, n.d.). Clarke in 1877 had
   denounced the "'endless reams' of drivel poured forth by Horatio Alger, Jr., and Oliver
   Optic"; Scharnhorst and Bales speculate that Alger named one of his villains "Clarke"
   shortly thereafter "in oblique reply" to the attack. See Scharnhorst and Bales, *Lost Life of
   Horatio Alger, Jr.*, 63, 118.
4. Another speaker formulated the problem thus: "The question to which good men who have
   studied library economy give different answers is, whether such books as those of which
   the writings of William T. Adams ('Oliver Optic'), and Horatio Alger, Jr., are examples
   among books provided for the young, and of Mrs. Southworth and Mrs. Hentz, among
   works wished for by older persons, ought to find a place in public libraries." S. S. Green,
   "Sensational Fiction in Public Libraries," *Library Journal* 4 (Sept.–Oct. 1879): 347.
5. T. W. Higginson, "Address of T. W. Higginson," *Library Journal* 4 (Sept.–Oct. 1879): 357.

people, because they tend to make them contented, cheerful and happy, because they tend to prevent crime by giving a taste for something better than the drinking saloon. Thus they make the whole community more safe and peaceful—they take the place of a police—they supplement the Public Schools.[6]

How, then, should libraries respond to the popularity of Alger and Optic? How can libraries fulfill their "police" function of maintaining public order through private reading?

Charles Francis Adams, Jr., who insisted that sensational fiction "emasculated" its readers, felt that using "public money" for the "wholesale purchase of trashy and ephemeral literature" was unjustified not so much because such literature should not be read, but because "those who wish to do so should be willing to pay for them, as they do for their theatres."[7] The public library is differentiated from the theater precisely by its public status, which is again defined as its separation from the market. Books that are "made to sell," Adams argues, belong in the market—subscription libraries and bookstores—and not in the public realm. The basis of this distinction lies in his interpretation of the market as an immoral reversal of the ideal scene of reading. Rather than the transparent medium of communication between boy and man, reader and author, characteristic of virtuous publicity, the literary mass market is governed by a reading practice that is dangerously unidirectional; the reader is read by the market, and thereby turned into a consumer. "The publisher of today," he argues, "understands the popular appetite almost perfectly well. . . . He studies the market, and not his own inner consciousness; the result is that he publishes what the market will take."[8]

Adams insists that there is nothing essentially immoral about this procedure, for it is the economic logic of capitalism and the basis of some of America's highest literary accomplishments—his example is *Harper's Monthly*. However, it is essential that one literary relation be kept apart from this dynamic: the public library's relation to children, especially boys. The books of Alger, Optic, and others should be relegated to the logic of the market and not allowed in the public library. Reading boys in public—the kind of judging of an audience that is essential to the targeting and creation of a male mass audience—is

6. James Freeman Clarke, "Address of James Freeman Clarke," *Library Journal* 4 (Sept.–Oct. 1879): 356

7. Charles Francis Adams, Jr., "Fiction in Public Libraries and Educational Catalogues," *Library Journal*, 331.

8. Ibid., 337. The result of this unidirectional reading is what the Appleton's Guide had warned against when it decried "the ready-made literature turned out by the fiction-mills. . . . Now, it is not right to call the consumers of stuff like this readers. Charles Lamb speaks of books which are not books, so these are readers who are not readers. They read with the eye alone, while the brain is inert." Penn, *The Home Library*, 28.

precisely the problem that the public library is designed to contain, because targeting boys erodes the distinction between the public and the market. Using Alger as his main example, he writes: "I fear the public libraries are, by degrees, approaching somewhat near to what it is not using too strong a term to call *pandering* "[9]

When Adams and others figure the relation between morally questionable books and their readers as a kind of pandering,—whether defined as "minister[ing] to the gratification of another's lust" or as catering to "the baser passions" in general[1]—and raise the specter of the public library operating on the model of "bread-and-circuses," their rhetoric condenses sexual and economic anxieties into a single worry about the meaning of male reading in the public sphere. Adams's fear is that an uncontrolled distribution of popular books like Alger's will collapse the public sphere into the mass market, thus making readers and citizens into consumers. Alger's books were at the center of this controversy, and yet they are not obviously any more mass cultural or sensationalistic than many others. The questions they aroused among nineteenth-century guardians of morality may have been due to the way his characters court the very relations Adams fears. Pandering is not a threat to the Alger boy. Indeed, as several critics have noted, the paradigmatic encounter between the boy and his older mentor is depicted as a kind of virtuous seduction, in which the boy's rewards are, at the least, "the pleasures of property." The encounter is equally and simultaneously an act of reading, of transparent communicability, in which each participant—again, almost always in a space like a street or a train—interprets the other's performance of virtuous masculinity. The model of transparent communicability such encounters offer to the reader entails the ambiguously economic and affective pleasures of the very pandering Adams decries.

Some of Alger's recent critics and biographers have read this dynamic as related to the event that occasioned Alger's decision to become a full-time, boy-book writer: his dismissal in 1866 from the ministry in Brewster, Massachusetts, for what the Unitarian Church report called "the abominable and revolting crime of unnatural familiarity with *boys*."[2] And, in fact, one of the few nineteenth-century

9. Adams, "Fiction in Public Libraries," 331. Emphasis added.
1. Both definitions are part of the *Oxford English Dictionary* entry under "pander."
2. Quoted in Scharnhorst and Bales, *The Lost Life*, 67. In light of this fact, it is easy to interpret as homoerotic Alger's claims to have all his life "made a close study of boys" as material for his books, and to have a rapport with his readers because "I have a natural liking for boys, which has made it easy for me to win their confidence and become intimately acquainted with them. Horatio Alger, "Writing Stories for Boys," 37. Such sentences are typical of the way the relation between male authors, books, and readers were figured in this period; another writer in the same series of essays that Alger wrote in proclaims that "I cannot write a book at all until I have actually made the intimate personal acquaintance" of its characters, "so that they will be confidential and tell me how they feel and what they

readers familiar with Alger's pederastic sexual history, a Brewster deacon named Solomon Freeman, articulated his antipathy to Alger by
linking the scandal to his writing. In a letter to the general secretary
of the church, Freeman expressed the fear that Alger's pernicious
influence carried through his fiction, voicing indignation that "he was
still permitted to contribute to the respectable periodicals, particularly those intended for boys to read." The danger lay not in the content of the stories, which the letter doesn't mention, but in Alger's
inexcusable desire to place his stories and himself in the public eye
after the scandal. Above all, Freeman declares, "his name should
never have appeared in any production before the public," and the
church secretary agreed that he was "sorry . . . at the readiness to
come forward into public so soon, on the part of Mr. Alger." Alger's
indiscreet desire to publicize his "familiarity with boys" persisted for
several years, for in 1870 Henry James, Sr., expressed surprise and
annoyance that "Alger talks freely about his own late insanity—which
he in fact appears to enjoy as a subject of conversation. . . ."[3]

The indignation of Freeman and James was echoed more than two
decades later in an 1893 issue of *The Literary World* by an anonymous reviewer who presumably knew nothing of the Brewster scandal. This writer proclaimed him or herself "indignant not only with
the writer, who might do something better than pour forth this
unceasing stream of sensational, impossible literature, but with the
boys who persistently read, enjoy, and talk them over." For that
anonymous writer, Alger is clearly guilty of a scandalously successful
pandering, one that produces enjoyment in its objects. However, the
reviewer acknowledges that "it is only fair to say that the writer
intends always to lay stress on the qualities of energy, truth, and manliness," implicitly granting Alger and his boys a marginal but recognizable masculinity but simultaneously demonstrating the instability
of masculinity's meaning.[4] I have been arguing here that late-
nineteenth-century shifts in the semantic and ideological connotations of the concepts of masculinity and publicity put the meaning
and stability of both terms into question. For many readers, Alger's
fantasies of masculine publicity came to epitomize the very transformations they seem designed to contain: the theatricalization and

---

mean to do." William O. Stoddard, "How to Write a Story for Boys.—1," *The Writer* 9
(Sept. 1895): 128.

   Alger's recent biographers have, with some justification, interpreted Alger's pederasty
as a motive for his literary production in general. My interpretation of homosocial erotics
in Alger is, however, closer to Michael Moon's conclusion that the way "his work manifests
male homosexuality" is an "encapsulation" of the way "corporate/capitalist America's long-
cherished myth" of upward mobility conceals its "male homoerotic foundations." Moon,
"The Gentle Boy," 107.

3. Scharnhorst and Bales, *The Lost Life of Horatio Alger, Jr.*, 72–73, 70.
4. Review of *In a New World*, by Horatio Alger, Jr., *The Literary World* 24 (2 Dec. 1893): 422.

putative "emasculation" of masculine character; the shift in the cultural meaning of writing for a male readership from an act of virtuous and transparent communication to a species of pandering; and the commodification of the reading public, its transformation into a mass audience.

It is unfortunately all too easy to see how these tensions resonate with current debates about the changing role of mass culture in the public sphere. To choose an obvious but nonetheless tempting target, I'd like to conclude by citing a paragraph from Allan Bloom's *The Closing of the American Mind*. This comes from the chapter on music:

> Picture a thirteen-year-old boy sitting in the living room of his family home doing his math assignment while wearing his Walkman headphones or watching MTV. He enjoys the liberties hard won over centuries by the alliance of philosophic genius and political heroism, consecrated by the blood of martyrs; he is provided with comfort and leisure by the most productive economy ever known to mankind; science has penetrated the secrets of nature in order to provide him with the marvelous, lifelike electronic sound and image reproduction he is enjoying. And in what does progress culminate? A pubescent child whose body throbs with orgasmic rhythms; whose feelings are made articulate in hymns to the joys of onanism or the killing of parents; whose ambition is to win fame and wealth in imitating the drag-queen who makes the music. In short, life is made into a nonstop, commercially prepackaged masturbational fantasy.[5]

Like his counterparts at the turn of the last century, Bloom tries to exert cultural authority precisely by claiming that mass culture has stripped men like himself of all such authority, which now presumably rests in the hands of "drag-queens." Bloom tries to control what we read and how we read it by putting forward a dystopian image of cultural reception, an image he juxtaposes with his own utopian vision of an enlightened, exclusively male public sphere, described in a chapter he names "Our Virtue." One implication of my argument is that such attempts can never really succeed because of how closely they are bound up with the phenomena they decry. Bloom expresses a fear of commodification in an extremely well-marketed, successful book; condenses his anxieties in the picture of a boy taking erotic pleasure in the supposedly passive consumption of mass culture; and opposes this scandalously homoerotic image to a male homosocial,

---

5. Allan Bloom, *The Closing of the American Mind: How Higher Education Has Failed Democracy and Impoverished the Souls of Today's Students* (New York, 1987), 74–75. Lawrence Grossberg interprets this quotation similarly, though not in the same historical framework in *We Gotta Get Out of this Place: Popular Conservatism and Postmodern Culture* (New York, 1992).

Enlightenment utopia. Like Noah Porter, Bloom claims that his ideal of masculine public virtue can counter the threats of mass culture, but he fails to recognize that the discourses he opposes to one another have been inextricably intertwined for more than a century, that Horatio Alger's public sphere was always a complex and contradictory fantasy.

HILDEGARD HOELLER

Freaks and the American Dream: Horatio Alger, P. T. Barnum, and the Art of Humbug†

> "It's my belief that you're a humbug," said the disappointed customer.
> "Thank you, sir, 'said Rough and Ready; 'I've been takin' lessons of Barnum, only I haven't made so much money yet." . . .
> "Don't do it again, my lad. It's wrong to humbug people, you know. By the way, do you ever come to the museum?"
> "Yes, sir."
> "Well, your joke is worth something. Here is a season ticket for three months."
>
> —Horatio Alger, *Rough and Ready*

When Horatio Alger lets P. T. Barnum suddenly appear as a character in *Rough and Ready*, the fourth volume of his *Ragged Dick* Series, he hints at a significant connection between Barnumesque humbug and his own fiction.[1] In Chapter XV, which "introduces a distinguished personage" (167), the newsboy Rough and Ready not only dishes up humbug to the customer looking for coverage of horrible disasters, but he also falsely claims that P. T. Barnum, who happens to be walking by, is Horace Greeley. The duped gentleman, who "keeps a seminary in the country," eagerly speaks with Barnum as if he were Greeley, commending him on his "luminous editorials" and their "most satisfactory exposition of the principles which I profess" (172). Barnum goes along with the joke but confronts the newsboy afterwards, chiding him that "to humbug people is wrong." Nonetheless, in the same breath he also rewards the boy with a free season pass because "the joke is worth something." Overtly, the deception compares Horace Greeley's journalism to Barnum's humbug; but, less directly, Alger might also be speaking about himself and his attempt to capitalize as a fiction writer on the lessons in the art of humbug he learned from P. T. Barnum.[2]

† From *Studies in American Fiction* 34.2 (Autumn 2006): 189–214. Copyright © 2006 Northeastern University. Reprinted with permission from Northeastern University.
1. Horatio Alger, *Rough and Ready* (Philadelphia: The John Winston Co., 1897), 169.
2. Neil Harris points out that this connection was rather usual. See *Humbug, The Art of P. T. Barnum* (Chicago: Univ. of Chicago Press, 1973), 172.

This essay argues that the similarities between Alger's fictional practices and P. T. Barnum's exhibition strategies are central in understanding both the nature and the success of Alger's most famous and quintessential rags-to-riches story, *Ragged Dick* (1868)— a context critics have overlooked. On the surface, Alger shows that Dick's education and improvement depend on his abandoning his favorite pleasures, such as going to Barnum's and to low theaters. Yet Dick's success, and the success of the novel, have much to do with the popularity and dynamics of freak shows. Partially designed by himself and partially by Alger, Dick is a freak, and our pleasure of reading about him is similar to the pleasure he himself seeks when he visits Barnum's museum. Ragged Dick is, like Tom Thumb, a charming miniature man, and his poverty and homelessness become curious and entertaining within this reduced scale. By offering his rags-to-riches story, the novel allowed its middle-class readers to indulge their curiosity and to face and appease fears about pressing social issues such as extreme urban poverty, immigration, the rise and threat of finance capitalism and its concomitant social mobility and fluidity. *Ragged Dick's* astounding success can be traced not so much to the professed message that any honest boy can make it to respectability and obtain the American dream with a lot of determination and a little bit of luck as to the way in which the novel, while professing this message, is also able to imply almost its direct opposite, namely that Dick is a freak and the American dream of rising from rags to riches a freak event. Dick's rise is an example of formidable Barnumesque humbug that happens only to those whom the middle-class audience enjoys and for whose performance they are willing to pay.

Alger's Anti-Freak Show Message

Explicitly, Alger's novel, like his character Barnum, considers all forms of humbug wrong; the narrator notes that Dick's greatest flaw is his love for entertainment and the way he squanders his money on shows and spectacles. The novel opens with Dick waking up late because he had gone to the Old Bowery the previous night. "Another of Dick's faults," Alger's narrator explains, "was his extravagance. . . . He earned enough to have supported himself comfortably and respectably," but Dick "was fond of going to the Old Bowery Theatre" and other places, and he likes to smoke, drink, and gamble.[3] It is central to Dick's rise to respectability that he stops spending his money on going to such shows. By the end of the novel, Dick proudly writes

---

3. Horatio Alger, *Ragged Dick* (New York: Signet Classic, 1990), 7. Hereafter cited parenthetically.

to his middle-class friend Frank that he "[hasn't] been to Tony Pastor's, or the Old Bowery, for ever so long" (172).

Alger's stance is, in most ways, hardly original. By the 1860s the Society for the Reformation of Juvenile Delinquents particularly concentrated on reforming the theaters and concert saloons because it saw them as "the breeding grounds of vice and lawlessness among the city's young people."[4] And we can find similar views in a budding literature written for middle-class audiences about urban poverty, and particularly "street arabs," which emerged on the market during the same time and which Alger's novels echoed.[5] For example, James McCabe warns in his 1872 *Lights and Shadows of New York Life* that "a large part of the earnings of the bootblacks is spent for tobacco and liquors. These children are regular patrons of the Bowery Theatre and the low-class concert halls. Upon reaching the age of seventeen or eighteen the bootblack generally abandons his calling, and as he is unfit for any other employment by reason of his laziness and want of skill, he becomes a loafer, a bummer, or a criminal."[6] Charles Loring Brace stresses in his 1872 *The Dangerous Classes of New York* that the poor urban boy's "more ideal pictures of the world about him, and his literary education, come from the low theatres, to which he is passionately attached."[7]

Alger clearly concurs with these authors. But unlike these other sources, Alger highlights Dick's particular fondness for Barnum's museum. "I'll guess I go to Barnum's tonight," Dick announces, "and see the bearded lady, the eight foot giant, the two foot dwarf, and the other curiosities, too numerous to mention" (19). When showing Frank around the city, Dick points it out: "Well, that's Barnum's. That's where the Happy Family live, and the lions, and the bears, and curiosities generally. It's a tip-top place. Haven't you ever been there?" (34). At the end of the novel, the now respectable Dick has stopped going to the theatres or to Barnum's museum, and, finding that his old rags are missing, he surmises that "maybe it's an agent of Barnum's" who has stolen them (184). Alger implies that Dick's rise to respectability means not only abandoning the low theatres but also cutting his ties to Barnum's museum.

This last implication, though, seems ironic in light of the fact that without his knowledge of Barnum's museum Alger's hero might never have risen in the first place. While Dick loves Tony Pastor's and the

---

4. Robert Snyder, *The Voice of the City: Vaudeville and Popular Culture in New York* (Chicago: Ivan Dee, 2000), 7.

5. Marcus Klein, *Easterns, Westerns, and Private Eyes* (Madison: Univ. of Wisconsin Press, 1994), 34.

6. James D. McCabe Jr., *Lights and Shadows of New York Life; or, Sights and Sensations of the Great City* (1872; Facsimile Edition New York: Farrar, Straus, and Giroux, 1970), 740.

7. Charles Loring Brace, *The Dangerous Classes of New York and Twenty Years' Work Among Them*, 3rd ed. (1880; repr. Montclair, New Jersey: Patterson Smith, 1967), 98.

Old Bowery Theatre and gets some of his sense of drama from these sources, his imagination and his presentation of himself are most strongly shaped by the freak exhibits of Barnum's museum.[8] His success is very much that of a freak. Just as in *Rough and Ready*, within the logic of Alger's *Rugged Dick*, the lessons his hero has learned from P. T. Barnum are definitely "worth something."

Ragged Dick, Self-Made Freak

Dick is full of humbug. Somewhat exasperated by studies of Alger, David Leverenz asks, "Why does nobody notice that this model of boyish honesty is lying all the time? Not only does Dick continuously fake upscale connections, but his linguistic bravado constitutes much of his appeal."[9] I agree that critics have not sufficiently discussed Dick's "linguistic bravado" as one of his important assets; like Leverenz, many contemporary observers stressed the abilities "street arabs" displayed with language and wit. But Alger specifically suffuses Dick's linguistic performance with references to Barnum's museum.

Contemporary books stressed the rhetorical abilities of bootblacks and newsboys and traced them to the boys' love for melodrama and theatre. Brace's *The Dangerous Classes* notes: "The street-boys, as is well-known, are exceedingly sharp and keen, and being accustomed to theatrical performances, are easily touched by real oratory, and by dramatic instruction." He emphasizes the boys' sense of irony and humor: "a more lighthearted youngster than the street-boy is not to be found. He is always ready to make fun of his own sufferings, and to 'chaff' others . . . he is merry as a clown, and always ready for the smallest joke, and quick to take 'a point' or to return a repartee."[1] Dick clearly has this "linguistic bravado" and sense of humor, but his bravado has a distinctly Barnumesque flavor.

Consider the first pages of the novel, in which the narrative focuses on Dick's verbal performance as he services a customer. "'Well, you know 'taint all clear profit,' said Dick, who had already set to work. 'There's the *blacking* costs something, and I have to get a new brush

---

8. Of course, there are strong connections between Barnum's museum and the theatrical conventions of the low theaters Alger mentions. The allusions to the Old Bowery Theatre and to Tony Pastor are particularly interesting in defining the context of Barnum's museum—and Alger's novel. As Robert Snyder points out, Barnum offered his museum as a respectable alternative to the Old Bowery Theatre, cleaning up its acts for middle-class audiences (7). Tony Pastor, who started his career as a child prodigy with Barnum, in turn opened his theater famously to clean up the acts of the low theaters and offer vaudeville entertainment suitable for middle-class audiences (Snyder, 12–13). See also Douglas Gilbert, *American Vaudeville: Its Life and Times* (New York: Dover, 1963), 103.

9. David Leverenz, "Tomboys, Bad Boys, and Horatio Alger: When Fatherhood Became a Problem," *American Literary History* 10 (1998), 232.

1. Brace, 79–80, 98. "Chaff": playful teasing.

pretty often.' 'And you have a large rent too,' said the gentleman
quizzically, with a glance at a large hole in Dick's coat. 'Yes, sir,' said
Dick, always ready to joke; 'I have to pay such a big rent for my manshun on Fifth Avenoo, that I can't affor to take less than ten cents a
shine' " (5). When the customer inquires about his tailor, Dick
responds; "The coat once belonged to General Washington . . . he
wore it all through the revolution, and it got torn some, 'cause he fit
so. When he died he told his widder to give it to some smart young
feller that hadn't got none of his own; so she gave it to me" (5–6).
Glenn Hendler comments that "Alger was intent on making [Ragged
Dick's] ideological ancestry clear" by linking Dick to the founding
father.[2] But in its immediate context the allusion seems more likely
to point to Barnum's humbug, since in the same breath Dick also
mythologizes his pants: "they was a gift from Lewis Napolean. Lewis
had outgrown 'em and sent 'em to me,—he's bigger than me, and
that's why they don't fit.' 'It seems you have distinguished friends.
Now, my lad, I suppose you would like your money' " (6). The episode
clearly shows that the customer pays for Dick's performance, which
in general participates in the model and humor of low theaters and
is, in specific ways, a very clever imitation of "perhaps the most profitable item [Barnum] ever stumbled upon: General Tom Thumb."[3]

Dick's jokes about size—claiming that he is smaller than Napoleon
and further exaggerating his smallness through Washington's coat—
suggest that he might be viewed as a midget, even though he is a
child; Thumb, too, was exhibited as a midget when he was still a
child. These methods of exaggeration—making children who were
presented as dwarfs younger than they were, or by adding height to
giants through hats and lifts—were "run-of-the-mill conventions of
the business."[5] Dick turns himself into an exhibit, a humbug performance for which the customer pays. His play with literal, corporeal
size is echoed in his verbal play with other relations such as insignif-
icant/significant, child/adult, servant/client, inferior/superior,
homeless vagrant/owner of a mansion on Fifth Avenue, bootblack-
ing/American business. In his interaction with this customer, Dick
uses techniques of exaggeration, deception, and humbug that Barnum used in his freak exhibits; Dick turns himself both in economic
and physical terms into a charming miniature man.

While Barnum's museum shared some of these techniques with
the tradition of low theaters, Dick's first narrated performance par-

2. Glenn Hendler, *Public Sentiments; Structures of Feeling in Nineteenth-Century American
Literature* (Chapel Hill: Univ. of North Carolina Press, 2001), 95.
3. Harris, 43.
4. Napoleon was 5 feet 2 inches and Washington was 6 feet 2 inches.
5. Robert Bogdan, *Freak Show: Presenting Human Oddities for Amusement and Profit* (Chicago: Univ. of Chicago Press, 1988), 97.

ticularly alludes to Tom Thumb's performances, such as his early imitations of Napoleon and a Revolutionary Soldier.[6] Dick's persona, like Thumb's, is astonishing because of "his distinguished friends," as the customer calls them. Barnum famously made huge business when Tom Thumb visited Buckingham Palace in the 1840s and met, and received gifts from, the royal family, including the Prince of Wales and the queen. "[T]he gifts . . . were placed on exhibition, and Tom Thumb's witty sallies were immediately publicized when he met the Duke of Wellington while dressed in the uniform of Napoleon, the duke asked him what he was thinking of and the general replied, 'I was thinking of the loss of the battle of Waterloo.'[7] This exchange, said Barnum, 'was of itself worth thousands of pounds to the exhibition.'"[8] Dick echoes these connections in this early scene and then again, even more explicitly, later in the novel: "'Oh indeed!' said Dick. 'You looked so much like the queen's picter what she gave me last Christmas in exchange for mine, that I couldn't help calling you by her name'" (83). And when Mickey Maguire asks him where he got his new clothes, Dick responds that "maybe the Prince of Wales gave 'em to me" (93). Dick clearly models himself after Tom Thumb; he even alludes here to the photographs freaks sold of themselves that became coveted collectors' items.[9]

But unlike Thumb, Dick is, of course, not physically a midget. He is rather what Robert Bogdan labels a "self-made freak," a new genre of freaks who unlike "form freaks" had no actual physical abnormalities but whose freak performance depended entirely upon presentation. By the 1860s, such self-made freaks had become increasingly common phenomena because freak exhibits had become so popular that there was a shortage of performers with actual physical abnormalities. For this type of exhibit the importance of autobiography became overwhelming, but in the end, as Bogdan emphasizes, these "self-made freaks" only highlighted what was true for all freaks: "Freaks were what you made them. How they were packaged, how they were dressed, how they acted, and what the audience was told about them—their presentation was the crucial element in determining their success, in making a freak." As the opening episode exemplifies, much of Dick's success depends

6. Bogdan, 150.
7. Battle of Waterloo, 1815, last action in Napoleonic Wars (1803–1815) in which the British under Wellington defeated the French under Napoleon I.
8. Harris, 96. Later Barnum put Thumb in great company again when he exhibited "wax figures of Napoleon, Victoria, Tom Thumb, Christ and his disciples, and many historical figures" (Harris, 165).
9. Bogdan reports that freaks customarily sold photographs of themselves. For example, "Lavinia Warren, Tom Thumb's wife, was referred to as the most photographed woman in the world. She ordered fifty thousand pictures of herself at a time . . . and these were widely available from photography vendors" (15).

entirely on this self-dramatization as a freak in the tradition of Bar-num's show.[1]

And like Tom Thumb's, Dick's success and appeal lie particularly in his sense of humor. While initially many freak exhibits were played straight, later in the nineteenth century they became more self-parodying and humorous, a mode that Tom Thumb mastered better (and earlier) than almost any other performer. "What made [the young Stratton] so charming as a young man was that he played his presentation so as to reveal to the audience that he was aware of the ludicrous poses he struck as they were. In this way they were not laughing at him; rather, they all laughed together."[2] Unlike many other exhibits, Tom Thumb made clear that he was "fully aware of the context in which [he was] viewed: much of Tom Thumb's appeal lay in the contrast between the small body and the sharp mind. Tiny as he was, he could hold his own in repartee with the Queen of England or draw a diminutive sword on her poodle when it threatened to bite."[3] Dick strikes exactly this note, laughing with the customer about his own absurd claims about himself.

This pose served several purposes: it prevented audiences from resenting or exposing the humbug as actual fraud; it alleviated any discomfort audiences might have felt when looking at a disabled person as a curiosity; and it helped the aggrandized presentation by put-ting the exhibited person, by way of his humor and intelligence, on the same level as the audience.[4] Dick's early performance in Alger's novel seems to accomplish exactly that—it allows the customer, as well as Alger's middle-class readers, to laugh away with Dick the pres-ence of his own abject poverty. In a way, Dick becomes an economic midget, one that middle-class Americans could increasingly not avoid seeing—particularly in New York City where the appalling living con-ditions of massive amounts of immigrants became more and more visible.[5] Voyeurism was a response to this increasingly obvious urban poverty, and Dick's performance eases the tensions Alger's audience may have felt about their own curiosity about the economically dis-abled, and particularly about homeless, impoverished children.

1. Bogdan, 239, 242, 95. Eric Fretz describes how nineteenth-century American culture began to "[celebrate] the individual's ability to stylize a public persona and assert these arti-ficially constructed identities into the public sphere"; "P. T. Barnum's Theatrical Selfhood and the Nineteenth-Century Culture of Exhibition," in *Freakery*, ed. Rosemarie Garland Thomson (New York: New York Univ. Press, 1996), 98. Barnum's exhibits and self-repre-sentation, as well as Dick's constructed identity, can be understood in this cultural con-text.
2. Bogden, 114, 152.
3. Harvey Blume, "Ota Benga and the Barnum Perplex," in *Africans on Stage*, ed. Bernth Lindfors (Bloomington: Indiana Univ. Press, 1999), 197.
4. Bogden, 114, 215.
5. This visibility was foregrounded later by Jacob Riis's *How the Other Half Lives* (1890; repr. New York: Dover Publications, 1971).

Fiction and Humbug: Horatio Alger as P. T. Barnum

If Dick models himself after Tom Thumb, then we can see Alger as taking on the role of P. T. Barnum, exhibiting his freak hero to his audience. In his preface, Alger emphasizes the seriousness of his intent by placing his work in the context of social reform, he "hopes that, while the volumes in this series may prove interesting as stories, they may also have the effect of enlisting the sympathies of his readers in behalf of the unfortunate children whose life is described, and of leading them to co-operate with the praiseworthy efforts of now making [sic] by the Children's Aid Society and other organizations to ameliorate their condition" (*Ragged Dick*, Preface, 1–2). Yet the narrator hints at the more voyeuristic aspects of the book later when he notes that "to gratify the curiosity of my young readers, I will put down the items with their cost" (89).[6] Even though the choice of exhibit seems innocuous enough—just numbers—Alger's choice of words is significant: the "gratification of curiosity" brings the book much closer to a spectacle, an exhibit of "curiosities" (34) as Dick calls Barnum's exhibits.

At best, Alger's novel balances education and amusement in the same way freak shows did; after all, they too "were heralded as more than frivolous amusement: they were morally uplifting, educational, and prudent."[7] This educational pretense was particularly relevant in the supposedly anthropological exhibits of savages, or the exotic mode of freak exhibits, to which Alger's narrative stance in *Ragged Dick* alludes. In this respect, too, Alger taps into an already existing market of books about urban poverty, which depicted the city as exotic and its urban poverty as a form of interesting savagery. At one moment in Brace's *Dangerous Classes* this stance becomes explicit, when he compares "street arabs" to Indians:

> There seemed to be a very considerable class of lads in New York who bore to the busy, wealthy world about them something of the same relation which Indians bear to civilized Western settlers. They had no settled home, and lived on the outskirts of society, their hand against every man's pocket, and every man looking on them as natural enemies; their wits sharpened like those of a savage, and their principles often no better. Christianity reared its temples over them, and Civilization was carrying on its great work, while they—a happy race of little heathens and barbarians—plundered, or frolicked, or led their roving life, far beneath.[8]

6. This exhibit may also allude to Thoreau's exhibit of his numbers in *Walden*, which might be seen as an American dream narrative.
7. Bogdan, 104.
8. Brace, 97.

Alger depicts Ragged Dick as such a "happy barbarian and heathen with sharpened wit who lives far beneath" the "civilization" of middle-class America; he uses an already known underworld, an "ominous geography" with its exotic savages, the street arabs, to which middle-class audiences wanted to 'travel' in their reading. Mrs. George C. Needham in her 1887 *Street Arabs and Gutter Snipes: The Pathetic and Humorous Side of Young Vagabon Life in the Great Cities, with Records of Work for their Reclamation* suggested the parallel appeal of freak shows and books about urban poverty: "The Arab hunter must be prepared for endless freaks and multiplied dodges, else he will find himself outwitted in the end."[9] Alger's novel shared its approach to its hero with these sources, and Alger knew that there was an audience eagerly reading reports of the adventures of "arab hunters" who dare to penetrate the jungle of urban poverty in pursuit of the freakish and exotic.

Alger uses an almost mock-anthropological voice to describe the strange customs of Dick and his likes, from his homelessness and dirtiness to his ignorance of the bible. "Washing the face and hands is usually considered proper in commencing the day, but Dick was above such refinement. He had no particular dislike to dirt, and did not think it necessary to remove several dark streaks on his face and hands" (4). Poverty and the lack of a home and sanitation seem here to be translated into a droll and primitive preference for dirt—a lack of a civilized need for cleanliness. Later, when Mr. Greyson tries to interest Dick in the church, Alger stresses the heathen aspect of his barbarian when he shows that Dick only responds to the music, the "children singing" (120). These emphases allow Alger to exhibit Dick as a specimen of a known other culture, a savage of the city. His exhibition of Dick is furthermore much in tune with the anthropological exhibits of non-Westerners in Barnum's museum, which did not aim at conveying actual knowledge of other cultures but which exoticized others and turned them into barbaric, savage freaks in order to make money.[1] Alger's novel, as so many other books about urban poverty, thus turned an economic issue into a cultural one, transforming the poor into an exotic race and exhibiting a poor, homeless American boy as a curious street arab, an invented urban savage.

Despite Alger's professed interest in arousing sympathy for homeless children, his mock-anthropological approach to Dick helps prevent identification of the middle class with the abysmal living conditions of a homeless, urban orphan; it fosters curiosity rather than sympathy, self-contentment rather than genuine concern or pity. In freak shows, Bogdan observes, "'Pity' as a mode of presentation

9. Quoted in Klein, 42.
1. Bogdan, 177.

was absent . . . Promoters capitalizing on pity would have developed presentations emphasizing how difficult life was for the poor exhibits, how unhappy they were; they would have explained how the admission charge would help pay the exhibits expenses, relieve their suffering, and even lead to a cure for their affliction. That approach, however, did not draw or please crowds. They did not fit in with the world of amusement, where people used their leisure and spent their money to have fun, not to confront human suffering."[2] In Barnum's "Some Account of General Tom Thumb," for example, pity is explicitly discouraged: "were he deformed, or sickly, or melancholy, we might pity him; but he is so manly, so hearty, and so happy."[3] Dick, like Thumb, appears manly, hearty, and happy, and so middle-class readers could enjoy his adventures without undue consideration for the actual plight of the urban poor.

Alger, like many reformers, professed—and most likely felt—great sympathy for New York's homeless boys, just as P. T. Barnum stressed his friendly relations to his exhibits.[4] Both men cast themselves in the roles of mentors and benefactors. Alger, who adopted and helped many homeless boys throughout his life, stressed that "a writer for boys should have an abundant sympathy for them" and should "exert a wholesome influence on his young readers."[5] Mr. Barnum, a pamphlet announces, "naturally feels the deepest interest in his protégé, and is unceasing in his care of him and attention to his welfare . . . Mr. Barnum suggested and carries out a system of education, moral and religious, which cannot fail of conducing greatly to the future happiness of his wonderful charge."[6] Nonetheless, by exoticizing their exhibits, both Alger's narrative stance and Barnum's exhibition strategies also introduced an element of exploitation into their relation to their exhibits.[7]

Alger could have borrowed his approach to Ragged Dick from Barnum's fictionalization of Tom Thumb because he both stressed, like Barnum, an anthropological context for Dick and insisted on the latter's specialness, his exceptional qualities. Ragged Dick is a wonder among street arabs just as Thumb was presented by Barnum as an amazing exception amongst people with unusual size. Barnum cre-

---

2. Bogdan, 277.
3. P. T. Barnum, "Some Account of General Tom Thumb, The Man in Miniature," Barnum's American Museum Pamphlet (1854), 6.
4. Exhibitor Sam Gumpertz, "freak show czar of Coney island and perhaps the most active twentieth-century importer of non-Western sideshow attractions" (Bogdan, 197), claimed: "I got along splendidly with these Dahomey tribesmen. I am lucky that I understand them . . . I like them instinctively. They seem to know that. We always get along. We are in sympathy, as the Latins say" (quoted in Bogdan, 198).
5. Horatio Alger, "Writing Stories for Boys," The Writer (March 1896), 37.
6. Barnum, "Some Account," 8.
7. For an extensive discussion of the exploitative nature of Barnum's relation to his performers, see David A. Gerber's "The 'Careers' of People Exhibited in Freak Shows: The Problem of Volition and Valorization," in Freakery, 38–54.

ated an elaborate exoticizing context for Thumb: "Ever since the commencement of the world," he opens a long mock-anthropological lecture in "Some Account of General Tom Thumb," "there has existed amongst all races of man, a common average as to height, size, and proportion." From there Barnum discusses races of giants and dwarfs: "The Patagonians[8] are men who average six feet nine in height; the early navigators said nine feet, but modern research has proved their estimate to be very erroneous." The pseudo-scientific voice claims the accuracy of "modern research" and gains credibility by apparently diminishing rather than exaggerating the height of these giants. Then Barnum turns to "communities of Dwarfs and Pigmies" such as Esquimaux, Lapplanders, and African pigmies. Barnum sets up this ornate mock-anthropological frame for Tom Thumb, only then to exhibit him as a different kind of phenomenon: "whatever people's opinions may be of the existence of pigmy nations, the occurrence of individual, although infrequent specimens of dwarfs, from the very remote period unto the present day, is placed beyond all doubt, both by authentic records of fact, and by living breathing witnesses in our own time." Barnum's description of Tom Thumb stresses that he is the only one in his family to differ in size and that he is not exotic.[9] Absurdly, Thumb is both part of a long, documented history of human races and a unique, individual exception. He is and is not part of a deviant race, just as Dick is described by Alger both as part of a "race" of "street arabs" and yet entirely different, a wonder in itself, that sets him apart from those other "street arabs" and brings him closer to the middle-class audience.

As this example shows, there was much of a fiction writer in Barnum. Barnum's humbug was his form of fiction, just as Alger's fiction might be seen as his form of humbug. Impresarios like Barnum "fabricated freaks' backgrounds, the nature of their conditions, the circumstances of their current lives, and other personal characteristics. The actual life and circumstances of those being exhibited were replaced by purposeful distortions designed to market the exhibit, to produce a more appealing freak." These fabricated stories about the freak exhibits were offered as "true life stories"—a form of literary or even scientific realism that mirrors Alger's supposedly realist fiction, which is "sketched from life" but does not aspire to "strict historical accuracy" (*Ragged Dick*, Preface, 1).[1] Indeed, it is easy to see Alger's depiction of Ragged Dick as a "purposeful distortion" of true urban poverty and homelessness "designed to market the exhibit, to produce a more appealing" image of the "street arab."

8. Inhabitants of Patagonia, a region primarily in South Argentina.
9. Barnum, "Some Account," 1–3.
1. Bogdan, 95, 105.

Harvey Blume argues that "the genres it was most crucial for Barnum to confound were those of fact and fiction"; "display, on the one hand, the claim of authenticity, on the other, are twin pillars of Barnumism and with them Barnum exemplifies the fixations of his age."[2] Alger's fiction strikes the same balance; on the one hand, it insists on its realism through footnotes and historical and geographical references, and by basing the characters of Johnny Nolan and Mickey Maguire on actual boys; and on the other hand, in the midst of all of this realist detail it displays to us the wonder of Ragged Dick—a pure fabrication.[3] And just as Alger managed to make the already known story of the "street arab" into an unprecedented success, Barnum managed to exhibit his freaks more successfully than anyone else did. Both Barnum and his disciple Alger had an ingenious sense for the humbug that the American public desired and would buy.

Amazing Respectability: Freaks and the American Dream

If Alger's fiction depends for its entertainment value on Dick's freakishness, what happens when Dick becomes increasingly respectable? Many readers have felt that the novel loses much of its charm when Dick rises in class, and one might surmise that Dick stops being a freak at that moment.[4] But the amazing respectability of freaks was also an important part of Barnum's freak shows. Many freaks—particularly performers who were small, large, or missed limbs—stressed their respectability in their exhibits and photographs and showed that the freak could lead a most normal, conventional life. For example, Tom Thumb was shown to lead a perfectly respectable life, just in miniature size, just as an armless performer might demonstrate how he could use his feet to sip a cup of tea, or the bearded lady would pose in a Victorian dress with her husband for a conventional family portrait. The appeal of these exhibits lay in the contrast between the one "freakish" feature (size, armlessness, or beard) and the conventions of middle-class life. These normalizing strategies became part of what Bogdan calls the "aggrandized mode" of exhibiting "form freaks," which "emphasized how, with the exception of the particular physical, mental, or behavioral condition, the freak was an upstanding, high-status person with talents of conventional and socially prestigious nature." In poses of such amazing respectability, freaks were also presented as physically normal, even

2. Blume, 194.
3. In his essay "Are My Boys Real?," *Ladies Home Journal*, November 1890, Alger stresses that he based his characters on real boys—with the exception of "Ragged Dick" whose name was real, "but I never knew the boy who bore it" (29). See also Gary Scharnhorst and Jack Bales, *The Lost Life of Horatio Alger, Jr.* (Bloomington: Indiana Univ. Press, 1985), 82.
4. For example, Gorman Beauchamp writes: "As Dick exchanges his rags for his respectability, the juice drains out of him; as he becomes good, he becomes gray." "Ragged Dick and the Fate of Respectability," *Michigan Quarterly Review* 31, no. 1 (1992), 332.

beautiful, apart from their one freakish feature.[5] Tom Thumb's appeal, in particular, had to do with the fact that he was perfectly shaped other than for his size; he was always advertised as having "nothing dwarfish in his appearance—he is a perfect man in miniature."[6] Dick also, Alger stresses, is normal other than for his one 'freakish' feature': his "raggedness." In the beginning the narrator affirms that "while Dick's appearance . . . was rather peculiar," "in spite of his dirt and rags there was something about Dick that was attractive. It was easy to see that if he had been clean and well dressed he would have been decidedly good-looking" (4). Like Tom Thumb, Dick is well built and good-looking. Barnum went further when he emphasized Thumb's full functionality by exhibiting Thumb with his wife and "their child," a baby that was supplied to the couple for exhibition purposes—a gesture Alger strangely mirrors and queers when he has his miniature couple, Ragged Dick and Henry Fosdick, come to some fruition after "nine months" and later adopt a child together.[7]

Beyond biological normalcy and ordinary respectability, the freak show emphasized that "the anomaly was a specific condition and did not reflect on the integrity or morality of the exhibit."[8] Alger parallels the attractiveness of Dick's body with the unusual integrity of his character: "He was above doing anything mean or dishonorable. He would not steal, or cheat, or impose upon younger boys, but was frank and straight-forward, manly and self-reliant. His nature was a noble one, and had saved him from all mean faults" (8).[9] Aggrandized in a Barnumesque way, Dick's integrity exceeds that of every other character.

This integrity and strength of the freak lend itself particularly to a blending of freak exhibits and American dream narratives. For many performers "the invented identify was so flattering that they strove to

---

5. Bogdan, 108–9.
6. Barnum, "Some Account," 5.
7. The wedding, staged in 1863, was a sensation of this kind; it stressed Tom Thumb's physical normality, his ability to lead a conventional respectable life. While much of the novel is homoerotic, Alger also hints at a heterosexual courtship when he has Dick meet Ida—Princess Ida was another famous performing midget—and Dick gets normalized into a middle-class drawing room and the early forms of heterosexual courtship. At the same time, as Michael Moon observes, Alger also hints at an impossible gestation period when he "specifies . . . [that] nine months after [Dick and Fosdick] move in together . . . Dick is said to bring forth a little bundle." Further, as Moon points out, the two boys adopt a child in the third volume of the series. Michael Moon, " 'The Gentle Boy from the Dangerous Classes': Pederasty, Domesticity, and Capitalism in Horatio Alger," *Representations* 19 (Summer 1987), 99.
8. Bogdan, 110.
9. In many ways, Ragged Dick fits the image of the noble savage, a concept that exotic exhibits relied upon (Bogdan, 178). But since Alger stresses that Dick is an exception amongst the street arabs, the emphasis on his honesty is also strongly reminiscent of the exhibition of form freaks.

become their stage persona."[1] Some actually did rise in class and gain respectability, and many exhibits incorporated an American dream narrative into their presentation. Performers were shown to be amazing examples of perseverance and determination, able to overcome formidable obstacles. For example, commenting on the armless wonder Charles Tripp, one of Barnum's exhibits, an editorial announced that "he was a real hero in every sense of the word and overcame odds in life that would have submerged many a man with less determination and spirit."[2] Similarly, the success of the armless Master Sanders K. G. Nellis as described in an 1840 magazine article was attributed to his industry and perseverance:

> He executes many other things with his feet, which a vast majority of mankind cannot with their hands, without long and arduous practice. *In him, we have an instance of what can be accomplished by a strong mind, aided by indomitable perseverance and untiring industry.*

Bogdan comments: "Such phrases suggested to onlookers that the exhibits' accomplishments and their ability to overcome disadvantages was a sign of their moral worth. The 'wonder' was not merely physical, it was the work of steadfast courage and perseverance."[3] Freak shows were able to tap into the moral component of the myth of the American dream by showing how freaks used their inner strength to overcome their outer challenges.

Alger depicts Ragged Dick in a similar way. First, Dick is transformed into outward respectability by cleaning up and changing, a wonder he connects to Barnum's show. "'Look at yourself,' said Frank, leading him before the mirror. 'By gracious!' said Dick, . . . 'It reminds me of Cinderella . . . when she changed into a fairy princess. I see it one night at Barnum's'" (24). But more importantly, Dick is the only character in the novel that has the inner strength to overcome obstacles. He has "energy, ambition, and natural sharpness" (175)—the very features Johnny Nolan, who is based on a historical figure, lacks. As Alger's own American Dream boy, Dick rises in a world in which "energy and industry are rewarded" (10), while Johnny Nolan and many others are left behind.

Indeed, most other characters are left behind.[4] In that sense, Alger's novel is as ambiguous about the American dream as freak shows were. Bogdan notes that "by flaunting normal accomplishments as

1. Bodgan, 147.
2. Quoted in Bogdan, 222.
3. Bogdan, 216 (emphasis Bogdan's), 217.
4. Henry Fosdick rises with Dick. But Alger describes Fosdick as much too timid to make it on his own (102), and furthermore Fosdick is a middle-class boy who had lived in "every comfort" until his father, a printer, drowned and left him orphaned (104). Fosdick thus will only be restored to his middle-class origin.

extraordinary, and by hailing people with disabilities as human wonders, aggrandized presentations probably taught the lesson that
achievement for people with differences was unusual rather than
common."[5] Alger's novel participates in this logic. Dick has to remain
a wonder just as Barnum's freaks did. His very success is linked to,
contingent upon, his wondrous otherness. Thus in Alger's novel, as in
freak shows, the freak can never be allowed entirely to assimilate without losing his or her value. He always has to remain framed and, in a
way, fictional; his value (entertainment and economic value) lies in a
careful balancing between otherness and assimilation.

Ragged Dick relies precisely on this complex dynamic of both exoticizing and aggrandizing its central exhibit. While the first half of the
novel mimics the exotic mode, the second half follows the normalizing strategies of freak shows. Aware that the second half can only
remain interesting as long as it is connected to the first, Alger needs
to remind the reader of Dick's otherness. While visual displays could
easily depict the simultaneity of freakishness and respectability, the
linearity of the novel and the fact that Dick has no physical abnormalities make it necessary for Alger continuously—and more and
more forcefully—to reinscribe Dick's exotic, freakish nature as the
latter becomes more and more respectable or normal. For example,
when Dick negotiates a position with Mr. Rockwell, the narrator
comments: "Dick was about to say 'Bully.' When he recollected himself, and answered, 'Very much'" (183). The "recollection" is clearly
Alger's, reminding the reader of Dick's otherness. Dick is only entertaining and appealing in the double persona of Richard Hunter/Ragged
Dick. For that purpose, Dick tells his friend Fosdick that he will keep
his bootblacking box and brush "'to remind me of the hard times I've
had, when I was an ignorant bootblack' . . . 'When, in short, you were
'Ragged Dick.' You 'must drop that name and think of yourself now
as—'Richard Hunter. Esq.,' said our hero, smiling'" (185). Having
Fosdick ask Dick to "drop" his name "Ragged Dick" is palpably
Alger's way of not dropping it; it allows the author once again to hint
at the interplay between the two personas, "Ragged Dick" and "Richard Hunter Esq.," asserting that, like "General" Tom Thumb, Dick
can be one only by virtue of the other. Dick's smile as well as Fosdick's
way of putting "Ragged Dick" and "Richard Hunter Esq." in quotation marks suggest that both boys recognize the performative aspects
of Dick's Cinderella-like "transformation." Finally, Alger reminds us
most forcefully of Dick's 'freakishness' when Dick, now out of his
Napoleon/Washington costume, exclaims in marked Ragged Dick
lingo: "somebody's stole my Washington coat and Napoleon pants.

5. Bogdan, 278–79.

Maybe it's an agent of Barnum's, who expects to make a fortun' by exhibitin' the valooable wardrobe of a gentleman of fashion" (184). Working against the linearity of a narrative that would truly describe a transformation from Ragged Dick to Richard Hunter—and thus would lose all Barnumesque appeal—Alger almost desperately tries to invoke simultaneity in the last pages so that we can read Dick's respectability as an integral part of his freak performance and so that Alger himself can make a fortune by exhibiting 'his hero's' rise from rags to amazing respectability.[6]

In some ways, Alger applied the same exhibition strategy to his own public persona, which depended on the double existence of his past as a pederast and his later, amazingly respectable life as child benefactor and author of juvenile fiction. Already physically exceptional for his short stature (at five feet two inches), Alger after his scandalous dismissal from the ministry for having molested boys had become in many ways himself a freak. (P. T. Barnum also exhibited himself in his own museum as an amazingly respectable "freak.") And his own rise to respectability balanced his otherness and his assimilation quite deliberately and carefully. His fiction turned a freakish abnormality, his propensity to abuse boys, into a profitable enterprise, even after his dismissal. Glenn Hendler points out that Alger's public reacted against his "inexcusable desire to place his stories and himself in the public eye after the scandal" and notes that "Alger's indiscreet desire to publicize his 'familiarity with boys' persisted for several years, for in 1870 Henry James, Sr, expressed surprise and annoyance that 'Alger talks freely about his own late insanity—which he in fact appears to enjoy as a subject of conversation.'"[7] In the context of Barnum's museum, Alger's strategy makes sense: he exoticized himself in order to stress his amazing and newfound respectability. Like P. T. Barnum Alger tried to remain in control of the show, exhibiting both himself and his novelistic hero as freaks who were able to overcome many obstacles and reach a curious, wondrous, freakish respectability.

6. The strain in these last pages hints at the problems Alger will face in the subsequent volumes of the "Ragged Dick" series. Alger tries to solve that problem by introducing new freaks, but none have the charm of Dick. Ragged Dick remained as unique in his appeal as Tom Thumb did. Alger "could not have guessed," write Scharnhorst and Bales, "that, at the modest age of thirty-five, he had written his best book, and that he would try in vain the remainder of his life to surpass it"(87).

7. Hendler, 431. Scharnhorst and Bales stress in their biography of Alger that after this incident Alger remained silent about this issue for the rest of his life; see *The Lost Life of Horatio Alger, Jr.* (Bloomington: Indiana Univ. Press, 1985), 70. It should be noted, though, that Alger published a thinly-veiled poem about his "sin" in 1872 ("Friar Anselmo," *New York Weekly* August 5, 1872).

The Cultural Work of Alger's Freak Fiction

In *Sideshow U.S.A.*, Rachel Adams argues that "freak shows performed important cultural work by allowing ordinary people to confront, and master, the most extreme and terrifying forms of Otherness
they could imagine, from exotic dark-skinned people, to victims of
war and disease, to ambiguously sexed bodies." They provided "a
stage for playing out many of the country's most charged social and
political controversies, such as debates about race and empire, immigration, relations among the sexes, taste and community standards of
decency."[8] Alger's *Ragged Dick* was such a success, and has remained
such a central American text, because like freak shows it allowed in
its middle-class readers "to confront, and master, the most extreme
forms of Otherness they could imagine": extreme urban poverty and
the traps and wonders of an emerging finance capitalism that promised both an exhilarating and frightening social mobility and rootless
fluidity.[9]

One "extreme and terrifying form of Otherness" for an 1868
middle-class audience clearly was the rapidly increasing population
of the urban, immigrant poor. While such poor adults people the
background of Alger's fiction, through his invented "street arab" Ragged
Dick, the problem of extreme urban poverty gets literally both diminished in size—miniaturized—and humorized and colored so as to
appear exotic rather than pathetic. As Lindsay Smith puts it in her
discussion of Victorian photographs of "street arabs," the child
becomes a "reduced form of ethnic other."[1] Furthermore, Ragged
Dick is also the least foreign street "arab" in the book. Much of the
terror of this growing urban and impoverished population was that it
was largely made up of immigrants. This fear of immigration is both
registered and solved in Alger's novel through the novel's latent anti-
Irish message.[2] For example, Alger portrays Mr. Nolan, Johnny's
father, as "a confirmed drunkard, [who] spent the greater part of his
wages for liquor. His potations made him ugly, and inflamed a temper never very sweet, working him up sometimes to such a pitch of
rage that Johnny's life was in danger. Some months before, he had
thrown a flat-iron at his son's head with such terrific force that unless
Johnny had dodged he would have not lived long enough to obtain a
place in our story" (12–13). Later, Dick encounters the "stout, red-

---

8. Rachel Adams, *Sideshow U. S. A.* (Chicago: University of Chicago Press, 2001), 2–3.
9. It also hints at another kind of otherness: a vaguely homoerotic lifestyle amongst the street
   arabs. For a discussion of that aspect of the novel see Moon.
1. Lindsay Smith, *The Politics of Focus* (Manchester: Manchester Univ. Press, 1998), 111.
2. John G. Cawelti notes that "the old maxim 'No Irish Need Apply' still held for Alger"; see
   Apostles of the Self-Made Man (Chicago: Univ. of Chicago Press, 1965), 110. Scharnhorst
   relates that Alger's own adoptive fatherhood had "distinct ethnic overtones. He was proud
   of the Anglo-Saxon descent of all the boys he adopted" (125).

faced" Mrs. Mooney, and her servant Bridget and rents a room in their dirty and neglected house, where everything is described as unclean, "ragged," and in ill repair (84). And then there is Dick's rival Mickey Maguire, "a stout, red-haired, freckled-faced boy of four-teen," who "by his boldness and recklessness, as well as his personal strength, which was considerable, had acquired an ascendancy among his fellow professionals, and had a gang of subservient followers, whom he led to acts of ruffianism, not infrequently terminating in a month or two at Blackwell's Island" (91). Ragged Dick is clearly marked as different from any of these Irish characters. Like Tom Thumb, he is not like other "midgets"; there is nothing dwarfish (for-eign) about him. He is a perfect American Anglo-Saxon man in minia-ture, supported by Mr. Greyson and Mr. Rockwell, and winning the war against the Irish most literally in his fight with Mickey Maguire and his gang.[3] Dick's American dream narrative assuages any fear of the rise of a growing immigrant population.

This ethnic agenda of the novel serves to mitigates the potentially threatening implications of a secular American dream narrative that asserts that everyone can make money and rise in class—a message for which Alger, and particularly *Ragged Dick*, have become famous. As Alan Trachtenberg asserts, Alger is often seen as "the single-minded ideologue for acquisitive capitalism."[4] Or, as Albert McLean puts it, "money becomes, in [the] simplified, magical world of the Alger story, an all-effecting, all-moving *mana* of life."[5] Part of the novel does indeed connect Dick's rise to the accumulation of money. On the first page, Dick awakens to the idea—typical of industrial capitalism—that time is money. From there, Dick's rise is connected to his saving money; "once the hero begins to 'rise' and achieves a modicum of domestic stability," Michael Moon observes, "the activ-ity or habit that is represented as being indispensable to and initiat-ing his personal ascendancy is 'saving.' "[6] Throughout the novel, Alger gives us literally an account of Dick's change in spending habits, and his rise to respectability is seemingly parallel to his rising account bal-ance. Here Alger overtly follows closely the dogma of the Children's Aid Society, which posited that "the desire for accumulation . . . is the base of all civilization." The society "broke up" street boys' "espe-cial vice of money-wasting" by having them open savings accounts so that "the small daily deposits accumulated to such a degree" that they

---

3. For a discussion of anti-Irish sentiments in New York City see Michael A. Gordon, *The Orange Riots: Irish Political Violence in New York City Between 1870 and 1872* (Ithaca: Cornell Univ. Press, 1993).
4. Alan Trachtenberg, Introduction to *Ragged Dick* (New York: Signet Classic, 1990), vii.
5. McLean, 9.
6. Moon, 99.

would begin to feel a "sense of property" and develop a desire to accumulate more.[7]

But what makes Alger's novel fascinating is that Alger is not entirely comfortable with this economic agenda; indeed, his novel ultimately resists it.[8] Repeatedly, Alger almost apologizes that his hero could possibly be seen as a capitalist. For example, when accounting for Dick's savings, he writes: "At the end of nine months therefore, or thirty-nine weeks, it will be seen that he had accumulated no less a sum than one hundred and seventeen dollars. Dick may be excused for feeling like a capitalist, when he looked at the long row of deposits in his little bank-book" (136).[9] A little later, Alger again feels compelled to exonerate Dick from being a capitalist: "He was beginning to feel the advantages of steady self-denial, and to experience the pleasures of property. Not that Dick was likely to be unduly attached to money. Let it be said to his credit that it had never given him so much satisfaction as when it enabled him to help Tom Wilkins in trouble" (147). The narrator's encomium bristles with ideological tension and contradictions. Alger mitigates Dick's "pleasures of property" by making it an expression of "steady self-denial"; and he gives "credit" to his hero by showing that the money "gave" Dick "so much" satisfaction only when it is *given* away. Alger mixes gift and market economy and accumulation of wealth or self-interest and self-denial to rescue his hero from being a "capitalist."

While Alger thus registers some discomfort with an undue reverence for the merely "capitalist" virtues of earning, saving, and accumulation, his novel consistently exposes the wondrous and dangerously duplicitous nature of finance capitalism. As Dick shows Frank Wall Street, the narrator comments: "The reader would be astonished if he could know the amount of money involved in transactions which take place in a single day in this street" (68). This wondrousness is linked, throughout the text, with the sense of finance capitalism as swindle and deception, particularly through Dick's continuous references to owning Erie railroad stock. Right in the opening scene, Dick jokingly mentions that he has no change because "all my money's invested in the Erie Railroad." The customer replies that "that's unfortunate," going along with Dick's joke but also affirming that all Americans have been victims, and been impoverished by, the Erie Railroad scandal (6). Later, Dick mentions his Erie shares again to Frank. A stranger, "Samuel Snap, No.—Wall Street," overhears them and offers Dick

<hr />

7. Brace, 104–5.
8. For a full-fledged account of a long history of capitalist "misreadings" of the novel see Gary Scharnhorst, "Demythologizing Alger," *Markham Review* 10 (Fall 1980–Winter 1981), 20–27.
9. The reference to nine months hints at more organic patterns of creation, gestation, and giving birth—a cycle of life rather than a merely linear, numerical accumulation of wealth.

shares in the "Excelsior Copper Mining Company, which possesses one of the most productive mines in the world." (37). The "tall, gaunt" (36) stranger promises that "it's sure to yield fifty per cent. on the investment. Now, all you have to do is sell out your Erie shares, and invest in our stock, and I'll insure you a fortune in three years"(37).[1] When the stranger leaves, Frank comments: "Perhaps you earn your money more honorably than he does, after all, . . . some of these mining companies are nothing but swindles, got up to cheat people out of their money" (37). The stranger, an agent from Wall Street, embodies the treacherousness of finance capitalism that the novel affirms throughout. And Dick's continuous mention of Erie Railroad stock in his invented public persona connects one of finance capitalism's most famous scandals with Dick's own freak performance.

Alger's warning, particularly in connection with the Erie Railroad scandal, was designed to fall on very fertile ground with a middle-class audience in 1868, when the scandal had the entire nation rattled.[2] Charles Francis Adams summed up its cultural importance: "no better illustration of the fantastic disguises which the worst and most familiar evils of history assume as they meet us in the actual movements of our own day could be afforded than was seen in the events attending what are known as the Erie wars of the year 1868." It was, in Adams' words, "a strange conflict that convulsed the money market, occupied the courts, agitated legislature, and perplexed the country." For Adams, the events surrounding the Erie railroad scandal "touch very nearly the foundations of common truth and honesty without which that healthy public opinion cannot exist which is the life's breath of our whole political system."[3] What was most threatening about the Erie scandal was that it violated honesty and common truth since it confronted the public with "a fantastic disguise" they could not penetrate.

P. T. Barnum himself capitalized on the public's fear of an emerging finance capitalism in an outrageously ironic move. A master of all the wiles of capitalism and often seen as the inventor of modern advertising techniques himself, Barnum took on capitalism and its "greedy financiers" as one of the "humbugs of the world" about which he warned his readers as much as about "mediums, animal magnetists, [and] religious maniacs."[4] Terence Whalen calls this stance

---

1. Dick mentions his Erie shares again on page 113. They become a kind of standing joke in the novel.
2. See Robert Sobel, *Panic on Wall Street: A History of America's Financial Disasters* (London: The MacmillanGroup, 1968), 128–35.
3. Charles Francis Adams, Jr., and Henry Adams, *Chapters of Erie* (1871; repr. Ithaca: Great Seal Books, Cornell Univ. Press, 1956), 3.
4. Harris, 215.

"capitalist irony," which "involves a satiric self-awareness on the part of a narrator who has made a killing in the market, [while] this self-awareness exposes the illusory or arbitrary nature of an entire economic system."[5] Barnum's ludicrous posture towards capitalism contained exactly the kind of irony that Alger attributed to Barnum's attitude towards his own museum in his appearance in the Rough and Ready novel. And Alger's own stance towards capitalism actually resonates with Barnum's ridiculous pose. Alger, like Barnum, warns of finance capitalism as a dangerous form of humbug because it meddles with truth and fiction, the very modes that both men continually manipulated themselves. But Alger also—rather sincerely—offers its readers an alternative economic logic: the logic of gift exchange.

Recall that Alger stresses that to his "credit" Dick felt pleasure in property only when it was connected to the possibility of giving, of helping others (147). Surprisingly, Alger's novel—so often read as an endorsement of capitalist entrepreneurship—is structured not so much around consistent earnings but around a series of gift transactions.[6] These transactions—voluntary, spontaneous, coincidental, and moral—are what allow Dick to rise, not his increased ability to save and work. This pattern of gift transactions—from buying drinks to receiving clothes to receiving and giving money—reaches its climax in the end, when Dick, risking his own life, rescues a boy who fell in the water. This final gift of life allows Dick finally to rise into respectability. Alger stresses that Dick's motive in this instance is not monetary: "He no sooner saw the boy fall than he resolved to rescue him. His determination was formed before he heard the liberal offer made by the boy's father. Indeed, I must do Dick the justice to say that, in the excitement of the moment, he did not hear it at all, nor would it have stimulated the alacrity with which he sprang to the rescue of the little boy" (178). Thus, the economic logic of the novel—as Dick's motivation in this final scene—is ultimately neither that of finance capitalism nor that of working and saving; rather, it is the logic of the gift.

Noting the importance of luck in the novel, Alan Trachtenberg argues that "the real magic and charm of *Ragged Dick* is the way the narrative makes money and desire coincide. There is something fabulous and otherworldly about such consistency. In Horatio Alger's

5. Terence Whalen, Introduction, *The Life of P. T. Barnum* (1855; Urbana: Univ. of Illinois Press, 2000), xvi–xvii.
6. Malcolm Cowley noted as early as 1945 that "I cannot understand how [Alger] should come to be regarded as the prophet of business enterprise" (quoted in Scharnhorst, "Demythologizing Alger," 20). While critics have repeatedly noted that Alger is not endorsing capitalism in a way people generally believe, none has written about the consistent way in which Alger depicts and explains at length the workings of gift exchange.

world, once mistaken by readers young and old for America itself, all good wishes come true."[7] The "fabulous" and "otherworldly . . . consistency" of the novel is its faith in the gift—a faith that allows Alger's readers to replace the fearful vision of a fluid social mobility with the faith in a moral order in which they, themselves, are in control in so far as they can choose to give or not. That Dick's rise is dependent on a series of gift transactions—transactions that often defy the spirit of capitalism entirely and that become freak accidents in an alienated urban environment—alleviates possible anxieties about a threatening upheaval of social classes, an uncontrollable society in which everyone, who speculates on the right stock, can make it overnight.[8] Far from making it on his own, Dick rises because he performs for the rich and gets selected again and again, based on his personal gifts.

Freak shows, too, rewarded gifts. Looked at through an economic lens, what made freak shows so wondrous was that they exhibited an incredible, unbelievable reversal of values; they turned an absence of value, such as a handicap, into a phenomenal value, a gift: a freakishness that could be sold in exhibits and pictures. This astonishing reversal of value is concomitant with the curious spectacle of finance capitalism, which also manipulates value in extraordinary, spectacular, even freakish ways. Both freak shows and an emerging finance capitalism offered to the amazed American middle class a comedy of values that turned ordinary into extraordinary and played with both fact and fiction to create value and to arouse in them both interest and speculation. But the freak show was much safer than the world of Wall Street; freaks always remained freaks, able to succeed only through the consent of the audience. Their amazing respectability might have almost reassured the audience that the American dream was a rare, freakish, staged event, which happened only as long as they paid the performer.

Just as Rachel Adams claims of freak shows, Alger's novel was, and has remained, "a stage for playing out many of the country's most

---

7. Trachtenberg, xx. W. T. Lhamon, Jr., also stresses the importance of luck in the novel; see "Horatio Alger and American Modernism: The One-Dimensional Social Formula," *American Studies* 17, no. 2 (1976), 19.
8. This fear is explicitly addressed in McCabe's *Lights and Shades of New York*. In a chapter on "Stock Gambling" McCabe writes: "Fortunes are made quicker and lost more easily in New York than in any place of the world. A sudden rise in stocks, or a lucky venture of some other kind, often places a comparatively poor man in possession of great wealth. Watch the carriages as they whirl through Fifth Avenue, going and returning from the park. The are as elegant and sumptuous as wealth can make them. The owners, lying back amongst the soft cushions, are clad in the height of fashion. By their dresses they might be princes and princesses. This much is due to art. Now mark the coarse features, the ill-bred stare, the haughty rudeness which they endeavor to palm off for dignity. Do you see any difference between them and the footman in livery on the carriage box? Both master and man belong to the same class—only one is wealthy and the other is not. But the footman may take the place of the master in a couple of years, or less time. Such changes may seem remarkable, but they are very common in New York" (281).

charged social and political controversies." It is this quality that has transformed it from an ephemeral piece of juvenile fiction into an iconic American text. On April 6, 2001, when President George Bush congratulated winners of the Horatio Alger award, he still emphasized the centrality of Alger's message: "The Horatio Alger Society is dedicated to really one of the basic truths about this country, and I hope this home remains dedicated to the same truth. In America, we believe in the possibilities of every person. It doesn't matter how you start out in life; what really matters is how you live your life. That has always been our creed." And while the president acknowledges that Alger's stories "were just stories" that "had a point and showed young readers the way," he remarks in the very next sentence that "such stories are still written in America, in every town and city, every day and in real life"[9] Unlike Barnum's museum, Alger's freak fiction amazingly never quite lost its credibility, cultural centrality, and respectability. Alger is still a household word in American ideology. Perhaps this is so because Alger's juvenile fiction/humbug offers a version of the American Dream that no middle-class American needs to fear.

9. "President Bush Congratulates Winners of Horatio Alger Awards." <www.white-house.gov/news/releases/2001/04/20010418-4.html>. The Horatio Alger Association's Award recognizes those who "demonstrate individual initiative and a commitment to excellence—as exemplified by remarkable achievements accomplished through honesty, self-reliance, and perseverance" (website, section on Horatio Alger Award).

Horatio Alger, Jr.: A Chronology

1832   Horatio Alger, Jr. is born in Boston on January 13, first child of Reverend Horatio Alger and Olive Fenno.

1833   Birth of sister Olive Augusta.

1836   Birth of brother James.

1840   Birth of invalid sister Annie.

1842   Birth of brother Francis. Alger enters grammar school in Chelsea.

1844   Alger's father is bankrupt, and the family leaves Chelsea.

1845   Alger senior becomes minister in Marlborough, signs a petition of protest against slavery, and Alger attends preparatory school there.

1846   Alger is examined for admission to the freshman class at Harvard University.

1848   Alger begins to attend lectures at Harvard, entering the class of 1852.

1849   Alger publishes his first works, essays and a poem, in the Boston *Pictorial National Library*.

1852   Alger graduates eighth in a class of 88, with Phi Beta Kappa honors. Unable to find a job and determined to become a writer he returns home.

1853   Begins to publish occasional pieces in the *Monthly Religious Magazine* and in the *Christian Register*; his work begins to appear regularly in the Boston *True Flag*. Alger also adopts pseudonym "Carl Cantab." In September he enters theological school; in November he withdraws and starts to work for the *Boston Daily Advertiser*, a job he quits after a few months.

1854   Begins to write sentimental romances for *True Flag* under the pseudonym "Charles F. Preston."

1854–56   Accepts a teaching position at the Grange, a private boarding school for boys in Rhode Island, and continues to publish stories and occasional poems.

1855   Alger's first book appears: *Bertha's Christmas Vision: An Autumn Sheaf*, an anthology of eleven stories and eight poems.

1856   Becomes principal of local academy in Deerfield, Massachusetts, from May to September, then works as a private tutor.

1857   Second book, the long satirical poem *Nothing to Do: A Tilt at our Best Society*, appears in summer. Alger enters Cambridge Theological School and publishes more serial fiction under the Preston and Cantab pseudonyms.

1860   Alger graduates from divinity school in the spring.

1860–61 Alger graduates and travels with college classmate Reverend Charles Vinal and his nineteen-year-old cousin Cyrus Alger Sears to Liverpool for a trip through Europe from September 5 through June 12.

1861   Alger decides not to enlist, preaches in congregations in Dover and South Natick, and in December moves to Cambridge and begins work as a private tutor. He becomes a propagandist for the Northern cause, writing at least eighteen war ballads.

1862   Writes a Civil War poem from the point of view of a woman that could be a reference to his relationship with Joseph F. Dean, a sixteen-year-old man he met in October 1859, who enlisted and with whom he kept up a correspondence.

1863   Alger, drafted, appears for physical examination on July 29 and is exempted due to height (5 feet 2 inches) and near-sightedness. Becomes recording secretary of the New England Historic-Genealogical Society on August 5.

1864   Alger's first novel, *Frank's Campaign*, a juvenile fiction, appears in November and is well received. Alger becomes minister to the First Unitarian Church and Society of Brewster, Massachusetts, on November 13.

1865   By summer Alger contributes juvenile stories to monthly juvenile magazine *Student and Schoolmate*; publishes another novel, *Paul Prescott's Charge*, in September 1865.

1866   Rumors begin to circulate about Alger. Charges are brought against Alger for sexually abusing boys in his parish, which he does not deny. Alger is dismissed. That spring, Alger is obliged to earn his living exclusively by writing; he publishes stories and novels, including *Timothy* and *Helen Ford*. Moving to New

York City, Alger begins to study the "street arabs" there and gets involved with the Five Points mission, the YMCA, and the Newsboys' Lodging House, which was opened in 1854 by the Children's Aid Society.

1866   Publishes poem "Friar Anselmo's Sin" on April 20.

1867   First installment of *Ragged Dick* appears in *Student and Schoolmate* in January. The novel is so successful that by April 1867 Alger is exclusively engaged by *Student and Schoolmate*.

1868   *Ragged Dick* appears in book form in May.

1867–73   Alger publishes eighteen juvenile novels, including five more in the "Ragged Dick" series.

1869   In January Alger moves in with the family of banker Seligman to tutor his five sons until 1876.

1872–78   Two dozen of Alger's old stories for adults are reprinted in *Gleason's*.

1873–77   Twelve new stories appear. Alger borrows heavily from the writings of Benjamin Franklin, James Fenimore Cooper, Charles Dickens, Herman Melville, and Mark Twain.

1873   Takes his parents, brother Frank, sister Augusta, and her husband on a tour of Europe at his expense.

1875   Publishes verse selection *Grand'ther Baldwin's Thanksgiving* in the fall.

1876   Alger leaves the Seligman household and lives in boarding houses.

1877   Novels have become formulaic, and his sales drop. Alger heads toward California on February 1 to collect data for a projected "Pacific series" of juvenile westerns; by March he begins to write *Joe's Luck*, finishes the novel that year, and it appears in 1878. Brother Frank dies April 17; mother dies, late August. Alger returns to New York December 5. James Freeman Clarke delivers speech against sensational juvenile fiction at the opening of a branch of the Boston Public Library, begins an anti-Alger campaign among librarians.

1881   Alger writes and publishes juvenile biography of President James Garfield, entitled *From Canal Boy to President*, which sells well. He informally adopts New York city street boy Charlie Davis.

1882   Alger finishes the Pacific series.

1883   A second informally adopted street boy, John Downie, moves into Alger's flat.

1886–94   Alger publishes thirty serials in *The Golden Argosy* under the pseudonym "Arthur Lee Putnam."

1894   Alger begins to take care of John Downie's younger brother, Edward. Based on a survey by the ALA, 34 out of 140 libraries do not carry Alger novels in 1894.

1896   Alger leaves New York to retire to Natick. He suffers from bronchitis and is weakened and overworked.

1898   Alger designates Edward Stratemeyer as a ghost writer to finish his uncompleted work.

1899   Alger dies on July 18 in his sister's house in Natick of heart disease. Over the next decade Stratemeyer completes and publishes eight more novels under Alger's name.

Selected Bibliography

REFERENCE AND BIBLIOGRAPHIES

Scharnhorst, Gary, Jack Bales, and Herbert R. Mayes. *Horatio Alger, Jr.: An Annotated Bibliography of Comment and Criticism.* Scarecrow Author Bibliographies 54. Metuchen, NJ: Scarecrow, 1981.
Horatio Alger Resources <www.washburn.edu/sobu/algerres.html>.
Horatio Alger Society <www.ihot.com/~has/alger.htm> (this site contains a list of first editions).

BOOKS ABOUT HORATIO ALGER, JR.

Gardner, Ralph D. *Horatio Alger, or the American Hero Era.* Mednota, IL: Wayside, 1964.
————, *Horatio Alger; or The American Hero, including Road to Success: The Bibliography of the Works of Horatio Alger.* New York: Arco, 1978.
Hoyd, Edwin P. *Horatio's Boys: The Life and Work of Horatio Alger, Jr.* Radnor, PA: Chilton, 1974.
Scharnhorst, Gary, with Jack Bales. *The Lost Life of Horatio Alger, Jr.* Bloomington: Indiana University Press, 1985.
Tebbel, John. *From Rags to Riches: Horatio Alger, Jr. and the American Dream.* New York: Macmillan, 1963.
Westgard, Gilbert K, II. *Alger Street: The Poetry of Horatio Alger, Jr.* Boston: Canner, 1964.

SELECTED FULL-LENGTH ARTICLES

For shorter articles on all aspects of Horatio Alger's life and work, see scholarly publications and notes in *Newsboy,* listed in the MLA bibliography.

• indicates a work included or excerpted in this Norton Critical Edition.

Bales, Jack. "Herbert R. Mayes and Horatio Alger, Jr.: The Story of a Unique Literary Hoax." *Journal of Popular Culture* 8 (1974): 317–19.
Beauchamp, Gorman. "*Ragged Dick* and the Fate of Respectability." *Michigan Quarterly Review* 31.3 (Summer 1992): 324–45.
• Hendler, Glenn. "Pandering in the Public Sphere: Masculinity and the Market of Horatio Alger." *American Quarterly* 48.3 (Sept. 1996): 415–38.
• Hoeller, Hildegard. "Freaks and the American Dream: Horatio Alger, P. T. Barnum, and the Art of Humbug." *Studies in American Fiction* 34.2 (Autumn 2006): 189–214.
Lhamon, W. T. Jr. "Horatio Alger and American Modernism: The One-Dimensional Social Formula." *American Studies* 17.2 (1976): 11–27.
Miner, Madonne M. "Horatio Alger's *Ragged Dick*: Projection, Denial, and Double-Dealing." *American Imago: Studies in Psychoanalysis and Culture* 47.3–4 (Fall–Winter 1990): 233–48.
• Moon, Michael. "'The Gentle Boy from the Dangerous Classes': Pederasty, Domesticity, and Capitalism in Horatio Alger." *Representations* 19 (Summer 1987): 87–110.
Nackenoff, Carol. "Of Factories and Failures: Exploring the Invisible Factory Gates of Horatio Alger, Jr." *Journal of Popular Culture* 25.4 (Spring 1992): 63–80.
• Scharnhorst, Gary. "Demythologizing Alger." *Markham Review* 10 (Fall 1980–Winter 1981): 20–27.
Schroeder, Fred. "America's First Literary Realist: Horatio Alger, Junior." *Western Humanities Review* 17 (1963): 129–37.
Schwartzman, Roy. "Recasting the American Dream Through Horatio Alger's Success Stories." *Studies in American Culture* 23.2 (Oct. 2000): 75–91.
• Walsh, Mary Roth. "Selling the Self-Made Woman." *Journal of American Culture* 2 (Spring 1979): 52–60.